DIGITAL CRIMINOLOGY

The infusion of digital technology into contemporary society has had significant effects for everyday life and for everyday crimes. *Digital Criminology: Crime and Justice in Digital Society* is the first interdisciplinary scholarly investigation extending beyond traditional topics of cybercrime, policing and the law to consider the implications of digital society for public engagement with crime and justice movements. This book seeks to connect the disparate fields of criminology, sociology, legal studies, politics, media and cultural studies in the study of crime and justice. Drawing together intersecting conceptual frameworks, *Digital Criminology* examines conceptual, legal, political and cultural framings of crime, formal justice responses and informal citizen-led justice movements in our increasingly connected, global and digital society.

Building on case study examples from across Australia, Canada, Europe, China, the UK and the United States, *Digital Criminology* explores key questions including: What are the implications of an increasingly digital society for crime and justice? What effects will emergent technologies have for how we respond to crime and participate in crime debates? What will be the foundational shifts in criminological research and frameworks for understanding crime and justice in this technologically mediated context? What does it mean to be a 'just' digital citizen? How will digital communications and social networks enable new forms of justice and justice movements? Ultimately, the book advances the case for an emerging digital criminology: extending the practical and conceptual analyses of 'cyber' or 'e' crime beyond a focus foremost on the novelty, pathology and illegality of technology-enabled crimes, to understandings of online crime as inherently social.

Anastasia Powell is Associate Professor in Criminology and Justice Studies at RMIT University. Anastasia's research explores the intersections of gender, violence, justice, technology and digital culture. Her previous co-authored and solo-authored books include: *Sexual Violence in a Digital Age* (2017) and *Sex, Power and Consent: Youth Culture and the Unwritten Rules* (2010); as well as the co-edited books *Rape Justice: Beyond the Criminal Law* (2015) and *Preventing Sexual Violence* (2014).

Gregory Stratton is Lecturer in Criminology and Justice Studies at RMIT University. Gregory also manages the *Bridge of Hope Innocence Initiative* at RMIT, a collaboration between academics, university students and lawyers who investigate claims of wrongful conviction. His research examines wrongful conviction, state crime, media and crime, and identity in the digital age.

Robin Cameron is Lecturer in Criminology and Justice Studies at RMIT University. Robin is also the manager of the Bachelor of Criminal Justice at RMIT. Robin's research focuses on security through an examination of gender, race and violence in urban and online spaces. His books include: *Subjects of Security: Domestic Effects of Foreign Policy in the War on Terror* (2013) and the co-edited book *Human Security and Natural Disasters* (2014).

"*Digital Criminology* pushes the boundaries past conventional cybercrime studies by casting its gaze towards the profound transformation of social relations in a 'digital society'. It develops a new programme for criminological inquiry, one that appreciates how the landscapes of crime, justice, and social conflict are being reshaped. Original, ambitious, and challenging – this is an important and timely book."

— *Majid Yar, Professor of Criminology, Lancaster University*

"*Digital Criminology* provides a bold, critical framework to challenge the existing paradigms of criminological inquiry. The authors reconceptualize the issues in light of the state of the Internet and technology use in the 21st century and propose a new way to view technological deviance that must be read by scholars and practitioners alike."

— *Thomas J. Holt, Professor, School of Criminal Justice, Michigan State University*

"This volume serves as a foundational primer for a truly technosocial criminology, one that moves beyond narrow conventions of cybercrime and more fully engages the emergent harms, inequalities, justice, and activism that make up global digital societies. *Digital Criminology* is an interdisciplinary feat – a must-read for anyone who seeks to do work on media and crime in the contemporary moment."

— *Michelle Brown, Associate Professor, Department of Sociology, The University of Tennessee*

DIGITAL CRIMINOLOGY

Crime and Justice in Digital Society

Anastasia Powell • *Gregory Stratton* • *Robin Cameron*

Routledge
Taylor & Francis Group

NEW YORK AND LONDON

First published 2018
by Routledge
711 Third Avenue, New York, NY 10017

and by Routledge
2 Park Square, Milton Park, Abingdon, Oxon, OX14 4RN

Routledge is an imprint of the Taylor & Francis Group, an informa business

Library of Congress Cataloging-in-Publication Data
Names: Powell, Anastasia, author. | Stratton, Gregory, author. | Cameron,
Robin, 1982- author.
Title: Digital criminology: crime and justice in digital society/Anastasia
Powell, Gregory Stratton, Robin Cameron.
Description: New York, NY: Routledge, 2018. | Includes index.
Identifiers: LCCN 2018001651 (print) | LCCN 2018002672 (ebook) |
ISBN 9781315205786 (master) | ISBN 9781138636736 (hbk) | ISBN
9781138636743 (pbk)
Subjects: LCSH: Criminology. | Social justice. | Social movements. |
Internet–Social aspects.
Classification: LCC HV6025 (ebook) | LCC HV6025.P657 2018 (print) |
DDC 364–dc23
LC record available at https://lccn.loc.gov/2018001651

ISBN: 978-1-138-63673-6 (hbk)
ISBN: 978-1-138-63674-3 (pbk)
ISBN: 978-1-315-20578-6 (ebk)

Typeset in Bembo
by Sunrise Setting Ltd, Brixham, UK

MIX
Paper from
responsible sources
FSC   FSC® C013985
www.fsc.org

Printed in the United Kingdom
by Henry Ling Limited

CONTENTS

PREFACE

The infusion of digital technology into contemporary society has had significant effects for everyday life and for everyday crimes. *Digital Criminology: Crime and Justice in Digital Society* is the first interdisciplinary scholarly investigation extending beyond traditional topics of cybercrime, policing and the law to consider the implications of digital society for public engagement with crime and justice movements. Drawing together intersecting conceptual frameworks, *Digital Criminology* examines conceptual, legal, political and cultural framings of crime, formal justice responses and informal citizen-led justice movements in our increasingly connected, global and digital society. Much criminological engagement with computer and cybercrime has, to date, been largely insular; and lacking in a critical and interdisciplinary engagement with fields such as sociology, computer science, politics, journalism, media and cultural studies. In *Digital Criminology*, we argue that such insularity is particularly detrimental to advancing a new generation of scholarship concerning technology, crime, deviance and justice in digital society. Throughout this book, we position *digital society* as a useful theoretical framework that not only draws together the largely disparate scholarship on technosocial crime and justice within criminology, but also expands our disciplinary concepts, understandings and empirical examinations of crime and justice in the digital age.

Throughout *Digital Criminology*, we explore case study examples such as peer and corporate surveillance, crowdsourced investigations, crime 'selfies', social media hate, 'viral' justice, digilantism and hashtag activism. Building on these case studies from across Australia, Canada, Europe, China, the United Kingdom and the United States, the book explores key questions including: What are the implications of an increasingly digital society for crime and justice? What effects will emergent technologies have for how we respond to crime and participate in crime debates? What will be the foundational shifts in criminological research and frameworks for understanding crime and justice in this technologically mediated context? What does it mean to be a 'just' digital citizen? How will digital communications and social networks enable new forms of justice and justice movements? Ultimately, the book advances the case for an emerging digital criminology: extending the practical and conceptual analyses of 'cyber' or 'e' crime beyond a focus foremost on the novelty, pathology and illegality of technology-enabled crimes, to understandings of crime as inherently *technosocial*. Here, we seek to reinvigorate and extend criminological analysis of digital technologies and their role not only in the commission of crimes but the emergence of unfamiliar and/or extended harms, cultures of inequality and hate, as well as issues of justice, citizen participation and crime policy activism.

This book will be essential reading for scholars and students in criminology seeking to push the conventional boundaries of cybercrime and to engage in a social, cultural and political examination of crime and justice in digital society.

ACKNOWLEDGMENTS

We are grateful to many of our colleagues, friends and family for their support and assistance throughout the development of this book. The development of this book was funded, in part, by an Australian Research Council (ARC)-funded Discovery Early Career Researcher Award (DE160100044) titled *Crime and Justice by Social Media: Citizen Engagements with Justice Online*. The views expressed here are ours and not those of the funding agency or the Australian government. We are extremely grateful to have had funding support from the ARC for this research and also the support of our institution, RMIT University (Melbourne, Australia), which has allowed us the time and resources to complete this work. In particular, we'd like to thank our head of department, Dr Michele Ruyters, for her unwavering support of our work and for fostering a very fruitful research culture in Criminology and Justice Studies at RMIT. This research culture has been made all the more supportive through the lively contributions of academic, professional and student staff members within the Criminology and Justice Studies department at RMIT. We are also very grateful to numerous peers, colleagues and reviewers who have provided advice and guidance on various aspects of our work on this topic over the past few years.

This book represents a platform for our emerging research agenda into crime and justice in digital society. Aspects of our initial conceptual development have also previously been published in the scholarly articles: 'Crime and Justice in Digital Society: Towards a 'Digital Criminology'?' in the *International Journal for Crime, Justice and Social Democracy*; and 'Following #JillMeagher: Collective Meaning-Making in Response to Crime Events via Social Media' in *Crime, Media, Culture*. We thank the editors of these journals, and our anonymous peer reviewers in particular, for their feedback and support of our research and the development of our thinking in this field. We further express our sincere gratitude to the editorial team at Routledge, in particular Irene Bunnell and Ellen Boyne, for their patience and support throughout the production process. Thanks also to our manuscript editor Helena Bond, whose expertise and astute advice have proven so valuable in the final stages of production of this book. We also thank Caitlin Overington, Tully O'Neill, Alexander Waters and Naomi Pfitzner for their wonderful research assistance work. Finally, thanks to many colleagues within Criminology who have been wonderful mentors, supporters and critical friends, including: Adam

Sutton, Fiona Haines, Murray Lee, Kerry Carrington, Sharon Pickering, Stuart Thomas, Nicola Henry, Asher Flynn, Ruth Liston and Peta Malins.

Anastasia would further like to thank her sisters, Desiree and Kathleen, for their friendship and support. Thank you also to Matthew and Alexander for understanding the obsession of an academic with her work.

Gregory extends his thanks to his friends and family for their assistance, encouragement and support during a time that saw loved ones gained and lost. A mention should be made to the interns and staff at the Innocence Initiative, particularly Michele, Alyssa and Monique, who were able to pick up the slack during the writing process. Finally, a special thank you to Holly, Henry and Max, whose continued patience and love is greatly appreciated and reciprocated.

Finally, Robin would like to thank all the many thoughtful friends, colleagues and students whose thoughts he has greatly benefitted from sharing. In particular, since his last book he has grown wiser from exchanges with Pete, James and Tom; Hussein and Sahar; Jon and Myles; Hannah, Margaret and John and, as always, his family.

1

INTRODUCTION

Criminology and the Digital Society

Introduction

On Friday 20 January 2017, Donald John Trump was inaugurated President of the United States. While his first year in office has been marred by controversy, the 2016 election also highlighted the ubiquity of digital technologies within contemporary society. Indeed, both the Trump and Clinton campaigns not only navigated the political trail by harnessing digital platforms such as Twitter to convey their messages, but were also hampered through various digital disruptions despite careful management by campaign organisers. Take, for example, a selection of key issues raised throughout the Trump and Clinton campaigns: accusations of Russian hacking that resulted in a WikiLeaks release of Democratic National Committee and John Podesta emails (Healy, Sanger, & Haberman, 2016; Perlroth & Shear, 2016; Sanger & Shane, 2016); the consequential FBI investigation into Clinton's use of private servers (Federal Bureau of Investigation, 2016; Jacobs, Siddiqui, & Ackerman, 2016); photos that were taken in the polling booth as a potential Federal crime (Crockett, 2016); the 'doxing' by Trump of Senator Lindsey Graham by releasing his personal contact information without consent (Gass & Lerner, 2015); the appearance of 'fake news' and claims of a 'post-truth' world (Hogan, 2016; Howard, 2017; Subramanian, 2017); and the rise of social media as the foremost agenda-setting source in politics that had previously been dominated by print, radio and television news media (Enli, 2017; Johnson, 2016; Ott, 2017).

Yet Trump's prolific use of Twitter, in particular, has emerged as both highly controversial and highly influential since the election result. Scholars from across politics, sociology and cultural studies, as well as media and communications, are already examining various aspects of Trump's social media discourse and citizen engagements with it (Enli, 2017; Johnson, 2016; Ott, 2017). While some have noted that Trump's 'amateur' style may have been read culturally as more 'authentic' than traditional political discourse and thus added to his popularity (Enli, 2017), others have criticised the Trump campaign for inciting fear and hatred of 'the other' in its messaging (Ott, 2017; Speed & Mannion, 2017). Texas Tech University Professor of Communications Brian Ott (2017, p. 65), for example, has argued that the 'Age of Twitter virtually guaranteed the rise of Trump', adding that, 'public discourse simply cannot descend into the politics of division and degradation on a daily basis without significant consequence'. Ott's analysis is remarkable for its pessimistic view of social media, which he describes as a toxic 'contagion', noting that 'Tweets do more than merely reflect sexism, racism, homophobia, and xenophobia; they spread those ideologies like a social cancer' (p. 64). Yet his pessimism about the impacts of social media are not unfounded, with a Pew Internet Survey reporting that one in five US social media users changed their minds about a political issue or a candidate for office because of something they read on social media (Duggan & Smith, 2016). Moreover, the mainstream news media's increasing treatment of Twitter itself as a source of news and information has arguably cemented Twitter's agenda-setting function in which opinion and 'alternative facts' are circulated and recirculated as both factual and newsworthy (Ott, 2017; Speed & Mannion, 2017).

Across the Atlantic, and the UK vote to leave the European Union (referred to as 'Brexit', a portmanteau of 'Britain' and 'exit') in June 2016 has likewise raised questions about the influence of 'fake news', social media 'echo chambers' (Colleoni, Rozza, & Arvidsson, 2014; McPherson, Smith-Lovin, & Cook, 2001) and the populist politics of fear and hate in a post-truth world (Lockie, 2017; Peters, 2017; Speed & Mannion, 2017).[1] As Diyana Dobreva and Martin Innes (2016) identify, the 'leave' campaign made many inaccurate claims about the damage that immigration and open borders had caused in Britain: appealing to emotions of fear of foreign 'invaders' and towards a conservative nationalism. Again, such rhetoric is not without social consequences: according to statistics released by the National Police Chiefs' Council (NPCC), reported hate crimes increased by 57% following the Brexit vote, a trend some argued was exacerbated by social media discourse (Debrova & Innes, 2016). Yet in a post-truth world, as suggested by Ewen Speed and Russell Mannion (2017, p. 250), swift policy reforms can be made based on the 'personal whims and prejudices' of a charismatic leader and at the expense of a secure evidence base, appealing instead to 'a populism built on "walls" and fear of the "other"'. Though politicians have, before now, certainly been documented as spin-doctoring the facts to suit a political agenda, 'the post-truth politician manufactures his or her own facts . . . [with] an authoritarian impulse that promises to be both reckless and destructive — an impulse all too comfortable with the deployment of propaganda, vilification and intimidation' (Lockie, 2017, p. 1).

Though social media discourse cannot be understood as the *cause* of hate-based populism, neither are such digital platforms free of influence in co-producing and amplifying cultures and practices of bigotry, racism and misogyny. At the same time, the post-truth turn of populist politics may result from growing social exclusion and from a cultural backlash in which some groups within the community resent the multiculturalism and perceived displacement of traditional social values by successive waves of progressive social and cultural change (Inglehart & Norris, 2016; Speed & Mannion, 2017). The post-truth turn is also described as a reaction against, and rejection of, 'evidence-based' politics and the 'elitist experts' who espouse them (Lockie, 2017). Take, for instance, the notorious rebuke by Michael Gove, the UK's justice secretary, on Sky News when discussing the role of expert advice in the Brexit decision (Gilman, 2016): 'I think people in this country have had enough of experts'.

As sociologist Stewart Lockie (2017, p. 2) argues, 'usage of the term "post-truth" may well be novel, but there is nothing novel about the authoritarian impulse implicit in such open contempt for truthfulness . . . Propaganda has long been a favoured tool among demagogues and colonialists — misleading information and dehumanizing rhetoric the legitimating force behind dispossession, repression, coercion and violence'. Indeed, criminologists too have long identified and problematised both the turn towards 'populist punitiveness' (Bottoms, 1995; Simon, 2007) and the claims that 'almost nothing works' in response to criminal offending, thus calling into question the role of the criminological 'expert' (Martinson, 1974). Criminologists have also long recognised the 'affective versus effective' tensions within law and criminal justice policy (Freiberg, 2001) in which political appeals to emotion and values often carry greater weight than evidence-based policy design. Each of these threads in criminological thinking and analysis bears distinct parallels to the contemporary populist, post-truth political context. Certainly, criminologists should be concerned about the potential for social media discourses to interact with and amplify populist politics in ways that may shape and influence not just politics generally but law and criminal justice policy in particular (Aas, 2013; Milivojevic & McGovern, 2014; Powell, 2014).

Of course, the ways in which digital technologies are enmeshed with the social, structural and cultural practices of law, crime and justice are many and varied — extending well beyond the politics of social media. For example, the 'perpetual contact' (Katz & Akhaus, 2002) that is facilitated by digital devices can be linked to the *perpetration* of crime, such as robberies and assaults facilitated by virtual 'lures' in the augmented reality game Pokemon Go (Criddle, 2016). At the same time, the constant connectivity via internet-enabled wearable devices ('wearables'), as well as via social media, has contributed to the *investigation* of crimes. While police are increasingly employing 'open source intelligence-gathering' via social media and other publicly accessible data sources, everyday citizens are also following crime 'in real time' and seeking to actively contribute to ongoing criminal investigations. Meanwhile, the role of imagery in the perpetration, aftermath and cultures of criminality has shifted noticeably in the digital age: from photographs of crime victims being posted on social media (Ford, 2016); to blackmail and extortion of victims via threats to release humiliating or nude photographs and/or video (Henry, Powell, & Flynn, 2017); to streaming crimes including murder and rape for a public audience in real time via Facebook Live (Sulleyman, 2017). These are just some examples that illustrate the role of digital technologies in a wide range of offending and victimisation. Of equal concern are broader issues of persistent social and digital inequalities as they relate to crime and justice.

From a criminological perspective, the ways in which social media and other digital technologies permeated the Trump election, the Brexit vote and continue to pervade a variety of emerging harms and injustices in our global, digital world, further expose underlying substantive issues of power inequality, racism, bullying, misogyny, surveillance, digital privacy and digital security. Although criminology currently offers tools to explore some aspects of criminality in the digital age, such as cybercrime, cyber-terrorism and cyber-warfare, its tools are limited in their focus on the internet or 'cyberspace' as a distinct driver of criminality. Yet the examples discussed in this chapter, and indeed throughout this book, demonstrate the centrality of digital technologies in modern political and social life, such that it is increasingly impractical to isolate the practices and impacts of the 'digital' from 'society' and vice versa. It is here that criminology has arguably yet to fully engage.

In this book, we seek to reinvigorate and extend criminological analysis of digital technologies and their role not only in the commission of crimes but in the emergence of unfamiliar and/or extended harms, cultures of inequality and hate, as well as issues of justice, citizen participation and crime policy activism. To do so, we argue that criminology must engage more thoroughly with interdisciplinary perspectives from across science and technology, politics and cultural studies, as well as media and communications, in seeking to understand and respond to crime, justice and injustice in digital society.

What is Digital Society?

Unsurprisingly, the transformative impact of digital information and communication technologies in society has become a focus of interdisciplinary study. Unlike earlier conceptualisations of cyberspace (as compared with 'real', 'terrestrial' or 'meat' space) as a distinct sphere of experience, the concept of digital society refers to the integrated whole represented by digital technologies and society — a whole that is more than the sum of its parts. In order to avoid the limitations and distracting vagueness of previous emphasis on the digital, we advocate Heather Horst and Daniel Miller's (2013, p. 5) proposal that, rather than distinguish between digital and analogue behaviours (see Grabosky and Smith, 2001), 'digital' can refer to anything and everything that can be developed through, or reduced to, the binary, that is the 1s and 0s of data. By avoiding any fixed characteristic of the nature of the digital, we are able to adopt a 'heterogeneous understanding of the digital', which emphasises the various ways in which it can be mobilised and deployed, even lived (Ruppert, Law, & Savage, 2013, p. 40). This use of 'digital' encapsulates the capacities of new technologies to produce emergent social relations and doings, rather than suggesting that it replaces or exists outside of human interaction (Ruppert et al., 2013). 'Digital', in this framework, does not refer only to computers, nor is it limited to code. Rather, it allows for expanded understandings and acknowledgements of the intersections between technologies and the social. In short, it recognises the potential for a digital society.

An understanding of the mutual and reciprocal shaping of technology and society is core to the concept of digital society as we employ it throughout this book. We do not view digital technologies as mere tools of human action and interaction, nor as deterministic of human action and interaction; we seek to conceptualise the *technosocial* nature of contemporary social and political life. So the 'digital society' becomes a shorthand for the fundamental nature of the technological, structural and social changes in the contemporary society in which we live; while 'technosociality' captures the processes, cultures and practices that characterise our day-to-day lives. Drawing in part on broader studies of technology and society (STS), and in part on the sub-field of digital sociology, we identify the dual concepts of digital society and technosociality as fundamental to — and indeed a launching pad for — emerging criminological theory, research and policy development that extend beyond the cybercriminologies of the past.

The concepts of digital society and technosociality both offer insights into technologically-mediated sociality, which has been underexamined within criminology. These concepts are not in themselves new, but rather signal a range of explanations of the mutual relationship between technology and society that have been offered through interdisciplinary concepts, such as: the network society (Castells, 1996, 2010, 2012), information and knowledge society (Hassan, 2008; Stehr, 1994; Webster, 1995), information age (Lash, 2002), cyberculture (Lévy, 2001) and cybersociety (Jones, 1995). Such concepts seek to understand the rapid transformative effect of information, communication and digital technologies on social and political life.

Manuel Castells' highly influential concept of the network society, for example, acknowledges that 'Technology does not determine society . . . nor does society script the course of technological change' (Castells, 1996, p. 5). Castells (2010, p. 5) has referred to processes of digitalisation of society — in which the relationships between the digital and the social are so enmeshed that 'technology is society, and society cannot be understood or represented without its technological tools'. Acceptance of this premise recognises the digital as both a tool and a space in which technologies have shaped cultural artefacts, arrangements and activities, both online and offline (Deuze, 2006).

It is for reasons such as this that sociologists Kate Orton-Johnson and Nick Prior (2013b, p. 2) contend that research of a digital society can no longer be restricted to the study of 'an exotic, esoteric or autonomous cyberspace' because of the 'new intersections, continuities and flows between the social and the digital'. Evidence of this is seen throughout everyday life, perhaps most clearly in the way people's social engagements with one another have embraced digital technologies and disintegrated online and offline boundaries of behaviour (Baym, 2015).

Acknowledging the mutual shaping of society and digital technologies carries with it a number of further observations about life in a digital society. Computers, mobile phones, web-based platforms, social media, wearable technologies, navigational technologies and the Internet of Things, among other digital innovations, demonstrate the integration of technology that often goes unnoticed in our everyday lives. Thrift's (2004, 2005) conceptualisation of the 'technological unconscious' offers a useful explanation of why the relationship between digital technology and everyday life can be underexamined from certain perspectives. The 'technological unconscious' refers to the operations of technologies and information that have moved beyond mediation to constitute central interactions and associations to produce everyday assumptions surrounding its use (Thrift, 2005). The use of the modern automobile represents an example of the 'technological unconscious' offered by Thrift (2004): in the hundred plus years of the automobile's history, the experience of driving has become familiar, then been taken for granted and absorbed into our collective and technological unconscious (Thrift, 2004). In the digital society, this unconscious acceptance is being furthered with advances in technologies such as GPS and Bluetooth, which are becoming second-nature in our driving experience. Looking forward a further 100 years, it is entirely possible that emerging technologies of autonomous vehicles will be likewise taken for granted. For Thrift (2004, p. 46), the importance of technology in this context rests in the construction of embodied cues and gestures that work beyond simple cultural codes. Instead, they are ingrained within communicative registers and memory, helping to shape our experiences and becoming one with those experiences.

By acknowledging how technology is absorbed, unnoticed in everyday life, digital technology offers a 'new media ontology' (Lash, 2007), which accounts for a shift to a society where the digital actively shapes lifestyles, social interactions and environments. Beer (2009, p. 987) contends that this proposal is useful to diversify social scientific research to incorporate technological advances within, and not separate to, human agency. As sociologist Roger Burrows (2009) suggests:

> . . . the 'stuff' that makes up the social and urban fabric has changed — it is no longer just about emergent properties that derive from a complex of social associations and interactions. These interactions are now not only mediated by software and code they are becoming constituted by it (p. 451).

When reflecting on distinctions between online and offline, the ubiquity of the digital can also be recognised as the culmination of a convergence culture (Hay & Couldry, 2011; Jenkins, 2006, 2014). Where once convergence referred to the increasing ability of technologies to 'talk' to each other, convergence now also represents how technologies and people are able to connect simultaneously. As German media theorist Norbert Bolz notes 'a computer that is worn as a dress, serving as an information assistant, that is the direction of paradigm shifts determined by the progressive digitization of our lives' (Bolz, 2011, p. 14, cited in Kyslova & Berdnyk, 2014).

The emerging sub-discipline of digital sociology further explores the 'digitisation' of society and the implications for the wider discipline across both theoretical and methodological approaches. For academics, the digital in this sense not only offers new ways of organising social and political life, but also new ways of *analysing* it (Law, Ruppert, & Savage, 2011). Sociologist Deborah Lupton (2013, 2015), for example, has long championed digital sociology as exploring four key areas: (i) professional digital practice; (ii) sociological analyses of digital media use; (iii) digital data analysis; and (iv) critical digital sociology. As professional digital practice, Lupton describes the changing role of the academic in digital society, such that using digital media tools is increasingly an important part of their sociological and reflective practice, as well as using them to build networks, to publicise and share research findings and to instruct students. Sociological analysis of digital media use, meanwhile, refers to researching the ways in which people's use of digital media technologies contributes towards configuring their sense of self, their embodiment and their social relations. It also examines the role of digital media in the creation or reproduction of social institutions and structure. Third, digital data analysis, including 'big data' such as social media, are an important source for sociologists of both quantitative and qualitative research. Finally, Lupton (2013, 2015) calls for scholars to undertake reflective critical sociological analysis of digital technologies through the prism of social and cultural theory that engages with concepts of power and inequality. Yet, to date, much digital sociology has focused on changes in technology as a tool of sociological inquiry.

For the sociologist, the digital society has brought with it a time of rapid socio-cultural and socio-technical change that allows the discipline to emphasise 'critical, distinctive, and thick' investigations of emergent digital phenomena (Beer & Burrows, 2007, p. 11). Yet, as sociologist Noortje Marres (2013) notes:

> Digital sociology is not just about theorizing the digital society, and it is not just about applying social methods to analyse digital social life. The relations between social life and its analysis are changing in the context of digitization, and digital sociology offers a way of engaging with this (n.p.).

Indeed, the digital sociological approach seeks to recognise the importance of interdisciplinary collaboration; drawing from communication studies, cultural studies, science and technology studies (STS), computer science, and internet studies to re-examine the core traditions and concerns of sociology, including power and inequalities across social, economic and cultural structures and practices (Orton-Johnson & Prior, 2013a).

Unlike concepts such as cybersociety and information society, those who use the term digital society tend not to propose a new era, or even a unique perspective. Cultural studies theorist Adrian Athique (2013, p. 15) offers the use of 'the digital' as a means to allow for the overlap and acceptance of other concepts, like the network society or the digital age. While other prefixes could be used to explain the processes discussed here, they provide specific meanings and limitations that sometimes underplay the agency of human activity. We use 'digital society' to refer to the technological, structural and social changes highlighted in all these theories. Digital society acknowledges the cultural, political and affectual dimensions of social life that intersect both the information and network society theories. Using the concept of the digital society as the lens to focus our research encourages us to think about the social, political and cultural consequences of digital technologies rather than the constant evolution of the technologies themselves.

Towards a Digital Criminology

There is much that an explicitly criminological encounter with digital society could bring to analyses of crime, justice and injustice. Yet progressing empirical and theoretical development in this field will require both a re-engagement with criminology's interdisciplinary foundations (Garland, 2011) and a shift beyond some of the limitations of conventional 'cybercriminologies'. Indeed, as we go on to discuss more deeply in Chapter 2, much criminological engagement with 'cybercrime' has concentrated on key focus areas such as theft, identity fraud, bullying, terrorist extremism and child sexual exploitation material. Beyond the common issue of focus, however, is an interrelated set of conceptual underpinnings that have become dominant within cybercriminologies. In particular, the *online/offline dichotomy* that is so frequently reproduced within cybercrime and cybercriminological theorising and research. While such a concept made some sense in the early 1990s when online communications and 'virtual communities' were emerging, the dichotomy is already far less useful in the context of contemporary digital society. Building on our earlier work (Powell & Henry, 2017; Stratton Powell, & Cameron 2017), we argue that it makes little sense to talk about 'virtual' as opposed to 'terrestrial' space when one considers that so much of our face-to-face and online social interactions are embedded within, and reinforce, one another. As such, a key thread woven throughout this book is the challenge of moving beyond such 'online/offline', 'cyber/real' or 'virtual/terrestrial' dichotomies.

Hand in hand with a conceptual break from online/offline, then, is the challenge for criminology to examine a broader range of crime, justice and injustice issues that typify the *integration of the digital* in everyday life. As criminologist Sheila Brown notes: 'there is quite simply no such thing as a "technological" crime (such as a "cyber crime") as distinct from an "embodied" crime' (Brown, 2006, p. 236). Indeed, many core societal issues of criminological concern — such as power, agency, inequality and access to justice — not only continue but are changed through their interaction with digital technologies (Van Dijk, 2013, p. 100). While sociological, political and technological studies have substantially theorised the nature of *digital social inequality* (Halford & Savage, 2010), such examinations are arguably underdeveloped in criminology: both equity of access and equity of participation are important issues in society generally, with implications for crime and justice.

Our proposed shift towards a *digital* criminology represents more than a mere substitution of the prefix 'cyber' with a preferred and more contemporary alternative. Many scholars within internet research areas clearly demarcate different eras of technological innovations, referring to Web 1.0, 2.0, 3.0, for instance; each of which has clear characteristics that have also brought shifts in theories and research over time (as discussed further in Chapter 2). While the distinction between digital and cyber may seem inconsequential to some, we suggest, along with others outside of criminology, that digital is a descriptor that encapsulates various waves of technological innovation and that can better stand the test of time. Much like Lupton (2013, p. 5), our preference in referring to the digital acknowledges that, though 'cyber' was the choice in vogue in the 1990s, as technologies have become more pervasive, ubiquitous and mobile, digital better encapsulates both the 'old' notions of cyber and contemporary shifts and advances in technology and sociality. Moreover, a focus on the digital, as the central and continuing element in technology, avoids the pitfalls of constructing theory to the whim of technological innovation and steers instead towards lived experience that includes all technology. Thus the centrality of the technosocial relationship becomes more apparent as reliance upon the digital increases in everyday life (Lash, 2001).

By focusing on *digital* society over other prefixes such as cyber or virtual, we invite criminologists to move beyond framing 'computer', 'cyber' or 'virtual' crime and justice as fundamentally distinct from, or indeed oppositional to, 'non-technological' forms of crime and justice. At the same time, encouraging research under the concept of digital *society* draws the criminological imagination towards an exploration of the relational, cultural, affective, political and socio-structural dimensions of crime and justice that are reproduced, reinstitutionalised and potentially resisted, in both familiar and unfamiliar ways. Part of our motivation for using 'society', over other similar and popular suffixes such as 'age' or 'era', is to deliberately invoke analyses of social inequalities, socio-cultural practices and socio-political factors that underpin crime and justice more broadly and that demonstrably persist as our lives become increasingly digital. We propose that this conceptual focus on digital society also opens up several new and rapidly emerging foci for criminological theory and research. We identify seven avenues for the study of crime, deviance and justice in a digital society, drawing on examples from interdisciplinary research across sociology, cultural and media studies, journalism, policing and surveillance studies, as well as law and criminology — which are briefly described below, and many of which are further explored throughout this book. We do not claim these to constitute a comprehensive list, but rather an invitation to further develop the field.

Digital Spectatorship

Just as traditional media and crime scholarship has highlighted a tendency for crime media consumers to be more punitive in their attitudes towards crime and justice, there is potential for technological advancements to increase the immersion of crime news in our daily lives and for this to be associated with an amplification of 'penal populism' (Quilter, 2012). The potential for increased spectatorship is itself facilitated in large part by social media, as well as by our 'perpetual contact' via wearable technologies and the Internet of Things that provide live access to crime and justice news as events unfold. The capacity to follow crime 'in real time' has further implications with respect to intensifying misperceptions and fear of crime, as well as calling on everyday citizens to more actively participate in crime news as eye-witnesses and citizen journalists (Allan, 2013).

Digital Investigation and Evidence

Digital technologies offer opportunities for a range of actors to explore and investigate criminal behaviour in both online and offline settings. Data that have been stored or transmitted on digital devices are increasingly used to explore how offences occurred or assist in elements such as providing an alibi or proving intent (Casey, 2011, p. 7). The utility of technologies other than the personal computer, such as mobile, personal and wearable devices, that expand the repertoire of investigators and traditional law enforcement agencies has recently emerged in the discussion of digital evidence (Chaikin, 2006). For example, wearable fitness technologies have been introduced as evidence in criminal trials to identify the location of key figures in the case at the time of the crime (Gottehrer, 2015; Rutkin, 2015). Importantly, digital evidence is collected and used in ways that require an in-depth understanding of the investigation process. Digital investigations raise new and important questions over how evidence is collected, retained and regulated in relation to privacy and individual liberties (Kerr, 2005, p. 280). Online platforms such as Facebook provide government agencies with new opportunities for investigation, and the monitoring and policing of these platforms can represent a form of surveillance creep (Trottier, 2014, p. 79). This was evident during the 2011 Vancouver riot, when both police and Facebook users drew on posted content and collaborated to identify suspected rioters (Trottier, 2014).

Digital Justice and 'Digilantism'

The democratising effect of digital technologies has enabled state agencies to engage with the public in ways that were unavailable before. The use of social media by police (Goldsmith, 2015; McGovern & Lee, 2012) and the courts (Johnston & McGovern, 2013; McGovern, 2011) both encourage access and engagement with the justice system, whilst also causing problematic and potentially disruptive effects on traditional justice processes such as the involvement of juries in the court system (Aaronson & Patterson, 2012; Browning, 2014). At the same time, digital society has also encouraged 'informal' justice practices and community responses in relation to crime. For example, legal scholar Corien Prins (2011) has advocated for a sub-field of e-victimology exploring how digital participation facilitates both new practices for self-help and self-activism and new threats to victims' well-being and privacy. Similarly, criminologists Anastasia Powell (2014, 2015a, 2015b) and Bianca Fileborn (2014) have examined emerging 'informal justice' practices of victim-survivors and their advocates in response to sexual violence and street harassment, operating in civil society. Some scholars have raised concerns about informal justice processes embracing the use of technologies: highlighting the potential for a digital media 'pillory' (Hess & Waller, 2014) and 'digilantism' (Van Laer & van Aelst, 2009), which can result in injustices, harassment and violence towards alleged offenders. Also labelled 'viral justice' (Aikins, 2013; Antoniades, 2012; Thompson, Wood, & Rose, 2016), such analyses suggest a need to further examine the nature and impacts of citizen-led justice practices that are enabled by digital participation.

Digital Surveillance

Digital technologies open new opportunities for state-sanctioned surveillance, occasioning both sociological and criminological critiques of the powers enabled by such technologies (Bauman & Lyon, 2012; Graham & Wood, 2003; Lyon, 2003). Furthermore, government breaches of their citizen's privacy, due process and individual liberties are increasingly being discovered and subject to judicial scrutiny (Bauman et al., 2014; Margulies, 2013), intensifying the critique of all state-sanctioned surveillance. At the same time, agents of power within criminal justice systems are increasingly tracked, documented and held accountable for their actions and responsibilities (Bradshaw, 2013; Marx, 2003; McGrath, 2004). In addition to surveillance of the powerful, the digital society allows peer-to-peer or lateral digital surveillance, which monitors crime from collectives rather than from positions of privilege (Smyth, 2012; Trottier, 2012). For example, 'crowdsourced surveillance' represents a 'socio-technical assemblage' of citizens, police and private institutions that allows for criminological investigation of the relationship between these technologies and responses to, and prevention of, crime (Trottier, 2014, p. 81).

Digitally Embodied Harms

A growing literature is exploring issues of spatiality and embodiment as they relate specifically to the harms of gendered and sexual violence (Henry & Powell, 2015), as well as racial, sexuality and/or gender-identity based hate (Citron, 2014; Mann, Sutton, & Tuffin, 2003; Zempi & Awan, 2016). The harassment, violence and hate speech experienced by such groups take place not only via digital communications but in a specific context of broader patterns of violence and abuse that persist and are perpetuated by cultures and structures of inequality, marginalisation and exclusion. While typologies of 'cyber' versus 'real' harassment, violence and hate speech can serve to minimise harms enabled by communications and online technologies, we argue that understanding these harms situated in digital society better captures the lived experiences of marginalised communities and the operation of power and violence across every aspect of their daily lives.

Digital Engagement

Expanding beyond cultural criminology and media-crime scholarship, the portability, ubiquity and perpetual contact of digital technologies allow the public to adopt new 'gatewatching' roles (Bruns, 2003, 2005). In accessing the range of diverse media content available to them, publics are now able to (re)consume, (re)produce and (re)publish through digital technologies that offer new opportunities for criminologists to explore (Bruns, 2003, 2005). These opportunities exist in a variety of platforms, such as social media (Facebook, Twitter, Instagram), traditional media sources (television, radio, print) and online media sources (websites, blogs, forums). One example can be found in criminologists Sanja Milivojevic and Alyce McGovern's 2014 analysis of Facebook users' responses to Melbourne woman Jill Meagher's assault and murder, in which they identify disruptive narratives from the public that shifted the traditional media's all-too familiar and predictable victim-blaming tropes to provide a counter-framing that refocused the emphasis onto men's violence against women.

Digital Social Inequalities

Threaded throughout each of the above potential foci of criminological research are persistent themes of social inequalities, such as the intersections of race, class, gender and sexuality. While unequal technosocial relations may be facilitating new practices and cultures of racial and gender-based harms in particular (Mann et al., 2003; Powell & Henry, 2016), the capacity and nature of resistance to these harms and to broader racial and gender inequalities has arguably been changed by digital communications in significant ways. The capacity for marginalised communities to 'watch the watchers', i.e. to share video evidence of private abuses and police brutality, to organise via both tweets and streets to protest continued racial and gender inequalities; these are not merely technological shifts but an invigoration of social justice movements in a broader political context of disenchantment. Understanding the nature, impacts and justice movements of digital–social inequalities is thus a further crucial research topic within the field of digital criminology.

Structure of the Book

There is much to be gained in criminological theory and research from connecting the largely disparate threads of technology, sociality, crime, deviance and justice; we suggest that 'digital society' provides a useful starting place from which to advance such broad scholarship in the discipline. It is our intention to reinvigorate an ongoing conversation within the discipline and provide a framework for situating emerging theoretical and empirical crime and justice scholarship within a digital criminology.

The following two chapters continue framing our conceptual approach to digital criminology, and how it intersects with existing bodies of criminological research, as well as cross-disciplinary perspectives on digital technologies and society. In Chapter 2, *At the Crossroad*, we provide a brief history of cybercriminologies and summarise the key features of digital society, before moving on to an elaboration of critical and cultural criminologies as they relate to crime and justice in digital society. In Chapter 3, *A Global Context*, we propose that the challenges new digital technologies pose to individuals, communities and states are as much conceptual as they are to do with law enforcement and security, particularly in the context of increasing transnationalisation of crime.

The remaining chapters explore key issues for a digital criminology. Chapter 4 examines *Crime in Real Time*; engaging with a criminological perspective on the 'crowd' and citizen participation following, and potentially contributing to, investigations of crimes as they occur. In Chapter 5, *Liminal Images*, we discuss the meanings of, and responses to, images of crime in the context of digital technologies, focusing on participatory social media in particular. Chapter 6, *Networked Hate*, engages with the socio-cultural production and reproduction of gendered, racial and religious hate.

In the final two substantive chapters, we consider justice responses, both formal and informal, as well as justice activism, in digital society. Chapter 7, *Informal Justice*, considers the implications of citizen engagement across issues including informal justice, 'viral justice' and digital vigilantism (or digilantism). In Chapter 8, *More than a Hashtag*, we discuss the intersections of deliberative democracy, punitive politics and justice activism via social and other digital media. Finally, in the Conclusion (Chapter 9), we draw together the key themes and concepts developed across the book, identifying future directions for digital criminology.

Conclusion

In an edited collection titled *What is Criminology?* (Bosworth & Hoyle, 2011), David Garland argued that, to the detriment of our discipline, criminology is losing its dialogic nature of cross-disciplinary engagement and needs to be regularly infused with empirical and theoretical innovation from the outside. Much criminological engagement with digital crime has, to date, been likewise largely insular: lacking critical and interdisciplinary engagement with disciplines such as sociology, computer science, politics, journalism and media and cultural studies. This, we suggest, is particularly detrimental to advancing a new generation of scholarship concerning technology, crime, deviance and justice in digital society. Throughout this book, we position digital society as a useful theoretical framework that not only draws together the largely disparate scholarship on technosocial crime and justice within criminology but also expands our disciplinary concept, understanding and empirical examinations of crime and justice.

The potential avenues for digital criminological research presented here are intended to encompass and substantially expand the traditional foci of computer crime and cybercrime scholarship, while at the same time representing a provocation for continued development of the field. While there are many social and technological theoretical frameworks and disciplinary influences that may invigorate criminological research, what underlies many of them is a fundamental recognition that the influences of technology on contemporary crime and justice cannot be understood either as mere tools or as operating in a separate sphere of experience. Rather, here we have deployed the concept of 'digital society' to emphasise: the embedded nature of technology in our lived experiences of criminality, victimisation and justice; the emergence of new technosocial practices of both crime and justice; and the continued relevance of social, cultural and critical theories of society in understanding and responding to crime in a digital age.

As such, 'digital criminology' refers to the rapidly developing field of scholarship that applies criminological, social, cultural and technical theory and methods to the study of crime, deviance and justice in our digital society. Rather than necessarily a sub-discipline per se, we advocate that digital criminology may provide a fruitful platform from which to expand the boundaries of contemporary criminological theory and research. Our intention is twofold: to foster a broad and ongoing conversation within the discipline that cuts across technology, sociality, crime, deviance and justice; and to inspire new conceptual and empirical directions.

Note

1   In 2016, the Oxford English Dictionary made 'post-truth' its international word of the year, defining it as relating to or denoting 'circumstances in which objective facts are less influential in shaping public opinion than appeals to emotion and personal belief'.

References

Aaronson, D. E., & Patterson, S. M. (2012). Modernizing jury instructions in the age of social media. *Criminal Justice*, *27*(4), 26–35.

Aas, K. F. (2013). The ad and the form: Punitiveness and technological culture. In J. Pratt, D. Brown, M. Brown, S. Hallsworth, & W. Morrison (Eds.), *The new punitiveness: Trends, theories, perspectives* (pp. 150–166). London: Routledge.

Aikins, M. (2013, 28 June). Viral justice. *The New York Times*. Available at www.latitude.blogs.nytimes. com/2013/06/28/viral-justice/ (last accessed 29 November 2017).

Allan, S. (2013). *Citizen Witnessing: Revisioning Journalism in Times of Crisis. Key Concepts in Journalism.* Cambridge, UK: Polity.

Antoniades, A. (2012, 14 September). Viral justice: Domestic abuse victim calls out attacker on Facebook. *Takepart.* Available at: www.takepart.com/article/2012/12/14/viral-justice-domestic-abuse-victim-calls-out-attacker-facebook (last accessed 29 November 2017).

Athique, A. (2013). *Digital media and society: An introduction.* Cambridge, UK: Polity.

Bauman, Z., Bigo, D., Esteves, P., Guild, E., Jabri, V., Lyon, D., & Walker, R. B. (2014). After Snowden: Rethinking the impact of surveillance. *International Political Sociology*, *8*(2), 121–144.

Bauman, Z., & Lyon, D. (2012). *Liquid surveillance: A conversation.* Cambridge, UK: Polity.

Baym, N. K. (2015). *Personal connections in the digital age* (2nd ed.). Cambridge, UK: John Wiley & Sons.

Beer, D. (2009). Power through the algorithm? Participatory web cultures and the technological unconscious. *New Media & Society*, *11*(6), 985–1002.

Beer, D., & Burrows, R. (2007). Sociology and, of and in Web 2.0: Some initial considerations. *Sociological Research Online*, *12*(5). doi: 10.5153/sro.1560.

Bosworth, M., & Hoyle, C. (Eds.). (2011). *What is criminology?* (pp. 298–317). Oxford: Oxford University Press.

Bottoms, A. (1995). The philosophy and politics of punishment and sentencing. In C. Clarkson, & R. Morgan (Eds.), *The politics of sentencing reform* (pp. 17–49). Oxford: Oxford University Press.

Bradshaw, E. A. (2013). This is what a police state looks like: Sousveillance, direct action and the anti-corporate globalization movement. *Critical Criminology*, *21*(4), 447–461.

Brown, S. (2006). The criminology of hybrids: Rethinking crime and law in technosocial networks. *Theoretical Criminology*, *10*(2), 223–244.

Browning, J. G. (2014). Should voir dire become voir Google? Ethical implications of researching jurors on social media. *SMU Science and Technology Law Review*, *17*(4), 603–629.

Bruns, A. (2003). Gatewatching, not gatekeeping: Collaborative online news. *Media International Australia Incorporating Culture and Policy: Quarterly Journal of Media Research and Resources, 107*(1), 31–44.

Bruns, A. (2005). *Gatewatching: Collaborative online news production.* New York: Peter Lang Publishing.

Burrows, R. (2009). Afterword: Urban informatics and social ontology. In M. Foth (ed.), *Handbook of research on urban informatics: The practice and promise of the realtime city* (pp. 450–454). Hershey: IGI Global.

Casey, E. (2011). *Digital evidence and computer crime: Forensic science, computers, and the internet.* Cambridge, UK: Academic Press.

Castells, M. (1996). *The network society* (Vol. *469*). Oxford: Blackwell.

Castells, M. (2010). *The rise of the network society: The information age: Economy, society, and culture* (Vol. *1*, 2nd ed.). West Sussex: Wiley-Blackwell.

Castells, M. (2012). *Networks of outrage and HOPE: Social movements in the internet age.* Cambridge, UK: Polity Press.

Chaikin, D. (2006). Network investigations of cyber attacks: The limits of digital evidence. *Crime, Law and Social Change, 46*(4–5), 239–256.

Citron, D. K. (2014). *Hate crimes in cyberspace.* Cambridge, MA: Harvard University Press.

Colleoni, E., Rozza, A., & Arvidsson, A. (2014). Echo chamber or public sphere? Predicting political orientation and measuring political homophily in Twitter using big data. *Journal of Communication, 64*(2), 317–332.

Criddle, C. (2016, 29 August). Robberies, thefts, assaults and driving offences among hundreds of crimes involving Pokemon Go logged by police in July. *The Telegraph.* Available at: www.telegraph.co.uk/news/2016/08/29/robberies-thefts-assaults-and-driving-offences-among-hundreds-of/ (last accessed 29 November 2017).

Crockett, Z. (2016, 8 November). *Your ballot selfie could get you arrested in these states. Here's where it's legal and illegal.* Available at: www.vox.com/policy-and-politics/2016/10/25/13389980/ballot-selfie-legal-illegal (last accessed 29 November 2017).

Deuze, M. (2006). Participation, remediation, bricolage: Considering principal components of a digital culture. *The Information Society, 22*(2), 63–75.

Dobreva, D., & Innes, M. (2016). 'Second wave de-liberalisation' and understanding the causes and consequences of Brexit's implications for policing. *Democrazia e Sicurezza-Democracy and Security Review, VI*(4), 21–54.

Duggan, M., & Smith, A. (2016). *The political environment on social media.* Washington, DC: Pew Research Center. Available at: www.pewinternet.org/2016/10/25/the-political-environment-on-social-media/ (last accessed 29 November 2017).

Enli, G. (2017). Twitter as arena for the authentic outsider: Exploring the social media campaigns of Trump and Clinton in the 2016 US presidential election. *European Journal of Communication, 32*(1), 50–61.

Federal Bureau of Investigation. (2016). *FBI records: The vault (Hillary R. Clinton).* Available at: https://vault.fbi.gov/hillary-r.-clinton (last accessed 29 November 2017).

Fileborn, B. (2014). Online activism and street harassment: Digital justice or shouting into the ether? *Griffith Journal of Law & Human Dignity, 2*(1), 32–51.

Ford, H. (2016). Plano man killed girlfriend, posted picture on Facebook: PD. *NBC 5.* Available at: www.nbcdfw.com/news/local/Plano-Man-Arrested-For-Killing-Girlfriend-Police-381326061.html (last accessed 29 November 2017).

Freiberg, A. (2001). Affective versus effective justice instrumentalism and emotionalism in criminal justice. *Punishment & Society, 3*(2), 265–278.

Garland, D. (2011). Criminology's place in the academic field, David Garland. In M. Bosworth & C. Hoyle (Eds.), *What is criminology?* (pp. 298–317). Oxford: Oxford University Press.

Gass, N., & Lerner, A. B. (2015). Donald Trump gives out Lindsey Graham's cellphone number. *Politico.* Available at: www.politico.com/story/2015/07/donald-trump-gives-out-lindsey-grahams-cell-phone-number-120414 (last accessed 29 November 2017).

Gilman, D. (Director). (2016, June 3). *EU: In or out?* [Television broadcast]. UK: Sky News.

Goldsmith, A. (2015). Disgracebook policing: Social media and the rise of police indiscretion. *Policing and Society, 25*(3), 249–267.

Gottehrer, G. (2015). Connected discovery: What the ubiquity of digital evidence means for lawyers and litigation. *Richmond Journal of Law & Technology, 22*(3), 1–27.

Grabosky, P. N., & Smith, R. G. (2001). Digital Crime in the Twenty-First Century 1. *Journal of information ethics*, *10*(1), 8.

Graham, S., & Wood, D. (2003). Digitizing surveillance: categorization, space, inequality. *Critical Social Policy*, *23*(2), 227–248.

Halford, S., & Savage, M. (2010). Reconceptualizing digital social Inequality. *Information, Communication & Society*, *13*(7), 937–955.

Hassan, R. (2008). *The information society: Cyber dreams and digital nightmares*. Cambridge, UK: Polity.

Hay, J., & Couldry, N. (2011). Rethinking convergence/culture. *Cultural Studies*, *25*(4–5), 473–486.

Healy, P., Sanger, D. E., & Haberman, M. (2016). Donald Trump finds improbable ally in WikiLeaks. *New York Times*. Available at: www.nytimes.com/2016/10/13/us/politics/wikileaks-hillary-clinton-emails.html (last accessed 29 November 2017).

Henry, N., & Powell, A. (2015). Embodied harms: Gender, shame, and technology-facilitated sexual violence. *Violence against women*, *21*(6), 758–779.

Henry, N., Powell, A., & Flynn, A. (2017). *Not Just 'Revenge Pornography': Australians' Experiences of Image-Based Abuse. A Summary Report*. Available at: Melbourne, Australia: RMIT University.

Hess, K., & Waller, L. (2014). The digital pillory: Media shaming of 'Ordinary' people for minor crimes. *Continuum*, *28*(1), 101–111.

Hogan, B. (2016). How Facebook divides us. *The Time Literary Supplement*. Available at: www.the-tls.co.uk/articles/public/facebook-trump-brexit/ (last accessed 29 November 2017).

Horst, H., & Miller, D. (2013). The digital and the human: A prospectus for digital anthropology. In H. Horst & D. Miller (Eds.), *Digital anthropology* (pp. 3–38). New York: Berg.

Howard, P. (2017). *Reuters: Facebook and Twitter's real sin goes beyond spreading fake news*. Available at: www.oii.ox.ac.uk/blog/reuters-facebook-and-twitters-real-sin-goes-beyond-spreading-fake-news/ (last accessed 29 November 2017).

Inglehart, R., & Norris, P. (2016). *Trump, Brexit, and the rise of populism: Economic have-nots and the cultural backlash* (HKS Faculty Research Working Paper No. RWP16-026). Harvard: Harvard Kennedy School.

Jacobs, B., Siddiqui, S., & Ackerman, S. (2016, 29 October). Newly discovered Emails relating to Hillary Clinton case under review by FBI. *The Guardian*. Available at: www.theguardian.com/us-news/2016/oct/28/fbi-reopens-hillary-clinton-emails-investigation (last accessed 29 November 2017).

Jenkins, H. (2006). *Convergence culture: Where old and new media collide*: New York: New York University Press.

Jenkins, H. (2014). Rethinking 'Rethinking Convergence/Culture'. *Cultural Studies*, *28*(2), 267–297.

Johnson, S. (2016, 11 November). Donald Trump Tweeted Himself into the White House. *The Conversation*. Available at: www.theconversation.com/donald-trump-tweeted-himself-into-the-white-house-68561 (last accessed 29 November 2017).

Johnston, J., & McGovern, A. (2013). Communicating justice: A comparison of courts and police use of contemporary media. *International Journal of Communication*, 7, 1667–1687.

Jones, S. (1995). *Cybersociety*. London: Sage.

Katz, J. E., & Aakhus, M. (Eds.). (2002). *Perpetual contact: Mobile communication, private talk, public performance*. Cambridge, UK: Cambridge University Press.

Kerr, O. S. (2005). Digital evidence and the new criminal procedure. *Columbia Law Review*, *105*(1), 279–318.

Kyslova, O., & Berdnyk, E. (2014). New media as a formation factor for digital sociology: The consequences of the networking in the society and the intellectualization of the communications. *Studies of Changing Societies*, *2013*(3), 67–106.

Lash, S. (2001). Technological forms of life. *Theory, Culture & Society*, *18*(1), 105–120.

Lash, S. (2002). *Critique of information*. London: Sage.

Lash, S. (2007, 5–6 September). *New new media ontology*. Presentation at toward a social science of Web 2.0, York, UK.

Law, J., Ruppert, E., & Savage, M. (2011). *The double social life of methods*. (CRESC Working Paper No. 95). Milton Keynes: Centre for Research on Socio-Cultural Change (CRESC), Open University.

Lévy, P. (2001). *Cyberculture* (Vol. 4). Minneapolis, MN: University of Minnesota Press.

Lockie, S. (2017). Post-truth politics and the Social Sciences. *Environmental Sociology, 3*(1), 1–5.

Lupton, D. (2013). *Introducing digital sociology.* Sydney: University of Sydney.

Lupton, D. (2015). *Digital sociology.* London: Routledge.

Lyon, D. (ed.). (2003). *Surveillance as social sorting: Privacy, risk, and digital discrimination.* London: Routledge.

Mann, D., Sutton, M., & Tuffin, R. (2003). The evolution of Hate. Social dynamics in white racist newsgroups. *Internet Journal of Criminology, 1,* 1–32.

Margulies, P. (2013). NSA in global perspective: Surveillance, human rights, and international counterterrorism. *The Fordham Law Review, 82*(5), 2137–2167.

Marres, N. (2013). *What is digital sociology?* Available at: www.csisponline.net/2013/01/21/what-is-digital-sociology/ (last accessed 29 November 2017).

Martinson, R. (1974). What works? - Questions and answers about prison reform. *The Public Interest, 35,* 2–54.

Marx, G. T. (2003). A tack in the shoe: Neutralizing and resisting the new surveillance. *Journal of Social Issues, 59*(2), 369–390.

McGovern, A. (2011, 17 May 2010). *Tweeting the news: Criminal justice agencies and their use of social networking Sites.* Paper presented at the Australian and New Zealand Critical Criminology Conference Proceedings, Sydney, New South Wales.

McGovern, A., & Lee, M. (2012). Police communications in the social media age. In P. Keyzer, J. Johnston, & M. Pearson (Eds.), *The courts and the media: Challenges in the era of digital and social media* (pp. 160–174). Ultimo: Halstead Press.

McGrath, J. E. (2004). *Loving big brother: Performance, privacy and surveillance space.* Abingdon, UK: Psychology Press.

McPherson, M., Smith-Lovin, L., & Cook, J. M. (2001). Birds of a feather: Homophily in social networks. *Annual Review of Sociology, 27*(1), 415–444.

Milivojevic, S., & McGovern, A. (2014). The death of Jill Meagher: Crime and punishment on social media. *International Journal for Crime, Justice and Social Democracy, 3*(3), 22–39.

Orton-Johnson, K., & Prior, N. (Eds.). (2013a). *Digital sociology: Critical perspectives.* Hampshire, UK: Palgrave–Macmillan.

Orton-Johnson, K., & Prior, N. (2013b). Introduction. In K. Orton-Johnson, & N. Prior (Eds.), *Digital sociology: Critical perspectives* (pp. 1–12). Hampshire, UK: Palgrave Macmillan.

Ott, B. L. (2017). The age of Twitter: Donald J. Trump and the politics of debasement. *Critical Studies in Media Communication, 34*(1), 59–68.

Perlroth, N., & Shear, M. D. (2016, October 20). Private security group says Russia was behind John Podesta's email hack. *New York Time.* Available at: www.nytimes.com/2016/10/21/us/private-security-group-says-russia-was-behind-john-podestas-email-hack.html (last accessed 29 November 2017).

Peters, M. (2017). Education in a post-truth world. *Educational Philosophy and Theory, 49*(6), 563–566.

Powell, A. (2014, 24–27 November). *Pursuing Justice Online: Citizen Participation in Justice via Social Media.* Refereed Proceedings at The Australian Sociological Association Conference, *Challenging Identities, Institutions and Communities,* Adelaide, Australia.

Powell, A. (2015a). Seeking informal justice online: Vigilantism, activism and resisting a rape culture in cyberspace. In A. Powell, N. Henry, & A. Flynn (Eds.), *Rape justice: Beyond the criminal law* (pp. 218–237). Hampshire, UK: Palgrave Macmillan.

Powell, A. (2015b). Seeking rape justice: Formal and informal responses to sexual violence through technosocial counter-publics. *Theoretical Criminology, 19*(4), 571–588.

Powell, A., & Henry, N. (2016). Technology-facilitated sexual violence victimization: Results from an online survey of Australian adults. *Journal of Interpersonal Violence,* 1–26. doi: 10.1177/0886260516672055.

Powell, A., & Henry, N. (2017). *Sexual violence in a digital age.* Basingstoke: Palgrave Macmillan.

Prins, C. (2011). Digital tools: Risks and opportunities for victims: Explorations in e-victimology. In R. Letschert & J. Van Dijk (Eds.), *The new faces of victimhood. Globalization, transnational crimes and victim rights* (pp. 215–230). Netherlands: Springer.

Quilter, J. (2012). Responses to the death of Thomas Kelly: Taking populism seriously. *Current Issues in Criminal Justice, 24*(3), 439–448.

Ruppert, E., Law, J., & Savage, M. (2013). Reassembling social science methods: The challenge of digital devices. *Theory, Culture & Society, 30*(4), 22–46.

Rutkin, A. (2015). It's a fitbit, your honour. *New Scientist, 225*(3002), 17.

Sanger, D. E., & Shane, S. (2016, December 9). Russian hackers acted to aid Trump in election, U.S. says. *The New York Times.* Available at: www.nytimes.com/2016/12/09/us/obama-russia-election-hack.html (last accessed 29 November 2017).

Simon, J. (2007). *Governing through Crime.* New York: Oxford University Press.

Smyth, S. M. (2012). The new social media paradox: A symbol of self-determination or a boon for big brother? *International Journal of Cyber Criminology, 6*(1), 924–950.

Speed, E., & Mannion, R. (2017). The rise of post-truth populism in pluralist liberal democracies: Challenges for health policy. *International Journal of Health Policy Management, 6*(5), 249–251.

Stehr, N. (1994). *Knowledge societies.* London: Sage.

Stratton, G., Powell, A., & Cameron, R. (2017). Crime and Justice in Digital Society: Towards a 'Digital Criminology'?. *International Journal for Crime, Justice and Social Democracy, 6*(2), 17–33.

Subramanian, S. (2017, 15 February). Welcome to Veles, Macedonia, fake news factory to the world. *Wired.* Available at: www.wired.com/2017/02/veles-macedonia-fake-news/ (last accessed 29 November 2017).

Sulleyman, A. (2017, 27 April). Facebook live killings: Why the criticism has been harsh. *The Independent.* Available at: www.independent.co.uk/life-style/gadgets-and-tech/features/facebook-live-killings-ai-artificial-intelligence-not-blame-fatalities-murders-us-steve-stephens-a7706056.html (last accessed 29 November 2017).

Thompson, C., Wood, M., & Rose, E. (2016). *Viral Justice: Survivor Selfies, Internet Virality and Justice for Victims of Intimate Partner Violence.* Paper presented at the British Society of Criminology 2016 Conference: Inequalities in a Diverse World, Nottingham, England.

Thrift, N. (2004). Driving in the city. *Theory, Culture & Society, 21*(4–5), 41–59.

Thrift, N. (2005). *Knowing capitalism.* London: Sage.

Trottier, D. (2012). *Social media as surveillance: Rethinking visibility in a converging world.* Abingdon, Oxon, UK: Routledge.

Trottier, D. (2014). Crowdsourcing CCTV surveillance on the internet. *Information, Communication & Society, 17*(5), 609–626.

Van Dijk, J. A. G. M. (2013). Inequalities in the network society. In N. Prior & K. Orton-Johnson (Eds.), *Digital sociology: Critical perspectives* (pp. 105–124). Houndmills, Basingstoke, Hampshire: Palgrave Macmillan.

Van Laer, J., & van Aelst, P. (2009). Cyber-protest and civil society: The internet and action repertoires of social movements. In Y. Jewkes & M. Yar (Eds.), *Handbook of internet crime* (pp. 230–254). Portland, Oregon: Willan Publishing.

Webster, F. (1995). Information and the idea of an information society. In F. Webster (Ed.), *Theories of the information society* (1st ed., pp. 6–51). London: Routledge.

Zempi, I., & Awan, I. (2016). *Islamophobia: Lived experiences of online and offline victimisation.* Bristol, UK: Policy Press.

2

AT THE CROSSROAD

Cyber, Critical and Cultural Criminologies

Introduction

Criminology has a long tradition of examining both the socio-structural and socio-cultural bases of crime and justice. Emerging in the late 1960s, critical criminologies have sought to illuminate the various ways in which crime, and the institutions of crime control, 'reflect and reproduce patterns of power, inequality, exploitation and exclusion' (Yar, 2012c, p. 52). Cultural criminologies, meanwhile, have grown in breadth and popularity since the mid-1990s, focusing on the intersections of culture and crime: 'to account for the culture and subcultures of crime, the criminalization of cultural and subcultural activities, and the politics of these processes' (Ferrell & Sanders, 1995, pp. 3–4). Throughout this book, we advocate a reinvigoration of criminological research that extends beyond conventional 'cybercrime'. Indeed, as Danish criminologist Katja Franko Aas (2016) observes, 'Criminologists have been, with some exceptions, relatively slow to take on board, or at least to systematically theorize, the technologically-mediated nature of our sociality.' To do so, we suggest, requires inspiration from interdisciplinary theories, concepts and approaches. As such, we position digital criminology not as a new sub-discipline, but as a critical and cultural criminological orientation to crime and justice in a digital society.

Digital criminology represents the intersection of critical, cultural and socio-technical theory and research. The purpose of this chapter, then, is first to provide a brief history of cybercriminologies, and then to summarise the key features of digital society, before moving on to discuss critical and cultural criminologies as they relate to crime and justice in digital society. In doing so, we consider how these conceptual frameworks might be further developed by the addition of socio-technical concepts, before moving on to elaborate some fruitful avenues for digital criminological theory and research in subsequent chapters.

A Brief History of Cybercriminologies

The internet has long-reaching origins: from advances in computing in the 1950s; to the earliest electronic mail (and spam) in the 1970s; to the first messages sent via the US-military-funded

ARPANET in 1969; to online communications within private, closed networks in the 1980s; to the global web in the 1990s (Leiner et al., 2009). Indeed, technological developments and their associated implications for crime and criminology can be charted across three broad periods: the 'pre-web' era of the 1980s to early 1990s, the 'global web' era of the 1990s to early 2000s and the 'social web' era from the mid-2000s to the present day. We do not intend to suggest that the challenges and opportunities for crime and criminological scholarship presented by each era are replaced or discontinued with the next, but that each period brings with it unique advances in technology that have particular impacts for crime and that can be broadly linked with associated shifts in criminological thinking and research.

Pre-web Era: 1980s to 1991

It was not until the 1980s that personal computers[1] were widely adopted in workplaces and public institutions in the developed West (Ceruzzi, 2003). From the 1980s onwards, however, the information and activities of governments, education institutions and corporations were rapidly computerised and associated with greater electronic data storage, as well as increased connectivity within closed internal and private networks (Ceruzzi, 2003; Williams, 1997). Criminology in this pre-web era (1980s to 1991) recognised that such widespread computer availability and electronic data storage, combined with internally networked workstations and dial-in connections, had opened up governments, corporations and educational institutions to new forms of crime through technology misuse. Computer-related economic crimes (including financial data theft and identity fraud), 'eavesdropping' and the interception of confidential communications, and the security and privacy of confidential information systems, as well as software piracy via illegal disk-based copies, were among the predominant concerns of the time (Clough & Mungo, 1992; Sieber, 1986). As computer technology was predominantly adopted in public and corporate organisations, these emerging harms were largely associated with white collar crime (Croall, 1992; Kling, 1980; Montgomery, 1986).

The pre-web period also marked the first legislative steps to address computer-enabled crime. For example, one of the earliest laws that defined computer crime was passed in Florida in the United States in 1978 in response to the fraudulent printing of winning tickets at a dog racing track using a computer (Hollinger & Lanza-Kaduce, 1988). This law was notable because it defined all unauthorised access to a computer as an offence, regardless of whether or not there was malicious intent (Casey, 2011, p. 35). By 1983, another 20 states had introduced computer crime legislation. The US federal *Computer Fraud and Abuse Act* of 1984 criminalised various forms of unauthorised computer access of information. Information relating to defence or foreign relations matters was regarded as a felony offence, whereas intrusions designed to access or alter all other non-classified forms of information were regarded as misdemeanors (Griffith, 1990, p. 460). Similar computer crime laws were subsequently introduced elsewhere. In Australia, for instance, a 1989 amendment to the *Crimes Act* outlined three categories of computer 'hacking' crimes: mere access, without seeking out or altering specific information; access without initial intent but opportunistically seeking or altering information; and access with intent to seek or alter specific information. In England, meanwhile, it was 1990 before the first criminal statute to tackle the misuse of computers was passed (Wasik, 1991). Consistent with many legislative frameworks, the very act of using a computer to breach a network or database was highlighted as an offence, regardless of specific intent (Greenleaf, 1990, p. 21). A tension running throughout the debates that led to these initial legal reforms was the question of whether the act of computer misuse or unauthorised access itself should be specifically criminalised, in addition to the equivalent terrestrial or analogue crimes that may result.

Global Web Era: 1990s to 2000s

The modern World Wide Web went live to a global public on 6 August 1991 (Leiner et al., 2009). While understanding and legislating computer crime typified criminological research of the 1980s and early 1990s, the 'global web' era (1990s to 2000s) brought an associated shift towards internet and cybercrime research. The increased accessibility of online information sharing and communications that the global web brought for everyday users was widely recognised as creating new and massively expanded opportunities for crime as 'the perpetrators who attacked machines through machines . . . started attacking *real humans* through the machines' (Jaishankar, 2011, p. 26, emphasis added). Thus, while financial fraud, data theft, information privacy and identity crime remained (and remain) persistent themes in criminological research, the attention of cybercrime scholars broadened to include interpersonal harms such as online child sexual exploitation and child pornography (Armagh, 2001; Esposito, 1998; Mitchell et al., 2010), both of which had become the focus of much public and policy concern.

The scope and focus of cybercrime scholarship in the global web era is well captured by David Wall's (2001) original and highly influential typology, which comprises four categories of cybercrime:

(1) *cybertrespass*, incorporating unauthorised access to a computer system, network or data source, such as through on-site system hacking, online attacks and/or malicious software (malware);
(2) *cyberdeception and cybertheft*, including financial and data thefts, intellectual property thefts and electronic piracy. Such crimes may be facilitated through fraudulent scams, identity fraud and malware;
(3) *cyberporn and cyberobscenity*, referring to the online trading of sexually expressive material and including sexually deviant and fetish subcultures, sex work, sex trafficking, sex tourism and child sexual grooming and exploitation material; and
(4) *cyberviolence*, referring to the various ways that individuals can cause interpersonal harms to others. Such harms include cyberstalking, cyberbullying, cyberharassment and communications that support prospective acts of violence or terror, such as threats of personal violence, bomb talk or circulating instructions for making explosives and other weaponry (Wall, 2001).

These categories can be understood according to a common categorisation in cybercrime research: the first category represents computer-focused acts (i.e. directed at the machine), while the latter three are more readily described as computer-assisted acts (Jewkes & Yar, 2010; Smith et al., 2004). Wall's early work (2001) identified that the internet had influenced crime across these categories in at least three broad ways. First, by providing a platform for communications that may enable and sustain existing harmful and criminal activities, such as drug trafficking, hate speech, stalking and sharing information on how to offend. Second, through enabling participation in a transnational environment that provides new opportunities and expanded reach for criminal activities which would be subject to existing law in sovereign states. Third, the distanciation of time and space creates potentially new, unbounded, contestable and private harms, such as the misappropriation of imagery and intellectual property. In particular, he suggested that the shrinking role of the state and the relative ungovernability of cyberspace (discussed further in Chapter 3) present particular challenges both for policing 'virtual communities' and for the discipline of criminology more broadly (Wall, 1997). Wall argued that, while the new cyberspace offered enormous democratising potential, 'there are also many opportunities for new types of offending' and that the internet posed a 'considerable threat to traditional forms of governance and . . . to traditional understandings of order' (Wall, 1997, p. 208).

Despite this broad potential focus for criminology, in practice much cybercriminology has focused on financial crimes, identity fraud and threats to market and state security: the first three aspects of Wall's (2001) typology. Interpersonal violence has received much less attention by comparison. While there are a plethora of studies on cyberbullying, these are focused almost exclusively on minors (aged 17 years or under) and young adults (up to 24 years), and they are undertaken more often in the contexts of psychology, social work and education than criminology itself. Similarly, the many studies on cyberstalking originate largely from within psychological frameworks. In both instances, these fields of research have come to dominate work on cyberviolence to the relative neglect of a broader range of interpersonal violences and their intersections with digital technologies, including: intimate partner violence, sexual violence, racially and/or sexuality based harassment and/or hate crime, as well as more traditional criminological concerns, such as male-to-male violence.

In addition to restricted *topics* of analysis, much criminological research has focused on cybercrimes, cybercriminality and cyber law enforcement with very few studies seeking to apply or adapt criminological *theory* to such research (see Holt & Bossler, 2014, 2015 for a discussion of these limitations). The works that have undertaken such conceptual development have drawn predominantly on a handful of 'rational choice', deviant lifestyle and subcultural theories of crime (for reviews see Diamond & Bachman, 2015; Holt & Bossler, 2014). In particular, Lawrence Cohen and Marcus Felson's 1979 Routine Activity Theory (RAT) features so often in cybercrime theorising that it might be described as the prevailing orthodoxy in such research (Holt & Bossler, 2008; Hutchings & Hayes, 2008; Pyrooz et al., 2015; Reyns et al., 2011; van Wilmsen, 2011; Yar, 2005). For example, as criminologist Peter Grabosky (2001) explains:

> [o]ne of the basic tenets of criminology holds that crime can be explained by three factors: motivation, opportunity, and the absence of a capable guardian . . . derived initially to explain conventional "street" crime, it is equally applicable to crime in cyberspace (p. 248).

While not all criminologists agree on the applicability of the theory to cybercrime (Jaishankar, 2008; Yar, 2005), its dominance is arguably highly influential in framing the focus of much research with regards to identifying the motivations of individual cyber offenders, 'target hardening' and identifying 'risky' online victim behaviours, as well as the challenges of law enforcement (as a form of guardianship), a trend which has continued in computer and cybercriminologies. Indeed, in a recent review of the current state of cybercrime scholarship, Thomas Holt and Adam Bossler (2014, p. 21), describe how the preceding 20 years of criminological research have predominantly focused on the study of the 'impact of technology on the practices of *offenders*, factors affecting the *risk of victimization*, and the applicability of *traditional theories* of crime to *virtual offences*' (emphasis added).

Social Web Era: 2000s to present

With the millennium came Web 2.0 and the 'social web' (2000s to present) as online communications became increasingly collaborative, with expanded capacity for user-generated content development and sharing, as well as online social networking. Between 2002 and 2010, there was an explosion of social networks and image-sharing platforms, including Friendster, MySpace, Facebook, YouTube, Twitter, Tumblr and Instagram. Research into cyberbullying, cyberstalking and online harassment rapidly expanded over this period as the relative ease, anonymity and reach of online communications was associated with continuing concerns regarding invasive and threatening communications (Pittaro, 2007; Reyns et al., 2011; Spitzberg & Hoobler, 2002), particularly in relation to vulnerable groups such as children and young adults.

As the social web expanded, so too did the 'deep web' and 'dark web'; a shorthand for content on the internet that is not indexed by standard search engines (and is thus not searchable) and/or that is protected by layers of encryption and other security mechanisms (Bergman, 2001). While not *all* content on the dark web is necessarily, or by definition, illicit, the concealment of such underground networks provides the ideal environment for activities such as: illicit content, including child exploitation material; criminal organising, such as by terrorist or organised crime networks; and black markets, trading in items such as malware and illicit drugs (Martin, 2014; Sugiura, 2018; Yip et al., 2013). A growing focus of cybercrime research has thus been to identify and understand the nature and patterns of such online criminal social networks (Brewer, 2017; Décary-Hétu & Dupont, 2012; Holt, 2013; Westlake & Bouchard, 2016).

A further feature of the social web era is the increasingly mobile web, with smartphones and wearable technology becoming ever-more common — almost ubiquitous — and simultaneously collecting expansive 'big data' about our selves, our identities and our everyday lives. Criminological research has also sought to engage with these increasingly automated, algorithmic and computational capacities as they relate to crime data analytics, law enforcement and justice system practices (Berk, 2008; Birks et al., 2012; Brantingham, 2011). Though there is, as yet, a comparative dearth of criminological research that has begun to empirically and critically explore the range of challenges and opportunities presented by 'big data' analytics. Most recently, Janet Chan and Lyria Bennett Moses (2016, p. 25) note the relatively small engagement from criminologists with big data research, which tends to lie in two main areas: social media data analysis and the uptake of computer modelling/algorithms as a predictive tool in police and criminal justice decision making. They suggest that criminologists, and social scientists more broadly, must increasingly collaborate with technical experts to further progress this field.

Breaking Through the Binaries of Online/Offline and Real/Virtual

As the preceding discussion shows, we believe that there are notable gaps in the current field of cybercrime research (Aas, 2007a,b; Hayward, 2012; Holt & Bossler, 2014). Despite more than ten years since the rise of the social web, criminological scholarship remains focused on computing and internet technologies as either themselves the *targets* of crime or as mere *tools* in the commission of otherwise familiar and recognisable crimes. The topics and foci of much of the cybercrime research are likewise limited in scope. An overview of both seminal and contemporary works — books, edited collections and journal special issues — over the past 20 years yields recurring topics including: hacking, data theft, online fraud and scams, digital piracy, child exploitation materials ('pornography'[2]), online sex work, cyberbullying, cyberstalking, cyberterrorism and online extremism; as well as challenges for cyber legislation and law enforcement (Grabosky & Smith, 1998; Holt, 2011; Jaishankar, 2011; Wall, 2007). There are also cybercrime works on topics including information privacy and data surveillance

(Thomas & Loader, 2000; Yar, 2013), though these are fewer. Little cybercrime scholarship engages with persistent social inequalities, or the digital divide, as it relates to crime (Halford & Savage, 2010); therefore, few studies explore the unequal nature, impacts and responses towards cybercrimes and other digital harms with respect to gender, gender-identity, race and/or sexuality (notable exceptions include Halder & Jaishankar, 2012; Powell & Henry, 2016; Mann et al., 2003; Sutton, 2002). Indeed, in their recent review of cybercrime scholarship, Holt and Bossler (2014) make no mention of technology-enabled and online violence against women (despite discussing studies on harassment, stalking and bullying, which they overtly associate with juvenile victims and offenders), nor internet hate such as racially motivated hate speech or harassment focused on sexuality and/or gender-identity. This does not indicate an oversight of their review but the dearth of cybercrime research that has engaged with violence against marginalised and/or minority communities.

There clearly remains an inherent dualism, in which cybercrimes continue to be framed as a mirror or the online double of their terrestrial counterparts, differing perhaps by medium and reach but not by nature: trespass becomes *cyber*trespass, theft becomes *cyber*theft, bullying becomes *cyber*bullying, terrorism becomes *cyber*terrorism. But the foregrounding of the cyber, itself a direct reference to internet and 'virtual' technologies, obscures the diverse and embedded nature of digital data and communications in contemporary societies (Aas, 2007b). Jaishankar (2007, p. 2), for instance, describes the field of cybercriminology itself as studies of 'cyber crime, cyber criminal behaviour, cyber victims, cyber laws and cyber investigations', as if these categories were all readily or neatly distinguishable from a 'non-cyber' equivalent.

Yet, in a groundbreaking article featured in *Theoretical Criminology*, Sheila Brown challenged such computer criminology and cybercriminology to look outside of its conventional disciplinary frameworks and look instead 'towards theories of the *technosocial*' (2006, p. 227 emphasis added). Analyses of cybercrime, she suggests, are caught up in false distinctions between 'virtual' and 'embodied' crime; seeking to develop and translate 'old' legal and theoretical frameworks to understand the 'new' crimes in cyberspace. Brown argues that, within criminology, 'nowhere is captured the vision of the crucial nature of the world as a human/technical hybrid . . .' (Brown 2006, p. 227), in which all crime occurs in networks, which vary only in degrees of virtuality/embodiment. Drawing variously on social and technology theorists such as Bruno Latour (1993), Scott Lash (2002), Donna Haraway (1991) and Manuel Castells (1996, 2001), Brown posited a need for criminologists to understand crime and criminality at the increasingly blurred intersections of biology/technology, nature/society, object/agent and artificial/human. Computing and information theories, she argued, 'will increasingly infuse both domains of Law and Criminology' (Brown 2006, p. 236) as social theory is not in itself sufficient to analyse and understand crime in contemporary societies.

Key Features of Digital Society

In order to further conceptualise contemporary crime and justice, in this section we first consider some of the key features of digital society that come to bear on an emerging *digital criminological* scholarship. Then, we elaborate further on possible intersections with innovative and emerging research and theory within critical and cultural criminologies. Many researchers across politics (Papacharissi, 2010; Ruppert, Law, & Savage, 2013; Wilhelm, 2000), media and communications (Berry, 2012; Miller, 2011), as well as digital sociologies (Lupton, 2014; Marres, 2017), have sought to summarise the distinctive features of the digital age; and, naturally, our discussion in this chapter is not novel in this respect. Yet, we do find it useful to weave together some of these disparate bodies of literature and concepts to engage the criminological imagination further. In doing so, we identify eight key themes of digital society that inspire reflections on crime and justice, each of which we now describe as a prelude to the discussion and analysis that follows throughout the book as a whole.

'Perpetual Contact', Convergence and Omnipresence

Among the key features of the digital age are the global networking and portability of internet-enabled devices, such that individuals are in 'perpetual contact' (Katz & Akhaus, 2002). Though the first smartphones, with programmable operating systems, internet access, emailing and web-browsing capabilities, were released in the mid-1990s, it was not until 2007, with the launch of the Apple iPhone, that smartphones began their rise as a dominant consumer communications device (Cecere, Corrocher, & Battaglia, 2015). Further integrated features such as wi-fi connectivity, Bluetooth, file storage, GPS, motion sensors, advanced operating systems capable of supporting a wide range of software applications, as well as increasingly powerful still and video cameras (including a secondary front-facing camera for video-calling and 'selfie' mode), have all contributed to the 'full convergence between computing and communications' (Cecere et al., 2015, p. 165). Changes in communications, sociality and behaviours associated with people having this advanced portable computer in their hand everywhere they go have not gone unnoticed by social and political scientists. From the ease of communicating via social media for everything from the banal to the personal and the political (Bonilla & Rosa, 2015; Goggin, 2014; Ibrahim, 2015), to promoting 'selfie' culture (Diefenbach & Christoforakos, 2017; Lim & Lim, 2016; Murray, 2015; Senft & Baym, 2015), to location tracking during disasters (Bruns & Burgess, 2013; Jasmontaite & Dimitrova, 2017), to tracking health and fitness (Goldstein, Thomas, Wing, & Bond, 2017; Kaiser, Harrington, & Turakhia, 2016; Kim et al., 2016), to concerns about the impacts on mental well-being and personal relationships (Bayer, Campbell, & Ling, 2016; Harwood, Dooley, Scott, & Joiner, 2014; Miller, 2012; Misra, Cheng, Genevie, & Yuan, 2016); many scholars have noted that the rapid and extensive uptake of smartphones will be looked back on as one of the defining technological shifts of our time.

Among the implications of the software applications (apps) available on smartphones is the presence of social media as an integrated form of communication and consumption in everyday life. Distinctions between 'old' and 'new' media as sources of news and information are increasingly blurred. Where once the generation of news and other media content was top-down and hierarchical, with citizens' roles narrowly defined as passive consumers, the new media is typified by its horizontal and 'two-way' networks of interaction and user-content generation (Yar, 2012a; see also Miller, 2011). Journalism, cultural studies and politics scholars alike have discussed, at length, the contradictory implications of such *media convergence* (Hay & Couldry, 2011; Jenkins, 2006). As media scholars Henry Jenkins and Mark Deuze (2008) explain:

> shifts in the communication infrastructure bring about contradictory pulls and tugs within our culture. On the one hand, this 'democratization' of media use signals a broadening of opportunities for individuals and grassroots communities to tell stories and access stories others are telling, to present arguments and listen to arguments made elsewhere, to share information and learn more about the world from a multitude of other perspectives. On the other hand, the media companies seek to extend their reach by merging, co-opting, converging

and synergizing their brands and intellectual properties across all of these channels. In some ways, this has concentrated the power of traditional gatekeepers and agenda setters and in other ways, it has disintegrated their tight control over our culture (p. 6).

Of course, it is not only smartphones and social media that keep us 'constantly connected' (Harwood et al., 2014). Today, numerous devices, including 'wearables' (such as fitness trackers, smart watches and other smart jewellery), household goods (such as televisions, refrigerators and home management systems), as well as the more conventional portable computing devices (such as laptops and tablets), are all increasingly networked. Referred to broadly as the Internet of Things (IoTs), this omnipresent internet connectivity is further associated with data-sharing and data-gathering practices that mark an additional key feature of digital society.

Permanence, Digital Footprints and Dataveillance

A further implication of the IoTs and its associated data-sharing and data-gathering practices is an ever increasing 'digital footprint'. Many scholars have noted the prominence of the 'quantified self' formed as individuals engage with numerous apps, trackers and tools (Lupton, 2013; Swan, 2013). Clearly, this mounting social data can be 'collected, analysed and visualized' by social scientists (Housley et al., 2014) and thus presents research and methodological opportunities for digital sociology (Lupton, 2014) and, indeed, digital criminology (Smith, Bennett Moses, & Chan, 2017); however, it also presents very real challenges for privacy and human rights. Indeed, as noted by Gordon Fletcher, Marie Griffiths, and Maria Kutar (2011, p. 1): 'individuals passively volunteer personal information while government and commercial organisations aggressively amass these snippets into correlated data'. Not only do we as individuals contribute to our own potential surveillance in digital society, but increasingly, we engage in mutual surveillance of each other ('lateral surveillance', discussed further in Chapter 3). The 'human data trail now begins . . . prior to conception and continues after death' (Fletcher et al., 2011, p. 1) as disparate threads of individuals' data are retained, stored and increasingly linked in ways that were not necessarily intended by the subjects of this extensive networked dataveillance (Degli Esposti, 2014; Van Dijck, 2014).

Yet, beyond concerns with privacy alone, scholars have also noted the negative social effects of this permanence in the 'big data' society. For instance, US scholars Jean-Francois Blanchette and Debra Johnson (2002) advocate for the 'social benefits of forgetfulness', noting that American society has been founded on a culture of 'forgive and forget' that enables people to make a fresh start and change the course of their lives. As they highlight:

> In the paper-and-ink world, the sheer cumbersomeness of archiving and later finding information often promoted a form of institutional forgetfulness—a situation with parallels to human memory. The forgetfulness of the paper-and-ink world was implicit in the material being of institutions, the available storage space, the budget for cabinets, etc. Often the institution's memory/forgetfulness was not even recognized as a policy issue but dealt with as a matter of physical facilities. In many cases, as storage technologies have gained in practicality, ease of remote access, and lowered in price, the shift to an electronic medium changed the default position from one of forgetfulness to one of memory.
>
> (Blanchette & Johnson, 2002, p. 34)

Continuing concerns over the permanence of social data and its impacts on individuals' human rights have promoted a global debate over whether people should have a 'right to be forgotten' in the digital age. In 2014, the Court of Justice of the European Union (EU) ruled that individuals do indeed have the right, under certain conditions, to request that search engines remove links to personal information about them. According to subsequent guidance released by the European Commission, 'this applies where the information is inaccurate, inadequate, irrelevant or excessive for the purposes of the data processing', furthermore that 'interference with a person's right to data protection could not be justified merely by the economic interest of the search engine' (European Commission, 2014, n.p.). Though such privacy and data protection rights are thus recognised in the EU, there is far from global agreement on the issue. In the United States in particular, debates regarding the European 'right to be forgotten' have noted the potential conflict with freedom of speech principles (Bennett, 2012; Gajda, 2017; Mantelero, 2013).

Echo Chambers, Filter Bubbles and 'Algorithmic Sociality'

Social commentators and scholars alike have identified the self-affirming nature of individuals' online engagement. For instance, US legal scholar Cass Sunstein (2004, 2009, 2017), has noted that one of the more striking features of digital society is the capacity for users to actively curate and 'filter' what they see. Such filtering he describes as a 'mixed blessing'; simultaneously allowing individuals to filter out 'noise' in an increasingly information-heavy digital life and restricting engagement with a diversity of topics and points of view. 'The implication,' Sunstein suggests, 'is that groups of people, especially if they are like-minded, will end up thinking the same thing they thought before—but in more extreme form, and sometimes in a much more extreme form' (Sunstein, 2004, p. 58). In this way, a 'filter bubble' may contribute to further polarising of public sentiment and political ideology, in ways that are not only damaging for democratic engagement but that amplify cultures of hate (discussed further in Chapter 6). Indeed, several studies have found evidence that individuals tend to actively choose and 'follow' news outlets that are aligned with their own political opinions (Garrett, 2009; Iyengar & Hahn, 2009; Munson & Resnick, 2010).

The role of digital technology in content curation and consumption in digital society is not simply a neutral tool in the hands of users. Rather, digital media and online platforms are explicitly 'designed to introduce bias' (Marres, 2017, pp. 103–104). Increasingly, search engines, online news media and social networks personalise content for their users through machine-learning models (Agichtein, Brill, & Dumais 2006; Chan & Bennett Moses, 2016; Das, Datar, Garg, & Rajaram, 2007; Hannak et al., 2013). This automation effectively creates 'filter bubbles' (Pariser, 2011) through which 'algorithms inadvertently amplify ideological segregation by automatically recommending content an individual is likely to agree with' (Flaxman, Goel, & Rao, 2016, p. 299). British sociologist Daniel Smith (2017) further provides an account of *algorithmic sociality*, noting the ways in which interactive processes of joint human–machine content curation are determining how we experience and enact social relations (see also Skeggs & Yuill, 2016). Meanwhile, in Australia, in an analysis of Facebook 'fight pages', criminologist Mark Wood (2016, 2017) refers to a social media 'technological unconscious'; noting that every time we click 'Like' we are simultaneously responding to and reinforcing a social algorithm that will determine not only which content we continue to be presented with but also the content presented to others who are 'like us' (the 'like economy', Gerlitz & Helmond, 2013). Thus, echo chambers, filter bubbles and algorithmic sociality all reinforce and potentially amplify individuals' and communities' beliefs, attitudes, sentiment and practices; including potentially deviant and criminal subcultures (Smith et al., 2017).

Spatiality, Temporality and 'Virality'

It has frequently been observed that digital technologies have shifted our experience of time and space. A global network of digital communications has, according to some sociologists and technologists, facilitated a dispersal of social connections that are increasingly characterised by 'loose', 'weak' or 'liquid' social ties (Bauman, 2000; Kavanaugh, Reese, Carroll, & Rosson, 2005; Turkle, 2012). In short, the strength of our social ties can be seen as a combination of the amount of time, emotional intensity, intimacy and reciprocity involved (Granovetter, 1973). Strong ties thus involve greater intimacy, investment and mutuality, as well as frequent interactions across multiple settings and/or contexts; weak ties are characterised by sharing of resources or information rather than affective and mutual confidences (Wellman, 1992). Granovetter (1973) famously argued for the strength of weak ties. If individuals are only connected through strong ties in localised cliques, then their capacity for sharing information and driving innovation and coordinated action is limited (Granovetter, 1973).

The internet has a positive potential for increasing weak ties between individuals and communities across the globe, which might inspire information, innovation, coordination and overall *cohesiveness* in the social network (Kavanaugh, 2003). While such shifts in *spatiality* associated with online communications may have a positive impact on weak ties, other scholars have repeatedly noted the ways in which participation in distributed networks creates a new kind of sociality in which people live 'alone together' (Turkle, 2012). Dispersed spatial networks offer the capacity to develop and maintain strong distal ties, while one's immediate proximal ties may be weak. As some scholars have highlighted, rather than investing in and maintaining strong ties in networks physically close to us, technology enables us to invest more in relationships with individuals far away, perhaps people who we have never met face-to-face. This is not necessarily a negative shift — though many psychologists have warned that the growth of weak ties, *at the expense of* strong ones, may have negative effects on social cohesion (Baek, Bae, & Jang, 2013).

In addition to considerations of spatiality, a new *temporality* further characterises participation in digital society. As suggested by Anthropologists Yarimar Bonilla and Jonathan Rosa (2015) in discussing justice movements on social media:

> E-mail, television, radio, and print have long managed to open up windows into the experience of social movements, but the dialogicality and temporality of Twitter create a unique feeling of direct participation. Twitter allows users who are territorially displaced to feel like they are united across both space and time (p. 7).

The sense of immediacy and extended reach of digital society has facilitated a further cultural trend in which content sharing can 'go viral': spreading rapidly through social networks as hundreds of thousands, even millions, of users replicate and distribute the original posts. The viral uptake of some internet memes provides a vivid example. Memes, more broadly, have been explained by Richard Dawkins (1976) as:

> ...a unit of cultural transmission, or a unit of imitation ... Imitation, in the broad sense, is how memes can replicate. But just as not all genes that can replicate do so successfully, so some memes are more successful in the meme-pool than others (pp. 203–205).

Dawkins (1976) went on to describe how memes spread and are transmitted, 'like a virus', from person to person while constantly undergoing 'natural selection' and variation. This propagation of cultural memes — whether a scientific theory, a political idea, a tune, a fashion or a catchphrase — can thus be understood as a series of copies. Each is a variation, adaptation or copy of the last, as a collective whole existing and continuing to self-perpetuate in societies over longer periods of time. What makes one meme persist while another fades, whether in terms of rapid and widescale uptake or becoming embedded in socio-cultural practices over centuries, is 'how acceptable it is to the population' (Dawkins, 1976, p. 194).

Like memes generally, internet and digital media memes, which may include 'viral' videos, online catchphrases, images, as well as cultural practices (such as 'happy slapping', 'planking' and 'neknomination'),[3] become sites for community cultural meaning-making and boundary-setting (Gal, Shifman & Kampf, 2016). Some such memes may fade as short-lived fads, but many endure: their variations and adaptations being replicated across societies and over time. Thus, such memes can reflect social norms among peer groups, local communities and societies broadly; constituting a practice of norm creation and/or reproduction (Shifman, 2014). Some commentators and scholars have gone further, observing that 'viral memes are capable of doing lasting damage' (Godwin, 1994, n.p; see also Giardina, Denzin, & Kien, 2013), particularly as sites for the transmission of social ills such as racist and sexist extremism (Powell & Henry, 2017). At the same time, though content that elicits a negative emotional response spreads faster than positive content (Guadagno, Rempala, Murphy, & Okdie, 2013), virality and memetic culture are not always inherently negative (see Chapter 4). For instance, feminist scholars and some criminologists have identified the positive potential of 'survivor selfies' in the context of domestic and/or sexual violence to drive new practices of informal and 'viral' justice (Powell, 2015a, 2015b; discussed further in Chapters 7 and 8).

Visual Communication and Conversations

Images carry particular importance in contemporary digital society. Indeed, such is the influence of the visual in day-to-day modern life that some social theorists have suggested that imagery is becoming a central practice through which we communicate (van House, 2011); others refer to social image-sharing as a form of 'visual conversation' (Katz & Crocker, 2015). Where once we wrote or telephoned to share our experiences with loved ones, family and friends, increasingly we share updates via photos and videos on public, quasi-public and private social media networks and other digital applications.

The widespread availability, ease of use and 'perpetual contact' (Katz & Aakhus, 2002) of digital camera-enabled devices is associated with similarly widespread image-taking and sharing practices. Now 'images can be made any time, any place, without prior planning ... what is considered photo-worthy has expanded to include the everyday' (van House, 2011, p. 127). Indeed, for van

House (2011), self-representation through making, showing, viewing and talking about images forms part of how we *enact our selves* and contributes to the construction of collective social norms. The ways in which image-sharing and visual conversation might be implicated in both perpetration of, and community responses to, crime and justice are further explored in Chapter 5.

Corporatisation and 'Private' Public Space

In digital society, public and private life seem to be fusing in radical new ways. First, individuals are increasingly documenting and sharing images of private life with broader publics, as described above. Second, the *ways* in which such content is shared further blur the traditional public/private divide. While some social media platforms might be considered largely public spaces (such as Twitter), others require a login to access and further enable users to restrict their shared content to select groups and individuals (such as Facebook and Google+). Moreover, as individuals, we frequently shift seamlessly — both deliberately and sometimes unknowingly — between public and restricted content-sharing on our social media networks (Bruns & Highfield, 2015; Papacharissi, 2010).

In all cases, these platforms, whether public, quasi-public, or 'private' (to the extent that content is not visible by those outside of the user's selected group), are developed, administered and regulated by private corporations. Thus, in social institutional terms, social media spaces might all be considered simultaneously both public and private because whatever the user's expectation — open public access or user-determined privacy — in practice, it is ultimately the private companies who regulate these spaces, determining who has access, which content is to be shared, how widely it is viewed (such as through algorithmic content moderation described above) and on what grounds it is removed. In this corporatisation of both public and private life, companies such as Facebook and Google engage in practices of 'networked authoritarianism' and 'corporate censorship' (Mackinnon, 2013), arguably in place of the declining role of the terrestrial state (further discussed in Chapter 3). Indeed, Anthony Wilhelm (2000) has long problematised the privatisation of public online space and the ways in which the political interests of citizens give way to corporate and commercial interests. The majority of citizens' digital participation occurs in privately owned and regulated spaces, rather than in a democratic online agora (Tidwell, 1999).

Digital Social Inequalities

Access to communications technology, the first-level 'digital divide', differs by country, locale, socio-economic factors, education and race, as well as by gender (International Telecommunication Union, 2016). For example, while developed countries have high population-level internet access at 81%, developing countries have roughly half this access at 40.1% (International Telecommunication Union, 2016). Yet developing regions are home to 2.5 billion internet users, compared to one billion users in the developed world (International Telecommunication Union, 2016). Such inequalities are a serious concern, as reduced internet access has flow-on effects, including reduced access to education, economic, social and civic engagement opportunities (Antonio & Tuffley, 2014).

Among those who have internet access, concerning differences in internet use and online experiences emerge (Büchi, Just, & Latzer, 2015; van Deursen & van Dijk, 2014; Halford & Savage, 2010): the second-level 'digital divide'. Studies are increasingly examining purposes and parity of participation across age, socio-economic status, gender, sexuality and race. For example, studies consistently demonstrate that younger groups use technology at higher rates and more often for entertainment and social purposes than older groups, while lower educated groups tend to use communications technology for entertainment purposes more than those with higher education. In these studies, more highly educated groups were more likely to report transactional or commercial uses of technology than lower educated groups, while men continued to report both more frequent and more entertainment-based internet use than women, whose online engagements are typically more relational (Büchi, Just, & Latzer, 2015). Certainly, it appears that some groups are more likely to have negative experiences of online participation, marked by harassment and abuse, for example. Several studies have identified gender, sexuality and race-based harassment and abuse across various platforms, including social media, online communities and virtual gaming environments (Fox & Tang, 2014; Jane, 2014; Powell & Henry, 2017). Some explanations for this second-level divide include identifying technology itself as a 'classed', 'gendered' and 'raced' space developed by, for the purposes of, and largely used by, white middle-class men (Wajcman, 2004). Conversely, as suggested by Halford & Savage (2010), a key challenge facing contemporary societies is to promote *digital social inclusion*, so that all groups are able to benefit from the education, workforce, economic, civic and social opportunities that online participation opens up.

Democratisation and Participatory Politics

Media and legal scholars, political scientists and sociologists have variously studied changes in the nature of communications with the advent of user-generated content, and in particular social media. Such user-generated and participatory media have variously been described as promoting democratic citizen participation in public life (Loader & Mercea, 2011); exposing state crime, such as cases of police brutality or military misuse of force (Reilly, 2013); facilitating revolutionary action against autocratic government regimes (Christensen, 2011); supporting police investigations and evidence-gathering (Trottier, 2012; Williams et al., 2013); monitoring communications of suspected terrorist networks by the State (Oh, Agrawal & Rao, 2011); and aiding crisis responses during natural disasters (Bruns & Burgess, 2013). These analyses traverse disciplinary boundaries, including politics, law, criminology, sociology, computer sciences, media and cultural studies. Overall, the implication is that social media, in particular, represents a powerful tool for an increasingly *citizen-led* and *participatory* politics. While the traditional news media is routinely subject to critique for having 'weakened public life and civic engagement, alienating citizens' (Haas & Steiner, 2001, p. 24), social media has been heralded as having transformed the capacity for more participatory and democratic modes of citizen engagement in public life (Loader & Mercea, 2011; Yar, 2012a).

In particular, many scholars have noted the potential for citizen participation via social media to enable representation of marginalised and/or disempowered social groups whose voices are often unheard in traditional media and public discourse (Papacharissi, 2010). Rather than representing a singular online forum, social media may be better described as providing multiple opportunities for 'counterpublic' communications (Boyd, 2011; Bruns, Enli, Skogerbo, Larsson, & Christensen, 2016; Powell, 2015a, 2015b; Renninger, 2014; Rentschler, 2014). This conceptualisation of the function of social media as a democratising force builds on the work of feminist theorist Nancy Fraser (1990) who, in critique of Jurgen Habermas' notion of a singular public sphere of communicative action, suggested that subordinated social groups form their own parallel public spheres, which she refered to as 'subaltern counterpublics'. Fraser described the emancipatory potential of such counterpublics which, she said, are not separatist subcultures but rather 'aspire to disseminate one's discourse into ever-widening arenas' (Fraser, 1990, p. 67). Fraser (1990) further asserted that, in stratified societies in which the democratic ideal of participatory parity is not fully realised for subordinated groups, subaltern counterpublics serve a dual function:

> On the one hand, they function as spaces of withdrawal and regroupment; on the other hand, they also function as bases and training grounds for agitational activities directed toward wider publics … This dialectic enables subaltern counterpublics partially to offset, although not wholly to eradicate, the unjust participatory privileges enjoyed by members of dominant social groups in stratified societies (p. 68).

This positive take on the potential of online participation to act as a 'virtual town square' (Kavanaugh, Perez-Quinones, Tedesco, & Sanders, 2010), extending democratic engagement among otherwise marginalised groups, is of course, not without criticism. Perhaps most famously, media scholar Evgeny Morozov (2009, 2011) has urged caution in interpretations of the internet, social media and online activism as fundamentally a force for freedom. Instead, Morozov points to the myriad ways in which democracy is threatened by authoritarianism in the form of consumerism and corporatisation, both of which have only expanded in the digital age. We cannot, he said, tweet our way to freedom (Morozov, 2011).

Internet freedom itself presents particular tensions for criminologists. On the one hand, law enforcement in the context of global and organised cybercrime requires state oversight, regulation and intervention. From a cybercriminological perspective, user anonymity, encryption, location spoofing and other features of deep web and dark web participation are more appropriately viewed through a lens of suspected illicit activity, than as the tools of democracy. Yet, such a view potentially places cybercriminology on the side of increased government control and an expanding 'securitization of cyberspace' (Morozov, 2011; discussed further in Chapter 3), rather than engaging critically with concerns over privacy, human rights and internet freedom.

On the other hand, the democratising potential of online participation to open up debates about crime and justice, to challenge the punitive law-and-order politics of contemporary liberal democracies (see Chapter 1) and to promote alternative discourses of inclusion and social justice are exciting prospects for criminology. And they are particularly exciting for *critical criminologies*, whose foundation lies in critiques of power, inequality and the role of the state.

Critical and Cultural Criminologies in Digital Society

Critical criminologies represent a collection of perspectives on crime and institutions of criminal justice including the state apparatus that oversees them (Muncie, 2000; Schwendinger & Schwendinger, 1970; Yar, 2012c). Whether focusing on 'conflict', 'radical', 'abolitionist', 'decriminalising' or other lenses, the core of all critical criminologies is a counterpoint to individualist explanations of crime. Instead, critical criminologies seek to uncover and challenge the socially and structurally produced context of inequalities in power that define crime itself, underpin its causes and are profoundly implicated in responses to it. As Majid Yar explained, critical criminology 'owes much of its organising assumptions to an earlier appropriation of Marxist ideas' (Yar, 2012c, p. 53). In 1916, Dutch criminologist Willem Bonger, for example, outlined the relationships between capitalism and class inequalities, on the one hand, and crime and justice, on the other, in *Criminality and Economic Conditions* (Bonger, 1916). Bonger argued that capitalism itself created a culture of individualism, materialism and greed at the same time as 'the criminal justice system emerged as a social institution that criminalizes the greed of the poor while ignoring the greed of the wealthy' (Welch, 1996, p. 44).

In keeping with its roots as a criminology that interrogates the role and actions of the state, as well as the exercise of power in societies, contemporary critical criminologies are organised around a core concern with *social harms*, rather than with more narrowly defined *crimes* and *crime control* (Muncie, 2000; Yar, 2012c). As criminologist John Muncie (2000, p. 1) further explained, 'a vast range of harms — sexism, racism, imperialism, economic exploitation and so on — could and should be included as the focal concern of an area of study called criminology'. Thus, the uniting themes of critical criminology might be broadly understood as a concern with collective harms, human rights and social justice.

The focus on harms rather than crimes, as well as collective harms and human rights concerns, are important inclusions for our purposes here. The digital criminology that we have in mind is also a critical criminological approach, taking as its central focus the intersections of technologies and social harms, as well as a broader concern with justice and injustice beyond the state. Such a focus, we believe, represents a crucial counterpoint to the dominant individualist, rationalist-actor and crime control concerns of conventional cybercriminologies.

At the same time as attempts to control cybercrime seek to enhance law enforcement and extend the global reach of criminal law through international cooperation in the fight against cybercrime, critical criminologies suggest caution. For example, who might be the casualities of the 'war' on cybercrime? Are privacy concerns, human rights and interpersonal harms sidelined by an overwhelming concern with state security, the globalisation of cybercrime and counterterrorism? To what extent might rhetorics of 'risk' and cyber 'law and order' contribute to further and over-criminalisation of already marginalised communities? In this, we are guided by the provocative question posed by criminologists Herman and Julia Schwendinger in their 1970 article: are we, as criminologists, 'Defenders of order or guardians of human rights?' (Schwendinger and Schwendinger, 1970). These are significant questions for a digital criminology, and ones we explore throughout this book.

Yet, it is not only a concern with structural inequalities, social harms, human rights and justice beyond the state that we seek to embed within digital criminological approaches to crime and justice. In light of the key features described earlier, it appears apparent that the socio-structural and the socio-cultural have become enmeshed in powerful ways in digital society.

Cultural criminology, meanwhile, as its founding advocates identify, can be understood as a distinct subtype of critical criminology (see Ferrell, Hayward, Morrison, & Presdee, 2004). As Jeff Ferrell (2013, p. 258) defined it, cultural criminology is an 'orientation designed especially for critical engagement with the politics of meaning surrounding crime and crime control, and for critical intervention into those politics'. Ferrell further identified three spheres of cultural criminological focus: situations or meaning in interactions, subcultural meanings and media and popular culture. And yet, these spheres themselves arguably take on new meanings in light of the features of digital society; in particular, convergence and visual conversations.

Some cultural criminologists have sought to identify the significance of the 'digital turn' in socio-cultural representations and considered the complex interactions of images as both producers and reproducers of meanings about crime (Ferrell , Hayward & Young, 2008; Hayward & Presdee, 2010). Keith Hayward (2012), for example, has identified the problematic narrow scope of conventional cybercrime scholarship and called for further criminological engagement with spatial and socio-technical theory. Rather than taking a cybercrime focus on technology as a tool of diffusion that has increased criminal opportunities and networks, he suggests that 'a better way of thinking about digital/ online (criminal) activities is as a *process*, namely as phenomena in constant dialogue and transformation with other phenomena/technologies' (Hayward, 2012, p. 455, emphasis in original). Hayward, for example, drawing on Actor-Network Theory (Latour, 1993, 2005) and Castells' (1996) networked 'space of flows', among others, notes the potential for communication technologies 'to alter the way we experience the sense of *being* in an environment' (emphasis in original, 2012, p. 456).

Other scholars have explored how the social web may be changing the culturally constructed nature, and socially constituted practices, of crime and deviance (Jewkes, 2007; Jewkes & Yar, 2010, 2013; Surette, 2015). Yar (2012b), for example, makes a persuasive case for considering the impact of communications technologies and new media as itself a *motivator* of criminality. In discussing the practice of 'happy slapping', Yar (2012b, p. 252) argues that 'crucial to understanding this phenomenon is the role played by participants' desire to be seen, and esteemed or celebrated, by others for their criminal activities'. He argues that this 'will-to-represent' one's transgressive self is linked to broader trends both of a self-creating subjectivity associated with processes of de-traditionalisation (Beck & Beck-Gernsheim, 2002; Giddens, 1991) and the ready availability of new media platforms for such self-creation (Yar, 2012b, p. 251).

Though much cultural criminology has focused on the ways that images of crime, criminality and the criminal are produced and represented in news media, as well as in fiction and popular culture, an emerging sub-field of visual criminology explores the increasingly blurred distinction between 'real' and 'imagined' images of crime in digital society (Brown, 2014; Carrabine, 2011, 2012; Young, 2012, 2014). Such engagement with images is an important perspective for digital criminology, and one which we take up in more detail in Chapter 5.

A further task, then, for digital criminology is to examine the ways in which the digital has become enmeshed with the *experiences*, *meanings* and *images* of crime and justice, whether from the perspective of victims, perpetrators, the criminal justice system or citizen engagement beyond the state. In so doing, it is important not to lose sight of varying degrees to which digital technologies are integrated in offending, victimisation and justice; at the same time as such integration may reflect broader trends in digital participation and culture in everyday life. In digital society, criminologists arguably need to engage with interdisciplinary perspectives on digital technology and sociality, not only to better understand crime and justice in this context but also so as not to overstate the unique contribution of technological practices in crime itself.

Conclusion

In briefly charting these sub-disciplinary boundaries, it is important to recognise that the demarcations between them are not solid; they are better represented as clusters of criminological engagement, which blur and bleed into each other at the edges. Nonetheless, we suggest that critical and cultural criminological scholarship has yet to fully engage with some of the emerging cultural trends of digital society and with its key elements, which have become integral to everyday life and consequently feature in everyday crime and (in)justices.

Underscoring digital criminology is an exploration of the ways in which *technosocial* cultures and practices come to bear — not only directly on crime and criminal justice but on social harms, social justice, inequality and meaning-making in digital society. Arguably, where conventional cybercrimi-nologies have fallen short is that much of the field succumbs to degrees of *techno-criminal determinism* and of *individualism*. By this, we mean that the research questions asked, and the types of analyses and understandings provided, suggest that the changes of most importance for criminology arise from the opportunities for crime created by technologies themselves, as well as the challenges for law enforcement in detection and response. A further common feature is to draw on psychological frameworks and positivist methods to explore why the individual 'cybercriminal' might be drawn to these opportunities or susceptible to their temptations. By comparison, other transformations in crime and justice remain underexamined, and much research is lacking in an interdisciplinary lens through which to develop alternative concepts, questions and analyses.

But what if criminologists were to turn this engagement with techno-criminal determinism and individualism on its head? What if we were to take, as our starting point, an understanding of the socio-structural, socio-cultural and socio-technical bases of crime and justice?

When we approach criminological research from this position, through the concepts of *digital society* and *technosociality*, new avenues for exploration emerge. Technology, for example, is not under-stood to cause racism or race-based hate speech (as discussed in Chapter 6); but race certainly orders contemporary digital life in particular ways. Furthermore, the interaction of racism with new social technologies produces not only individual criminal acts, but also social practices of communication and action that can, and do, result in collective harms. Here, technology is understood neither as a cause of harm nor as a tool of harm, but rather as enmeshed in both pre-existing and newly emerg-ing social practices. Though this chapter has sought to position an emerging digital criminological framework through its relationship to existing cyber, critical and cultural criminologies, much of its discussion has remained within the level of individual and interpersonal crimes; albeit positioning these within their broader structural context. Yet, a further critical issue for criminology is the chal-lenges that a digital society — which is, after all, also a global society — presents for state-based understandings of crime and justice. In the following chapter, we consider global framings of 'risk', 'state security' and 'state harms' in the context of a digital society.

Notes

1 Personal computing workstations, such as the Xerox Alto in 1973, the Sun 1 in 1982, and the Apple Macintosh 128k in 1984, can be differentiated from the centralised, stationary early computers. These personal com-puting workstations were also among the first to use a graphical user interface, which did not require specific knowledge of command-line programming, and thus radically opened up computing to individual users both through portability and ease of use (Goldberg, 1988).

2 While some criminological and other research continues to refer to 'child pornography', we reject such terminol-ogy on the basis that it minimises the seriousness of these crimes. Indeed, according to Liddell and Powell (2015), there are at least three key problems with not calling these images what they are: online child abuse material or child exploitation material. First, calling these images 'pornography' creates a false distinction between the viewing of images and the contact sexual abuse of a child. Second, it creates confusion by aligning the images with legally acceptable forms of pornography. And third, it contributes to the normalisation of child sexual assault.

3 'Happy slapping' refers to a meme originating in the UK in 2004, in which an individual or group of teens or young adults would film what were typically minor assaults (such as slapping or hitting a victim), and then post the recordings online. 'Planking' refers to a photo-based meme that gained popularity in 2011. It involved lying face down with arms held to the sides (like a plank of wood) in unusual and often dan-gerous public spaces, photographing the scene and then sharing the image online. Finally, according to KnowYourMeme.com: 'Neknominate', also known as Neck and Nominate in the UK, is a drinking game

in which 'participants record themselves partaking in a physically extreme activity after chugging alcoholic beverages and challeng[ing] others to outdrink them in the identical fashion'. Each of these internet memes has been implicated in a small number of extreme and violent instances that have resulted in rapes, homicides and/or accidental deaths. 'Happy slapping' assaults, for example, have included sexual assault and murder (Ching, Daffern, & Thomas, 2012; Saunders, 2005).

Recommended Further Reading

McGovern, A. (2015). Introduction: Crime, media and new technologies. *Current Issues in Criminal Justice*, 27(2), 137.

McGuire, M. R. (2016). Cybercrime 4.0: Now what is to be done? In R. Matthews (Ed.), *What is to be done about crime and punishment? Towards a 'public Criminology'* (pp. 251–279). Basingstoke: Palgrave Macmillan.

Smith, G. J., Bennett Moses, L., & Chan, J. (2017). The challenges of doing criminology in the big data era: towards a digital and data-driven approach. *The British Journal of Criminology*, 57(2), 259–274.

References

Aas, K. F. (2016). Preface. In D. Robert, & M. Dufresne (Eds.), *Actor-network theory and crime studies: Explorations in science and technology* (pp. ix–xii). London: Routledge.

Aas, K. F. (2007a). Analysing a world in motion: Global flows meet 'criminology of the other'. *Theoretical Criminology*, 11(2), 283–303.

Aas, K. F. (2007b). Beyond 'the desert of the real': Crime control in a virtual (ised) reality. In Y. Jewkes (Ed.), *Crime online* (pp. 160–178). Cullompton, UK: Willan Publishing.

Agichtein, E., Brill, E., & Dumais, S. (2006). *Improving web search ranking by incorporating user behavior information.* Paper presented at the 29th Annual International ACM Sigir Conference on Research and Development in Information Retrieval, Seattle, WA.

Antonio, A., & Tuffley, D. (2014). The Gender Digital Divide in Developing Countries. *Future Internet*, 6(4), 673–687.

Armagh, D. S. (2001). Virtual child pornography: Criminal conduct or protected speech. *Cardozo Law Review*, 23(6), 1993–2010.

Baek, Y. M., Bae, Y., & Jang, H. (2013). Social and parasocial relationships on social network sites and their differential relationships with users' psychological well-being. *Cyberpsychology, Behavior, and Social Networking*, 16(7), 512–517.

Bauman, Z. (2000). *Liquid Modernity*. Cambridge: Polity.

Bayer, J. B., Campbell, S. W., & Ling, R. (2016). Connection cues: Activating the norms and habits of social connectedness. *Communication Theory*, 26(2), 128–149.

Beck, U., & Beck-Gernsheim, E. (2002). *Individualisation*. London: Sage.

Bennett, S. C. (2012). The right to be forgotten: Reconciling EU and US perspectives. *Berkeley Journal of International Law*, 30(1), 161.

Bergman, M. K. (2001). White paper: the deep web: surfacing hidden value. *Journal of Electronic Publishing*, 7(1), 1–17. doi: 10.3998/3336451.0007.104.

Berk, R. (2008). How you can tell if the simulations in computational criminology are any good. *Journal of Experimental Criminology*, 4(3), 289–308.

Berry, D. (Ed.). (2012). *Understanding Digital Humanities*. Basingstoke: Palgrave Macmillan.

Birks, D., Townsley, M., & Stewart, A. (2012). Generative explanations of crime: Using simulation to test criminological theory. *Criminology*, 50(1), 221–254.

Blanchette, J. F., & Johnson, D. G. (2002). Data retention and the panoptic society: The social benefits of forgetfulness. *The Information Society*, 18(1), 33–45.

Bonger, W. A. (1916). *Criminology and economic conditions*. Boston: Little, Brown.

Bonilla, Y., & Rosa, J. (2015). # Ferguson: Digital protest, hashtag ethnography, and the racial politics of social media in the United States. *American Ethnologist, 42*(1), 4–17.

Boyd, D. (2011). Social network sites as networked publics. In Z. Papacharissi (Ed.), *A networked self: Identity, community and culture on social network sites.* New York: Routledge.

Brantingham, P. L. (2011, September). *Computational criminology.* Keynote address to the European Intelligence and Security Informatics Conference, 12–14 September. Athens, Greece: IEEE.

Brewer, R. (2017). Controlling crime through networks. In P. Drahos (Ed.), *Regulatory theory: Foundations and applications* (pp. 447–464). Canberra: Australian National University Press.

Brown, S. (2006). The criminology of hybrids Rethinking crime and law in technosocial networks. *Theoretical Criminology, 10*(2), 223–244.

Brown, M. (2014). Visual criminology and carceral studies: Counter-images in the carceral age. *Theoretical Criminology, 18*(2), 176–197.

Bruns, A., & Burgess, J. (2013). Crisis communication in natural disasters: The Queensland floods and Christchurch earthquakes. *Twitter and Society, 89*, 373–384.

Bruns, A., & Highfield, T. (2015). From news blogs to news on twitter: Gatewatching and collaborative news curation. In S. Coleman, & D. Freelon (Eds.), *Handbook of digital politics* (pp. 325–339). Cheltenham, UK: Edward Elgar.

Bruns, A., Enli, G., Skogerbo, E., Larsson, A. O., & Christensen, C. (Eds.). (2016). *The Routledge companion to social media and politics.* London: Routledge.

Büchi, M., Just, N., & Latzer, M. (2016). Modeling the second-level digital divide: A five-country study of social differences in Internet use. *New Media & Society, 18*(11), 2703–2722.

Carrabine, E. (2011). Images of torture: Culture, politics and power. *Crime, Media, Culture, 7*(1), 5–30.

Carrabine, E. (2012). Just images: Aesthetics, ethics and visual criminology. *The British Journal of Criminology, 52*(3), 463–489.

Casey, E. (2011). *Digital Evidence and Computer Crime: Forensic Science, Computers, and the Internet.* Cambridge, England: Academic Press.

Castells, M. (1996). *The information age: Economy, society, and culture. Volume I: The rise of the network society.* Malden: Wiley Blackwell.

Castells, M. (2001). *The Internet galaxy: Reflections on the Internet, business, and society.* Oxford, New York: Oxford University Press.

Cecere, G., Corrocher, N., & Battaglia, R. D. (2015). Innovation and competition in the smartphone industry: Is there a dominant design? *Telecommunications Policy, 39*(3), 162–175.

Ceruzzi, P. E. (2003). *A history of modern computing.* Cambridge, MA: MIT Press.

Chan, J., & Bennett Moses, L. (2016). Is big data challenging criminology? *Theoretical Criminology, 20*(1), 21–39.

Ching, H., Daffern, M., & Thomas, S. (2012). Appetitive violence: A new phenomenon? *Psychiatry, Psychology and Law, 19*(5), 745–763.

Christensen, C. (2011). Twitter revolutions? Addressing social media and dissent. *The Communication Review, 14*(3), 155–157.

Clough, B., & Mungo, P. (1992). *Approaching zero: Data crime and the computer underworld.* London: Faber & Faber.

Croall, H. (1992). White collar crime. *Criminal justice and criminology,* Bristol: Open University Press.

Das, A. S., Datar, M., Garg, A., & Rajaram, S. (2007). *Google news personalization: Scalable online collaborative filtering.* Paper presented at the 16th International Conference on World Wide Web, Banff, Alberta, Canada.

Dawkins, R. (1976). *The Selfish Gene.* Oxford: Oxford University Press.

Décary-Hétu, D., & Dupont, B. (2012). The social network of hackers. *Global Crime, 13*(3), 160–175.

Degli Esposti, S. (2014). When big data meets dataveillance: The hidden side of analytics. *Surveillance & Society, 12*(2), 209–225.

Diamond, B. & Bachmann, M. (2015). Out of the beta phase: Obstacles, challenges, and promising paths in the study of cyber criminology. *International Journal of Cyber Criminology, 9*(1), 24–34.

Diefenbach, S., & Christoforakos, L. (2017). The selfie paradox: Nobody seems to like them yet everyone has reasons to take them. An exploration of psychological functions of selfies in self-presentation. *Frontiers in Psychology, 8*(7), 18–31.

Esposito, L. C. (1998). Regulating the Internet: The new battle against child pornography. *Case Western Reserve Journal of International Law, 30*(2/3), 541–564.

European Commission. (2014). Factsheet on the "Right to be Forgotten" ruling (C-131/12). Retrieved from Brussels. Available at: www.ec.europa.eu/justice/data-protection/files/factsheets/factsheet_data_protection_en.pdf (last accessed 29 November 2017).

Ferrell, J. (2013). Cultural criminology and the politics of meaning. *Critical Criminology, 21*(3), 257–271.

Ferrell, J., Hayward, K., Morrison, W., & Presdee, M. (Eds.). (2004). *Cultural criminology unleashed.* London: Routledge.

Ferrell, J., Hayward, K., & Young, J. (2008). *Cultural Criminology: an invitation.* London: Sage.

Ferrell, J., & Sanders, C. (Eds.). (1995). *Cultural criminology.* London: Glasshouse Press.

Flaxman, S., Goel, S., & Rao, J. M. (2016). Filter bubbles, echo chambers, and online news consumption. *Public Opinion Quarterly, 80*(S1), 298–320.

Fletcher, G., Griffiths, M., & Kutar, M. S. (2011). A day in the digital life: A preliminary sousveillance study retrieved from New York. Available at: www.ssrn.com/abstract=1923629.

Fraser, N. (1990). Rethinking the public sphere: A contribution to the critique of actually existing democracy. *Social Text, 25*(26), 56–80.

Fox, J., & Tang, W. Y. (2014). Sexism in online video games: The role of conformity to masculine norms and social dominance orientation. *Computers in Human Behavior, 33*, 314–320.

Gal, N., Shifman, L., & Kampf, Z. (2016). "It Gets Better": Internet memes and the construction of collective identity. *New Media & Society, 18*(8), 1698–1714.

Gajda, A. (2017). Privacy, press, and a right to be forgotten in the United States. Tulane Public Law Research Paper No. 17-11. Retrieved from Tulane, United States. Available at: www.ssrn.com/abstract=2976529 (last accessed 29 November 2017).

Garrett, R. K. (2009). Echo chambers online? Politically motivated selective exposure among internet news users. *Journal of Computer-Mediated Communication, 14*(2), 265–285.

Gerlitz, C., & Helmond, A. (2013). The like economy: Social buttons and the data-intensive web. *New Media & Society, 15*(8), 1348–1365.

Giardina, M. D., Denzin, N. K., & Kien, G. (2013). Media Memes and Prosumerist Ethics. *Cultural Studies ↔ Critical Methodologies, 13*(6), 554–561.

Giddens, A. (1991). *Modernity and self-identity: Self and society in the late modern age.* Stanford, CA: Stanford University Press.

Godwin, M. (1994) Meme, Counter-Meme, *Wired.* Available at: www.wired.com/wired/archive/2.10/godwin.if.html (last accessed 29 November 2017).

Goggin, G. (2014). Facebook's mobile career. *New Media & Society, 16*(7), 1068–1086.

Goldberg, A. (Ed.). (1988). *A history of personal workstations* (No. 04; QA76. 17, G6.). New York: ACM Press.

Goldstein, C. M., Thomas, J. G., Wing, R. R., & Bond, D. S. (2017). Successful weight loss maintainers use health tracking smartphone applications more than a nationally representative sample: Comparison of the National Weight Control Registry to Pew Tracking for Health. *Obesity Science & Practice, 3*(2), 117–126.

Grabosky, P. N. and Smith, R. G. (1998). *Crime in the Digital Age: Controlling Telecommunications and Cyberspace Illegalities.* Sydney: The Federation Press.

Grabosky, P. N. (2001). Virtual criminality: old wine in new bottles? *Social & Legal Studies, 10*(2), 243–249.

Granovetter, M. S. (1973). The strength of weak ties. *American Journal of Sociology, 78*(6), 1360–1380.

Greenleaf, G. (1990). Computers and crime-the hacker's new rules. *Computer Law & Security Review, 6*(2), 21–22.

Griffith, D. S. (1990). The Computer Fraud and Abuse Act of 1986: A measured response to a growing problem. *Vanderbilt Law Review, 43*(2), 453–490.

Guadagno, R. E., Rempala, D. M., Murphy, S., & Okdie, B. M. (2013). What makes a video go viral? An analysis of emotional contagion and internet memes. *Computers in Human Behavior, 29*(6), 2312–2319.

Halder, D., & Jaishankar, K. (2012). *Cyber crime and the victimization of women: laws, rights and regulations*. Hershey, PA: IGI Global.

Halford, S., & Savage, M. (2010). Reconceptualizing digital social inequality. *Information, Communication & Society, 13*(7), 937–955.

Hannak, A., Sapiezynski, P., Kakhki, A. M., Krishnamurthy, B., Lazer, D., Mislove, A., & Wilson, C. (2013, 13–17 May 2013). Measuring personalization of web search. Paper presented at the 22nd International Conference on World Wide Web, Rio de Janeiro, Brazil.

Harwood, J., Dooley, J. J., Scott, A. J., & Joiner, R. (2014). Constantly connected—The effects of smart-devices on mental health. *Computers in Human Behavior, 34*, 267–272.

Haas, T., & Steiner, L. (2001). Public journalism as a journalism of publics: Implications of the Habermas-Fraser debate for public journalism. *Journalism: Theory, Practice & Criticism, 2*(2), 123–147.

Haraway, D. J. (1991). A cyborg manifesto. In *Simians, Cyborgs, and Women: The Reinvention of Nature* (pp. 149–181). New York: Routledge.

Hay, J., & Couldry, N. (2011). Rethinking convergence/culture. *Cultural Studies, 25*(4–5), 473–486.

Hayward, K. & Presdee, M. (Eds.). (2010) *Framing crime: Cultural criminology and the image*. Abingdon, UK: Routledge.

Hayward, K. J. (2012). Five spaces of cultural criminology. *British Journal of Criminology, 52*(3), 441–462.

Hollinger, R. C., & Lanza-Kaduce, L. (1988). The process of criminalization: The case of computer crime laws. *Criminology, 26*(1), 101–126.

Holt, T. J. (Ed.). (2011). *Crime On-line: Causes, Correlates and Context*. Durham: Carolina Academic Press.

Holt, T., & Bossler, A. M. (2008). Examining the Applicability of Lifestyle-Routine Activities Theory for Cybercrime Victimization. *Deviant Behavior, 30*(1), 1–25.

Holt, T. J. (2013). Examining the forces shaping cybercrime markets online. *Social Science Computer Review, 31*(2), 165–177.

Holt, T. J. & Bossler, A. M. (2014). An assessment of the current state of cybercrime scholarship. *Deviant Behavior, 35*(1), 20–40.

Holt, T. J., & Bossler, A. M. (2015). *Cybercrime in Progress: Theory and Prevention of Technology-enabled Offenses*. New York: Routledge

Housley, W., Procter, R., Edwards, A., Burnap, P., Williams, M., Sloan, L., . . . Greenhill, A. (2014). Big and broad social data and the sociological imagination: A collaborative response. *Big Data & Society, 1*(2), 1–15.

Hutchings, A., & Hayes, H. (2008). Routine activity theory and phishing victimisation: who gets caught in the net. *Current Issues Criminal Justice, 20*(3), 433–452.

Ibrahim, Y. (2015). Instagramming life: Banal imaging and the poetics of the everyday. *Journal of Media Practice, 16*(1), 42–54.

International Telecommunication Union. (2016). *ICT facts and figures 2016*. Geneva. Available at: www.itu.int/en/ITU-D/Statistics/Documents/facts/ICTFactsFigures2016.pdf (last accessed 29 November, 2017).

Iyengar, S., & Hahn, K. S. (2009). Red media, blue media: Evidence of ideological selectivity in media use. *Journal of Communication, 59*(1), 19–39.

Jaishankar, K. (2007). Establishing a theory of cyber crimes. *International Journal of Cyber Criminology, 1*(2), 7–9.

Jaishankar, K. (2008). Space Transition Theory of cyber crimes. In F. Schmallager, & M. Pittaro, (Eds.), *Crimes of the Internet* (pp. 283–301). Upper Saddle River, NJ: Prentice Hall.

Jaishankar, K. (Ed.). (2011). *Cyber criminology: exploring internet crimes and criminal behavior*. Boca Raton, FL: CRC Press.

Jane, E. A. (2014). 'Back to the Kitchen, Cunt': Speaking the unspeakable about online misogyny. *Continuum, 28*(4), 558–570.

Jasmontaite, L., & Dimitrova, D. (2017). Online disaster management: Applicability of the European data protection framework and its key principles. *Journal of Contingencies and Crisis Management, 25*(1), 23–30.

Jenkins, H. (2006). *Convergence culture: Where old and new media collide*. New York: New York University Press.

Jenkins, H., & Deuze, M. (2008). Editorial. *Convergence: The Journal of Research into New Media Technologies, 14*(1), 5–12.

Jewkes, Y. (Ed.). (2007). *Crime online* (pp. 160–178). Cullompton, UK: Willan Publishing.

Jewkes, Y., & Yar, M. (Eds.) (2010). *Handbook of Internet Crime*. London: Routledge.

Jewkes, Y., & Yar, M. (Eds.). (2013). *Handbook of Internet Crime*. Online: Routledge.

Kaiser, D. W., Harrington, R. A., & Turakhia, M. P. (2016). Wearable fitness trackers and heart disease. *JAMA Cardiology*, *1*(2), 239–239.

Katz, J. E., & Aakhus, M. (2002). *Perpetual contact: Mobile communication, private talk, public performance*. Cambridge, UK: Cambridge University Press.

Katz, J. E., & Crocker, E. T. (2015). Selfies | Selfies and Photo Messaging as Visual Conversation: Reports from the United States, United Kingdom and China. *International Journal of Communication*, *9*, 1861–1872.

Kavanaugh, A. (2003). Community networks and civic engagement: A social network approach. *The Good Society*, *11*(3), 17–24.

Kavanaugh, A. L., Reese, D. D., Carroll, J. M., & Rosson, M. B. (2005). Weak ties in networked communities. *The Information Society*, *21*(2), 119–131.

Kavanaugh, A., Perez-Quinones, M. A., Tedesco, J. C., & Sanders, W. (2010). Toward a virtual town square in the era of Web 2.0. In Hunsinger, J., Klastrup, L., & Allen, M. (Eds.), *International handbook of internet research*. (pp. 279–294). Dordrecht: Springer.

Kim, J., Lim, S., Min, Y. H., Shin, Y. W., Lee, B., Sohn, G., ... Shin, S. Y. (2016). Depression screening using daily mental-health ratings from a smartphone application for breast cancer patients. *Journal of Medical Internet Research*, *18*(8), e216.

Kling, R. (1980). Computer abuse and computer crime as organizational activities. *Computer Law Journal*, *2*(1), 403–427.

Lash, S. (2002). *Critique of information*. London: Sage.

Latour, B. (1993). Ethnography of a high-tech case. In P. Lemonnier (Ed.) *Technological Choices: transformation in material cultures since the neolithic* (pp. 372–398), London: Routledge.

Latour, B. (2005). *Reassembling the social: An introduction to actor-network-theory*. New York: Oxford University Press.

Leiner, B. M., Cerf, V. G., Clark, D. D., Kahn, R. E., Kleinrock, L., Lynch, D. C., ... Wolff, S. (2009). A brief history of the internet. *ACM SIGCOMM Computer Communication Review*, *39*(5), 22.

Liddell, M. & Powell, A. (2015). 'What's in a Name? Child abuse material is not 'Pornography', *The Conversation*, August 13. Available at: www.theconversation.com/whats-in-a-name-online-child-abuse-material-is-not-pornography-45840 (last accessed 29 November 2017).

Lim, W. M., & Lim, W. M. (2016). Understanding the selfie phenomenon: Current insights and future research directions. *European Journal of Marketing*, *50*(9/10), 1773–1788.

Loader, B. D., & Mercea, D. (2011) Networking democracy? Social media innovations and participatory politics. *Information, Communication & Society*, *14*(6), 757–769.

Lupton, D. (2013). Quantifying the body: Monitoring and measuring health in the age of mHealth technologies. *Critical Public Health*, *23*(4), 393–403.

Lupton, D. (2014). *Digital sociology*. London, UK: Routledge.

MacKinnon, R. (2013). *Consent of the networked: The worldwide struggle for internet freedom*. New York: Basic Books.

Mann, D., Sutton, M., & Tuffin, R. (2003). The evolution of hate. Social dynamics in white racist newsgroups. *Internet Journal of Criminology*, *1*, 1–32.

Mantelero, A. (2013). The EU proposal for a general data protection regulation and the roots of the 'Right to be Forgotten'. *Computer Law & Security Review*, *29*(3), 229–235.

Marres, N. (2017). *Digital sociology: The reinvention of social research*. Cambridge: Polity Press.

Martin, J. (2014). *Drugs on the dark net: How cryptomarkets are transforming the global trade in illicit drugs*. Basingstoke: Palgrave Macmillan.

Miller, V. (2011). *Understanding digital culture*. London: Sage Publications.

Miller, G. (2012). The smartphone psychology manifesto. *Perspectives on Psychological Science*, *7*(3), 221–237.

Misra, S., Cheng, L., Genevie, J., & Yuan, M. (2016). The iPhone effect: The quality of in-person social interactions in the presence of mobile devices. *Environment and Behavior*, *48*(2), 275–298.

Mitchell, K. J., Finkelhor, D., Jones, L. M., & Wolak, J. (2010). Growth and change in undercover online child exploitation investigations, 2000–2006. *Policing & Society*, *20*(4), 416–431.

Montgomery, J. (1986). Computer crime. *American Criminal Law Review, 24*(3), 429–438.

Morozov, E. (2009). The internet: A room of our own? *Dissent, 56*(3), 80–85.

Morozov, E. (2011). *The net delusion: The dark side of internet freedom.* London: Allen Lane Publishing.

Muncie, J. (2000). Decriminalizing criminology. In G. Lewis, S. Gewirtz, & J. Clark (Eds.), *Rethinking social policy* (pp. 217–228). London, UK: SAGE Publications.

Munson, S. A., & Resnick, P. (2010). *Presenting diverse political opinions: How and how much.* Proceedings of the Sigchi Conference on Human Factors in Computing Systems, pp. 1457–1466, ACM.

Murray, D. C. (2015). Notes to self: The visual culture of selfies in the age of social media. *Consumption Markets & Culture, 18*(6), 490–516.

Oh, O., Agrawal, M., & Rao, H. R. (2011). Information control and terrorism: Tracking the Mumbai terrorist attack through twitter. *Information Systems Frontiers, 13*(1), 33–43.

Papacharissi, Z. (2010). *A private sphere: Democracy in a digital age.* Cambridge: Polity Press.

Pariser, E. (2011). *The filter bubble: What the internet is hiding from you.* New York: Penguin.

Pittaro, M. L. (2007). Cyber stalking: An analysis of online harassment and intimidation. *International Journal of Cyber Criminology, 1*(2), 180–197.

Powell, A. (2015a). Seeking informal justice online: Vigilantism, activism and resisting a rape culture in cyberspace. In Henry, N., Powell, A., & Flynn, A. (Eds.), *Rape Justice: Beyond the Criminal Law* (pp. 218–237). Basingstoke: Palgrave Macmillan.

Powell, A. (2015b). Seeking rape justice: Formal and informal responses to sexual violence through technosocial counter-publics. *Theoretical Criminology, 19*(4), 571–588.

Powell, A., & Henry, N. (2016). Policing technology-facilitated sexual violence against adult victims: police and service sector perspectives. *Policing and Society, 28*(3), 291–307. doi: 10.1080/10439463.2016.1154964.

Powell, A., & Henry, N. (2017). *Sexual Violence in a Digital Age.* Basingstoke: Palgrave Macmillan.

Pyrooz, D. C., Decker, S. H., & Moule Jr, R. K. (2015). Criminal and routine activities in online settings: Gangs, offenders, and the Internet. *Justice Quarterly, 32*(3), 471–499.

Reilly, P. (2013). Every little helps? YouTube, sousveillance and the 'anti-Tesco' riot in stokes croft. *New Media & Society, 17*(5), 755–771.

Renninger, B. J. (2014) "Where I Can Be Myself. . .Where I Can Speak My Mind": Networked counterpublics in a polymedia environment. *New Media & Society, 17*(9), 1513–1529.

Rentschler, C. A. (2014). Rape culture and the feminist politics of social media. *Girlhood Studies, 7*(1), 65–82.

Reyns, B. W., Henson, B., & Fisher, B. S. (2011). Being pursued online applying cyberlifestyle–routine activities theory to cyberstalking victimization. *Criminal Justice and Behavior, 38*(11), 1149–1169.

Ruppert, E., Law, J., & Savage, M. (2013). Reassembling social science methods: The challenge of digital devices. *Theory, Culture & Society, 30*(4), 22–46.

Saunders, R. (2005). Happy slapping: Transatlantic contagion or home-grown, mass-mediated nihilism. *The London Consortium, 1*, 1–11.

Schwendinger, H., & Schwendinger, J. (1970). Defenders of order or guardians of human rights? *Issues Criminology, 5*(2), 123–157.

Senft, T. M., & Baym, N. K. (2015). Selfies introduction: What does the selfie say? Investigating a global phenomenon. *International Journal of Communication, 9*(19), 1588–1606.

Shifman, L. (2014). *Memes in digital culture.* Cambridge, MA: MIT Press.

Sieber, U. (1986). *The International Handbook on Computer Crime.* Chichester, UK: Wiley.

Skeggs, B., & Yuill, S. (2016). The methodology of a multi-model project examining how facebook infrastructures social relations. *Information, Communication & Society, 19*(10), 1356–1372.

Smith, D. R. (2017). The tragedy of self in digitised popular culture: The existential consequences of digital fame on Youtube. *Qualitative Research, 17*(6), 699–714.

Smith, G. J., Bennett Moses, L., & Chan, J. (2017). The challenges of doing criminology in the big data era: Towards a digital and data-driven approach. *The British Journal of Criminology, 57*(2), 259–274.

Smith, R., Grabosky, P., & Urbas, G. (2004). *Cyber Criminals on Trial.* Cambridge, UK: Cambridge University Press.

Spitzberg, B. H., & Hoobler, G. (2002). Cyberstalking and the technologies of interpersonal terrorism. *New Media & Society, 4*(1), 71–92.

Sugiura, L. (2018). *Respectable Deviance and Purchasing Medicine Online: Opportunities and Risks for Consumers.* Basingstoke: Palgrave Macmillan.

Sunstein, C. R. (2004). Democracy and filtering. *Communications of the ACM, 47*(12), 57–59.

Sunstein, C. R. (2009). *Going to extremes: How like minds unite and divide.* Oxford: Oxford University Press.

Sunstein, C. R. (2017). *#Republic: Divided democracy in the age of social media.* Princeton, NJ: Princeton University Press.

Surette, R. (2015). Thought bite: A case study of the social construction of a crime and justice concept. *Crime, Media, Culture, 11*(2), 105–135.

Sutton, M. (2002). Race hatred and the far right on the Internet. *Criminal Justice Matters, 48*(1), 26–27.

Swan, M. (2013). The quantified self: Fundamental disruption in big data science and biological discovery. *Big Data, 1*(2), 85–99.

Schwendinger, H., & Schwendinger, J. (1970). Defenders of order or guardians of human rights. *Issues Criminology, 5*(2), 123–158.

Thomas, D. and Loader, B. (Eds.). (2000). *Cyber crime: Law enforcement, security and surveillance in the information age.* London: Routledge.

Tidwell, A. (1999). The virtual agora: Online ethical dialogues and professional communities. *First Monday, 4*(7), 6–14.

Trottier, D. (2012). Policing social media. *Canadian Review of Sociology/Revue Canadienne de Sociologie, 49*(4), 411–425.

Turkle, S. (2012). *Alone together: Why we expect more from technology and less from each other.* New York: Basic books.

Van Deursen, A. J., & Van Dijk, J. A. (2014). The digital divide shifts to differences in usage. *New Media & Society, 16*(3), 507–526.

Van Dijck, J. (2014). Datafication, dataism and dataveillance: Big data between scientific paradigm and ideology. *Surveillance & Society, 12*(2), 197.

Van House, N. A. (2011). Personal photography, digital technologies and the uses of the visual. *Visual Studies, 26*(2), 125–134.

Van Wilsem, J. (2011). Worlds tied together? Online and non-domestic routine activities and their impact on digital and traditional threat victimization. *European Journal of Criminology, 8*(2), 115–127.

Wajcman, J. (2004). Gendered by design. *Internet Issue Brief, 2*, 11–12.

Wall, D. (1997). Policing the Virtual Community: The Internet, Cyberspace and Cyber-Crime. In Francis, P., Davies, P. & Jupp, V. (Eds.) *Policing futures* (pp. 208–236). Basingstoke: Palgrave.

Wall, D. (2001). Cybercrimes and the Internet. In Wall, D. (Ed.) *Crime and the Internet.* (pp. 1–17). New York: Routledge.

Wall, D. (2007). *Cybercrime: The transformation of crime in the information age* (Vol. 4). Cambridge: Polity.

Wasik, M. (1991). *Crime and the Computer.* Oxford, England: Clarendon Press.

Welch, M. (1996). Critical criminology, social justice, and an alternative view of incarceration. *Critical Criminology, 7*(2), 43–58.

Wellman, B. (1992). Which ties provide what kinds of support? *Advances in Group Processes, 9*, 207–235.

Westlake, B. G. & Bouchard, M. (2016). Liking and hyperlinking: Community detection in online child sexual exploitation networks. *Social Science Research, 59* (September), 23–36.

Wilhelm, A. G. (2000). *Democracy in the digital age: Challenges to political life in cyberspace.* New York: Routledge.

Williams, M. L., Edwards, A., Housley, W., Burnap, P., Rana, O., Avis, N., . . . Sloan, L. (2013). Policing cyber-neighbourhoods: tension monitoring and social media networks. *Policing and Society: An International Journal of Research and Policy, 23*(4), 461–481.

Williams, M. R. (1997). *A History of Computing Technology.* Los Alamitos, CA: IEEE Computer Society Press.

Wood, M. A. (2016). 'I Just Wanna See Someone Get Knocked the Fuck Out': Spectating affray on Facebook fight pages. *Crime, Media, Culture, 14*(1), 23–40.

Wood, M. A. (2017). Antisocial media and algorithmic deviancy amplification: Analysing the id of Facebook's technological unconscious. *Theoretical Criminology, 21*(2), 168–185.

Yar, M. (2005). The novelty of 'Cybercrime': An assessment in light of routine activity theory. *European Journal of Criminology, 2*(4), 407–427.

Yar, M. (2012a). E-Crime 2.0: The Criminological landscape of new social media. *Information & Communications Technology Law, 21*(3), 207–219.

Yar, M. (2012b) Crime, media and the will-to-representation: Reconsidering relationships in the new media age. *Crime, Media, Culture, 8*(3), 245–260.

Yar, M. (2012c). Critical criminology, critical theory and Social Harm. In S. Hall & S. Winslow (Eds.), *New directions in criminological theory* (pp. 52–65). London: Routledge.

Yar, M. (2013). *Cybercrime and society* (2nd ed.). Thousand Oaks, CA: SAGE Publications.

Yip, M., Webber, C., & Shadbolt, N. (2013). Trust among cybercriminals? Carding forums, uncertainty and implications for policing. *Policing and Society, 23*(4), 516–539.

Young, A. (2012) I. Visualising law in the digital age: Arrested by the image. *New York Law School Review, 57*(1), 77–205.

Young, A. (2014). From object to encounter: Aesthetic politics and visual criminology. *Theoretical Criminology, 18*(2), 159–175.

3

A GLOBAL CONTEXT

Networks, Corporations and States

Introduction

Since the attacks on the World Trade Center, New York, on 11 September 2001, the US government has been engaging in extensive surveillance and pervasive datamining. The ensuing 'global war on terror' declared by the Bush administration has been associated with the 'rise of the surveillance state' by scholars, technologists and political commentators alike (Balkin, 2008; Balkin & Levinson, 2006). Throughout the 2000s, various leaks and disclosures have been made regarding the extent of this surveillance, such as warrantless telephone wiretapping, and various forms of 'dataveillance' through the retention, mining and searching of individuals' data (Solove, 2007, 2011). Among them is the now infamous 'Snowden revelations' of 2013, in which former government contractor Edward Snowden leaked details of the US National Security Agency (NSA) and Federal Bureau of Investigation (FBI)'s activities (Lyon, 2014). Snowden revealed surveillance practices involving the telephone metadata of millions of Americans, as well as the NSA's PRISM program, which allowed the US government access to the servers of technology giants such as Apple, Facebook, Google, Microsoft, Skype, Yahoo and YouTube, through 'back doors' created with the help of the companies themselves (Landau, 2013; Lyon, 2014) and used to monitor the communications of non-US citizens, as well as those who communicated with them. Such surveillance, government proponents argue, is a necessary trade-off of individual citizens' rights to *privacy*, for the greater good of increased *security* and the potential prevention of future mass harms in a context of the threat of global terrorism. Yet, rather than targeted surveillance directed only at those suspected of engaging in terrorist-related activities, what the Snowden leaks showed was that governments, especially those of America, Britain and Canada, have been engaging in remarkably large scale monitoring of *whole populations* of citizens (Lyon, 2014). The approach of US intelligence agencies was reportedly: 'Collect it all, process it all, exploit it all, sniff it all, know it all' (NSA Collection Posture revealed in Snowden documents, in Crampton, 2015).

The assumption that citizens' human rights, such as privacy, can and should be readily traded for greater 'security' is itself a contested point in both political and scholarly fields. Professor of Law at George Washington University, Daniel Solove (2007, 2011), provides a useful critique of one of the all-too-common refrains of citizens in response to discovering that the government is mass monitoring their private information: *If you've got nothing to hide, then what do you have to fear?* (see also Schneier 2009, 2015; Stone, 2010). The problem, argues Solove, lies in the very question itself. For the most part, the question fails to understand the many and varied impacts that surveillance and dataveillance can have both on individuals and on societies more broadly; including the exposure of individuals to potentially greater *insecurity* from misuse and abuse of their information, either by governments or by others who gain unlawful access (Solove, 2007). Failure to appreciate the implications of mass monitoring is understandable, since the risk posed by surveillance activities of private and state authorities is itself hard to conceptualise; for most citizens, while it is omnipresent, its effects are never felt. Data security expert Bruce Schneier meanwhile, responds to the 'nothing to hide' argument by turning the question on its head: 'If I'm not doing anything wrong, then you have no cause to watch me' (2009, n.p.).

Such arguments regarding the balancing of privacy and security concerns are naturally of interest to digital criminology, which is concerned about the potential for technosocial *harms* (as opposed to narrowly defined *crimes*, as discussed in Chapter 2) within and beyond the nation state. Yet, in order to fully appreciate the context and implications of such concerns, it is also necessary to understand the broader global context of shifting technosocial relations of risk, security, surveillance and the state in digital society. More specifically, the shifts in structures of power, governance and regulation between the domain of nation states (the conventional focus of much criminological research) and those of global corporations have particular implications for how we conceptualise harms and injustice in a digital society. This chapter explores these tensions, providing a necessary backdrop to the further examination of crime, deviance, justice and injustice in subsequent chapters. In particular, we suggest that technologically mediated interactions in digital society do not occur solely, or even primarily, within the familiar terrains of domestic society and typical state-based criminological framings. Digital society is, in this sense, embedded in a variety of normative contexts and subject to a range of regulatory systems; both formal and informal, as well as local and global.

We then explore some of the major global regulatory logics that can be applied to 'risky' interactions within digital society. In particular, in this chapter, we highlight the emergence of competing modes of regulation in a digital society as the local increasingly becomes interconnected with the global. The following section outlines how the diffusion of global networks throughout contemporary life challenges national and bounded policies and techniques designed to create order and provide protection. The latter rely on the state to authorise law and the judiciary, delineate territory and maintain a monopoly on the use of force as part of a social contract. In the first instance, the increasingly omnipresent surveillance regimes designed to gather information about digital society in order to generate profit (corporate surveillance) and identify threats (state surveillance) pose an outsized risk to freedom and privacy because immediate forms of harm are hard to identify. The second challenge to this traditional mode of regulation is the bilateral policies and transnational regimes that deregulate economies and facilitate trade in order to increase market efficiency and foster innovation but actually give corporate entities heretofore unparalleled power and profit that is greatly disproportionate to the wider citizenry. The final challenge to the traditional mode of regulation is the influence of diplomacy, statecraft and military might, intended to manage insecurity caused by conflicts between states. The securitisation of new or unfamiliar elements of digital society makes them more likely to be interpreted as foreign threats to national security. Having highlighted the unsuitability of these global regulatory schemes for understanding and managing interactions within a digital society, we will outline a citizen-led approach to regulation that more accurately reflects the lived lives of everyday digital citizens.

Crime in Global Networks

There is no doubt that the increased connectivity inherent in our digital technologies creates new risks and dangers. The very nature of global digital networks opens up individuals and nations to harms enacted across the borderless spaces of online communications and information flows. Yet, exactly how to conceive of these risks and dangers, let alone how to respond to them, is far from settled. Increasingly, it appears, governments are conceptualising and responding to cybercrime through a securitised, militaristic frame of reference (as we discuss further below). In short, incursions in cyberspace are considered foremost as threats to nation states: whether as threats to their economies (such as in financially-motivated and/or organised crime) or as threats to their national security (such as in espionage and/or threats to critical infrastructure), or both. The lines demarcating cyber*crimes* as a distinct form of threat have arguably become blurred with those of cyber*security*, cyber-*war* and cyber-*terrorism*. In part, this blurring can be understood in the context of shifting ideas about the 'spatiality' of digital society — to put it differently, uncertainty around the question of 'Where is the internet?' As a relatively recent development in human communication, digital networks appear to occupy a different space to 'real life'. This gives rise to a tendency to treat digital networks as existing either in a virtual place that is 'not real' or in a foreign, dangerous space. Understanding that digital networks are not separate to, but in fact overlaid upon, everyday life is vital to understanding the nature of digital society.

Shifts in Place, Space and Time

In order to understand how familiar everyday contexts are increasingly overlaid with technological communications, it is important to understand the implications of networks in shifting our experience of place, space and time. Manuel Castells' seminal theorising of these new connections and disconnections dates back nearly thirty years but continues to offer useful insights. Vitally, Castells offered an account of the effects of global networks on local sense of place that captured the distinction between 'virtual' and 'real' life but did not rely on an *online/offline dichotomy* (as discussed in Chapter 1) that treats digital interactions as occurring in a separate space, alternate to the material space we inhabit. The virtual versus material real dichotomy tendency evident in initial utopian theorisations of interactions via digital communications, seen in many popular culture representations of the internet, has been repeated in many accounts of cybercrime and cybersecurity. Castells counselled against the notion of virtualised or vanishing space, highlighting instead the importance of 'reconceptualiz[ing] new forms of spatial arrangements under the new technological paradigm' (1996, p. 13). Material conceptions of space are important to Castells for three reasons. First, there is not a move to an alternate place beyond the place of origin and destination of sender and receiver, but an instantaneous linking of the two territories. Second, technologically facilitated connections still rely on material infrastructure located in various places across the network. Third, space is not erased: rather its meaning is altered, along with that of time, as distant places become connected and the time between becomes shared (Castells, 1996). In this sense, distant places and their respective senses of time become shared in the moment of connection.

This connecting of disparate places, however, does create a new experience of space: that of the 'flow'. There are two observable understandings of space bound up together in Castells' account. The first is the space of places: the everyday lived experience of most individuals in their immediate surrounds. This space is tied to history and culture (Castells, 2000) and also to social and political control (Castells, 1996). The second is the space of flows, which can be described as 'the material arrangements that allow for simultaneity of social practices without territorial contiguity. It is not a purely electronic space, not what Batty has called a "cyberspace", although cyberspace is a component of the space of flows' (Castells, 1999, p. 295). The space of flows comprises both the lines of communication enabled by software platforms and the hardware and infrastructure that underpin it (Castells, 1996). A key point of distinction is that the space of places and the space of flows are not competing or oppositional conceptions of space. This has been true right from the initial formation of the internet (Castells, 1989). Society does not exist exclusively in one or the other, but rather they are mutually productive. They are dialectical rather than dichotomous spaces, where place shapes flow and flow shapes place (Castells, 2000). To understand the dialectic of space of flows and space of place within the scope of a criminological inquiry, it is important to appreciate how the modes of regulation and control bound up in the materiality of flows beyond the state interact with more traditional regulations and control of place within the state.

The 'Darker Sides of Globalisation'[1]

The new forms of movement and connection enabled by globalisation pose both conceptual and practical challenges for criminological thinking. As critical criminologist David Friedrichs ominously suggested in 2007, '[e]arly in the 21st century, a spectre haunts the field of criminology; the spectre of globalization' (p. 4). He was alluding to the conceptual challenge for criminological thinking to shift its focus from initial concerns with response of local authorities to crime, to the need for a state or federal response to serious and complex crimes, and then again towards a global setting, where state sovereign authority and territory are less equipped to respond to, and contain the effects of, globalisation (Friedrichs, 2007). Australian criminologist Russell Hogg argues that these challenges stem from commitment to a 'Hobbesian Criminology', which sets out the 'taken-for-granted intellectual parameters and political horizons of criminology' (Hogg, 2002, p. 192; Morrison, 2006). These parameters include a concept of crime as that which is defined by authority of the state, the idea of justice as resulting from the rules, institutions, processes and punishments of the state, and the idea of a nation that is delineated by territorial borders and unified by the formal legal system (Hogg, 2002). While these parameters capture the venerable traditions of criminological thinking within the state and its commitment to ensuring a civilised space, they also set up certain implicit assumptions about the 'uncivilised' nature of non-citizens and global processes that exist beyond its borders (Morrison, 2006, p. 2).

Not only does this state-centric view of crime struggle with the complexity of globalisation, it also reflects a Euro-centric worldview that is itself implicated in an earlier dark history of globalised colonial rule. Nigerian criminologist Biko Agozino suggested it is no coincidence that 'criminology is concentrated in former colonising countries, and virtually absent in the former colonised countries' because this reflects a history of 'criminology [a]s a social science that served colonialism' (2003, p. 1). Moving beyond the territorial and conceptual borders of the state means coming to grips with these histories of violence and their enduring effects. According to Australian criminologist Chris Cunneen '[t]he criminological imagination falters when confronted with genocide and dispossession, with the peoples who demand that their radical difference, their laws, their customs, their alterity to the west be recognized' (Cunneen, 2011, p. 251). To think beyond these limits, a decolonisation of criminology needs to occur through a counter-colonial or post-colonial approach that, at the very least, recognises the specific forms of power and control that exist in different global contexts (Agozino, 2004). The effects of globalisation are not producing 'a flat, generic entity, which can be zoomed in and out at will, the complex nature of the contemporary world order presents us with a patchwork of unequal geographies, frictions and spaces of difference' (Aas, 2012b, p. 17). A criminological approach to digital networks, which are inherently global, must be able to recognise the overlapping and often competing forms of regulation and control that occur within territories constrained by borders, how these interact with histories of violence and dispossession and the effects this has on digital society.

The practical challenge is that this expanded focus opens criminology up to a range of new, complex and often very serious concerns that need to be responded to in the absence of any overarching supranational authority. As legal scholar Mark Findlay set out in an early account, '[g]lobalization creates new and favourable contexts for crime' (Findlay, 1999, p. 1). The first step towards a global criminology can be seen in the field of 'comparative and transnational criminology' (Barak, 2000; Beirne & Nelken, 1997; McDonald, 1995; Reichel & Albanese, 2004; Sheptycki & Wardack, 2005). The premise of this method is that not only does it draw countries into comparison in order to reveal specificities of crime and control in different contexts, but it also adopts a critical reflective approach to cultural differences that highlights forms of harm that might otherwise be taken for granted because of their structural nature or overlooked due to cultural bias (Beirne, 1997). Importantly, however, it draws attention to common transnational problems faced by nations and reveals the cross-border nature of harm and crime (Barak, 2000). Cultural difference and transnationality, of course, are not separate categories, as criminologist Susanne Karstedt (2001) highlighted: cultural histories and patterns of contemporary inequality play a major role in determining the nature and intensity of global phenomena, and they need to be integrated into the comparative criminological approach. The breadth of this global comparative methodology has gradually broadened so that it not only looks beyond the state at global interconnectedness but also 'below the city' to recognise the multiple layers of governance spanning the supranational to the local (Pakes, 2010, p. 19).

The development of a global perspective on criminology has been further developed in studies of specific forms of transnational harm. Criminologists Sharon Pickering and Leanne Weber (2006, 2011) highlight the complex challenge posed by the movement of people across borders in search of physical and economic security, drawing attention to the role played by global structural inequalities in producing these conditions and the limitations of state policies that criminalise border-crossing as an attempted solution. This example highlights a contradiction within the traditional approach to crime control in the face of globalisation, namely that at the very moment the challenges of global migration and asylum-seeking become most pronounced, the state reverts most forcefully to its least progressive modes of dealing with crime (Weber & Bowling, 2008). This response takes the form of delineating otherness along racial lines by subjecting those seeking refuge to increasingly tough border security measures and treating migrants and refugees within the state as criminals (Weber & Bowling, 2008). This creates 'innumerable points of insecurity and suspicion of foreign populations', resulting in a 'simultaneous "securitization" and "criminalization" of migration' (Aas, 2007, p. 289).

Another example of transnational crime that requires an understanding of global networks is harms against the environment. The field of 'green criminology' attempts to understand how corporate and state economic interests generate harms that are local in their impact but enabled by global interconnectedness (Lynch, 1990; South & Beirne, 1998). White has directly tackled the global dimension of this field in his 'eco-global criminological' approach, which offers 'a framework of analysis where the emphasis is on the ecological, the transnational and questions of justice. The substantive focus of eco-global criminology is transgressions against ecosystems, humans and animals' (White, 2011, p. 19). The challenge for criminology here is to expand its boundaries to encompass a broad range of *harms* as *crimes*, particularly as many are occurring at a scale and pace that elude existing policing and justice processes (White, 2009). In drawing attention to causes, White highlights 'the destructive nature of global capitalism, the role of the nation state (and regional and global regulatory bodies), and inequality and discrimination as these relate to class, gender, race and nonhuman animals' (White, 2013, p. 22). Crime in global networks can therefore be seen as structural in nature but varied in impact according to various kinds of vulnerability. The production of environmental damage highlights how important it is to broaden the concept of crime while also maintaining a 'simultaneous view of global and local levels' (Aas, 2013, p. 220). The approach adopted here in *Digital Criminology* can be understood as a continuation of concern with transnational harms such as these that are, at once, local and global.

The challenge of globalisation for criminology can also be seen in the limited effectiveness of the traditional approaches to seeking justice. State-based responses to globalisation are not static: 'global crime agendas are now being reordered and security priorities realigned' but they are still 'defined by criminalization and the restoration of global security', which are traditional domestic and foreign policy responses to fears and threats. In 2008, Findlay suggested that this is an insufficient reconceptualisation of what justice should look like in an increasingly global era and instead that 'crime and punishment are constructed and employed to govern the globe' (Findlay, 2008, p. xi). Far from achieving justice, these responses that are grounded in 'sharp distinctions between the domestic and the international matters are themselves becoming a major source of injustice' (Aas, 2007, p. 297). The best way forward, according to criminologist Katja Franko Aas, is to recognise that '[t]he growing awareness of global interconnectedness represents an impetus to develop methodological, theoretical and conceptual approaches which transcend the established ethnocentric frameworks and are built on a more expansive and inclusive geographical imagination' (Aas, 2012b, p. 8). Drawing on the work of Nancy Fraser, Aas proposes a 'rescaling' of the focus of justice away from the geographical location of people within a nation state, towards a concern for the structures and frameworks that govern them, taking it as a given that these are increasingly global (Aas, 2012a, p. 236). The sections that follow articulate how changing flows through digital networks are regulated both within and beyond state borders, in line with this global criminological outlook.

Risk and the Surveillance Society

The new connections and interactions enabled by digital networks are shifting the patterns of fears and risks. New social phenomena are being criminalised or securitised as people are at once connected to new cultural and political movements and disconnected from those they once knew. Reframing risks as crimes or threats to security is an attempt to 'solve' global social change that is highly invasive, shifting social norms and reorienting cultural relations around collective fears and dangers. It is not just that many individuals are denied freedoms in the pursuit of security, this reframing changes the collective conception of what it means to be free. This is a fertile environment for negative encounters with 'otherness' as the distant becomes close and the familiar becomes unfamiliar. All the while, conflict, disorder and change do not abate, adding to the sense that we live in an ever more insecure and dangerous world. The truth may be that we do. But do our fears really line up with the risks? The digital society poses a challenge simply in determining whether what we perceive as new fears are misperceptions of new risks, changing perceptions of existing risks or actual increases in risk.

The advent of powerful digital technologies has given rise to expansive forms of surveillance that pose significant dangers to a free society. As sociologist Ulrich Beck suggests, 'there has never been a situation like this in human history, where this level of surveillance can go beyond social and territorial units. It is a fundamentally global issue because of the new possibilities of the digital age' (Beck, 2014, n.p.). The conception of risk that Beck invoked here is grounded in his notion of 'risk society' — the ways in which pursuit of progress by government and private actors generates significant unanticipated dangers to the world in which we live; dangers that we are not collectively equipped to anticipate or respond to effectively. As Beck (1992) suggests,

> in contrast to all earlier epochs (including industrial society), the risk society is characterised essentially by a lack: the impossibility of an external attribution of hazards. In other words, risks depend on decisions, they are industrially produced and in this sense politically reflexive (p. 183).

New technological advances are allowed to be potent organising principles within society because they offer immediate utility or profit but obscure the likely damaging consequences, for example, toxic pesticides (Beck, 1992). Such misperceptions, or lack of awareness of risk, are likely to increase when it comes to global or transnational issues due to different cultural perceptions of social issues and the fact that faraway problems are less likely to resonate with people (Beck, 1999). Societies operate according to many logics or rationalities, yet they often are unable to rationally or accurately determine their corresponding risks.

The expanding global systems of state and corporate surveillance are a key example of misperception of risk. Whereas other discussions of risk, such as striking a balance between the benefits and the dangers of nuclear power, typically result from a major catastrophe, the negative consequence of surveillance occurs largely without anyone noticing because it 'does not focus on, result from or repeatedly refer to a catastrophe which is physical and real in time and space' (Beck, 2013, n.p.). The power of surveillance is obscured to a large degree because the nature of its operation has evolved. First, from the centralised notions of power and authority represented by Bentham's panopticon and 'Big Brother', in which the few watch the many; second, to more distributed notions of lateral surveillance and synopticon, in which the many watch the few; and finally, to the dispersed technosocial networks, or 'surveillance assemblages', of algorithmic surveillance in which almost anyone watches almost everyone. These three conceptual modes of surveillance have not replaced one another in a linear fashion but coexist, further obscuring their cumulative operation and effects.

French philosopher Michel Foucault published his now famous book *Surveiller et Punir: Naissance de la Prison* in 1975. It was subsequently translated into English, and re-published in 1977 under the title *Discipline and Punish: The Birth of the Prison* (1991), and has been highly influential in the sociology of social control, including within criminology. Foucault's book opens with a vivid account of a violent execution carried out in Paris in 1757, suggesting that it was through the 'great spectacle' of torturous physical punishment that the state authority demonstrated its power and exerted control of its citizenry. He contrasts this with the power of authority's gaze and the subsequent compulsion for self-discipline in modern societies, drawing on the metaphor of the 'panopticon'. Developed by 18th century English philosopher Jeremy Bentham, the panopticon is a design for a prison in which a single, central guard tower surveys a surrounding ring of prison cells. The prisoners, never certain if the guard is looking their way, are prompted to engage in self-disciplining behaviour — in case they are the ones currently being watched. For Foucault (1984), the panopticon was an analogy for the effects of power exercised through social institutions, in which they induced 'a state of conscious and permanent visibility that assures the automatic functioning of power' (Foucault, 1991, p. 201). This Foucauldian, and indeed Orwellian, notion of the disciplinary gaze of 'Big Brother' has been hugely influential on the popular and academic conceptualisation of surveillance. When one considers state surveillance practices such as CCTV, the metaphor of the panopticon and the disciplinary effects of never knowing if someone is watching — and, if so, who — remain analytically helpful within criminology. Yet, despite the continued relevance of surveillance in rendering populations permanently visible, the panopticon is, in many respects, outmoded in the digital age (Farinosi, 2011; Gilliom & Monahan, 2013; Lyon, 1994; Mathiesen, 1997). The surveillance regimes of countries such as the United States (described at the start of this chapter) are notably more expansive than was imagined by either Foucault or Orwell, both in that they are increasingly global in reach and, crucially, that they are not operated only by singular, sovereign states.

In digital society, surveillance occurs at levels of detail and breadth previously unimaginable — facilitated through online participation in applications such as social media platforms that most participate in largely unreflexively (Pridmore & Zwick, 2011; Trottier & Lyon, 2012). This expansive conception of surveillance has been articulated effectively by British sociologist and surveillance theorist David Lyon, who described it as 'the focused, systematic and routine attention to personal details for purposes of influence, management, protection or detection' (Lyon, 2007, p. 14). Norwegian sociologist Thomas Mathiesen (1997), meanwhile, articulated that we do indeed live in societies where the 'few see the many', in the classic panopticon model of social control. But increasingly with the development of mass media, to which we might now add digital media, '*the many see and contemplate the few*' (Mathiesen, 1997, p. 219, emphasis in original). As such, Mathiesen argued that not only does panopticism characterise surveillance and social control in modern societies but simultaneously a synopticism: in effect, a two-way *viewer society*.

Yet, arguably, digital society goes further, with citizen-consumers also willingly engaging in new modes of 'participatory surveillance': mutual sharing and watching that has come to feature in what Albrechtslund (2008) described as an empowering way of maintaining friendships and constructing identities (see also Fuchs, Boersma, Albrechtslund, & Sandoval, 2013). While media scholar Anders Albrechtslund (2008) conceptualised this participatory and social surveillance in the digital age as positive in its democratising potential, other scholars are less convinced. Media scholar Mark Andrejevic (2005), for instance, similarly identified an increasingly 'peer-to-peer' or 'lateral surveillance' but argued that it reinforces and extends the gaze of the state. Individuals are, in effect, 'invited to become spies' in a society where 'everyone is to be considered potentially suspect' (Andrejevic, 2005, p. 494).

Finally, surveillance scholars have further engaged with French philosopher Gilles Deleuze's (1992) concept of the 'control society', suggesting that power operates less through centralised panoptic systems or 'total institutions' (Foucault, 1982) and more through flexible, dispersed, interconnected and distributive 'flows' (Erwin, 2015; Rice, 2017). Together, these flows form a 'surveillant assemblage' (Haggerty & Ericson, 2000) that permeates and impacts on all aspects of both public and private life. Drawing on Deleuze and his collaborator Felix Guattari, sociologists Kevin Haggerty and Richard Ericson (2000) describe assemblages as comprising:

> discrete flows of an essentially limitless range of other phenomena such as people, signs, chemicals, knowledge and institutions. To dig beneath the surface stability of any entity is to encounter a host of different phenomena and processes working in concert (p. 608).

In digital society, the surveillant assemblage thus comprises big data collection, predictive algorithmic analysis, multiple data sources (including video, biometric, demographic, and geographic data), as well as the practices and uses of multiple agencies — both private and public — to track, monitor and actively shape individuals' behaviours and interactions (Erwin, 2015). Understood in these terms, the level of surveillance of the digitally mediated interactions of everyday individuals is incredibly extensive. Moreover, in the context of digital society, surveillance and the monitoring of populations has also arguably shifted its purpose: from the population control concerns of nation states, to the market- and profit-driven concerns of increasingly corporate 'digital sovereigns' (see below).

The Corporatisation of Digital Networks

Sovereign states have put in place processes that enable corporations to operate across national borders with relative ease. The last 30 years of trade policies — pushed through a series of bilateral agreements and through multilateral organisations such as the World Trade Organization (WTO), International Monetary Fund (IMF) and World Bank — have seen corporations gain levels of access to local and foreign markets not seen since colonialism. Often portrayed as removing regulation to enable efficiency, so-called free trade operates through removing certain subsidies and tariffs while leaving in place, or even increasing, restrictions on the conduct of states and individuals. These 'free trade' policies are put forward as a mode of social and economic governance designed to foster productivity based on an efficient markets hypothesis, which holds that supply and demand will best allocate capital and labour to the most profitable sectors of the global economy. These policies have contributed to spectacular growth in certain parts of the 'developed world' and also brutal poverty and living conditions in 'developing' economies. The consequences of this ascendant corporate power for the digital society have been significant. A digitally mediated society is inherently transnational, as it is not constrained by territorial borders. Global communications platforms are as likely to be regulated according to their own operating principles and emergent cultural norms as by the day-to-day behaviour of the locality of individual users. To understand these new modes of regulation, this section seeks to understand globalisation not as an inevitable freeing of markets from regulation but rather as a set of policies implemented in order to facilitate a neoliberal worldview.

There are many ways of critically engaging with the regulatory effects of neoliberalism, all of them contested and reflecting particular goals and worldviews. A liberal perspective on neoliberalism sees it fundamentally in contest with Keynesian social democracy. Within this contest, sociologist Anthony Giddens suggested that social democracy failed to understand the efficiency of the market in sending signals to producers and consumers in favour of state planning and intervention (Giddens, 1998). Neoliberal policies, in turn, fail to understand the social basis of the market and, by unleashing the logic of competitive economic exchange, undermine the communal norms that underpin society, ultimately fragmenting the coherence of the societies that allow markets to function. Giddens' suggestion was that a liberal compromise, a 'third way' consensus, could be made to protect those parts of society under threat from the market (Giddens, 1998, p. 70). From a Marxist perspective, neoliberal policies are incoherent, ultimately failing to adhere to neoliberalism's own prescriptions. According to political geographer David Harvey, neoliberalism is an 'unstable and contradictory political form' (Harvey, 2005, p. 64) that even the most ardent adherent cannot fully implement. The United States, a vocal advocate of neoliberalism, regularly runs large budget deficits, protects its markets and continues to commit huge government spending to areas such as defence and security. Likewise, the EU states often run budget deficits and act collectively to protect sectors of the economy, such as agriculture. The outlook predicted by Harvey was that policies necessary to maintain the coherence of neoliberalism would become increasingly authoritarian and needed to be resisted through collective democratic struggle (Harvey, 2005). Another lens through which to interpret neoliberal policies sees it as the contemporary dominant ideological variant of globalisation. The focus of Manfred Steger's critique was to highlight how the broad array of policies united under the rhetoric of neoliberalism varied considerably from country to country (Steger & Roy, 2010). In order to challenge the logic of neoliberalism and the seeming 'common sense' basis of these policies, Steger highlighted the many alternate forms of globalisation that were being facilitated through new cultures and technologies and that could constitute a more socially-oriented vision of globalisation that he called 'justice globalism' (Steger, Goodman, & Wilson, 2013).

Regulatory Capitalism

A further critical frame through which to understand neoliberal policies is in historical terms, focusing on the emergence of the many international regulatory frameworks (Braithwaite, 2000). The foremost proponents of this approach, criminologist John Braithwaite and his frequent collaborator Peter Drahos, avoided the use of the term neoliberalism altogether, preferring to call the forms of regulation that have occurred within capitalism in recent decades 'regulatory capitalism' (Braithwaite, 2005). The historical arc that Braithwaite traced (2006) began on the European continent in a feudal economy where local landholders exercised monopoly control of their territories and order was created through force of arms. This was followed by what Braithwaite terms the 'police economy' during the 16th to 19th century transition to capitalism, during which time order was maintained by local private police officers, whose primary role was to ensure orderly conditions for trade and commerce (2006, p. 411). The *laissez faire* economy of the 19th century was much more open and free of regulation than the contemporary era; indeed, Braithwaite describes it as 'unregulable' (Braithwaite, 2006, p. 413). In order to regain some measure of control over the economy and to create control by state institutions, the welfare state, or what Braithwaite terms the 'provider state', was introduced in western Europe and the United States to maintain capitalism in the face of the increasing popularity of socialist ideas. This led the state to regulate more and more aspects of day-to-day life (2006, p. 415). Throughout the 20th century, Western states encouraged the creation of large business enterprises, leading to the rise of regulatory capitalism and the increased corporatisation of everyday life. According to Braithwaite (2008), in the era of regulatory capitalism, more of the governance that shapes the daily lives of most citizens is corporate governance than state governance. The corporatization of the world is both a product of regulation and the key driver of regulatory growth, indeed of state growth more generally (p. 4).

Viewed in these terms, corporatisation can be understood explicitly as a mode of regulating human activity to gain profit, as opposed to freeing markets to make them more efficient.

National laws and global agreements intended to facilitate the success of businesses and corporations in the digital economy function as means of regulating those activities. Summarising the findings of their lengthy tome, Braithwaite and Drahos describe 'the globalization of business regulation broadly as the globalization of the norms, standards, principles, and rules that govern commerce and the globalization of their enforcement' (Braithwaite & Drahos, 2000, p. 10). Writing in the early stages of the emergence of the information economy, Drahos (1995) hypothesised a pessimistic possible future of the regulation of intellectual property and media industries, in which the rights of corporations greatly outweighed the rights of individuals, to the great detriment of the development of knowledge and human freedom. The year he projected this pessimistic future was 2015, and the regulatory scheme he outlined looks a great deal like that of the present.

> [I]f abstract objects fall out of the intellectual commons and are enclosed by private owners, private, arbitrary, unchecked global power will become part of life in the information society. A world in which seed rights, algorithms, DNA, and chemical formulas are owned by a few, a world in which information flows can be coordinated by information-media barons, might indeed be information feudalism.
>
> (Drahos, 1995, p. 221)

This concept of information feudalism was further developed by Drahos and Braithwaite as it became clear the emergent global information economy was continuing on a path to the portentous future Drahos had envisioned. The regulatory system was not one that succeeded even in the terms it set out; information feudalism, they suggested, 'is a regime of property rights that is not economically-efficient and does not get the balance right between rewarding innovation and diffusing it' (Drahos & Braithwaite, 2002, p. 219). Furthermore, it benefits corporations excessively at the expense of the broader public who contribute to its success; 'like feudalism, it rewards guilds instead of inventive individual citizens. It makes democratic citizens trespassers on knowledge that should be the common heritage of humankind, their educational birthright' (Drahos & Braithwaite, 2002, p. 219). This disadvantageous system of regulating the contemporary knowledge economy can be seen clearly in regards to a number of important elements of the systems that underpin the digital society.

The presence of these corporate regulations and their effect on the digital society, however, is not always readily evident. This gives rise, as with the case of surveillance, to unforeseen risk and control within digital society that are not appropriately reflected in the level of concern, resistance or policy response. This is, in part, due to the operative norms within these communities. The notion of ownership and control is antithetical to the rhetoric and operative logic of the internet, which is widely understood as open, dynamic and, to a degree, ungovernable. Indeed, the foundational principle of the internet was that information should be free. The key architects of the early web held a utopian libertarian worldview, believing that the internet had the ability to be a profoundly liberatory force for social change and would enable new kinds of human communities that were not confined by the limitations of territory and authority. This gave rise to a tremendous vibrancy and investment in new hardware, software and networks, but also gave rise to certain contradictions that inadvertently enabled corporations to achieve unprecedented levels of profit and exercise new kinds of control. Freedom, however, means different things to different people when it comes to networks. Media scholar Rebecca MacKinnon suggests that internet freedom is 'like a Rorschach inkblot test: different people look at the same ink splotch and see very different things' (MacKinnon, 2012, pp. 187–188). The real meaning of the maxim that 'information should be free' quickly became a key point of contention. Does free information mean that there should be no cost, or can it just mean that information is convenient and ubiquitous? Does it mean that there should be no restrictions on the networked activities of corporations and citizens or that users should have equal rights? This tension within the notion that information should be free generates conflict between internet utopians and powerful corporate content owners. A commitment to the principle that content on the internet should be free of cost leads to behaviour that, from the perspective of owners of intellectual property, is criminal. Ultimately, legislators and regulators have agreed with these corporations and defined accessing and uploading content subject to copyright without authorization or payment via the internet as digital piracy.

Networked Authoritarianism

MacKinnon adopted a balanced account of the opportunities and risks provided by new networked technologies. She embraced the optimism of social movement researchers Jennifer Earl and Katrina Kimport (2011) in her belief in the power for digital technologies to facilitate positive social change. She located the internet as potentially a new stage in the evolution of democratic practice, suggesting the 'digital commons is the virtual equivalent of Toqueville's civil society, through which citizens can mobilise to express their interests and protect their rights' (MacKinnon, 2012, p. 17). While MacKinnon believed that the internet could be a force for positive change, she echoed the concerns of other commentators such as Evgeny Morozov (2011) regarding the potential for loss of freedom when powerful corporations and states collaborate at the expense of popular social movements. She warned of a 'networked authoritarianism' emerging in countries such as China, where increased citizen participation via the internet meant that 'public debate and even some forms of activism are expanding on it, while at the same time, state controls and manipulation tactics have prevented democracy movements from gaining meaningful traction' (MacKinnon, 2012, p. 42). This is not just a problem of authoritarian countries: collaboration between states and corporations in the United States has meant that 'standards of oversight, due process, and accountability have been eroded in ways that have made it easier for government agencies to abuse power and more difficult for citizens to hold abusers accountable' (MacKinnon, 2012, p. 76). The risks, however, do not only lie with the ability of technology to enable authoritarian tendencies.

The corporatisation of the internet also has a range of more subtle effects. The influence of corporate regulation of networked flows can be seen most literally and directly in the behaviour of businesses and the ownership and control of intellectual property and user data. At a broad and diffuse level, however, it equally shapes and controls the behaviour and norms of all members of digital society who use these platforms. The ability to determine community standards policies and the form and function for communicating via digitally networked communications means that 'companies are even more powerful because not only do they create and sell products, but they also provide and shape the digital space upon which citizens increasingly depend' (MacKinnon, 2012, p. 11). The move away from open access to proprietary platforms 'created a new, globally networked public sphere that is largely shaped, built, owned, and operated by the private sector. Digital platforms, services and devices now mediate human relationships between citizens and governments' (MacKinnon, 2012, p. 9). So, while privately-owned social media platforms are nominally facilitating democratic engagement, they are primarily optimised for data retention, advertising exposure and other profit-making strategies. In this sense, the networked tools of liberation are the same as those that surveil and control the digital society.

A further critical point MacKinnon made is that corporations control the digital networks. Concepts such 'Googledom' and 'Facebookistan' are employed to convey the increasing influence that these corporations have over digital society, but perhaps MacKinnon overstates their power with the concepts of 'digital sovereigns' and 'sovereigns of cyberspace'. While these corporations are powerful, the nature of their power is very different from that of a sovereign, since they do not exercise the same regulatory powers. As this chapter seeks to demonstrate, these are distinct regulatory modes. As explained in earlier sections of this chapter, the response to crime in a conventional setting might involve imprisonment or punishment of citizens and their surveillance and classification in order to prevent or mitigate certain risks. As we will explain in the next section of this chapter, the external regulatory mode of the sovereign involves diplomatic agreements and threats, or actual deployment, of military force. This is not to invalidate MacKinnon's point, but rather to suggest that these equally potent forms of regulation are quite distinct and produce quite different effects when they are applied in the digital society.

Surveillance Capitalism and 'Big Other'

American sociologist and technology theorist Shoshana Zuboff poignantly foreshadowed the implications of increasingly corporate 'digital sovereigns' (in MacKinnon's terms). In her influential 1988 book, *In the Age of the Smart Machine*, she articulated 'Zuboff's three laws' of information computing. First, everything that can be automated will be automated (Zuboff, 1988). Second, everything that can be informed will be informed. Third, and of most relevance here, 'every digital application that can be used for surveillance and control will be used for surveillance and control, irrespective of its originating intention' (Zuboff, 2013, n.p.). Zuboff's three laws underpin an emerging logic of capital accumulation that she describes as *surveillance capitalism*: a 'new form of information capitalism [that] aims to predict and modify human behaviour as a means to produce revenue and market control' (Zuboff, 2015, p. 75). Rather than the panopticon-style of surveillance typified by 'Big Brother', Zuboff identifies a new kind of sovereign power emerging in the information age: 'Big Other' (2015). Big Other emerges in the context of pervasive computer mediation, in which people's interactions, experiences and behaviours are commodified: reborn as data that are collectable, knowable and manipulable, and resulting in behaviour modification through rewards and punishments distributed by 'a new kind of invisible hand' from which there is no escape (Zuboff, 2015):

> False consciousness is no longer produced by the hidden facts of class and their relation to production, but rather by the hidden facts of commoditized behavior modification. If power was once identified with the ownership of the means of production, it is now identified with the ownership of the means of behavioral modification (p. 82).

A key implication of surveillance capitalism, then, is that while the accumulation of information (from the deeply sensitive to the seemingly banal) is automatically analysed and fed back into the network to improve the 'consumer experience' (and thereby increase corporate profit margins), there is a simultaneous *merging of corporate and state surveillance apparatuses* (Giroux, 2015). The dual promises of greater security from the state and greater convenience from technology corporations have arguably acculturated the vast bulk of citizen-consumers 'into accepting the intrusion of surveillance technologies and privatised commodified values into all aspects of their lives' (Giroux, 2015, p. 156). At the same time, the extent, nature, accessibility and uses of this personal information are not transparent; information that consumers share willingly with private companies in return for convenience, may be, in turn, shared with state authorities, as citizens are 'now considered as both potential terrorists and a vast consumer market' (Giroux, 2015, p. 156). As Zuboff (2015, p. 86) further describes: 'Since Edward Snowden, we have learned of the blurring of public and private boundaries in surveillance activities including collaborations and constructive interdependencies between state security authorities and high tech firms'.

Paradoxically, private corporations ultimately motivated by market interests (and not transparent, independent, socially-governed authorities) seem to be emerging as the arbiters of human rights and freedoms — so as long as it serves the purpose of profit. Take, for instance, the 2016 legal case between technology giant Apple and the FBI, in which Apple refused to comply with a court order that would override the security features of an iPhone belonging to a deceased suspected terrorist (Etzioni, 2016). The iPhone in question was suggested by the FBI to potentially contain data relevant to investigations into accomplices and financing. Further complicating matters was the fact that the device was not owned by the suspect but by a company he was employed by. This case reflects three intersecting concerns that are of interest to this chapter: namely, the regulatory and normative influence of profit-seeking behaviour by corporations, the pursuit of national security by states and the call for privacy and access to a free and open internet by digital citizens. The position adopted by Apple in this case temporarily aligns with that of digital citizens in challenging the threat to privacy posed by the FBI demands.

Digital Threats to National Security

The increased concern with cybersecurity and cybercrime has meant that the techniques developed for dealing with foreign threats are being used to understand a range of activities that occur in digital society. This section sets out how the foreign policy logic of diplomacy and military deterrence are functioning as regulatory mechanisms to police unwanted or unfamiliar activities. The regulatory logic of foreign policy seeks to govern how nation states or their proxies interact with one another. It differs from domestic policy in being primarily directed at other sovereign entities, which it has no formal right to rule, rather than at citizens or corporations within its borders, which it does have a right to rule. Because inter-state relations are between nominally equal entities rather than according to a hierarchy, the regulatory mode primarily relies on a consequence-based approach, premised on notions of deterrence. That is, if a state does not act in accordance with expected diplomatic conduct, or challenges another's national interest, concerned state(s) will send signals that it has violated expected international norms or is a national security threat. This can lead to loss of face or potentially could be used for leverage in negotiations. In extreme cases, where there are already underlying tensions or it is interpreted as an attack, it can give rise to military tensions or outright conflict. Foreign policy as a mode of regulation was never designed to be applied to non-state actors, as threats to national security were traditionally conceptualised as only those things that could pose an existential danger to the nation state. With the increasing prominence of non-state actors in global affairs, there has been an increased tendency to 'securitise' other challenges and threats.

Securitising Digital Networks

The concept of securitisation offers an insight into how non-state actors, whether they be threatening or just unfamiliar, come to be treated as serious, or even existential, threats. The study of securitisation began as a conceptualisation of how countries could pursue security through non-military means. In doing so, it sought to 'explor[e] the logic of security itself, to find out what differentiates security, and the process of securitisation, from that which is merely political' (Buzan, 1997, p. 13). Security concerns from this perspective are not merely objective but rather constructed through 'speech acts' (Balzacq, 2005, p. 171). According to international relations scholar Olve Waever, 'it is by labelling something a security issue that it becomes one' (Waever, 2004, p. 13). Securitisation can therefore be understood as 'the intersubjective establishment of an existential threat with a saliency sufficient to have substantial political effects' (Lausten & Waever, 2000, p. 708). Viewed more critically, securitisation is now a term used to describe how non-state issues become constructed as threats to national security (McDonald, 2008).

Cybersecurity is a good example of this securitisation taking place. Framing potential damage to specific, critical infrastructure as a potential threat to the existence of the country enables attacks emanating from digital sources to be treated as threats to national security. Lene Hansen and Helen Nissenbaum suggested that what creates the perception of the 'potential magnitude of cyber threats is the networked character of computer systems', meaning that the danger is conceivably limitless (Hansen & Nissenbaum, 2009, p. 1161). Thus, specific threats can be reframed as general ones. 'The information infrastructure, including its physical and cybercomponents, is often named as a concrete target of cyber-terror and, more generally, of cyber-threats,' security studies scholar Myriam Dunn Cavelty (2007, p. 30) wrote. The securitisation is evident because

> a danger has been constructed that emanates from an enemy who is located outside of the US, both in geographic terms and in moral terms. This picture of a dangerous *other* reinforces the idea of the nation as a collective self. The use of phrases like *our computers* or *our infrastructure* amplifies this effect, the referent object of security is the entire US society.
>
> (Cavelty, 2007, p. 30, emphasis in original)

As a consequence, the regulatory strategies of foreign policy — deterrent techniques of threatening military force or prosecution for serious crimes — can be directed towards non-state actors employing digital means.

The securitisation of a broad array of activities can be seen in recent US cybersecurity policy. A 2011 Department of Defense report suggested that the Pentagon would deem computer-based incursions on digital infrastructure or cyberattacks by foreign actors as an 'act of war' (Department of Defense, 2011). The range of possible responses by the US military would not be limited to digital attacks but could also include conventional kinetic means. According to the report, we will respond to hostile attacks in cyberspace as we would to any threat to our country. We reserve the right to use all necessary means — diplomatic, informational, military and economic — to defend our nation, our allies, our partners and our interests.

(Department of Defense, 2011)

Responding to questions on the report, a Pentagon spokesperson added that the 'response to a cyber-incident or attack on the US would not necessarily be a cyber-response. All appropriate options would be on the table' (Sanger & Bumiller, 2011). Speaking anonymously to *Wall Street Journal* reporters, a Pentagon official elaborated: 'if you shut down our power grid, maybe we will put a missile down one of your smokestacks' (Gorman & Barnes, 2011). This securitising rhetoric is a clear attempt to deter all digital actors by treating hacking as a threat to national security that can be responded to with conventional military means. Speaking at a House Armed Services Committee hearing in June 2016, Acting Assistant Secretary of Defense for Homeland Defense and Global Security Thomas Atkin admitted that the point at which cyberattacks would be considered an act of war 'has not been defined' and that they were 'still working toward that definition' (Jordan, 2016, n.p.). In the interim, the Pentagon is using the phrase 'act of significant consequence' to describe what would trigger an act of war. According to Atkin's testimony at the hearing, 'as regards an act of significant consequence, we don't necessarily have a clear definition . . . but we evaluate it based on loss of life, physical property, economic impact and our foreign policy' (Jordan, 2016, n.p.). While this strong military language is nominally directed at state actors, it may not always be clear what demarcates a state from a non-state hacker.

Hackers as a Threat to National Security

Attribution of hacks to state actors, whether it be public or for internal, classified purposes, is often quite complicated. Even the most notorious and high-profile intrusions, such as the Stuxnet hack that caused an explosion in the Iranian Natanz nuclear facility, the hack on the Estonian government that shut down the parliament, bureaucracies, banks and the media or the Democratic National Congress (DNC) email server leak, the perpetrators have not been confirmed, even though major superpowers are suspected. No one has publicly admitted to the Stuxnet attack, in spite of reverse engineering of the code suggesting that it was most likely the United States and/or Israel. Many in the US government suggest that Russia was involved in both the Estonia attack and DNC leak, but nothing has been proven. Prominent cryptographer Bruce Schneier (2009) suggests that attribution is not so clear and straightforward because, while

> Russian hackers were indisputably the major instigators of the attack, the only individuals positively identified have been young ethnic Russians living inside Estonia, who were angry over the statue incident. Poke at any of these international incidents, and what you find are kids playing politics (n.p.).

This is not to deny the role played by states in these intrusions, but it complicates matters that they are operating through third parties. Beyond such notorious attacks with immediate, real-world consequences or high levels of disruption to critical infrastructure, the picture is even murkier.

The rhetorical labelling power of securitisation can be turned against governments by activist groups to garner popular attention. Hacker collectives such as Anonymous regularly declare 'war' on their targets, which often include government assets and corporate systems that could be considered critical infrastructure. Both media and government alike buy into this publicity seeking, treating these campaigns as serious national security threats to developed countries. While it is not likely that this would rise to the level of an 'act of significant consequence', the FBI has described Anonymous and other related groups as having conducted cyberattacks (FBI, 2012). While 'cyberattack' is a commonly used term within the media and government, it is a hyperbolic metaphor to describe what is ultimately the hacking of information stored in databases. The war analogy is simply not a useful way of understanding the nature of the phenomenon. If cyberattacks were understood more accurately as incidents that caused physical damage or disruption to critical infrastructure, and cyberwar were understood as a retaliatory cyberattack in response to an initial breach, the actual number of occurrences would be relatively low. According to James Andrew Lewis (2011), as of 2011 'there have been no cyber wars and perhaps two or three cyber attacks since the Internet first appeared'. While this number may have grown significantly since then, the actual scale of the problem that can be meaningfully understood through a military lens is relatively low compared to the far greater number that are carried out by 'black hat' hackers for financial gain or as a challenge for 'grey hat' hackers looking to test their skills.

While the effectiveness of US cybersecurity policy in creating effective deterrents against hacking is unclear, what is clear is the effect this language has on elements of the digital society. The language used by the Pentagon may have a clear and decisive tone, but the lack of clear definition of what constitutes an act of war introduces a degree of uncertainty. For strategic deterrence to be effective, it relies upon clarity and transparency in regards to exactly what line cannot be crossed. More pertinent to this discussion, however, is that this uncertainty shows a lack of conceptual clarity around what kind of cyberattack can be regarded as equivalent to a kinetic attack. The broad point that this chapter is seeking to raise is that this conceptual confusion arises because it is assumed that like is being compared to like, and it is just a matter of determining what are equivalent acts. Conventional warfare and cyberattacks, however, should not be regarded as equivalent acts in order to construct a deterrence regime. The rhetorical linking of warfare and hacking should be better understood as an analogy that acts as a securitising metaphor designed to regulate a broad range of new technologies used by non-state and state activities as if they were the conventional activities of states using military technology. The warfare metaphor is an all-too-common rhetorical labelling device — war on crime, war on drugs, war on terror — in each case the function is to position some party as a foreign threat to a domestic population. Criminologist Kevin Steinmetz posits that this kind of language has framed hackers as 'pathological, aberrant, deviant monsters lurking in the wires — the contemporary boogeyman on which to heap our anxieties about technology and social change' (Steinmetz, 2016, p. 214) In this case, however, a broad range of non-state actors, many of whom may be ordinary citizens, are being treated as akin to a foreign enemy. Thus, corporate espionage, black-hat hacking, whistle-blowing and even poor internet security by government employees may be ascribed an intent to undermine national security when its actual motives are unknown or unclear. This runs the risk, at its most apocalyptic, of triggering actual war — potentially even nuclear war — through the actions of non-state actors.

The securitisation of digital networks engenders a range of effects beyond those it immediately targets. As with the corporatisation of digital networks, the concern from a digital criminological perspective is not just with those non-state actors that it directly re-casts as threats to national secu-rity, but also with the wider socialisation of norms that operate according to the regulatory logic of foreign policy. Robin Cameron (2013) articulates how the logic of foreign policy can become diffused throughout society, exerting a form of social control beyond the intended international audience. As has been discussed in this section, the foreign policy pronouncements of US cybersecurity are clearly and forcefully directed at an intended international audience of state actors and malevolent proxies in order to establish a sufficient deterrent to create security from cyberattacks. The receiving audience, however, is not limited to these actors, especially as these logics become embedded into everyday social norms. Foreign policy in this sense is not only foreign, it is also inverted in its domestic effects and lateral in its suffusion through networks (Cameron, 2013). In this more subtle regulatory mode, foreign policy functions less as a deterrent and more as logic that is 'written into the lines of conflict between social groups,' where it becomes

> a regulatory mechanism by ascribing a familiar safety to certain groups of people and an alien danger to others. In short, the ruptures of domestic politics become securitised in order to conform with the measures designed to protect against foreign threats.
>
> (Cameron, 2013, p. 91)

This effect of the foreign policy script can be seen, for instance, in the readiness to link hacks with foreign governments and, more subtly, in the tendency to link disagreeable viewpoints as a threat to the collective way of life of the nation. The divisiveness and distanciation that occurs in many networked interactions poses serious challenges for a common sense of collective identity in the digital society.

Citizen-led Regulation

The digital criminology approach adopted here seeks to engage with the complex new forms of interactions that can be enabled locally and globally by digitally mediated communications technology. By drawing attention to the increasingly ubiquitous overlay of digital communications on regular physical interactions, this approach seeks to incorporate the global space of flows as an additional analytical layer to the local criminological space of place. Because of the unboundedness of these digital flows that enable us to instantly communicate with increasing numbers of people across the world, it effectively extends the spatial concern of criminology beyond the bounds of the state territory. As it does so, it also begins to encompass a wider range of not only unfamiliar human behaviour and new social norms but also a wider set of practices that could be considered criminal, given the dif-fering approaches to crime and justice in other countries. In this way, the approach of digital crimi-nology seeks to deepen and broaden how crime and harm are understood.

The rise of the digital society has seen new communities emerge that are, at once, apart and con-nected. This may seem, at face value, to be something of a logical fallacy, but the rise of immersive digital communication has meant that intimate connections can be made across vast spatial distances while, at the same time, these technologies may also create interpersonal distance between people who may have otherwise maintained face-to-face relations. This sense of being 'alone together' as internet studies scholar Sherry Turkle (2012) described it, sees people become disconnected even while they may be in relative physical proximity to one another. On the other hand, however, the forces of global communications connect those who would otherwise be simply 'foreign', giving rise to a transnational sense of solidarity across disparate spaces and national cultures. The implication of a digital society is that people may be spatially apart but intersubjectively connected, and/or spatially together but intersubjectively disconnected. Turkle's conception of how people relate via networked social platforms and digital communications provides a useful account of the emotional life of the digital subject. This perspective, however, needs to be supplemented with an account of the wider structures that connect and disconnect people and the implications these have for how space and time are understood.

Returning to the work of Rebecca MacKinnon, discussed earlier, she concluded her book with suggestions for how a citizen-led approach to regulating the digital society might be pursued. MacKinnon cautioned against aspiring towards limiting the power of corporations and states from above through a 'global UN-like uber-government to manage and restrain cross-border power' on the grounds that the likelihood of traditional state sovereign power giving way to a supranational power is close to nil (2012, p. 223). Likewise, singular cases of 'Robin Hood-style cyber-vigilantism and digital guerilla warfare' from below are unlikely to be successful, as they will be criminalised, securitised or otherwise marginalised as aberrant actors (MacKinnon, 2012, p. 223). Rather, MacKinnon (2012) reminds us that

> the Internet is a human creation. Power struggles are an inevitable feature of human society. Democracy is about constraining power and holding it accountable. The Internet can be a powerful tool in the hands of citizens seeking to hold governments and corporations to account — but only if we keep the Internet itself open and free (p. xxvii).

Digital citizenship should be seen as an active and conscientious disposition of people towards digitally networked communication that enables participation in democratic processes.

Digital Citizenship

The first step towards an open and free internet, according to MacKinnon, is to make citizens within the digital society more aware and politicised. An important element of this is making them aware of the regulatory modes of corporate and state control that are being exercised via technology, as she put it, 'though the technology used for coordinating and organizing may be politically neutral, the context in which it is deployed is rarely so' (MacKinnon, 2012, p. 52). Ordinary citizens are typically rendered unaware of the regulations and controls that are in play as 'users' of seemingly free platforms or paying 'consumers' of software they think they own. Instead, MacKinnon suggests that a notion of citizenship within networks will be more empowering, an idea she refers to as being a 'netizen' (2012, p. 223). While the concept of citizenship within networks is not a formal devolution of state normally associated with citizenship, and the exact rhetorical framing or neologism used may be up for debate, such an outlook is undoubtedly vital for a more participatory approach to digital society.

MacKinnon's notion of digital citizenship highlights Castells' interest in the relationships between power, space and individuals in a network society. These relationships are increasingly distinguished through the concept of digital citizenship that requires an ability to participate in society online (Mossberger, Tolbert, & McNeal, 2007). Digital citizenship recognises that society is increasingly enacted in digital spaces by individual actors, communities, states, corporations, softwares and technologies (Isin & Ruppert, 2015). Moreover, this diversification of what it means to be a citizen has led to people living in digital society to claim rights in the same way that citizens currently claim rights through their nation states (Isin & Ruppert, 2015). In response to this emerging citizenship, some have raised the prospect of new digital human rights, such as the 'right to be forgotten' (Ambrose & Ausloos, 2013), and the reprioritisation of existing provisions, such as the right to privacy (United Nations General Assembly, 2015).

'Digital citizenship' can be understood in practical terms as a concern for what constitutes a just and dignified digital life. In the experience of many people, particularly members of vulnerable communities, interaction on the internet carries with it the potential for a whole host of digital harms to be experienced. Deep divisions that exist around gender and sexuality, race and religion come to the fore as people are digitally targeted for abuse that enacts real-world harm, as will be highlighted throughout the following chapters. Digital society is not abstract because the space of flows is intimately connected to the space of place. Digital citizenship can therefore be seen as an emerging human rights framework that protects and enables our ever more digital lives. In 2003, the United Nations (UN) convened a World Summit on the Information Society in Geneva, which, while unable to agree on rules for governing the internet, affirmed principles that the right to freedom and expression encompassed access to digital networks (World Summit on the Information Society, 2003). Furthermore, it recognised that this access was 'unevenly distributed between the developed and developing countries and within societies' (World Summit on the Information Society, 2003). In the intervening years, a campaign has grown to recognise access to the internet, or what is sometimes called the freedom to connect, as a human right. In 2011, the UN independent expert representative, known as a 'special rapporteur', for the promotion and protection of the right to freedom of opinion and expression advocated that this right be formalised, issuing a report calling on states and corporations to 'ensure that there is as little restriction as possible to the flow of information via the Internet' (La Rue, 2011, p. 19). In 2015, this right was affirmed when the UN General Assembly adopted a resolution, albeit non-binding, that 'the rights held by people offline must also be protected online' (United Nations General Assembly, 2015, p. 3). In other words, this freedom to connect must be accompanied by freedom from harm.

As we have seen in this chapter, however, digital networks are not spaces of pure freedom; they are subject to state and corporate regulation that are accompanied by various risks. The pursuit of human rights in digital society, then, is not as simple as affirming freedom to connect but also requires mitigation of these risks and protection from harms. What is encouraging about the statements by the special rapporteur and the resolution by the General Assembly is that the right to the internet is very much subsidiary to the central concern with privacy. The resolution (United Nations General Assembly, 2015) highlights that the:

> rapid pace of technological development enables individuals all over the world to use new information and communication technologies and at the same time enhances the capacity of governments, companies and individuals to undertake surveillance, interception and data collection, which may violate or abuse human rights (p. 2).

Building measures designed to protect people from surveillance and control into emerging human rights and global governance principles is an important step towards creating a digital society which rebalances power towards citizens. Another example can be seen in the 'right to be forgotten', which is a uniquely digital evolution of human rights. This ruling in 2014 by the Court of Justice in the European Union established that European citizens were entitled to have specific search engine results removed in order to protect individuals from data that is no longer relevant to their lives (Tirosh, 2017). In effect, this extends the right to privacy regarding information that is not publicly known to also include public information that is no longer relevant or applicable. Here, again, is evidence of how evolving notions of digital citizenship can shape human rights frameworks.

Conclusion

In this chapter, we have argued that the challenges new digital technologies pose to individuals, communities and states are as much conceptual as they are to do with actual insecurity, crime and danger. Three things are vital here: a proportional understanding of risk; a meaningful understanding of norms in their embedded context; and an approach to security that connects to the lived experiences of those who use technology. On one hand, increased use of digital technology facilitates the increasing transnationalisation of crime and harm, but on the other, it also facilitates new norms — some may be divergent, others just unfamiliar — that can disrupt existing modes of social control. The latter should not be lumped in at an analytical level with the former. The conceptual challenge is to theorise the criminological consequences of this shift towards modes of social interaction that are increasingly digital, and always potentially transnational, without simply adopting an outlook in which the unfamiliar is treated as a 'foreign' danger or threat. The conceptual challenge also extends to the question of how authorities — local, state and supranational — should respond at policy and operational levels.

The presence of modes of regulation shaped by governance that empowers corporations and the national security priorities that concern states show that citizens of the digital society often transcend the spatial regulations of the state, moving into the contested space of flows. Beyond the state, there are two logics that come into play and compete with the territorial space of place. The first is the competing interests of corporate power, in which companies individually or collectively lobby to shape and facilitate international trade agendas to maximise profits. The second is the regulatory logic of foreign policy associated with the competition between states. These two logics are not always separate, as maximisation of profit is increasingly framed as being in the national interest of states, and the collection of incredibly detailed data about individual users by corporations enables new insight into the lives of citizens for state agencies. To what degree corporate regulation or foreign policy shape digital society depends on what kind of actors and what forms of exchange are taking place in the space of flows. These two extraterritorial logics may seem a long way removed from the everyday life of a criminal, or for that matter a criminologist, and in many respects, this is true. But these global regulatory processes, and the norms associated with them, shape the lives of digital society as much as the domestic processes associated with traditional social control and criminal justice.

The approach of digital criminology is global in orientation but it also seeks to reorient the focus from nations and corporations to the emerging digital society. Crime control and criminology have a history of being brought to the service of the powerful, and many of the contemporary responses to new and unfamiliar technologies reflect this tendency. This chapter has highlighted the new regulatory techniques used by corporations and states that criminalise or securitise attempts by members of the emergent digital society to challenge what Bauman referred to as the 'extraterritoriality of the new global elite and the forced territoriality of the rest' (Bauman, 2000, p. 221). These responses focus attention on the threats to economies and security of nation states and seek to enable the continued accumulation of profit and capital of corporations. Accordingly, the justice that follows is justice for the wealthy and powerful, not for the vulnerable and disadvantaged. The case study chapters that follow tell different stories of digitally mediated life: stories that reflect people's experiences of the integration of their communities in global networks. In exploring these accounts, it is vital to retain the familiar experience of digitally mediated interpersonal harms and vulnerabilities. While this chapter has largely examined processes of global regulation through national security and corporatisation, we advocate that forms of regulation that ought to underpin digital justice should be concerned with the everyday harms that citizens experience in digital society – typically along the lines of gender, race, religion and structural economic inequality. Ultimately, the global justice envisioned by digital criminology is a socially meaningful justice for all people.

Note

1 Then US Secretary of State Colin Powell, cited in Urry (2002, p. 57).

Recommended Further Reading

Lyon, D. (2014). Surveillance, Snowden, and big data: Capacities, consequences, critique. *Big Data & Society, 1*(2), 1–13. doi:10.1177/2053951714541861.
MacKinnon, R. (2012). The netizen. *Development, 55*(2), 201–204.
Solove, D. J. (2007). I've got nothing to hide and other misunderstandings of privacy. *San Diego Law Review, 44*(4), 745–772.

References

Aas, K. F. (2007). Analysing a world in motion: Global flows meet 'criminology of the other'. *Theoretical Criminology, 11*(2), 282–303.
Aas, K. F. (2012a). (In)security-at-a-distance: Rescaling risk, justice and warfare in a transnational age. *Global Crime, 13*(4), 235–253.
Aas, K. F. (2012b). 'The Earth is one but the World is not': Criminological theory and its geopolitical divisions. *Theoretical Criminology, 16*(1), 5–20.
Aas, K. F. (2013). *Globalization and crime: Key approaches to crime* (2nd ed.). London: Sage.
Agozino, B. (2003). *Counter-colonial criminology: A critique of imperialist reason.* London: Pluo Press.
Agozino, B. (2004). Imperialism, crime and criminology: Towards the decolonisation of criminology. *Crime, Law and Social Change, 41*(4), 343–358.
Albrechtslund, A. (2008). Online social networking as participatory surveillance. *First Monday, 13*(3).
Ambrose, M. L., & Ausloos, J. (2013). The right to be forgotten across the pond. *Journal of Information Policy, 3*, 1–23.
Andrejevic, M. (2005). The work of watching one another: Lateral surveillance, risk, and governance. *Surveillance & Society, 2*(4), 476–497.
Balkin, J. M. (2008). The constitution in the national surveillance state. *Minnesota Law Review, 93*(1), 1–25.
Balkin, J. M., & Levinson, S. (2006). The processes of constitutional change: From partisan entrenchment to the national surveillance state. *Fordham Law Review, 75*(2), 489.
Balzacq, T. (2005). The three faces of securitization: Political agency, audience and context. *European Journal of International Affairs, 11*(2), 171–201.

Barak, G. (2000). Introduction: A comparative perspective on crime and crime control. In G. Barak (Ed.), *Crime and crime control: A global view.* Westport, CT: Greenwood Press.

Bauman, Z. (2000). *Liquid modernity.* Cambridge: Polity Press.

Beck, U. (1992). *Risk society: Towards a new modernity.* London: Sage Publications.

Beck, U. (1999). *World risk society.* Cambridge: Polity Press.

Beck, U. (2013). The digital freedom risk: Too fragile an acknowledgement. Available at: www.opendemocracy. net/can-europe-make-it/ulrich-beck/digital-freedom-risk-too-fragile-acknowledgment (last accessed 29 November 2017).

Beck, U. (2014). Five minutes with Ulrich beck: "Digital freedom risk is one of the most important risks we face in modern society". Available at: www.blogs.lse.ac.uk/europpblog/2014/04/02/five-minutes-with-ulrich-beck-digital-freedom-risk-is-one-of-the-most-important-risks-we-face-in-modern-society/ (last accessed 29 November 2017).

Beirne, P. (1997). Cultural relativism and comparative criminology. In P. Beirne, & D. Nelken (Eds.), *Issues in comparative criminology.* Aldershot: Ashgate.

Beirne, P., & Nelken, D. (Eds.). (1997). *Issues in comparative criminology.* Aldershot: Ashgate.

Braithwaite, J. (2000). The new regulatory state and the transformation of criminology. *British Journal of Criminology, 40*(2), 222–238.

Braithwaite, J. (2005). Neoliberalism or regulatory capitalism. *RegNet Occasional Paper No 5.* Available at: www. anu.edu.au/fellows/jbraithwaite/_documents/Articles/Neoliberalism_Regulatory_2005.pdf (last accessed 29 November 2017).

Braithwaite, J. (2006). The regulatory state? In S.A. Binder, R.A.W. Rhodes, & B.A. Rockman (Eds.), *The Oxford handbook of political institutions* (pp. 407–430). Oxford: Oxford University Press.

Braithwaite, J. (2008). *Regulatory capitalism: How it works, ideas for making it work better.* Cheltenham: Edward Elgar.

Braithwaite, J., & Drahos, P. (2000). *Global business regulation.* Cambridge: Cambridge University Press.

Buzan, B. (1997). Rethinking security after the cold war. *Cooperation & Conflict, 32*(1), 5–28.

Cameron, R. (2013). *Subjects of security: Domestic effects of foreign policy in the war on terror.* Basingstoke, UK: Palgrave.

Castells, M. (1989). *The informational city: Informational technology, economic restructuring, and the urban-regional process.* Oxford: Basil Blackwell.

Castells, M. (1996). An introduction to the information age. *Cities, 2*(7), 6–16.

Castells, M. (1999). Grassrooting the space of flows. *Urban Geography, 20*(4), 294–302.

Castells, M. (2000). *Rise of the network society* (2nd ed.). Oxford: Blackwell Publishers.

Cavelty, M. D. (2007). Cyber-terror: Looming threat or phantom menace? The framing of the US cyber-threat debate. *Journal of Information Technology and Politics, 4*(1), 19–36.

Crampton, J. W. (2015). Collect it all: National security, big data and governance. *Geo Journal, 80*(4), 519–531.

Cunneen, C. (2011). Postcolonial perspectives for criminology. In M. Bosworth & C. Hoyle (Eds.), *What is criminology?* Oxford: Oxford University Press.

Deleuze, G. (1992). Postscript on the Societies of Control. *October, 59*(1), 3–7.

Department of Defense. (2011). Department of defense cyberspace policy report. Available at: https://nsarchive2. gwu.edu/NSAEBB/NSAEBB424/docs/Cyber-059.pdf (last accessed 2 March 2018).

Drahos, P. (1995). Information feudalism in the information society. *Information Society, 11*(3), 209–222.

Drahos, P., & Braithwaite, J. (2002). *Information feudalism: Who owns the knowledge economy?* London: Earthscan Publications.

Earl, J., & Kimport, K. (2011). *Digitally enabled social change: Activism in the internet age.* Cambridge: MIT Press.

Erwin, S. (2015). Living by algorithm: Smart surveillance and the society of control. *Humanities and Technology Review, 34*, 28–69.

Etzioni, A. (2016). Apple: Good business, poor citizen? *Journal of Business Ethics,* 1–11.

Farinosi, M. (2011). Deconstructing Bentham's panopticon: The new metaphors of surveillance in the web 2.0 environment. *tripleC: Communication, Capitalism & Critique. Open Access Journal for a Global Sustainable Information Society, 9*(1), 62–76.

Federal Bureau of Investigation (FBI). (2012). Six hackers in the United States and abroad charged for crimes affecting over one million victims. Available at: https://archives.fbi.gov/archives/newyork/press-releases/2012/six-hackers-in-the-united-states-and-abroad-charged-for-crimes-affecting-over-one-million-victims (last accessed 29 November 2017).

Findlay, M. (1999). *The globalisation of crime: Understanding transitional relationships in context.* Cambridge: Cambridge University Press.

Findlay, M. (2008). *Governing through globalised crime: Futures for international criminal justice.* Collumpton: Willan Publishing.

Foucault, M. (1982). Subject and Power. *Critical Inquiry, 8*(4), 777–795.

Foucault, M. (1984). The birth of the asylum. *The Foucault Reader* (pp. 141–167). New York, NY: Pantheon Books.

Foucault, M. (1991). *Discipline and punish: The birth of the prison.* (A. French, Trans.). London: Penguin Books.

Friedrichs, D. O. (2007). Transnational crime and global criminology: Definitional, typological and contextual conundrums. *Social Justice, 34*(2), 4–18.

Fuchs, C., Boersma, K., Albrechtslund, A., & Sandoval, M. (Eds.). (2013). *Internet and surveillance: The challenges of Web 2.0 and social media* (Vol. 16). Routledge: London.

Giddens, A. (1998). *The third way: The renewal of social democracy.* Cambridge: Polity Press.

Gilliom, J., & Monahan, T. (2013). *Super vision: An introduction to the surveillance society.* Chicago: University of Chicago Press.

Giroux, H. A. (2015). Selfie culture in the age of corporate and state surveillance. *Third Text, 29*(3), 155–164.

Gorman, S., & Barnes, J. E. (2011). Cyber combat: Act of war. Available at: www.wsj.com/articles/SB10001424 052702304563104576355623135782718 (last accessed 29 November 2017).

Haggerty, K. D., & Ericson, R. V. (2000). The surveillant assemblage. *The British Journal of Sociology, 51*(4), 605–622.

Hansen, L., & Nissenbaum, H. (2009). Digital disaster, cyber security and the Copenhagen school. *International Studies Quarterly, 53*(4), 1155–1175.

Harvey, D. (2005). *A brief history of neoliberalism.* Oxford: Oxford University Press.

Hogg, R. (2002). Criminology beyond the nation state: Global conflicts, human rights and the 'new world order'. In K. Carrington, & R. Hogg (Eds.), *Critical criminology: Issues, debates, challenges.* Collumpton: Willan Publishing.

Isin, E., & Ruppert, E. (2015). *Being digital citizens.* London, UK: Rowman & Littlefield.

Jordan, B. (2016). US still has no definition for cyber act of war. Available at: www.military.com/daily-news/2016/06/22/us-still-has-no-definition-for-cyber-act-of-war.html (last accessed 29 November 2017).

Karstedt, S. (2001). Comparing cultures, comparing crime: Challenges, prospects and problems for a global criminology. *Crime, Law & Social Change, 36*(3), 285–308.

La Rue, F. (2011). Report of the special rapporteur on the promotion and protection of the right to freedom of opinion and expression. Human Rights Council, United Nations. Available at: www2.ohchr.org/english/bodies/hrcouncil/docs/17session/A.HRC.17.27_en.pdf (last accessed 29 November 2017).

Landau, S. (2013). Making sense from Snowden: What's significant in the NSA surveillance revelations. *IEEE Security & Privacy, 11*(4), 54–63.

Lausten, C. B., & O. Waever. (2000). In defence of religion: Sacred referent objects for securitization. *Millennium: Journal of International Studies, 29*(3), 705–739.

Lewis, J. A. (2011). Cyber attacks, real or imagined, and cyber war. Available at: www.csis.org/analysis/cyber-attacks-real-or-imagined-and-cyber-war (last accessed 29 November 2017).

Lynch, M. J. (1990). The greening of criminology: A perspective of the 1990s. *The Critical Criminologist, 2*(3), 11–12.

Lyon, D. (1994). *The electronic eye: The rise of surveillance society.* Minneapolis: University of Minnesota Press.

Lyon, D. (2007). *Surveillance studies: An overview.* Cambridge: Polity Press.

Lyon, D. (2014). Surveillance, Snowden, and big data: Capacities, consequences, critique. *Big Data & Society, 1*(2), 1–13. doi:10.1177/2053951714541861.

MacKinnon, R. (2012). *Consent of the networked: The worldwide struggle for internet freedom*. New York: Basic Books.

Mathiesen, T. (1997). The viewer society: Michel Foucault's 'Panopticon' revisited. *Theoretical Criminology, 1*(2), 215–234.

McDonald, M. (2008). Securitization and the construction of security. *European Journal of International Relations, 14*(4), 563–587.

McDonald, W. F. (1995). Globalization of criminology: The new frontier is the frontier. *Transnational Organized Crime, 1*(1), 1–22.

Mossberger, K., Tolbert, C. J., & McNeal, R. S. (2007). *Digital citizenship: The internet, society, and participation*. Cambridge, MA: MIT Press.

Morozov, E. (2011). *The net delusion: How not to liberate the world*. London: Penguin Books.

Morrison, W. (2006). *Criminology, civilisation and the new world order*. Abingdon, UK: Routledge.

Pakes, F. (2010). The comparative method in globalised criminology. *The Australian and New Zealand Journal of Criminology, 43*(1), 17–30.

Pickering, S., & Weber, L. (Eds.). (2006). *Borders, mobility and technologies of control*. Dordrecht: Springer.

Pickering, S., & Weber, L. (2011). *Globalization and borders: Death at the global frontier*. Basingstoke, UK: Palgrave.

Pridmore, J., & Zwick, D. (2011). Marketing and the rise of commercial consumer surveillance. *Surveillance & Society, 8*(3), 269–277.

Reichel, P., & Albanese, J. (Eds.). (2004). *Handbook of transnational crime and justice*. Thousand Oaks, CA: Sage.

Rice, R. M. (2017). Beyond interactivity: Critical/cultural surveillance scholarship, 10 years after Andrejevic. *Review of Communication, 17*(1), 37–55.

Sanger, D., & Bumiller, E. (2011). Pentagon to consider cyberattacks acts of war. Available at: www.nytimes.com/2011/06/01/us/politics/01cyber.html. (last accessed 29 November 2017).

Sheptycki, J., & Wardack, A. (Eds.). (2005). *Transnational and comparative criminology*. London: GlassHouse Press.

Schneier, B. (2015). *Data and Goliath: The hidden battles to collect your data and control your world*. New York, NY: WW Norton & Company.

Schneier, B. (2009). So-called cyberattack was overblown. Available at: www.mprnews.org/story/2009/07/10/schneier (last accessed 29 November 2017).

Solove, D. J. (2007). I've got nothing to hide and other misunderstandings of privacy. *San Diego Law. Review, 44*(4), 745–772.

Solove, D. J. (2011). *Nothing to hide: The false tradeoff between privacy and security*. New Haven, CT: Yale University Press.

South, N., & Beirne, P. (1998). Editor's introduction. *Theoretical Criminology, 2*(2), 147–148.

Steger, M. B., Goodman, J., & E. K. Wilson. (2013). *Justice globalism: Ideology, crises, policy*. London: Sage.

Steger, M. B., & Roy, R. K. (2010). *Neoliberalism: A very short introduction*. Oxford: Oxford University Press.

Steinmetz, K. F. (2016). *Hacked: A radical approach to hacker culture and crime*. New York, NY: New York University Press.

Stone, G. (2010). *Speaking out! Reflections on law, liberty and justice* (Vol. 1). Raleigh, NC: Lulu Publishing.

Tirosh, N. (2017). Reconsidering the 'right to be forgotten': Memory rights and the right to memory in the new media era. *Media, Culture & Society, 39*(5), 644–660.

Trottier, D., & Lyon, D. (2012). Key features of social media surveillance. In C. Fuchs, K. Boersma, A. Albrechtslund, & M. Sandoval (Eds.), *Internet and surveillance: The challenges of web 2.0 and social media*. New York, NY: Routledge.

Turkle, S. (2012). *Alone together: Why expect more from technology and less from each other*. Bradford: Basic Books.

United Nations General Assembly. (2015). Resolution on the right to privacy in the digital age, A/RES/69/166/. Available at: www.un.org/en/ga/search/view_doc.asp?symbol=A/RES/69/166 (last accessed 29 November 2017).

Urry, J. (2002). The global complexities of September 11th. *Theory, Culture & Society, 19*(4), 57–69.

Waever, O. (2004, March). *Aberystwyth, Paris and Copenhagen: New schools in security theory and the origins between core and periphery*. ISA Conference, Montreal.

Weber, L., & Bowling, B. (2008). Valiant beggars and global vagabonds: Select, eject immobilise. *Theoretical Criminology, 12*(3), 355–375.

White, R. (2009). Researching transnational environmental harm: Toward and eco-global criminology. *International Journal of Comparative and Applied Criminal Justice, 33*(2), 229–248.

White, R. (2011). *Transnational environmental crime: Towards an eco-global criminology.* Abingdon, UK: Routledge.

White, R. (2013). The conceptual contours of green criminology. In R. Walters, D. Solomon Westerhuis, and T. Wyatt (Eds.), *Emerging issues in green criminology: Exploring power, justice and harm.* London: Palgrave Macmillan.

World Summit on the Information Society. (2003). *Declaration of principles.* Geneva: WSIS. Available at: www.itu.int/net/wsis/docs/geneva/official/dop.html (last accessed 29 November 2017).

Zuboff, S. (1988). *In the age of the smart machine: The future of work and power.* New York, NY: Basic Books.

Zuboff, S. (2013). The surveillance paradigm: Be the friction – our response to the new lords of the ring. *The Frankfurter Allgemeine Zeitung,* 25 June 2013, Available at: www.faz.net/aktuell/feuilleton/the-surveillance-paradigm-be-the-friction-our-response-to-the-new-lords-of-the-ring-12241996-p2.html (last accessed 29 November 2017).

Zuboff, S. (2015). Big other: Surveillance capitalism and the prospects of an information civilization. *Journal of Information Technology, 30*(1), 75–89.

4

CRIME IN REAL TIME

Immediacy, Immersion and Engagement

Introduction

On the evening of 13 November 2015, a series of violent attacks on Paris's Stade de France, Bataclan Theatre, and a number of bars and restaurants, left 130 people dead and hundreds of others injured. The first of these attacks occurred at a France vs Germany football match, where Twitter user Johannes Müller was one of the first to respond to the suicide-explosion through any media, asking: 'Explosion im Stade de France grade? Wieder eine Bombe oder war das harmlos? Explosiv heute hier in Frankreich und im Stadion' ('Explosion in the Stade de France? Was it a bomb or was it harmless? Explosion today here in France, in the stadium'). Müller's tweet was posted a minute earlier than any traditional media source reported on the explosion — including the channels that were present broadcasting the match (BBC Trending, 2015). During the attacks, and throughout the evening in their aftermath, Parisians took to Facebook and Twitter to share and redistribute information on the violence taking place across the city. Witnesses and victims posted live updates from the sometimes chaotic scenes, detailing locations of shootings and describing and posting images of the crimes as they occured. In the initial aftermath of the attacks, traditional media sources (such as television, radio and print) were 'scrambled' in gathering information about the attacks, often relying on social media feeds to provide up-to-date, yet unverified, information (Koblin, 2015). While traditional media sources were slower to react, social media companies were providing the community with the means to track and monitor the locations of the violence, as well as check on the safety of friends in their network who may have been impacted by the attacks — not just locally within Paris, but also from abroad.

Unfortunately, these events in Paris are not unique. Yet, what is of interest in this chapter is the manner in which technosocial practices — facilitated in this case by mediums such as Twitter and Facebook — are increasingly employed by citizens in the immediate response to crime events as they unfold. These practices of rapid sharing of information, connections between those present at the scene and those afar, and the pull to follow a constant flow of updates, reflect the complex intersection between the technologies, the people involved in the incident and a global community.

Importantly, the intersection of these elements has the capacity both to *assist* and to *disrupt* law enforcement efforts and other justice responses in relation to crime. Furthermore, these technosocial practices of following 'crime in real time' have, in turn, enabled an emerging digital criminology to study the nature and potential impacts of both citizen and state agency engagement with crime events and their aftermath. Such research considers the justice implications of citizen engagement with crime in a digital society and the capacity of individuals and communities to participate and respond to crime events in ways that shape mainstream media and policy responses. This chapter explores these emerging practices, as well as the tensions and dilemmas they raise for criminologists, and indeed for crime, justice and citizen participation in digital society.

Following Crime Events as They Occur

The opportunity to examine 'crime in real time' is enabled by the immediacy and broad access of digital technology. What we mean by 'crime in real time' is the range of activities and responses that are facilitated by digital technology for everyday citzens to engage in their own monitoring, responding and sometimes investigation of crime events. Citizen-generated content shared via digital technologies, such as camera and internet-enabled mobile phones sharing to social networking sites, make readily available multiple points of view that may serve as a counterpoint to the those of state agencies (such as police and government departments) as well as traditional media (such as television, print and radio). The capacity for citizens to generate information sources of their own and to follow crime in real time represents a significant shift in the traditional relationship between media producers and audiences that has previously been characterised by a hierarchy of official knowledge sources on crime. By enabling audiences to actively engage with the entirety of the crime event (pre-event, during and post-event) and by including the voices of those affected, this shift in the knowledge hierarchy allows members of the public to offer uncensored, unsanitised, unfiltered versions of crime events. These 'participatory' engagements are often immediate and reflexive, developing and changing as new information is made available, and potentially changing the public's understandings, affectual responses and perceptions of crime as it occurs and in its immediate aftermath.

The data created via citizen's real-time engagements with crime events have also influenced how investigations into crime are conducted, allowing police agencies to incorporate multiple types of information as crimes progress. Such technologies have been embraced by agencies within the formal criminal justice system, empowering investigators with a diverse range of tools that assist in the identification of criminals, victims and crimes through observation of publicly shared material (referred to by some police agencies as 'open source intelligence'). In addition to social media sites, image-sharing platforms and website histories, other digital technologies such as personal fitness monitors, GPS data and mobile gaming have also been utilised by police, providing key evidence in their investigations in recent years. Such diversification of publicly shared sources of information has also enabled non-justice system actors (in other words, everyday citizens of digital society) to participate and contribute towards investigations in new ways. In this first section, we further explore some key case studies where the public has engaged with crime in real time: the 2015 Paris (France) attacks, the 2013 Boston (US) Marathon bombing, the 2011 London (England) riots and the 2012 murder of Jill Meagher in Melbourne (Australia). In so doing, we begin to examine some of the ways in which citizen participation, 'following' and even crowdsourced investigations may be influencing individuals' perceptions and meaning-making in response to crime, as well as formal and informal justice responses.

#PorteOuverte: The Paris Attacks

The 2015 attacks in Paris occurred within a time frame of approximately three hours; meaning that, for much of this time, official information about the victims was very limited. Yet, the role of digital technologies in relation to the attacks was not limited to the immediate news opportunities they offered. During the attacks, Facebook deployed its Safety Check for the first time in response to a crime (Facebook, 2015). Originally developed as a disaster response tool, Safety Check allowed users close to the attacks to mark themselves as safe; letting Facebook friends know with a single action. Local police also employed a similar tactic: publishing Twitter and Facebook emergency posts noting the seriousness of the incidents and recommending members of the public to limit their movements. The reach and utility of these messages can be seen in the tenfold increase of subscribers to the prefecture police account (@prefpolice) on the evening of 13 November 2015 (French National Assembly, 2016). Police social media accounts distributed information and advice to the community, such as 'Aux établissements recevant du public, de renforcer la surveillance des entrées et d'accueillir ceux qui en auraient besoin' ('At public sites, strengthen entry surveillance and accommodate those in need') (Préfecture de police, 2015).

The attacks also saw a unique real-time public response to crime, with the hashtag #PorteOuverte ('Open Door'). Just as Twitter became a site for information, #PorteOuverte became a spontaneous digital tool for people offering their homes to those in need during the immediate aftermath of the attack. The hashtag was used as a means of 'advertising' the opportunity to social media users in such a situation. Rather than an official emergency response, #PorteOuverte represented an emerging citizen-led solution. According to Twitter, the hashtag had been used one million times within ten hours of the attacks (Goel & Ember, 2015). Moreover, the coming days saw social media become a tool of solidarity, with responses like #PrayforParis and French flag profile filters used as expressions of solidarity with the victims of the attack and the French people. However, not all responses were harmonious: significant threats and anti-Muslim rhetoric were posted across social media (Magdy, Darwish, & Abokhodair, 2015), with social media activity ranging from individuals sharing hate-speech hashtags through to organised 'hacker' campaigns like #OpParis organised by Anonymous to expose potential terrorists and their sympathisers (Scaife, 2017) — see Chapter 7 for more about 'hacktivism'.

In the aftermath of the attacks, digital technologies informed much of the police investigation. Investigators were able to access abundant audio, visual and textual data recorded on mobile devices, which assisted in establishing what took place, the timings of events and the movements of those involved — both perpetrators and victims. In light of these investigations and subsequent official inquiries, it has also become apparent that mobile devices were integral to the planning, preparation and execution of the attack (French National Assembly, 2016). The ubiquity of digital technologies ensures their presence both during crime incidents and in their aftermath, as will be discussed in subsequent sections.

#BostonMarathon Bombings

On Monday 15 April 2013, two homemade bombs filled with shrapnel and hidden in backpacks that had been placed among crowds of marathon-watchers exploded within seconds of each other near the finish line of the 117th Boston Marathon. Media reports would later confirm that three spectators were killed in the blasts: 29-year-old Krystle Campbell, 8-year-old Martin Richard and

23-year-old Lu Lingzi; later, one police officer was shot and killed by the bombers as they attempted to flee (CBS News, 2013). More than 260 people were seriously wounded, including 17 who lost limbs as a result of the blast (Kotz, 2013; Moskowitz, 2014).

A five-day manhunt to identify and capture the two young men suspected of the bombings then sent the city of Boston into lockdown. On Thursday 18 April, police released CCTV images of two male suspects, one wearing a white baseball cap and the other a black cap, who they wanted to question in relation to the bombings. The two men were later identified as brothers Tamerlan Tsarnaev, aged 26, and Dzhokhar Tsarnaev, aged 19. According to media reports, on the morning of Friday 19 April, Tamerlan was killed in gunfire exchange with police, while Dzhokhar was still at large (BBC News, 2013; Miller, 2015; Ross, 2016). A 911 call to police ultimately led to the capture of Dzhokhar, four days after the bombing, hiding in a boat in a suburban backyard. A US federal jury unanimously sentenced him to death in May 2015.

Meanwhile, as the tragedy and subsequent police investigation were unfolding, citizens were sharing accounts of the events, as well as expressing their distress and grief for those impacted, with the hashtags #BostonMarathon and #PrayForBoston, which subsequently trended on Twitter. Additionally, amateur would-be detectives were taking to online platforms in an effort to identify the initially unknown suspects. A Reddit user started a discussion thread (or 'subreddit') /r/findbostonbombers and invited an online community of citizen 'sleuths' to assist in compiling information, including images from the day of the bombing, that might help the FBI track down the two suspects (Abad-Santos, 2013). Many spectators present on the Monday of the marathon had posted their photos and videos on image-sharing platforms such as Flickr, and any additional details gathered by both those present on the day and other citizens were further collated in an online spreadsheet (Abad-Santos, 2013). The eagerness of everyday citizens to contribute to the investigation led to several people being wrongly identified as the bombers, and their families were harassed as a result: a point we elaborate on further in latter sections of this chapter.

England 2011 Riots

On Saturday 6 August 2011, violent riots in Tottenham (a district of north London), were sparked after a police shooting that had killed 29-year-old Mark Duggan, a London born and bred man of mixed British and West Indian descent. It started initially as a peaceful protest of approximately 200 people outside the local Tottenham police station at 5:30 pm, the crowd demanding answers in the context of a history of black deaths in police custody (Lewis, 2011). As night fell, the growing crowd erupted into riots that would involve violence, looting and property damage spreading across north London suburbs and into several other cities in England (Lewis, 2011). The rioting ultimately lasted for four days, with five people killed and more than 2000 people arrested. By 9 pm on Saturday, a series of posts were emerging on Twitter with the hashtags #MarkDuggan, #Tottenham, #TottenhamRiots and, later, #LondonRiots (Ball & Lewis, 2011; Newburn, 2011; Procter, Vis, & Voss, 2013).

As the unrest spread to other cities, further hashtags such as #EnglandRiots, #BirminghamRiots and #ManchesterRiots also began to circulate. There was wide speculation about the role that social media networks had played in causing the riots, by allowing such widespread information sharing and incitement to violence (Newburn, 2011). Indeed, it was rumoured that government officials were discussing the potential to interrupt social media access in the event of a future riot or substantial civil disorder (Newburn, 2011). Yet, it would later emerge, through a joint research project between *The Guardian* and a London School of Economics team led by Professor of Criminology Tim Newburn, that in fact, the free messaging service on Blackberry phones (BlackBerry Messenger, or 'BBM') had been initially employed to communicate and plan in advance of the riots (Newburn, 2011; Procter et al., 2013; The Guardian & London School of Economics, 2011). Nonetheless, social media certainly played a role in documenting the riots, in identifying looters and in the subsequent clean-up efforts (Ball & Lewis, 2011; Blair, 2011). A Tumblr page titled 'Catch a Looter' and a Twitter hashtag #shopalooter encouraged the public to post videos and images that would help police to identify those involved in the riots (Blair, 2011; Denef, Bayerl, & Kaptein, 2013). Meanwhile, the hashtag #RiotCleanUp mobilised hundreds of individuals, companies and services to coordinate their efforts, with one twitterer posting 'Last night we needed Batman. This morning we need The Wombles. #londonriots #riotcleanup' (Ball & Lewis, 2011).

Murder of #JillMeagher

Finally, in Australia, the tragic disappearance, assault and murder of 29-year-old Irish woman Jill Meagher stands out as one of the first crime events where an Australian public followed along and interacted with the investigation via social media (Milivojevic & McGovern, 2014). It is a case that has continued to capture Australians' interest and become embedded in local collective memory. While much is now known regarding the events of the night in Melbourne that Jill Meagher was sexually assaulted and murdered by Adrian Bayley, at the time details were scant, as her disappearance escalated into local, national and international news.

On Friday 21 September 2012, Jill Meagher was recorded by CCTV cameras at around 5 pm as she left her office at the Australian Broadcasting Corporation (ABC) studios in Melbourne's Southbank with a female co-worker. Jill's night out with colleagues took her to a bar on Sydney Road in the inner suburb of Brunswick, only a short walk from the home she shared with her husband Tom Meagher. When Jill failed to return home that night, Tom searched the streets of Brunswick for her. Tom reported Jill missing to local police at around 6.00 am on Saturday 22 September, and the official search began. On Sunday 23 September, 'missing' posters were placed around Brunswick appealing to the public for any information that might help in the investigation. By 12.30 pm on Sunday, the public appeal went digital, with a Facebook group titled 'Help Us Find Jill Meagher' accumulating 90,000 followers in just four days, while the hashtags #jillmeagher and #meagher were two of the highest trending topics on Twitter across Australia (Ainsworth & Casey, 2012; Milivojevic & McGovern, 2014). On Tuesday 25 September, Victoria Police released CCTV footage depicting Meagher and other pedestrians, including 'the man in the blue hoodie' who was singled out as the main person of interest. This footage was subsequently posted and re-shared on social media and has now been viewed by millions of people across Australia and internationally (Little, 2015). By Thursday 27 September, police had identified and arrested 41-year-old Bayley, who led them to the site in the far north-west of Melbourne where he had buried Meagher's body. By Friday 28 September, Bayley appeared in court charged with rape and murder (see Powell, Overington & Hamilton, 2017).

From the initial report of the suspected crime and throughout the progress of the police investigation, citizens shared personal fears and accounts of 'near misses' that they had experienced on the streets of Melbourne; they contributed information and speculation throughout the trial and conviction of the perpetrator; and they engaged in calls for reform to criminal justice policy areas such as parole, violence against women and CCTV (Atmore, 2012; Bartels, 2013; Little, 2015; Milivojevic & McGovern, 2014; Thompson & Louise, 2014). Australian criminologists Sanja Milivojevic and Alyce McGovern argued that the public's engagement with the crime as it unfolded was facilitated by the 'sheer potential of social media's global reach and its practically unlimited audience' (2014, p. 29). Throughout the remainder of this chapter, we further elaborate on the nature, extent, reach and implications of such public engagement with crime in real time.

Technology and Immediacy in Response to Crime Events

While avoiding the hyperbole surrounding digital technologies and social media, the non-hierarchical immediacy of social media provides communities with instantaneous crime event information. The potential for crime-in-real-time information raises new challenges for old theoretical concepts, as well as revitalising criminology's approach to crime, media and technology in a digital age. Indeed, there are at least three ways in which the key features of digital society — as discussed in Chapters 2 and 3 — come to bear on formal and informal responses to crime in real time: public engagement with major events; disruption of traditional agenda-setting media; and immediacy and immersion of public participation in responding to crime.

Public Engagement with Major Events

Beyond criminology, there is a growing field of research into the ways the public engages with social media during times of crisis. Central to much of this investigation has been the development of big data analytics and attempts to parlay the wealth of information into social benefit. The field of disaster management clearly shows how social media has disrupted traditional response processes in times of crisis. Facebook and Twitter have been central in the burgeoning field of 'crisis informatics', a concern with the deployment of communications strategies to mobilise the public during emergencies (Palen & Anderson, 2016). Researchers have recognised that, in times of crisis, social media allows the public both to be informed and to have a voice in the spread of information, which can have positive and negative influences on disaster response (Gao, Barbier, & Goolsby, 2011; Palen & Anderson, 2016; Sutton, Palen, & Shklovski, 2008; Yates & Paquette, 2011).

Social media and search data have also been 'mined' to monitor disease epidemics and threats to the community. The use of digital technology in the surveillance and management of diseases has been supplemented with 'real-time' data drawn from social media, providing an insight into outbreaks as they unfold (Brownstein, Freifeld, & Madoff, 2009). In the past, disease-tracking was cumbersome, relying on data obtained from hospitals and medical professionals, which often created a delay between any predictive modelling, detailing and management of epidemics (Declich & Carter, 1994). With the rise of social media, the dominance of Google search and a range of disease-surveillance 'mashups', data can now be mined, categorised and analysed, offering real-time opportunities for health agencies to respond (Brownstein et al., 2009; Chunara, Andrews, & Brownstein, 2012; Culotta, 2010). Technologies like Google Flu Trends (GFT) even claimed to be able to provide real-time prediction of influenza patterns through analysis of search queries. Advocates of these methods see big data as a kind of 'collective intelligence' (Levy, 1997) in which citizens and technology share in the transformation of knowledge to the benefit of society. In this sense, a personal search for 'flu medications' becomes an element in a reciprocal exchange of information that is employed by both the individual (search for medication information) and the community (recognition of a potential flu sufferer). While many advocate a utopian view of trend management, these new analyses of big data have not been without their issues. For now, it seems that claims social media can offer any reliable predictive tools are too hyperbolic and based on limited evidence (Butler, 2013). For example, GFT had limited success, with inaccurate results (Santillana, Zhang, Althouse, & Ayers, 2014) that indicated a failure of the predictive modelling, and the site was closed in 2015.

The aforementioned use of technology demonstrates how the social sciences have embraced real-time data. Criminology has begun to develop similar approaches to citizen use of participatory online networks and digital technologies. Many opportunities exist in the analysis of user-generated content that may capture information about crime events, alleged offenders and police operations within peer groups and online communities. In this way, digital technologies disrupt the traditional models of information dissemination and community response to crime. No longer is citizen participation in response to crime events limited to the roles of victims, eyewitnesses and bystanders in the immediate vicinity; they are able to participate as crowds from anywhere in the world. In short, digital technologies make crime events seem closer, more relevant and more immediate to a far wider audience.

The ubiquity of communications technologies enables not only engagement but also active participation in the representation of crime events. When a crime occurs, the individuals involved have a detailed digital footprint prior to the events and are able to subsequently experience and respond via social media and digital platforms. The constant presence of technology means that, when a crime occurs, technology will be a fundamental ongoing element of the construction of crime scenes. At a broader level, the presence of technologies at crime events means that the wider public can become involved in a manner that is not possible without technology. Chapter 5 highlights the vital role that images can play in both perpetrating and extending the harms of crime, while Chapter 7 demonstrates how the public can pursue informal vigilante justice, for better or for worse.

Disruption of Agenda-setting News Media

Criminologists have long discussed the important role played by traditional media in making crime events accessible to the general public. For instance, criminologist Yvonne Jewkes (2011) noted that the news media is often the primary source of most people's experience of crime, and as such, it is central in developing public perceptions of crime. However, the work of Jewkes and many others in the field (e.g. Greer, 2007, 2012; Peelo, 2006) was largely established in a media environment reliant on asynchronous communication, not part of a 24-hour news cycle, nor distributed through the range of digital networks used today. Indeed the criminological conceptualisation of crime 'in the media' has tended to remain focused on the 'old' media era of print, radio and television, in which concepts such as 'newsworthiness', and the 'ideal victim' place immense responsibility on the shoulders of reporters and editors. Moreover, the traditional relationship between government officials and news media creates a stage-managed version of reporting, encompassing a range of stylistic devices, including press conferences, questions and answers, pre-prepared statements and even justice-agency produced content stylised in the same manner as traditional media sources. As a result of such practices, news media have long been understood as playing 'agenda-setting', 'gatekeeping' and 'framing' functions when it comes to reporting on issues of public and policy significance (Berkowitz, 1992;

McCombs & Shaw, 1972; Scheufele & Tewksbury, 2007). In effect, there is a feedback loop whereby the stories that get reported (in this case, crime and justice issues), and the ways in which they are reported, represent an interaction of news media imperatives to attract and hold audiences, policy-makers' political interests and a broader public's interest in crime.

The technosocial practices of following crime in real time have arguably disrupted the traditional agenda-setting role of the news media. This trend has not escaped a small but growing number of scholars, who are interested in the changing nature of crime 'sense-making' or 'meaning-making' in a digital society (Intravia, Wolff, Paez, & Gibbs, 2017; Kort-Butler & Habecker, 2017; Milivojevic & McGovern, 2014; Powell, Overington, & Hamilton, 2017). In their study of Australian Facebook users' interaction with both official police sources and media reporting of the Jill Meagher case (described above), Milivojevic and McGovern (2014) argue that social media participation can result in counter-narratives framed by citizens themselves that simultaneously resist and disrupt mainstream news reporting on crime issues. Furthermore, in response to some mainstream news stories that explicitly invoked 'victim-blaming' narratives (such as by questioning why Jill Meagher was walking home alone, drunk and late at night in the first place), Twitter users' presented their own counter-narrative reiterating the right of Melbourne women to #reclaimthenight (an appropriation of the annual feminist march to raise awareness of sexual violence) and walk the streets without fear (Powell et al., 2017).

The disruptive potential of social media is not, however, limited to the operation of counter-narratives in online space. Increasingly, mainstream news media are reporting on stories as they 'trend on Twitter' and appear to be influenced by the popular narratives that are forming in the digital agora. Moreover, the relationship between news media and social media is blurred and interactive. It is now common, for instance, when a major crime event occurs, for journalists to take to Twitter to report their own observations from the scene and, indeed, to share and re-distribute the tweets of citizen eye-witnesses before there has been sufficient time to fact-check the rapidly emerging accounts of what has happened. News reporting itself is also increasingly stylised on the social media format, represented as a series of short updates as information continues to develop. Furthermore, tweets sometimes come to substitute for direct news of major crime events. The 2015 Paris attacks, for example, were reported on BBC Trending, where the focus is specifically on how events unfold via social media. As the site notes: 'The order of events isn't different from other media reports, but to see it unfold online is to see the emotional and personal effect on ordinary people' (BBC Trending, 2015, n.p.). Despite the positive potential for social media to resist and disrupt traditional news media reporting on crime events, it would appear that mainstream media are actively closing the loop: influencing social media content on crime as well as reshaping news reporting in the form of a tweet or short blog. Some scholars have pointed to evidence that a lot of discussion on social media such as Twitter is actually just 'rehashing' content from the agenda-setting news media (Rogstad, 2016).

Immediacy and Immersion of Public Participation

Public participation in response to crime has been a fixture of criminological investigation, particularly in light of mediated representations. Technological advancements — whether they be the print, radio, television or more recent digital trends — have altered how members of the public, as an audience, perceive their relationship to crime. Peelo (2006) acknowledged the shifting nature of our relationship to crime with the concept of 'mediated witness' (discussed further below), placing audiences in the space of virtual victimhood rather than as direct victims of crime. This concept belongs to the era of passive media consumption that was reliant on editorial techniques and media selectivity to engage the public, who consumed stories as they were presented. One of the highlights of the digital society is that, while media stories are still consumed, the options available to audiences to respond and produce have been vastly increased. Digital technologies allow members of the public to become more involved in crime events and experience them as proximally closer than they actually were.

Where mediated witnesses in previous eras were passive consumers of stories, those living in digital society have an array of options to explore, follow and respond to instances of harm and crime. Thus, mediated witnesses move from the era of media *con*sumption to media *pro*sumption, meaning that audiences are not only consumers of content but are increasingly also producers (Ritzer & Jurgenson, 2010). In reference to the original incarnations of prosumption in media spaces, sociologists George Ritzer and Nathan Jurgenson (2010) explored user-generated content as a cultural artefact. Prosumption has been linked to the advent of Web 2.0 (Ritzer & Jurgenson, 2010), as advances in digital technologies such as YouTube and social networking sites have lowered the costs of production and distribution of content. From information shared on Wikipedia to fan-generated content, there are many examples of the intersection of market- or individual-generated content that is consumed but also reworked, converted, supplemented or improved upon by the consumer to produce an extension of the original (Ritzer & Jurgenson, 2010). Twitter and Facebook enable 'online citizen journalists to "prosume" new forms of information'; YouTube allows 'at-home video "produsers" 'to download, re-edit and upload innovative forms of entertainment; and the open source software movement enables hackers and amateur computer engineers to 'co-create open-source software' (Comor, 2010, p. 323). The expansion of user-generated content has allowed consumers and audiences greater levels of agency in relation to the cultural artefacts they consume, lessening the conceptual distance between the 'real' experience and that of the traditionally passive consumer. In many ways, the prosumer collapses traditional hierarchies of power and ownership, altering the asymmetries between creators and users, reporters and audiences, consumers and producers (Comor, 2010). For example, reporters are no longer the sole source of news, with platforms like Twitter allowing 'citizen journalists' the opportunity to submit stories to the public.

In relation to crime and justice, a side-effect of the turn towards prosumption can be seen in the emergence of 'web sleuthing' (Yardley, Lynes, Wilson, & Kelly, 2016). An extension of criminologist Keith Soothill's (1998) notion of the armchair detective, web sleuthing occurs when 'producer, consumer and subject' intersect with crime (Yardley et al., 2016). Digital technologies enable this relationship by lessening the limits of distance and access, meaning that online investigations and activities can 'have real world, embodied consequences' in spite of web sleuths not being at the site of the crime or formally involved in its investigation (Yardley et al., 2016). Web sleuthing is the popular criminological result of a digital society; it is 'an outcome of contemporary society's networked and multidimensional true crime infotainment experience, a manifestation of the norms and values of digital culture' (Yardley et al., 2016). Online sleuths embrace the digital society by creating groups devoted to their interests in investigating crime and injustice, whether identifying criminals, as at the 2013 Boston bombing, or investigating mysteries through popular culture in *Making a Murderer* and *Serial*.

Where digital technologies enable increased options for web sleuths and armchair detectives, these options reflect an increased agency of individuals. In being able to investigate crimes in a manner previously unavailable to them, the increased engagement of the public in online arenas alters their utility in the totality of the mediated environment surrounding crime. Matthew Williams, Pete Burnap, and Luke Sloan (2017) identify that social media, Twitter in particular, turns individuals into 'sensors' of offline phenomena. In their relationship with a particular crime, social media users engage with these platforms in four distinct ways: 'as victims; as first-hand witnesses; as second-hand observers (e.g. via media reports or the spread of rumour) and as perpetrators' (Williams et al., 2017). While the authors discuss sensors in the model of crime prediction and tracking, their conceptualisation of sensors offers insight into the types of data available to anyone responding to crime through social media networks.

The increased agency of the public is increasingly being recognised in shifting relationships between producers and consumers of crime media (Ellis & McGovern, 2016; Lee & McGovern, 2014; McGovern, 2011; Schneider, 2016). For instance, McGovern (2011) has argued that the converging factors of increasingly restricted public access to emergency radio scanners, the evaporation of crime-beat reporters and increased reliance on police-centric systems (such as the Police External Agencies Transfer System (PEATS) in NSW) have altered the traditional media environment, and citizen journalists fill the void. Social media enables the public greater immediacy in their engagement with crime events, bypassing the influence of journalists or police (Schneider, 2016).

Crime in Real Time and the Public

The omnipresence of digital technologies often means that members of the public are the first to distribute images of crime scenes. Digital media scholars Christopher Schneider and Daniel Trottier (2012, 2013) identified this in their study of the response to the 2011 Stanley Cup riots in Vancouver, where the public was invited to identify rioters by uploading images to a Facebook page. The evolution of the new media environment has taken much of the gatekeeper role away from editors and reporters and moved the power of information dissemination into the hands of the crowd (Allan & Thorsen, 2009; Goode, 2009; Williams & Delli Carpini, 2004). Participatory media like Twitter allow news and information to be distributed through 'broad, asynchronous, lightweight and always-on communication systems' that are 'enabling citizens to maintain a mental model of news and events' (Hermida, 2010, p. 299) in a 'networked public sphere' (Benkler, 2006). According to media scholar Alfred Hermida (2010, p. 298), the constant 'ambience' of social media enables a 'collective intelligence' that communicates instantly to share and discuss events via the technology. The nature of these platforms also encourages decentralised swarms of activity in response to events. New media environments ostensibly dissolve power relationships between creators and consumers as power and knowledge are dispersed among the community rather than reliant on traditional journalism's gatekeeping role (Bruns, 2005).

Participatory media such as Twitter, Facebook and Reddit have infiltrated the more traditional, established media organisations. Media organisations are now mining social media as a matter of routine journalistic practice for creating awareness, researching stories and measuring public sentiment across a range of interests (Broersma & Graham, 2012; Moon & Hadley, 2014; Paulussen & Harder, 2014). Moreover, social media is increasingly relied upon as support for a story, key 'newsworthy' information and, in some cases, the trigger of coverage (Broersma & Graham, 2013). Bruno identified this as the 'Twitter effect', in which social media, rather than traditional media, provides 'live coverage without any reporters on the ground, by simply newsgathering user-generated content available online' (Bruno, 2011, p. 8).

From a criminological perspective, the 2011 England riots offered a key, high-profile opportunity to view the shifting media landscape and disruptive effects of digital technologies. Technology scholar Farida Vis (2013) notes how traditional journalists embraced Twitter as a mode of reporting: using it to detail their own experiences, share opinions and request leads and sources for story developments. Meanwhile, the work of Emma Tonkin and colleagues (2012) further elucidates how big data sourced from social media networks can provide avenues of criminological exploration that expand beyond news and participatory media as a primary 'influencer' of crime in real time. As social media gains greater centrality in our everyday lives, big data are increasingly important for gaining a real-time understanding of patterns of crime and police responses to them (Baudains, Braithwaite, & Johnson, 2012). A study of 2.6 million tweets, 700,000 user accounts and 54 hashtags used during the 2011 London riots investigated how media reports, pictures, rumours and user reflections traversed Twitter (Procter et al., 2013). In this analysis, the researchers were able to conclude that Twitter assisted not only in inciting unlawful acts but also — and more importantly — in developing positive community responses, such as organising the clean-up after the riot (Panagiotopoulos, Bigdeli, & Sams, 2014; Procter et al., 2013). A significant finding of this work was the inadequacy of police response to social media leads, including distinguishing between reality and rumour (Procter et al., 2013). Sebastian Denef and colleagues (2013) have further identified that police Twitter and social media practices during the crisis detrimentally offered inconsistent, sometimes delayed, messages to the public and overstepped legal boundaries through practices shifting between rumour management, public awareness and investigation. Meanwhile, technology scholar Jeremy Crump (2011) has argued 'that the constraints of police culture have meant that Twitter has been used cautiously and as a reinforcement for existing means of communication' rather than being explored for its potential. Meanwhile, Rob Procter and colleagues (2013) conclude that the police were unable to make efficient use of the abundance of information available to them through social media during the riots. Research such as this highlights the potential to explore responses to crime with greater immediacy and effectiveness than traditional research methods and data collection techniques.

As technologies continue to improve, the potential to engage with crime in real time is increasing through a greater diversity of data sources that can converge to provide more depth and understanding. Again, the England riots of 2011 offer some insight here, as the public was quick to embrace a counter-response to identify rioters through 'riot accounts' such as @ManchesterRiots and @IDRioters. These accounts were embraced by Twitter users, who were encouraged to exchange news on events, support police and 'crowd-source identities of people caught on CCTV or camera phones apparently engaging in criminal activity during the riots' (Procter, Crump, Karstedt, Voss, & Cantijoch, 2013). In response to crime, social media offers the potential for the community to raise issues, voice concerns, collaborate with like-minded people and embrace agency by commenting, condemning and distributing information with greater expediency and efficiency than traditional media or government agencies (Procter et al., 2013, p. 427). When police engage in this discussion they implement a 'two-way communication strategy' that encourages 'information exchange' between officials and the community (Schneider, 2016). However, for all of the potential in the convergence of social media and more traditional digital technologies, Procter and colleagues (2013) raise ethical concerns over the consequences of pseudo-news networks that are prone to rumour and the outcomes that may result from erroneous and unverified information.

Citizen-led Investigations

While citizen participation offers compelling opportunities in response to crime, unmonitored citizen involvement has the potential to contribute to harm and victimisation. Examples such as the online response to the Boston Marathon bombing (15 April 2013) highlight the complexities of such engagement, demonstrating that, even when there may be a public benefit, the outcome can become obscured when participation interrupts official responses to crime. Importantly, this response had clear distinctions between the official and public investigations that intersected, not because of police but because of the digital technologies that enabled the public to monitor, investigate and pursue the offenders. By embracing these technologies, the public became aligned with professional services in pursuit of the criminals through the creation of an ad hoc nodal network via the internet (Nhan, Huey, & Broll, 2017). Where the police conducted their investigation through contemporary policing strategies, the public was engaged through media coverage, social media content and information gathered through police scanners.

The intensity of the public's engagement with the search for the perpetrators of the attacks highlights the potential for informal cyber-sleuths to fill deficiencies in law enforcement. Social media allowed an 'unprecedented' level of citizen participation in a crime investigation, facilitating 'the capturing and sharing of information, videos and photos between officials, bystanders and interested parties' (Andrea & Nicolas, 2014, p. 60). Facebook and Twitter enabled the public response 'by serving as a resource, communications and news hub, or a forum for finding support, and serving as additional "eyes and ears" for law enforcement' (Nhan et al., 2017, p. 357). The benefits of this crowdsourced information became immediately apparent with the array of social media images shared by bystanders from the scene of the crime following the incident (Cassa, Chunara, Mandl, & Brownstein, 2013). Consequently, images shared through social media, along with CCTV and video footage would become key assets in the search for Dzhokhar and Tamerlan Tsarnaev.

In the hours following the bombing, citizen participation moved beyond social media sites towards other online communities such as Reddit and 4chan. Of particular importance were Reddit discussions containing 'very detailed information concerning evidence publicly announced and even some evidence that was not announced' (Tapia, LaLone, & Kim, 2014, p. 271). Tapia and colleagues (2014) argue that, in many ways, Reddit out-performed the mainstream media when it came to the immediacy of content and community. For example, the Reddit community had established 'text-based communication, photographic evidence of the crime scene, food and shelter for those who had an account, as well as a timeline of events that was unmatched by the rest of the media' (Tapia et al., 2014, p. 272). However, for all the hyperbole surrounding citizen participation in the immediate aftermath of the bombing (Sutton et al., 2014), the influence that citizens participating via Reddit had on the general public was comparable to that of the law enforcement agencies and traditional media sources (Liu, Fraustino, & Jin, 2016; Olteanu, Vieweg, & Castillo, 2015). While some advocate the successes of the thread-based responses (Nhan et al., 2017, p. 357), social media also created confusion in the aftermath through the diversity of accounts and lack of hierarchical knowledge, forming what can be considered a 'conflictual media event' (Dayan & Katz, 1992; Hepp & Couldry, 2010; Mortensen, 2015).

Competing interpretations of events were central to the conflictual nature of the event. In the online investigations, participants in the Reddit community examined the photos posted online under the assumption the community could identify potential suspects that law enforcement may have missed (Nhan et al., 2017). While these searches were not problematic, and can be looked upon as potential examples of citizen participation acting as a 'hive mind', the unmoderated element of online space led to unexpected consequences. Most notable of these was the misidentification of potential suspects through unverified information. A great concern of the impact of the Boston Bombing misidentification is highlighted in research conducted by Professor Kate Starbird and colleagues (2014), who found that, even when errors are corrected, the correction has significantly less impact than the original misinformation presented. Moreover, the damaging effects of the errors or misidentification do not stem simply from a mistake by members of the public but from a complex interrelation between officials, the public and the media. For instance, the release of a grainy suspect photo by Boston police led to internet speculation about the likely identity, which was then further reported by media outlets.

Engagement Online and Official Investigations

Recognising that crime has a greater intimacy with the general public through digital media, criminal justice agencies have embraced digital technologies in their approaches to investigations. Incidents like the Boston Marathon bombing and the London riots have highlighted how digital technologies open opportunities for the public to explore and investigate criminal behaviour. Where footage and reactions to an event can be shared across digital platforms, the investigation following the aftermath of crime has also enabled real-time responses. Central to these opportunities is the wealth of data stored on digital devices, which expands the repertoire available to investigators to communicate with the community to recall events and elicit information with expediency. The materials collected during the event also become crucial evidence when developing cases against suspects.

When investigating crimes, digital technologies offer the chance to converge the 'bottom-up' approaches of web-sleuthing with the top-down approaches made by official agencies (Trottier, 2014). This convergence has extended traditional investigative practices that embrace the ubiquity of technology to crowdsource evidence about people suspected of criminal activity. For example, in response to the murders of six people in Bourke St Mall, Melbourne, Victoria Police opened a digital assessment management system that allowed the public to anonymously upload pictures or video of the incident (Bucci, 2017). The public appeal resulted in at least 70 videos and images by providing 'a forum and a means for people' to share 'imaging' with police (Bucci, 2017). Victoria Police Assistant Commissioner Steve Fontana acknowledges the potential in providing such access to the public, recognising that the shared video footage would have been critical 'if it had have been an ongoing event, and had we have not known who the person was at the time' (Bucci, 2017). Similar data were crowdsourced during the aftermath of the 2011 Vancouver Stanley Cup riots, where police and Facebook users drew on posted content and collaborated to identify suspected rioters (Trottier, 2014). Taking a different tack, after the murder of Lee Rigby, the UK House of Commons Intelligence Select Committee reflected upon social media content to explore the extent of opportunities that may have existed to detect and intercept the offenders prior to the attack (Innes, Roberts, Preece, & Rogers, 2016). And, moving away from social media, a range of other technologies — such as wearable fitness devices — have been introduced as evidence in criminal trials to identify the location of key figures in the case at the time of the crime (Gottehrer, 2015; Rutkin, 2015).

Responses to crimes, particularly high-profile crimes, have both highlighted the potential of digital investigation and raised serious privacy and security questions. Of concern in this discussion is how evidence is collected, retained and regulated in relation to individual liberties and for what purposes it may be used (Kerr, 2005). This concern has been raised when referring to the scope of official investigations through online platforms such as Facebook, where government agencies are granted ever more opportunities for investigation and monitoring — what Trottier refers to as 'surveillance creep' — under the guise of community protection and national security (Trottier, 2014, p. 79). Debates over surveillance and government access have been a continual point of contention in the post-9/11 landscape, with governments demanding 'backdoors' into digital technologies such as Facebook and mobile phones (as discussed in Chapter 3). Some tech companies have resisted such access, citing civil liberty concerns (Sorcher, 2015).

Populist Punitiveness and Fear of Crime

The capacity to follow 'crime in real time' has further implications with respect to intensifying misperceptions, 'virtual victimhood' and fear of crime. Criminologist Moira Peelo (2006, p. 160) developed the concept of 'mediated witness' to describe the authorial techniques utilised in media reporting that encourage readers to align themselves emotionally with the victim; a kind of 'virtual victimhood'. Though Peelo (2006) has used the concept to analyse the deliberately emotive reporting on violent crime by news media, the concept can also usefully be applied to consider the effects on social media users of immersion in crime events from the perspectives of victims, witnesses and bystanders. Psychological research following the 11 September 2001 terrorist attacks on the World Trade Center in New York City (which resulted in almost 3000 deaths and more than 6000 wounded) repeatedly found symptoms of acute and/or post-traumatic stress among not only those who witnessed the attacks or lived geographically nearby, but also those who had extended exposure to television coverage (Ahern et al., 2002; Blanchard et al., 2004; Schuster et al., 2001). Some researchers have identified a similar trend among those exposed to reporting of the 2011 Boston bombings, including those who followed the event via the internet (Comer, DeSerisy, & Grief Green, 2016; Garfin, Holman, & Silver, 2015). Heightened fear may be somewhat expected following such 'mega cases' (Soothill, Peelo, & Francis, 2002), or 'signal crimes' (Innes, 2004), which are repeatedly and widely covered, and which are simultaneously represented and interpreted as having important meanings and/or 'lessons' for society as a whole. As Peelo (2006) has earlier suggested, however, one of the impacts of immersive narratives and emotional engagement with crime events is to further politicise debates over crime policy and crime control. For example, in a US survey study with 918 university students, criminologist Jonathan Intravia and colleagues (2017) found that social media consumption was significantly related to students' fear of crime and perceptions of their safety. In particular, the researchers note the importance of criminological research into the ways that social media consumption may influence attitudes towards criminal justice policies and punitiveness. It would appear that social media, in particular, has a potential to exacerbate contemporary populist politics of fear and, as will be discussed further in Chapter 6, hate. Yet, to date, few studies have examined the affectual responses and potential trauma experienced through immersion in social media coverage of crime events.

A further affective impact of citizen engagements with crime in real time is the potential escalation of a particular kind of 'populist punitiveness' (Hogg, 2013; Quilter, 2012, 2014). For example, following the identification and arrest of Adrian Bayley for the murder of Jill Meagher, public discussions on Facebook and Twitter commented on the 'sickos' in this world, and that the courts would never be able to mete out the justice that was required in response to such a shocking crime (Milivojevic & McGovern, 2014; Powell et al., 2017). Narratives quickly emerged on social media supporting retaliative violence against Bayley in prison while he awaited trial and supporting a possible return of the death penalty in Australia, since there could be no rehabilitation for violent thugs such as he (Powell et al., 2017). Milivojevic and McGovern (2014), meanwhile, noted the ways that these popular narratives served to disrupt justice processes, as members of the public took to social media distributing Bayley's photo and declaring his guilt; threatening the alleged offender's due process rights and the impartiality of any subsequently-called jury. Furthermore, following Meagher's murder, the local State Government committed $3 million (AUD) in funding towards substantially extending the CCTV surveilliance network across the city, with a further committment of $50 million (AUD) made by the then Federal Opposition leader should he be elected to office (Milivojevic & McGovern, 2014). This is despite the dubious evidence of CCTV as an effective tool for the prevention, control or detection of crime (McGuire, 2012). Arguably, social media represents a powerful mechanism for the amplification of law and order discourses on crime and justice, as well as a ready tool for the politicisation of crime and justice issues (Powell et al., 2017) and, furthermore, promoting citizen vigilantism (discussed further in Chapter 7).

Ultimately, there is potential for the proliferation and immersive nature of crime news in our daily lives to amplify misinformation, fear of crime and 'penal populism' (Quilter, 2012). Yet, as Australian criminologist Russell Hogg (2013) argues, it is possible to 'rescue' the concept of populism from its critics. According to Hogg (2013), rather than continue the 'demonising of populism as an irrational intruder on healthy democratic practice' (p. 109), criminologists should engage more productively with populism as both a theoretical concept and a political practice. It is possible for populism, as a concept and as a legitimate (indeed inescapable) practice of political participation, to be directed at progressive crime and justice policymaking (Hogg, 2013). Legal scholar Julia Quilter (2012, 2014) makes a related case, highlighting the contradictory nature of contemporary crime and justice populism. According to Quilter, there is 'good reason' to be critical of 'penal populism' and the emotive rhetoric that appears so influential in the political and mass media landscape, with clear implications for an 'alarming explosion in prison populations across Western countries' (2014, p. 24). However, populist campaigns have also been deployed in service of progressive and non-punitive crime and justice policies — even presented as a counter-narrative to the 'law and order' politics so often presented by the agenda-setting news media (Quilter, 2014). Describing populism as a political practice that is characterised by simple, direct and jargon-free language (which, while it reduces the complexity of political issues also makes it comprehensible to a wider range of people), as well as appeals to public emotion, Quilter (2014) argues that this political repertoire can have positive potential to disrupt law and order rhetoric and renew crime policy debates (discussed in Chapter 8).

Challenges and Implications

This chapter has highlighted how digital technologies have opened opportunities to explore and respond to 'crime in real time'. Through responses to terrorism and other significant public crime events, we are seeing how technology and media consumption converge upon the entirety of crime events (pre-event, during and post-event). In our digital societies, we are discovering innovative ways of responding to crime, new methods of public engagement, disruption of traditional agenda-setting media and greater public immersion in crime events. Integral to these changes are technological advances in the form of mobile technologies, social media and information-sharing platforms, which allow near-instantaneous access to images and first-hand accounts from crime scenes. As demonstrated in this chapter, there is significant potential for 'crime in real time' to challenge old theoretical concepts, as well as to revitalise criminology's approach to crime, media and technology in the digital age.

Among the challenges is the sheer wealth of information that can be sourced from a dispersed audience for almost any event. With each incremental development of hardware, software and network technology, individuals have gained increased capacity to record and distribute their day-to-day lives. This capacity intersects with crime events both in the opportunistic recording of crime and in coordinated approaches to particular events. Video-recording technology was once the domain of an exclusive few who could afford it, and recording crime events would require the serendipitous presence of the bulky technology in the proximity of the event. Today, with video-camera technology embedded in mobile phones, and mobile phones in almost every adult's hand, anyone within proximity of a criminal event can record and transmit its occurrence. It is important also to understand the role of network technologies when discussing crime in real time: these have allowed crime events to be streamed directly to communities of users. Those who distribute recordings may do so to a limited audience (friends and family on social networks) or unknown potential audiences through live-streaming options across various platforms (Twitter/Periscope, Instagram, Facebook Live), the implications of which are further discussed in Chapter 5.

And the digital opportunities to engage with crime in real time are not limited to the visual experiences. Again, with the computational power that is increasingly available, a variety of ways to journal and chronicle crime events diffuses reporting power away from traditional media establishments into the hands of citizens with greater proximity and immediacy to the event. The potential for details of events to be distributed across platforms instantaneously provides the community with responses from those directly impacted by crime. It provides a platform for witnesses that once did not exist. For example, it has become common for witnesses of public crimes, perhaps particularly acts of mass violence and/or terrorism, to document what they have seen, identify key developments and display their emotional response to the event. In response to acts of terrorism, rather than rely on traditional communications, we have seen Facebook offer an emergency algorithm that allows those in the area to provide notices of their safety to friends and family in times of high anxiety. Similarly, the use of hashtags such as those in Paris and London can be recognised as journaling the immediate impact of a crime and facilitating local community organisation in real-time responses to crime. Rather than waiting for journalists to arrive at crime scenes, Facebook and Twitter platforms engage the community with eyewitness and proximate information.

More openly available visual and textual content has also disrupted how the general public responds to crime. The absence of gatekeepers for the content distributed has rearranged how people engage with the vast knowledge created. The combination of content creation, retention and networking capabilities of digital technologies has enabled networks of knowledge to emerge in response to crime in real time. We are able to establish tribes in response to crime, to investigate, empathise, mourn and vent as crimes unfold. These changes have been embraced by the traditional media, with news websites often providing running commentary and blogs citing tweets and Facebook posts as legitimate sources of information in times when coherent narratives have yet to be constructed. Similar approaches have begun to infiltrate traditional broadcast media, with not only user-generated information but also amateur video being lifted from these platforms and broadcast in crime reporting.

But, as the omnipresence and democratisation of digital technologies have enabled new responses to crime, they have done so in potentially problematic ways. In particular, the immediacy of technologies challenge core fundamentals of the criminal justice process. For example, a key concern for jury research has been how social media may exploit or expose the presentation of evidence and other information that may threaten the impartiality of jurors should they view it (Aaronson & Patterson, 2012).

The immediacy of responses to crime also raises concerns surrounding informal justice processes embracing the use of technologies (further discussed in Chapter 7). Central here is the potential for misinformation, such as that found on Reddit after the Boston Marathon bombing and elsewhere online. Meanwhile, journalism scholars Kristy Hess and Lisa Waller (2014) highlight the case of a 44-year-old Australian woman, who suffered a 'digital pillory' for a minor offence that was recorded and uploaded to YouTube. This particular case will be explored further in Chapter 7 but, for the purposes of the present chapter, it is clear that digital technologies and online spaces intensified public shaming, both by extending the time frame that the woman was infamous and by expanding the size and viciousness of the mob doing the shaming. Where incidents like this were once confined to 'news' in local regions or rumour amongst the community, digital technologies offer both an extended audience and a 'long-tail' of potential audiences who can access incriminating or humiliating images and the community response to them (Hess & Waller, 2014, p. 108).

Digital technologies extend the scope and intensity of public responses to crime that are ostensibly directed towards justice but cross over into a form of vigilantism (Huey, Nhan, & Broll, 2013; Nhan et al., 2017). Just as 'digital pillory' refers to the heightened public attention transgressors face through digital technologies, 'digilantism' refers to the use of these technologies to extend beyond attention into action (discussed further in Chapter 7). Trottier for instance, refers to digital vigilantism as 'a process where citizens are collectively offended by other citizen activity, and respond through coordinated retaliation on digital media, including mobile devices and social media platforms' (2017, p. 55). Digilantism has been adopted as an activist approach to achieve justice using a range of practices from hacktivism and denial-of-service (DoS) to trickery, persuasion, reputation assaults, public shaming and calls to action (Jane, 2017). While many digilantes seem to seek justice (Byrne, 2013; Jane, 2017; Nakamura, 2014), the situation arising from Reddit in responding to the Boston Marathon bombing demonstrates that justice-seeking behaviour can also result in injustices, harassment and violence towards alleged offenders.

Digilantism raises concerns between seeking justice and causing injustices. For the targets of digilantism, public responses are often unwanted, intense and enduring (Trottier, 2017). Moreover, these targets are often unaware of the scrutiny they have become subject to, sometimes even oblivious to the conflict or law-breaking that has elicited the retaliation (Trottier, 2017). In the search for the Boston bombers, Reddit users incorrectly identified Sunil Tripathi and Mike Mulugeta as a potential match for one of the images of the bombers (Kang, 2013). These false claims were not only shared across social media, independent news websites (notably Buzzfeed) and the traditional media, but also evidence of the error has long remained online (Kang, 2013). While the false accusations remain problematic, the error exposed further harm to Tripathi's family as he was, at the time, being registered as a missing person only to have his body found less than a week later. The online exposure of Tripathi as a suspect had immediate consequences for his family, who were then inundated with phone calls and media requests regarding their son's whereabouts and involvement in the crime (Kang, 2013).

Perhaps more positively, a further disruption afforded by technologies in response to crimes is that they offer creative avenues for alternative discourses, experiences and resistances. Where traditional media gatekeepers may have political, economic and personal agendas that influence news selection, digital technologies allow for choices on those agendas to be made by individuals in terms of the information they choose to consume. This active participation in news selection allows information that otherwise would not have been distributed to see the light of day. This may include violent crimes or police brutality that have gone unreported or the reprioritisation of the political agenda by citizens rather than gatekeepers. Public participation in major events via social media is not only a way of measuring sentiment and engagement, it also plays a role in social change. Of particular note here is the manner in which technologies have enabled democratic social movements around the world (Ghonim, 2012). Castells has witnessed social 'movements spread by contagion in a world networked by the wired Internet' (2012, p. 2). He argues:

> In our time, multimodal digital networks of horizontal communication are the fastest and most autonomous, interactive, reprogrammable and self-expanding means of communication in history ... the networked social movements of the digital age represent a new species of social movement.
>
> (Castells, 2012, p. 15)

In times of revolution and resistance, social media can be embraced by participants, with the technology allowing for spontaneous and reflexive organisation of protest events including directions to locations, how to act and — most importantly — providing 'the construction of an emotional narration to sustain their coming together in public space' (Gerbaudo, 2012, p. 12). The potential for such disruptive effects to further enable social justice activism are discussed in more depth in Chapter 8.

Conclusion

This chapter has explored various tensions inherent in greater citizen participation and engagement during and following crime events (Milivojevic & McGovern, 2014; Powell et al., 2017). On the one hand, there is a radical potential for citizen participation, following and engaging with crime in real time, to disrupt traditional and conservative narratives of crime and justice. In effect, citizen participation may form a resistance to 'penal populism' and, in its place, a new populism of equality and social justice in response to crime (as discussed in Chapter 1; see also Quilter, 2015). On the other hand, social media simultaneously represents a powerful mechanism for the amplification of law and order discourses on crime and justice and a ready tool for the further politicisation of crime and justice issues. The potential relationship between social media, citizen participation and the politics of crime and justice policy represents an important avenue for continued criminological research, and indeed, for digital criminology.

Recommended Further Reading

Powell, A., Overington, C., & Hamilton, G. (2017). Following #JillMeagher: Collective meaning-making in response to crime events via social media. *Crime, Media, Culture*. Advance online publication. doi:10.1177/1741659017721276.

Procter, R., Vis, F., & Voss, A. (2013). Reading the riots on Twitter: Methodological innovation for the analysis of big data. *International Journal of Social Research Methodology*, *16*(3), 197–214.

Trottier, D. (2014). Police and user-led investigations on social media. *Journal of Information Science*, *23*(1), 75.

Yardley, E., Lynes, A. G. T., Wilson, D., & Kelly, E. (2016). What's the deal with 'websleuthing'? News media representations of amateur detectives in networked spaces. *Crime, Media, Culture*, *14*(1), 81–109.

References

Aaronson, D. E., & Patterson, S. M. (2012). Modernizing jury instructions in the age of social media. *Criminal Justice*, *27*(4), 26.

Abad-Santos, A. (2013, April 22). Reddit's 'Find Boston Bombers' founder says 'It Was a Disaster' but 'Incredible', *The Atlantic*. Available at: www.theatlantic.com/national/archive/2013/04/reddit-find-boston-bombers-founder-interview/315987/ (last accessed 29 November 2017).

Ahern, J., Galea, S., Resnick, H., Kilpatrick, D., Bucuvalas, M., Gold, J. & Vlahov, D. (2002). Television images and psychological symptoms after the September 11 attacks. *Psychiatry*, *65*(4), 289–300.

Ainsworth, M. & Casey, B. (2012, September 28). Worldwide outpouring of grief after man arrested over Jill Meagher's disappearance. *The Australian*, p. 12.

Allan, S., & Thorsen, E. (2009). *Citizen journalism: Global perspectives* (Vol. 1). New York, NY: Peter Lang.

Andrea, H. T., & Nicolas, J. L. (2014). Crowdsourcing investigations: Crowd participation in identifying the bomb and bomber from the Boston marathon bombing. *International Journal of Information Systems for Crisis Response and Management (IJISCRAM)*, *6*(4), 60–75.

Atmore, C. (2012). What price a woman's life? *Australian Options*, *71*, 27–29.

Ball, J., & Lewis, P. (2011, December 8). Twitter and the riots: How the news spread, *The Guardian*.

Bartels, L. (2013). Parole and parole authorities in Australia: A system in crisis? *Criminal Law Journal*, *37*(6), 357–376.

Baudains, P., Braithwaite, A., & Johnson, S. D. (2012). Spatial patterns in the 2011 London riots. *Policing: A Journal of Policy and Practice*, *7*(1), 21–31.

BBC Trending. (2015). How the Paris attacks unfolded on social media. Available at: www.bbc.com/news/blogs-trending-34836214 (last accessed 29 November 2017).

Benkler, Y. (2006). *The wealth of networks: How social production transforms markets and freedom*. New Haven, CT: Yale University Press.

Berkowitz, D. (1992). Who sets the media agenda? The ability of policymakers to determine news decisions. In J. D. Kennamer (Ed.), *Public opinion, the press and public policy*. Westport, CT: Greenwood Publishing Group.

Blair, K. (2011, August 12). London turns to social media after riots, *AdWeek*.

Blanchard, E. B., Kuhn, E., Rowell, D. L., Hickling, E. J., Wittrock, D., Rogers, R. L., & Steckler, D. C. (2004). Studies of the vicarious traumatization of college students by the September 11th attacks: Effects of proximity, exposure and connectedness. *Behavior Research and Therapy*, *42*(2), 191–205.

Broersma, M., & Graham, T. (2012). Social media as beat. *Journalism Practice*, *6*(3), 403–419.

Broersma, M., & Graham, T. (2013). Twitter as a news source. *Journalism Practice*, *7*(4), 446–464.

Brownstein, J. S., Freifeld, C. C., & Madoff, L. C. (2009). Digital disease detection—Harnessing the web for public health surveillance. *New England Journal of Medicine*, *360*(21), 2153–2157.

Bruno, N. (2011). *Tweet first, verify later? How real-time information is changing the coverage of worldwide crisis events*. Oxford: Reuters Institute for the Study of Journalism, University of Oxford. Available at https://reutersinstitute.politics.ox.ac.uk/our-research/tweet-first-verify-later-how-real-time-information-changing-coverage-worldwide-crisis (last accessed 29 November 2017).

Bruns, A. (2005). *Gatewatching: Collaborative online news production*. New York, NY: Peter Lang.

Bucci, N. (2017, February 9 2017). Police seek Facebook tip to Gargasoulas' actions on day before Bourke St tragedy. Available at: www.theage.com.au/victoria/police-seek-facebook-tip-to-gargasoulas-actions-on-day-before-bourke-st-tragedy-20170209-gu94p9.html (last accessed 29 November 2017).

Butler, D. (2013). When Google got flu wrong. *Nature*, *494*(7436), 155.

Byrne, D. N. (2013). Digilantes and the frontier of radical justice online. *Radical History Review*, (117), 70–82.

Cassa, C. A., Chunara, R., Mandl, K., & Brownstein, J. S. (2013). Twitter as a sentinel in emergency situations: Lessons from the Boston marathon explosions. *PLoS Currents*, 5.

Castells, M. (2012). *Networks of outrage and hope: Social movements in the internet age*. Cambridge: Polity Press.

CBS News. (2013, April 17). Boston Marathon bombing victims. Available at: www.cbsnews.com/pictures/boston-marathon-bombing-victims/ (last accessed 29 November 2017).

Chunara, R., Andrews, J. R., & Brownstein, J. S. (2012). Social and news media enable estimation of epidemiological patterns early in the 2010 Haitian cholera outbreak. *The American Journal of Tropical Medicine and Hygiene*, *86*(1), 39–45.

Comer, J. S., DeSerisy, M., & Grief Green, J. (2016). Caregiver reports of internet exposure and posttraumatic stress among Boston-area youth following the 2013 marathon bombing. *Evidence-Based Practice in Child and Adolescent Mental Health*, *1*(2–3), 86–102.

Comor, E. (2010). Contextualizing and critiquing the fantastic prosumer: Power, alienation and hegemony. *Critical Sociology*, *37*(3), 309–327.

Crump, J. (2011). What are the police doing on Twitter? Social media, the police and the public. *Policy & Internet*, *3*(4), 1–27.

Culotta, A. (2010). *Towards detecting influenza epidemics by analyzing Twitter messages*. Paper presented at the Proceedings of the First Workshop on Social Media Analytics, Washington, DC.

Dayan, D., & Katz, E. (1992). *Media events: The live broadcasting of history*. Cambridge, MA: Harvard University Press.

Declich, S., & Carter, A. O. (1994). Public health surveillance: Historical origins, methods and evaluation. *Bulletin of the World Health Organization*, *72*(2), 285.

Denef, S., Bayerl, P. S., & Kaptein, N. A. (2013). *Social media and the police: Tweeting practices of British police forces during the August 2011 riots*. Paper presented at the Proceedings of the SIGCHI Conference on Human Factors in Computing Systems, Paris, France.

Ellis, J., & McGovern, A. (2016). The end of symbiosis? Australia police–media relations in the digital age. *Policing and Society*, *26*(8), 944–962.

Facebook. (2015). Paris terror attacks – facebook safety check. Available at: www.facebook.com/safetycheck/paris_terror_attacks (last accessed 29 November 2017).

French National Assembly. (2016). Board of inquiry report, No. 3922. Paris. 25 August, 2017. Available at: www.assemblee-nationale.fr/14/rap-enq/r3922-t2.asp (last accessed 29 November 2017).

Gao, H., Barbier, G., & Goolsby, R. (2011). Harnessing the crowdsourcing power of social media for disaster relief. *IEEE Intelligent Systems*, *26*(3), 10–14.

Garfin, D. R., Holman, E. A., & Silver, R. C. (2015). Cumulative exposure to prior collective trauma and acute stress responses to the Boston marathon bombings. *Psychological Science*, *26*(6), 675–683.

Gerbaudo, P. (2012). *Tweets and the streets. Social media and contemporary activism*. London: Pluto Press.

Ghonim, W. (2012). *Revolution 2.0. The power of the people is greater than the people in power. A memoir*. New York: Houghton Mifflin Harcourt.

Goel, V., & Ember, S. (2015). As Paris terror attacks unfolded, social media tools offered help in crisis, *New York Times*. Available at: www.nytimes.com/2015/11/15/technology/as-paris-terror-attacks-unfolded-social-media-tools-offered-help-in-crisis.html?mcubz=0 (last accessed 29 November 2017).

Goode, L. (2009). Social news, citizen journalism and democracy. *New Media & Society*, *11*(8), 1287–1305.

Gottehrer, G. (2015). Connected discovery: What the ubiquity of digital evidence means for lawyers and litigation. *Richmond Journal of Law & Technology*, *22*(3), 1–27.

Greer, C. (2007). News media, victims and crime. In P. Davies, P. Francis, & C. Greer (Eds.), *Victims, crime and society*. London: Sage.

Greer, C. (2012). *Sex crime and the media*. London: Routledge.

Hepp, A., & Couldry, N. (2010). Introduction: Media events in globalized media cultures. In N. Couldry, A. Hepp, & F. Krotz (Eds.), *Media events in a global age*. Abingdon: Routledge.

Hermida, A. (2010). Twittering the news: The emergence of ambient journalism. *Journalism Practice*, *4*(3), 297–308.

Hess, K., & Waller, L. (2014). The digital pillory: Media shaming of 'ordinary' people for minor crimes. *Continuum, 28*(1), 101–111.

Hogg, R. (2013). Punishment and 'the people': Rescuing populism from its critics. In K. Carrington, M. Ball, E. O'Brien, & J. Tauri (Eds.), *Crime, justice and social democracy: International perspectives*. Basingstoke: Palgrave Macmillan.

Huey, L., Nhan, J., & Broll, R. (2013). 'Uppity civilians' and 'cyber-vigilantes': The role of the general public in policing cyber-crime. *Criminology & Criminal Justice, 13*(1), 81–97.

Innes, M. (2004). Signal crimes and signal disorders: Notes on deviance and communicative action. *The British Journal of Sociology, 55*(3), 335–355.

Innes, M., Roberts, C., Preece, A., & Rogers, D. (2016). Ten "Rs" of social reaction: Using social media to analyse the "post-event" impacts of the murder of Lee Rigby. *Terrorism and Political Violence*, 30(3), 454–474. doi:10.1080/09546553.2016.1180289.

Intravia, J., Wolff, K. T., Paez, R., & Gibbs, B. R. (2017). Investigating the relationship between social media consumption and fear of crime: A partial analysis of mostly young adults. *Computers in Human Behavior, 77*, 158–168.

Jane, E. A. (2017). Feminist digilante responses to a slut-shaming on Facebook. *Social Media + Society, 3*(2).

Jewkes, Y. (2011). *Media & crime* (2nd ed.). London: SAGE.

Kang, J. (2013). Should Reddit be blamed for the spreading of a smear? *New York Times Magazine*, 25.

Kerr, O. S. (2005). Digital evidence and the new criminal procedure. *Columbia Law Review, 105*(1), 279–318.

Koblin, J. (2015). News media scrambles to cover paris shootings. *New York Times*. Available at www.nytimes. com/2015/11/15/business/media/paris-shooting-attacks-news-media-coverage.html (last accessed 29 November 2017).

Kotz, D. (2013). Health officials revise downward the number of injured in bombings to 264. Available at: www. bostonglobe.com/lifestyle/health-wellness/2013/04/23/boston-health-officials-revise-downward-number-injured-bombings/FT4QdismqFWr6pP23Y10qI/story.html (last accessed 29 November 2017).

Kort-Butler, L. A., & Habecker, P. (2017). Framing and cultivating the story of crime: The effects of media use, victimization, and social networks on attitudes about crime. *Criminal Justice Review*. Advance online publication. doi: 10.1177/0734016817710696.

Lee, M., & McGovern, A. (2014). *Policing and the media: Public relations, simulations and communications*. London: Routledge.

Levy, P. (1997). *Collective Intelligence*. New York, NY: Plenium Trade.

Lewis, P. (2011). Tottenham riots: a peaceful protest, then suddenly all hell broke loose. Available at www.the-guardian.com/uk/2011/aug/07/tottenham-riots-peaceful-protest (last accessed 29 November 2017).

Liu, B. F., Fraustino, J. D. & Jin, Y. (2016). Social Media Use During Disasters: How Information Form and Source Influence Intended Behavioural Response. *Communication Research, 43*(5), 626–646.

Little, J. M. (2015). Jill Meagher CCTV: Gothic tendencies in narratives of violence and gender justice. *Feminist Media Studies, 15*(3), 397–410.

Magdy, W., Darwish, K., & Abokhodair, N. (2015). Quantifying public response towards Islam on Twitter after Paris attacks. arXiv preprint arXiv:1512.04570.

McCombs, M. E., & Shaw, D. L. (1972). The agenda-setting function of the mass media. *Public Opinion Quaterly, 36*(2), 176–187.

McGovern, A. (2011). *Tweeting the news: Criminal justice agencies and their use of social networking sites*. Presented at Australia and New Zealand Critical Criminology Conference. Sydney, Australia.

McGuire, M. (2012). *Technology, Crime and Justice: The Question Concerning Technomia*. London: Routledge.

Milivojevic, S., & McGovern, A. (2014). The death of Jill Meagher: Crime and punishment on social media. *International Journal for Crime, Justice and Social Democracy, 3*(3), 22–39.

Moon, S. J., & Hadley, P. (2014). Routinizing a new technology in the newsroom: Twitter as a news source in mainstream media. *Journal of Broadcasting & Electronic Media, 58*(2), 289–305.

Mortensen, M. (2015). Conflictual media events, eyewitness image, and the Boston marathon bombing (2013). *Journalism Practice, 9*(4), 536–551.

Moskowitz, E. (2014). Long after Marathon blasts, survivor loses leg. Available at www.bostonglobe.com/metro/2014/11/11/long-after-marathon-bombings-survivor-loses-leg/urutULO5K3H33jlOGoLiNI/story.html (last accessed 29 November 2017).

Nakamura, L. (2014). 'I WILL DO EVERYthing That Am Asked': Scambaiting, digital show-space, and the racial violence of social media. *Journal of Visual Culture, 13*(3), 257–274.

Newburn, T. (2011). Reading the riots. *British Society of Criminology Newsletter, 69*(Winter), 12–14.

Nhan, J., Huey, L., & Broll, R. (2017). Digilantism: An analysis of crowdsourcing and the Boston marathon bombings. *The British Journal of Criminology, 57*(2), 341–361.

Olteanu, A., Vieweg, S., & Castillo, C. (2015). *What to expect when the unexpected happens: Social media communications across crises.* Paper presented at the Proceedings of the 18th ACM Conference on Computer Supported Cooperative Work & Social Computing, Vancouver, BC, Canada.

Palen, L., & Anderson, K. M. (2016). Crisis informatics—New data for extraordinary times. *Science, 353*(6296), 224–225.

Panagiotopoulos, P., Bigdeli, A. Z., & Sams, S. (2014). Citizen–government collaboration on social media: The case of Twitter in the 2011 riots in England. *Government Information Quarterly, 31*(3), 349–357.

Paulussen, S., & Harder, R. A. (2014). Social media references in newspapers. *Journalism Practice, 8*(5), 542–551.

Peelo, M. (2006). Framing homicide narratives in newspapers: Mediated witness and the construction of virtual victimhood. *Crime, Media, Culture, 2*(2), 159–175.

Powell, A., Overington, C., & Hamilton, G. (2017). Following #JillMeagher: Collective meaning-making in response to crime events via social media. *Crime, Media, Culture.* Advance online publication. doi:10.1177/1741659017721276.

Préfecture de police. (2015). Available at: www.twitter.com/prefpolice/status/665297982607261696 (last accessed 29 November 2017).

Procter, R., Crump, J., Karstedt, S., Voss, A., & Cantijoch, M. (2013). Reading the riots: What were the police doing on Twitter? *Policing and Society, 23*(4), 413–436.

Procter, R., Vis, F., & Voss, A. (2013). Reading the riots on Twitter: Methodological innovation for the analysis of big data. *International Journal of Social Research Methodology, 16*(3), 197–214.

Quilter, J. (2012). Responses to the death of Thomas Kelly: Taking populism seriously. *Current Issues in Criminal Justice, 24*(3), 439–448.

Quilter, J. (2014). Populism and criminal justice policy: An Australian case study of non-punitive responses to alcohol-related violence. *Australian & New Zealand Journal of Criminology, 48*(1), 24–52.

Quilter, J. (2015). Populism and criminal justice policy: An Australian case study of non-punitive responses to alcohol-related violence. *Australian and New Zealand Journal of Criminology, 48*(1), 24–52.

Ritzer, G., & Jurgenson, N. (2010). Production, consumption, prosumption. *Journal of Consumer Culture, 10*(1), 13–36.

Rogstad, I. (2016). Is Twitter just rehashing? Intermedia agenda-setting between Twitter and mainstream media. *Journal of Information Technology & Politics, 13*(2), 142–158.

Rutkin, A. (2015). It's a fitbit, your honour. *New Scientist, 225*(3002), 17.

Santillana, M., Zhang, D. W., Althouse, B. M., & Ayers, J. W. (2014). What can digital disease detection learn from (an external revision to) Google Flu Trends? *American Journal of Preventive Medicine, 47*(3), 341–347.

Scaife, L. (2017). *Social networks as the new frontier of terrorism: #Terror.* Abingdon: Routledge.

Scheufele, D., & Tewksbury, D. (2007). Framing, agenda setting, and priming: The evolution of three media effects models. *Journal of Communication, 57*(1), 9–20.

Schneider, C. J. (2016). *Policing and social media: Social control in an era of new media.* London: Lexington Books.

Schneider, C. J., & Trottier, D. (2012). The 2011 Vancouver riot and the role of Facebook in crowd-sourced policing. *BC Studies, 175,* 57–72.

Schneider, C. J., & Trottier, D. (2013). Social media and the 2011 Vancouver riot. In *40th anniversary of studies in symbolic interaction* (Vol. *40*, pp. 335–362). Emerald Group Publishing Limited.

Schuster, M. A., Stein, B. D., Jaycox, L. H., Collins, R. L., Marshall, G. N., Elliott, M. N., & Berry, S. H. (2001). A national survey of stress reactions after the September 11, 2001, terrorist attacks. *New England Journal of*

Medicine, 345(20), 1507–1512.

Soothill, K. (1998). Armchair detectives and armchair thieves. *The Police Journal, 71*(2), 155–159.

Soothill, K., Peelo, M., & Francis, B. (2002). Homicide and the media: Identifying the top case in the times. *The Howard Journal of Crime and Justice, 41*(5), 401–421.

Sorcher, S. (2015). The battle between Washington and Silicon Valley over encryption. Available at: www.csmonitor.com/World/Passcode/2015/0707/The-battle-between-Washington-and-Silicon-Valley-over-encryption (last accessed 29 November 2017).

Starbird, K., Maddock, J., Orand, M., Achterman, P., & Mason, R. M. (2014). Rumors, false flags, and digital vigilantes: Misinformation on Twitter after the 2013 Boston marathon bombing. *iConference 2014 Proceedings.* pp. 654–662. doi:10.9776/14308.

Sutton, J. N., Palen, L., & Shklovski, I. (2008). Backchannels on the front lines: Emergency uses of social media in the 2007 Southern California Wildfires. Proceedings of the 5th International ISCRAM Conference, Washington, DC.

Sutton, J., Spiro, E. S., Johnson, B., Fitzhugh, S., Gibson, B. & Butts, C. T. (2014). Warning tweets: Serial transmission of messages during the warning phase of a disaster event. *Communication & Society, 17*(6), 765–787.

Tapia, A. H., LaLone, N. J., & Kim, H. W. (2014). Run amok: Group crowd participation in identifying the bomb and bomber from the Boston marathon bombing. *Proceedings of the 11th International ISCRAM Conference,* University Park, Pennsylvania.

The Guardian & London School of Economics. (2011). Reading the riots: Investigating England's summer of disorder. *The Guardian.* Available at: www.theguardian.com/info/2011/dec/15/reading-the-riots-ebook (last accessed 29 November 2017).

Thompson, J. D. & Louise, R. (2014). Sexed violence and its (dis)appearances: Media coverage surrounding the murders of Jill Meagher and Johanna Martin. *Outskirts, 31*, 1–10.

Tonkin, E., Pfeiffer, H. D., & Tourte, G. (2012). Twitter, information sharing and the London riots? *Bulletin of the American Society for Information Science and Technology, 38*(2), 49–57.

Trottier, D. (2014). Police and user-led investigations on social media. *Journal of Law, Information, 23*(1), 75–96.

Trottier, D. (2017). Digital vigilantism as weaponisation of visibility. *Philosophy & Technology, 30*(1), 55–72.

Vis, F. (2013). Twitter as a tool for reporting breaking news. *Digital Journalism, 1*(1), 27–47.

Williams, B. A., & Delli Carpini, M. X. (2004). Monica and Bill all the time and everywhere: The collapse of gatekeeping and agenda setting in the new media environment. *American Behavioral Scientist, 47*(9), 1208–1230.

Williams, M. L., Burnap, P., & Sloan, L. (2017). Crime sensing with big data: The affordances and limitations of using open-source communications to estimate crime patterns. *The British Journal of Criminology, 57*(2), 320–340.

Yardley, E., Lynes, A. G. T., Wilson, D., & Kelly, E. (2016). What's the deal with 'websleuthing'? News media representations of amateur detectives in networked spaces. *Crime, Media, Culture, 14*(1), 81–109.

Yates, D., & Paquette, S. (2011). Emergency knowledge management and social media technologies: A case study of the 2010 Haitian earthquake. *International Journal of Information Management, 31*(1), 6–13.

5

LIMINAL IMAGES

Criminality, Victimisation and Voyeurism

Introduction

On a Saturday night in August 2013, two young men, Trent Mays and Ma'lik Richmond, sexually assaulted a 16-year-old woman. According to court reports, one of the men had sent pictures and text messages from his iPhone, including one of the young woman naked and unconscious with what appears to be semen on her chest (Ohio Court of Common Pleas, 2012). Mays and Richmond, both also 16 and players on the high school football team, would later be charged and found guilty of rape. Mays would also be charged and found guilty of dissemination of child pornography in relation to images that were taken and distributed of the sexual assault (Oppel, 2013). Several witnesses had also taken images that they subsequently shared with others via mobile phone, email and social media. In addition to the images themselves, the perpetrators, witnesses and their peers posted commentary minimizing the rape, as well as laughing at and blaming the victim. In one photograph, Mays and Richmond are seen carrying the clearly unconscious young woman by her wrists and her ankles, as her hair trails on the floor. The image, posted on Instagram by an ex-boyfriend of the victim, Cody Saltsman, was accompanied by a tweet: 'Never seen anything this sloppy lol' (Levy, 2013). Others who heard of the rape joined in on the public commentary by posting vicious tweets about the victim, including: 'Whores are hilarious', 'If they're getting "raped" and don't resist then to me it's not rape', and 'Song of the night is definitely Rape Me by Nirvana' (see Powell, 2015). Meanwhile, a friend of the young men who perpetrated the assault, Michael Nodianos, was recorded that same night laughing hysterically along with his peers about the rape, describing the unconscious young woman as 'dead' and saying 'there isn't any foreplay with a dead girl' and 'she's dead-er than OJ's wife' (Levy, 2013). In the background of the video, which was uploaded to YouTube, one of the young men can be heard saying 'That's not cool bro. That's like rape . . . they could go to jail' (Baker, 2013). But the group keeps laughing throughout the 12 minute video, as Michael continues saying 'she is so raped' and 'they raped her quicker than Mike Tyson', among other remarks. The cameraman can also be heard laughing and saying 'I'm gonna watch this every single day'. Given the nature of social networking, it is not surprising, though nonetheless distressing, that the victim herself was very much aware of what was being said about her and the sexual assault that she had experienced. According to media reports, she tweeted, 'I will officially never be able to trust a boy ever again,' and, "If someone is dangerously inebriated you help them out not take advantage of them . . .' and, 'Please everyone just drop it' (Levy, 2013). The images, video and remarks posted online suggest that the young men involved clearly understood that a sexual crime had been committed; they just didn't care — or didn't think anyone else would take it seriously.

That night in Steubenville, Ohio (United States), was not the first time, and nor would it be the last, that images of rape were taken by perpetrators and witnesses of the crime, then distributed via social media. Indeed, the distribution of images of violent crime by offenders themselves, as well as witnesses, peers and a wider public, has increased in prominence over the last ten years; arguably shifting in nature along with shifts in the digital tools available and emerging technosocial practices. There are a wide range of examples of crimes being recorded and/or distributed by offenders them-selves, by peers and participatory bystanders, by non-offending eye-witnesses (as discussed in Chapter 4) and through citizen surveillance by police and other agents of the state. Such images are liminal because they are often situated at the boundaries between *criminality* and *legality*: the image itself may be criminal (such as in existing crimes of child exploitation material and emerging crimes of image-based abuse) or legally understood only as the depiction or evidence of a crime. Images may also be taken either with the purpose of, or at least the effect of, extending the harms to those depicted (such as by harassing and blaming a victim, as described above) or, alternately, documenting such harms for the purposes of justice (whether formal or informal, as discussed in Chapter 7). Moreover, such thresholds of harmful, or 'just', purposes and effects are not fixed but malleable and may change as the images shift between contexts and audiences. As such, many images of crime taken in the moment, or used in practices of deviance and/or the facilitation of further harms, arguably exist in a space between criminality, on one hand, and 'justice', on the other. These criminal, and sometimes liminal, images are furthermore characteristic of the everyday forms of image-based communications that are typical of digital society. This chapter examines the implications of such liminal images in crime, criminality and justice in a digital society. In doing so, the chapter focuses on two key questions: How are digital images being used in the perpetration and aftermath of crimes, particularly violent crimes? And how can we understand these practices, and their potential effects, in the broader con-text of image-sharing and image-based communications in digital society? In exploring these key questions, the chapter draws on case study examples that exemplify differing technosocial practices: in particular, the taking and distribution of sexual assault and other crime 'selfie' images.

When Crime Goes Viral: Sexual Offending and Other Criminal 'Selfies'

Once, the mainstream news media had effectively a monopoly on the photographic and video imagery of real crimes; this has fundamentally changed in the context of digital society.

In 2006, in Melbourne, Australia, 12 teenage boys aged between 15 and 17 years and calling themselves the 'teenage kings of Werribee', filmed the sexual assault of a 16-year-old woman. The video showed the young men raping and sexually assaulting the victim, urinating on her, setting her hair on fire and kicking her clothes into a nearby river. The young men edited and produced a DVD of the assault with the title 'Cunt: The Movie', in which they can be heard saying: 'What the fuck, she's the ugliest thing I've ever seen,' and, 'Everyone's scared to go first, they don't want any diseases' (Powell, 2010; Powell & Henry, 2017; Yar, 2012). The 'Werribee DVD' was initially sold in local high schools for $5 and later emerged for sale on internet sites for up to $60; with excerpts also made freely available on YouTube (Powell, 2010). According to media reports, it took YouTube approximately three months to remove the video excerpts, with estimates that they had been viewed at least 9000 times (Ziffer, 2006). At the trial and sentencing of the young men responsible, the victim said she was terrified that she would be recognised in public after the distribution of the video and that her life had 'been changed forever' (Medew, 2007).

Yet, it was in 2013 that the distribution of sexual assault images and the associated harassment of victim-survivors gained widespread media attention. Such was the case in Dartmouth, Canada, where 17-year-old Rehteah Parsons took her own life after two years of harassment following the distribution of an image of her sexual assault via social media (Dodge, 2016). Meanwhile, in San Jose, USA, 15-year-old Audrie Pott was sexually assaulted by three boys at a party, who wrote harassing comments on her body with a marker and distributed a photo on social media (Dodge, 2016). Pott, too, took her own life after ongoing harassment in relation to the image. Also in 2013, this time in Auckland, New Zealand, a group of young men calling themselves the 'Roast Busters' intoxicated underage girls, gang raped them and took photos and videos of the rapes, which they posted on Facebook (Powell & Henry, 2017; Sills et al., 2016). Finally, in a case that appears to parallel that in Steubenville (Ohio, USA), four Vanderbilt University footballers have been charged after allegedly gang-raping an unconscious young woman in a campus dormitory. According to media reports, the men took photos and videos of the assault and sent them on to three other men — who have been charged with 'tampering with electronic evidence' for allegedly deleting the photos rather than cooperating with the police investigation (Culp-Ressler, 2013). Since that time, numerous cases involving sexual offenders taking and distributing images of sexual assault have been reported in the news media (Wellman, Reddington, & Clark, 2017). As we wrote this book, the rape of a 15-year-old girl by multiple perpetrators was streamed on Facebook Live and shared via Facebook Messenger (Gallardo, 2017). It is estimated at least 40 people viewed the live video before it was taken down; and yet no one reported the crime to police.

While such examples might be dismissed as rare exceptions in the practices of sexual violence, emerging evidence suggests that, in fact, amateur images taken at the time of an offence, whether they be live-streamed, video or photographs, are increasingly featuring in the perpetration of 'everyday' sexual violence. For example, in a 2015 issue of *Strategies: The Prosecutors' Newsletter on Violence Against Women* (US), Attorney Advisor Jane Anderson argues that 'image exploitation' is becoming increasingly common in sexual assault cases (Redden, 2016). Empirical studies are few and far between, though one survey of approximately 3000 Australian adults found that between 8 and 10% reported ever experiencing an unwanted sexual incident where an image (photo or video) was also taken and/or sent onto others (Powell & Henry, 2016a). In a related qualitative study, meanwhile, interviews with Australian police and other legal stakeholders suggested that images taken by offenders were becoming a common feature of reported sexual assaults (Powell & Henry, 2016b). Meanwhile, a separate study by Norwegian criminologists Sveinung Sandberg and Thomas Ugelvik (2016) analysed court decisions that described offenders taking images as part of the offence. They found that a majority of such cases involved sexual violence, including multiple and individual perpetrator sexual assaults and other instances of sexual abuse, which were photographed or filmed by perpetrators (Sandberg & Ugelvik, 2016). While it is difficult to gauge the true extent of such sexual assault imagery, it seems apparent that the practice extends well beyond the growing number of high-profile cases reported in the mainstream media.

More recently — indeed, in the last year alone — a series of other violent crimes have been covered by the mainstream news media, in which the incidents were live-filmed by offenders, apparently with the intention that they be viewed by a broad social media audience. Among them was the live broadcast in April 2017 by a man in Thailand as he killed his baby daughter before committing suicide, with the content reportedly being available to view for 24 hours before being taken down (Solon, 2017). Ten days earlier, some Facebook users witnessed the killing of Robert Godwin Snr (74 years), on Easter Sunday 16 April 2017, by Steve Stephens (37 years) in Cleveland, USA. Stephens broadcast live his intention to kill someone, before recording and uploading the act itself. 'I found somebody I'm about to kill,' Stephens said, as he pulled his vehicle up next to his victim, got out and shot him. According to media reports, the video continued to be viewable on Facebook for almost three hours before it was removed (Dreyfuss, 2017). Later that day, Stephens broadcast a live confession before he was found dead, having taken his own life (Crossley, 2017). Facebook apparently had not foreseen that its powerful new tool would be used for the live-streaming of very serious, violent crimes, including both rape and murder. The social media giant was reportedly ill-prepared for the content monitoring and curation that would be required (Dreyfuss, 2017).

Understanding the Sociality of Image-based Practices

As already identified in Chapter 2, several of the key features of digital society — including perpetual contact (Katz & Aakhus, 2002), the production–consumption nexus (or 'prosumption'), 'ubiquitous photography' and a blurring of public and private life — are themselves further enabled by the increasingly high-quality cameras integrated into smartphones. These camera and internet-enabled devices are carried about as a kind of 'social and cognitive prosthetic device' (Shanks & Svabo, 2014, p. 2): an extension of our embodied selves. It is through these technologies, as well as shifting social practices surrounding their use, that the spontaneous taking, sharing and redistribution of images of everyday life have become a normal part of the infrastructure and content of 'the digital superpublic' (Senft & Baym, 2015, p. 1589; Shanks & Svabo, 2014; van House, 2011). Indeed, like social media and user-generated content generally, some scholars suggest a democratising effect of widespread accessibility to cameras and internet-enabled devices in the palm of (almost) every hand; enabling citizen journalists to capture news and events that might otherwise go unreported (Allan & Peters, 2015; Gorin, 2015; Reading, 2011).

At the same time, the omnipresence of the camera-phone and associated image-sharing via social media has arguably extended the global mass media 'spectacle' (Couldry, Hepp & Krotz, 2009). Drawing on social theorist Guy Debord's (1967) *Society of the Spectacle*, media and cultural scholars have problematised the capitalist motives of mass media in representing news, events and information in spectacular form for the purpose of maintaining audience attention (and therefore advertising revenue) for as long as possible in an increasingly competitive global and 24/7 marketplace (Kellner, 2004, 2010). In the context of citizen-journalism, and the digital photographs made available by everyday participants and witnesses to extraordinary events, the spectacle has taken on new forms. While the mass media spectacle may come to a close, the record is preserved through multiple digital archives of images and first-hand accounts on social media and other content-sharing platforms, enabling an ongoing witnessing, memorialisation and citizen participation through revisiting the content and through its redistribution. Thus, the digitised spectacle allows unending vicarious experiencing of traumatic public events repeatedly over both distance and time (as discussed in Chapter 4).

In addition to communicating, and indeed reliving, public events, images have also become a central way in which we communicate personally. Through sharing images of ourselves and our daily lives, we engage in practices of self-identity, self-representation and relationality (Lee, 2016; van House, 2011) and tell 'visual stories' about our experiences (Shanks & Svabo, 2014, p. 1). Such 'visual conversations' (Katz & Crocker, 2017) are replacing, to a large extent, the written self-narratives of the pre-digital age. The visual is becoming so embedded in contemporary digital society that personal photographs are becoming more prolific, public and transitory — shifting in function from tools of memorialisation of significant people and events, to tools of instant and frequent communication of the mundane and the everyday (Shanks & Svabo, 2014; van House, 2011).

There has simultaneously been both celebration and denigration of the social function of the 'selfie' as a form of visual conversation in particular. Selfies, and to a lesser extent 'groupies', have been blamed for everything from youthful narcissism (Weiser, 2015), to low self-esteem and poor mental well-being (Wang, Yang, & Haigh, 2017), to reproducing harmful gender, race and class stereotypes (Senft & Baym, 2015; Williams & Marquez, 2015). Many selfies are undeniably purposefully curated: a tool in the social media practice of representing a partial and carefully constructed identity, with not all images 'making the cut' (Warfield, 2016). Certainly, selfies and groupies alike continue to represent aspects of the self-representation, family and friendship portraits, holiday snaps and significant life events that have typified the social practices of photography generally (van House, 2011). Perhaps more positively, self-images have also featured in counter-cultural practices of resistance to dominant social norms (Albury, 2015) and in digital activism (discussed further in Chapter 8). At the same, 'images can be made any time, any place, without prior planning ... support[ing] spontaneous, opportunistic image-making and experimentation' (Shanks & Svabo, 2014). Visual communication in digital society provides ample opportunity for immediate, unreflexive, 'in the moment' images to be taken and instantly shared.

The immediacy of visual communication has furthermore been examined by some media scholars as reflective of the spatial and embodied experience of both the production and consumption of self images in digital society (Pink, 2011). As communications scholar Paul Frosh (2015) identifies, there is a 'corporeal sociability' to the production and exchange of selfies; an invitation to one's network to share in a moment located in a particular time and place, as well as an invitation for viewers to respond not merely through 'likes' and comments but also through taking reaction selfies. Personal photography is increasingly 'live'; representing a real-time exchange between users in a network and, in doing so, simultaneously creating temporal and spatial connections that oscillate between 'now' and 'then', as well as 'here' and 'there' (Frosh, 2015).

The offering of video live-streaming tools within social media platforms is perhaps an inevitable development in the temporality and spatiality of visual communication. When launching *Facebook Live* on 6 April 2016, CEO Mark Zuckerberg described the live-streaming video application in this way:

> Live is like having a TV camera in your pocket. Anyone with a phone now has the power to broadcast to anyone in the world. When you interact live, you feel connected in a more personal way. This is a big shift in how we communicate, and it's going to create new opportunities for people to come together.
>
> (Zuckerberg, 2016)

The ability to broadcast live video was not itself new: Meerkat, Periscope and Facebook's earlier 'Mentions' service for premium users have allowed live video streaming since at least 2010. Yet, the uptake of Facebook is such that any new tool integrated for general users into the near-ubiquitous social media platform quite literally puts new technosocial practices at the fingertips of millions of citizens globally.

Among the first viral videos streamed on Facebook Live was that of a 37-year-old Texan woman, Candace Payne, demonstrating a mask of the Star Wars character Chewbacca, which roars every time the wearer opens their mouth, that she had bought for her son. The video, shared on 19 May 2016 and also known as the 'Chewbacca Mask Lady', live-streamed approximately three minutes of Candace in fits of giggles, interrupted by periodic Chewbacca 'roars' (BBC, 2016; Hern, 2017). As described by journalist for *The Guardian* Alex Hern (2017):

> In some ways, Payne's video set the precedent for how Live videos would evolve. For one thing, although the video was broadcast live, the overwhelming majority of its viewers came long after she had put the phone down and stopped broadcasting.

Indeed, it is largely through the function of Facebook's 'likes' and algorithms that content attracting user views and attention is rapidly pushed out through the social network to maximise user engagement and, in turn, advertising dollar potential (Bucher, 2017). In effect, it is a combination of human and technical agency that determines which content goes 'viral'.

Media scholar Nancy van House (2011), meanwhile, further suggests that images are not mere tools of human agency, but rather form part of a complex socio-technical system of human and non-human agents. Van House extends the work of Bruno Latour (1996, 2005), by suggesting that images such as photographs are not simply intermediaries, communicating or carrying a meaning as intended by human actants. Instead, such images:

> . . . often transform the meaning they are supposedly carrying. Photographs have always had the ability to convey a meaning other than the owner intended. Their meanings may change over time, for different viewers, in different contexts, in different associations with text and other images . . . photographs are potent agents of memory, relationship, self-presentation and self-expression across space and time, non-humans that are critical elements of important human activities.
>
> (van House, 2011, p. 132)

Likewise, technology researchers Theresa Senft and Nancy Baym (2015) describe the taking and sharing of selfies, in particular, as both photographic *objects* and a social *practice*. Selfies, as a gesture, not only may be intended to send different messages to different audiences but also 'may be dampened, amplified, or modified, by social media censorship, social censure, misreading of the sender's original intent, or adding additional gestures to the mix, such as likes, comments and remixes' (Senft & Baym, 2015, p. 1589). Once selfies are shared within the 'digital superpublic' (Senft & Baym, 2015), they take on a life of their own in which the images themselves and the technologies that connect and distribute them — as well as the human actors who produce, view and reproduce them — all form part of a network of social relations: a 'selfie assemblage' (Hess, 2015). As we note in Chapter 2, criminology, and cybercriminologies in particular, have largely struggled to engage with such socio-technical concepts, particularly those concepts that fundamentally challenge analyses of offender agency and 'rational choice'. Yet, we would suggest that an analysis of 'criminal selfies' within a digital criminology requires a technosocial approach that brings some of these key concepts together with more established critical, cultural and emerging 'visual' criminologies.

A Technosocial Criminology of Crime Images

Cultural criminologists such as Hayward (2010) have alluded to the significance of the 'digital turn' (which we see as the broader 'digital society') in socio-cultural representations of crime and considered the complexities of images as both producers and reproducers of meanings about crime. Much cultural criminology has focused on the ways images of crime, criminality and criminals are produced and represented in news media, fiction and popular culture (Ferrell, Hayward, Morrison, & Presdee, 2004). Yet an emerging sub-field of visual criminology explores the increasingly blurred distinction between 'real' and 'imagined' images of crime in digital society:

> While mug shots, surveillance photographs, and newspaper pictures of notorious criminals have long featured as part of the 'spectacle' of crime and punishment . . . Today, as criminals videotape their crimes and post them on YouTube, as security agents scrutinize the image-making of criminals on millions of surveillance monitors around the world . . . as images of brutality and victimization pop up on office computer screens and children's mobile phones . . . instead of simply studying 'images' we need a new methodological orientation . . . to understand and identify the various ways in which mediated processes of visual production and cultural exchange now 'constitute' the experience of crime, self, and society.
>
> (Hayward, 2010, pp. 2–3)

Indeed, within cultural and visual criminologies, several themes emerge in the literature regarding the potential functions of images, which are applicable to our discussions here and which we explore further in the following section.

Extension of Harm

Few criminologists have specifically examined what appears to be a significant cultural trend: taking and distributing perpetrator and bystander imagery of sexual assault (Dodge, 2016 Powell, 2010; Powell & Henry, 2017; Sandberg & Ugelvik, 2016; Wellman, Reddington, & Clark, 2017; Yar, 2012, for exceptions). Indeed, the nature, impacts and broader socio-cultural influences of sexual assault imagery and its online distribution are currently under-examined. Yet, according to recent work by feminist criminologists, technosocial practices increasingly associated with sexual assault in digital society arguably both amplify the harms to individual victims and reproduce broader socio-cultural support of sexual violence (Powell & Henry, 2017).

Sandberg and Ugelvik (2016) provide an integrated digital criminological approach to understanding criminal images. In this notable paper, they examine offenders' own use of imagery in the commission of their crimes, including the perspective of the potential criminogenic role of images and offenders' motivations in taking them, as well as broader socio-cultural concerns about the images' impacts and interpretations. They note first that, of the cases studied where images were referred to as a feature of the crime, a majority were images of a sex crime and/or of a sexual nature; and, second, that most of the images of sexual assault were not shared beyond the offenders themselves. This is not to suggest that because the image has not (yet) been distributed it is necessarily any less harmful to victims; indeed, following feminist theorist Judith Butler (2007), Sandberg and Ugelvik (2016) argue that the act of recording the assault is itself a way to further humiliate and extend the harm towards the victim:

> Forcing the victim to pose in degrading positions for the camera and in front of everyone present is a way to demonstrate ultimate power. The victim has to suffer violence, threats and sexual abuse, and is also made aware that this is filmed. The cold, penetrating gaze of the camera lens is, in effect, like a 'double rape'. Victims have no control over the future dissemination of the footage. The result is that they not only must cope with the effects of the assault, but . . . 'a kind of promise that the event will continue' in other forms, 'an infinite reiteration of the abuse' . . .
>
> (p. 8, citing Butler, 2007, p. 959)

Their analysis echoes that of previous feminist criminological research which has identified the harms to victims of sexual violence when images are taken as part of the offence (Dodge, 2016; Powell, 2010). Perpetrators of rape have long used various strategies to intimidate, harass and humiliate their victims, and arguably to prolong the experience of power and entitlement; recording and distributing images of the rape may, in some cases, represent an extension of these practices. Certainly, for many victims, the impact is both one of extended humiliation (Dodge, 2016; Powell & Henry, 2016b) and, as Sandberg and Ugelvik (2016) suggest, a 'second assault'. Thus, the very taking of photographs or video of a sexual assault compounds the trauma of the violence; regardless of whether the images are then circulated or how widely they are shared.

Criminogenic Technosociality and Memetic Deviance

That perpetrators are recording and distributing images constituting evidence of, and in some cases admission to, their crime itself warrants further explanation. It seems illogical for perpetrators of crimes to document evidence of their offence, and even less logical to make such images public. For crimes of sexual violence, such imagery may be used to facilitate a just outcome by the state by presenting evidence not only that the rape occurred (the imagery may demonstrate the victims' non-consent, for example) but also evidence of the perpetrators' state of mind. There can be no question of an accused not knowing that there was not consent (the *mens rea* element of which many rape cases fail to convince a jury, Larcombe 2011) if a photograph shows the perpetrator penetrating a clearly unconscious victim or he was found to be boasting about the rape to his peers on Twitter, Facebook or Instagram. Not only is there the possibility of inadvertently assisting police but, with sexual offences (more so, perhaps, than other criminal selfies), offenders are also exposed to the potential social stigma of outing themselves as 'sexually deviant'. Yet sexual offences occupy a contradictory space within public discourse. While some perpetrators are vilified as 'monsters' of heinous crimes, all too often the harms of sex offending are minimised in news media and popular discourse, while victims are routinely treated with suspicion and invalidation (Daly, 2014; Waterhouse-Watson, 2014).

Criminologist Majid Yar (2012) makes a persuasive case for considering the impacts of images shared via social media as potentially themselves a *motivator* of criminality. In other words, emerging technosocial practices may become criminogenic to the extent that they play a key role in causing an individual or groups to engage in crime. In discussing the practice of 'happy slapping', for instance, Yar (2012, p. 252) argues that 'crucial to understanding this phenomenon is the role played by participants' desire to be seen, and esteemed or celebrated, by others for their criminal activities'. 'Happy slapping' refers to a physical assault upon an unsuspecting victim, which is video recorded and subsequently distributed among peers and/or via online video-sharing platforms such as YouTube (Palasinski, 2013; Powell, 2010). Though many examples typify the namesake and literally involve running past and slapping the victim, more extreme incidents have included grievous bodily harm, rape, arson and murder (Palasinski, 2013). While some scholars have pointed to the replication of popular television culture encapsulated by programmes such as *Jackass* and *Bumfights* (Willett, 2009) as a cause for the social media trend, Yar (2012) identifies a deeper motivation. Drawing on the example of the Australian Werribee DVD case (discussed above), Yar suggests the recording of the sexual assault was not merely a replication, nor an accidental circumstance, of the offence but rather a key driver and cause of it. He considers the very purposeful way in which the perpetrators recorded, edited and distributed the video imagery of their crime; selling the 'film' on DVD complete with a self-ascribed 'R' rating and credits that listed the 'actors' involved on the back cover (2012, p. 253).

Meanwhile, in a highly publicised 2015 case, images of the rape of a 16-year-old woman in Houston (Texas, USA) were circulated via social media; extending the harm experienced by the victim and possibly, following Yar (2012), playing a motivating role in the offence itself. However, in this case, the circulation of images by witnesses, peers and then a broader online community went even further: becoming the subject of an internet meme. As discussed in Chapter 2, internet memes can be understood as a unit of cultural imitation and transmission, serving as sites of collective cultural meaning-making. Some images may 'go viral', being viewed and redistributed throughout a network without significant change or adaptation (Shifman, 2012). A meme, however, encapsulates a different structure of participatory culture, inviting *'extensive creative user engagement* in the form of parody, pastiche, mash-ups or other derivative work' (Shifman, 2012, p. 190, emphasis in original). In this case, the 16-year-old had been sexually assaulted by several men during a house party. The original images, which showed the unconscious and half-naked victim sprawled on the floor after the assault, were subsequently mimicked by an online community who posted photos of themselves in similar positions; along with the hashtag #JadaPose (see Bates, 2014; Powell, 2015). The narrative ridiculing that accompanied the images, such as 'hit that' and #THOT ('that hoe over there', Bates, 2014), further marked the memes' function as communicating a collective social and cultural norm. The #JadaPose meme minimised the rape and humiliated the victim through a process of imitation and transmission that served to remake the meaning of the sexual assault into a prank or joke.

A further observable feature of such mediated engagements with crime in digital society, then, is a kind of *memetic deviance*. More than the traditional 'copy-cat' crime, which is similarly inspired by emulating crimes depicted in the media (Surette, 2002), we use memetic deviance to refer to the rapid replication of a deviant, sometimes criminal, practice through a social network. Within this concept, 'happy slapping', as discussed above, can be understood not merely as a desire to be seen and celebrated by a community of online peers but reflecting the social and participatory logics evident in the '. . . popularity of mimicking in contemporary digital culture' (Shifman, 2012). In other words, it is not just the representation of a deviant identity, or the status that may be associated with it, but also the pleasure of participating in a movement, a wave of activity, that is experienced collectively over time and place. Yet, such memetic deviance facilitates an amplification of harm — whether it is the harm to the ridiculed victim (as in #JadaPose), the escalation of assaults as the meme spreads (as in happy slapping) or the encouragement of dangerous risk-taking behaviours (such as in #NekNominate or #Planking).

Memetic deviance also functions to communicate social and cultural norms such as dominant masculinities, sexism and racism. Take, for example, a 2013 internet meme, #Trayvoning, where young white men posted photos of themselves mimicking the deceased body of 17-year-old Trayvon Martin, an African-American boy who was fatally shot by George Zimmerman, a nightwatchman who was later acquitted of murder, claiming that that he used lethal force in 'self-defence' against the unarmed boy. The case prompted public outrage and exacerbated already poor race relations in the United States, adding to a series of cases of brutality and misuse of force by police or other authorities towards African-American citizens (discussed further in Chapter 8). The function of the meme was not only to mock the unjust death of Trayvon but to further communicate racist norms, transforming the injustice into 'a spectacle of white pleasure that further denies the humanity of black people' (Guerrero & Leonard, 2012, n.p.). In each of these cases, the wider social gender and racial norms combined with the nature of media spectacle and lax law enforcement response to provide an inverse deterrent to offending. In other words, within the current social practice of how images are used within specific parts of digital society, there exists a perverse incentive to document and share one's crimes.

Mediated Witness and Speaking Truths?

Scholars such as Michelle Brown (2014), Eamonn Carrabine (2011, 2012, 2014) and Alison Young (2014) have taken the further step of examining offender motivations and spectator engagements with photographic and video images of crime — amateur images often taken by offenders themselves that capture moments in horrific violent and other offences. Such images, their work suggests, can still be understood in terms of cultural artefacts that represent crime and are, in turn, interpreted within broader socio-cultural discourses in response to crime: the dominant cultural criminological 'frame'. Importantly, they can also be understood within the social context that leads to images being taken during a violent crime in the first place, as well as the meanings and impacts of societal spectatorship and engagement when the images come to be viewed more broadly.

Carrabine (2011) presents a compelling and insightful analysis of images depicting the sexual abuse and torture of prisoners at Abu Ghraib. The amateur 'trophy' snapshots of US soldiers torturing Iraqi prisoners were widely distributed through mainstream news media, as well as social media, blogs, wikis and other online platforms, evoking political debate within the United States and globally. Numerous research articles have since sought to make sense of the photographs themselves as simultaneously extending the humiliation and abuse of the prisoners, and opening a window onto the truth of the culture and practices of torture at the centre of US military action in foreign states (Andén-Papadopoulos, 2008; Carrabine, 2011). The images, Carrabine argues, are significant not only because 'they speak the truth of torture' (2011, p. 18) in ways that are remarkably consistent both with other wartime 'trophy' snapshots and with American lynching images, but also for what they reveal about the complexity of moral responses to such 'spectacles of suffering' (p. 19). Carrabine explores why the response to the images, once they became widely available via the global media, was not a consistent moral outrage. While previous studies have identified that we are increasingly desensitized to violence and atrocity in the context of contemporary media saturation (Mirzoeff, 2005),

Carrabine argues that 'grotesque violence is deeply embedded in human storytelling' (2011, p. 9). Indeed, as Carrie Rentschler (2004, p. 298) further identified, 'people can take voyeuristic pleasure or puerile interest in images of others' suffering ... closely resembling the appetite for vicarious sex in pornography'.

Similarly, Young (2007, 2010) noted that, as spectators, we are simultaneously repelled and compelled by crime and its images. Young (2010) suggests that criminology must attend to:

> The matrix of intersections between the spectator, the image, and the context of reception, with perhaps the most important factor in any instance being the possibility that the subject — including the legal institution as well as the individual — feels *addressed* by the image and thus bound up in a relation with it (p. 86, emphasis in original).

What Young (2007, 2010) suggests is an analytical approach taking account not only of the social meanings of images of crime (including cinematic representations and imagery of shared traumatic events such as 11 September 2001) but also of the affect and ethics of looking. She proposes that our spectatorship of images of crime should always be 'on trial'. How do we, the spectators, *feel* and *act* in response to viewing images of crime (whether fictitious or real)? 'There is of course a sense of ethical demand involved in witnessing – the demand that the *witness interpret what she sees*' (Young, 2007, p. 44, emphasis added). Young's (2007) analysis further suggests that there is a tension inherent in the meditated witnessing of crime 'selfie' images circulated via social media. As such, viewing crime images constitutes itself a virtual witnessing of a harm (Peelo, 2006; van Krieken, Hoeken, & Sanders, 2015), with an ensuing ethical demand to recognise that harm and to take action to mitigate or correct the injustice of it. At the same time, such is the cumulative impact of the crime and violence media spectacle that audiences become numbed, desensitized and/or indifferent to the harsh realities of violence and human suffering, lessening the call to empathy and action (Bushman, Chandler, & Huesmann, 2009; Dean, 2003; Scharrer, 2008).

A further complicating tension is that the torture and abuse at Abu Ghraib, as well as the various incidents of sexual assault described above, have not necessarily been responded to as serious criminal events of which the image itself is evidence. Rather, there remains a socio-cultural interpretability of such images of sexual violence and injustice.

On the one hand, like Carrabine's (2011) analysis cited earlier, the images can be read as 'speaking the truth' of violence. Sexual violence in particular, so often a hidden crime occurring in private space, is made brutally public when images of the crime are exposed. In a digital society, the widespread accessibility of camera and internet-enabled smartphones, and distribution of self-generated content in public or quasi-public networks, have combined to blur the public and private in ways that arguably open a window onto the extent of practices and cultures of sexual assault and abuse (Powell & Henry, 2017). The injustices of these largely gendered crimes are brought painfully into view, subjected to public scrutiny and are capable of motivating a shared response. In a discussion of sexual violence survivors' online truth-telling practices, Rentschler (2004, p. 68) describes a 'feminist response-ability' to respond to the evidence of rape culture that such disclosures represent. Following feminist philosopher Kelly Oliver (2001, p. 15) 'response-ability' refers to both 'the condition of possibility of response ... and the ethical obligation to respond and enable response-ability from others.' Arguably, though there is additional harm to victims when images of sexual assault are distributed, there is also the possibility and obligation to respond — to acknowledge the harm, to denounce it and to challenge the values of a society in which the actions of perpetrators are too often tolerated and condoned, while victims are overwhelmingly disbelieved and silenced.

On the other hand, images of sexual violence can be read as entertaining, humorous and/or a call to participate in commentary about the 'events' of a night out: not as a sexual assault at all. Indeed, as criminologists Keith Hayward (2010) and Chris Greer and Robert Reiner (2015) have suggested, it is often difficult to make clear distinctions between 'real' and 'imagined' images of crime; in this case, the similarities between amateur and non-consensual pornography may further obscure the interpretation of images of sexual assault. Arguably, for some spectators, images of sexual assault committed by their peers or those in their broader social network may well resemble other images consumed and interpreted as pornography and/or entertainment. Criminologists and sociologists alike have highlighted the ways in which much mainstream pornography simultaneously produces and reproduces cultural norms that fetishise and normalise violence against women (Dekeseredy & Corsianos, 2015; Dekeseredy & Olsson, 2010; Flood, 2009). The growth of amateur or user-generated pornography as a sub-genre means it may sometimes be difficult for someone receiving an image to determine whether a circulated nude or sexual image was originally taken and/or distributed with the consent of those depicted (Powell, 2010). And such difficulty in interpreting consent, or perhaps even thinking about the potential non-consensual nature of an image, occurs in a cultural context in which sexual autonomy is itself subject to wide interpretation (Powell & Henry, 2017). The prevailing societal norm — whether by police, other first responders, judiciary, news media or popular culture — is to presume that the victim consented, rather than to presume non-consent in the absence of clear and active communication otherwise. The multiple interpretations of sexual assault images, and the affective and (anti)ethical responses of many spectators, may further reflect and reproduce this societal norm in regard to consent (Powell, Henry, Henderson, & Flynn, 2013). Of course, this interpretability of acts of violence and injustice is not restricted to sexually violent crimes. As articulated by Butler (1993), the now famous video footage of police assaulting Rodney King in 1991 was not universally interpreted as evidence of state authorities' misuse of force, despite the footage becoming a key source for community protest and activism (discussed further in Chapter 8). Nor was it universally connected to the wider racist social structures of white supremacy that normalise and enable such crimes.

Masculinity, Entertainment and the Criminal Spectacle

Rather than functioning as 'bearing witness' to crime and injustice, the distribution of sexual assault images, in particular, often appears to function as a form of 'entertainment', inviting a broader audience to participate in the crime. In the *Georgetown Law Journal*, Legal scholar Kimberly Allen (2011) describes a 2009 case of sexual assault:

> . . . a 15-year-old student left her homecoming dance to join a drinking session on school property. She quickly became intoxicated and, over the next two hours, was attacked by as many as ten assailants who "laughed and took photos as they took turns" raping her. Detective Ken Greco, who had been in law enforcement for 29 years, called the incident "the worst thing [he'd] heard of" and a crime that "'shocked the conscience of responding officers.'" Equally shocking, however, is the fact that as many as two dozen bystanders witnessed the gang

rape, but none called the police. Some onlookers took photos with their cell phones, which suggests that they viewed the gang rape as a *spectacle* (p. 837, emphasis added).

Each of these cases speaks to the actions of participants, bystanders and witnesses to sexual assault. They had the capacity to directly intervene or to condemn the actions of the direct perpetrators, but instead contributed to the harms of the assault through taking and distributing images of it. In these examples, an audience appeared to view the sexual assault as though it was simply entertainment. There is little criminological research that has explored the individual motivations of such social media 'bystanding', or perhaps more aptly 'participation', in sexual assault or other violent crimes. In the case of sexual assault imagery, it is possible to draw some parallels with the more established literature on multiple perpetrator rape (Horvath & Kelly, 2009) and the role of 'spectators' to sexual violence (Allen, 2011; Horvath & Woodhams, 2013; Woodhams, Cooke, Harkins, & Silva, 2012).

Sexual violence scholars have long argued that multiple perpetrator rape is, in its essence, a group-oriented crime; it is a medium for direct perpetrators and their participating 'audience' to interact in a collective performance of masculinity which is based on the othering, humiliation and ridicule of the feminised victim (Franklin, 2013). As Anderson (in Redden, 2016, n.p.) describes: 'witnessing or videotaping a rape is not just being bystander. It's much more like buying a ticket to an event'. As such, the role of the audience is not merely incidental to the crime; it is a core motivator of it. As psychologist Karen Franklin (2013) further argues, 'admiring spectators' play a crucial role in multiple perpetrator rape:

> ... cheering, snapping photos, and shouting encouragement ... similar to the role of the fan at an athletic event, who — whether present in the spectator stand or learning of "their" team's victory from others — plays an important role in publicly affirming the players' dominance, or masculinity (p. 54).

Such analyses parallel feminist criminological scholarship on male peer support for violence against women (Dekeseredy & Schwartz, 2013, 2016; Schwartz & Dekeseredy, 1997) and performative masculinities. As Walter Dekeseredy and colleagues have argued, violence against women is more likely to occur in contexts in which male peer cultures minimise or actively condone violence and reinforce relations of male dominance and female objectification.

In a somewhat different example, criminologist Stephen Tomsen (2011) further presents a gendered analysis of *Felony Fights*, a series of DVDs with accompanying website and social media pages presenting 'ultra-violence at its finest'. Tomsen (2011) suggests the 'no rules' fighting between predominantly white, male, former convicts represents an internet-enabled shift towards serious, real, violence as, simultaneously, entertainment, public spectacle and 'protest masculinity' (Connell, 1995, p. 116). The celebration, consumption and cultural reproduction of underclass and violent masculinities extends its reach through a broader, willing audience who take 'evil delight in criminal acts' (Tomsen, 2011, citing Katz, 1988). While there may, on the one hand, be a pleasurable attraction to violence as a criminal spectacle (Carrabine, 2011; Young, 2010), what Tomsen (2011) further identifies is the role of online communities as host to an overwhelmingly masculine fascination with both sex and violence. Group participation in producing, recording and distributing fight videos represents not only a ritualised performance of a particular script of masculinity but one which explicitly seeks and receives the validation of a community of peers. Likewise, criminologist

Mark Wood (2018) draws on a related analysis of Facebook amateur fight pages, noting the codes of respectable masculinity and associated normative violence that are reproduced and celebrated by user commentaries on the sites; at the same time as 'fighting dishonourably' is constructed as feminine. Though gender, power and masculinity are central to these fights, their peer endorsement is not exclusively an all-male affair. Women also cheer on these violent performances, just as women and girls also participate in excusing perpetrators of sexual violence, and shaming and blaming their victims.

The Banality of the Criminal Selfie

Following the social functions of personal photography discussed above (van House, 2011; van House, Davis, Ames, Finn, & Viswanathan, 2005), we suggest that criminology must not overlook the far more banal roles of self- and life-imagery in the day-to-day. For example, Science and technology scholar Nancy van House identifies key social motivations for photo taking and sharing practices, including: personal and group memory, relationship creating and maintenance and self-representation. Each of these motivations carries particular significance for the issues discussed here. One might extrapolate, for instance, that photos of a shared crime might be motivated by shared group memory or 'memorialisation' of the event, in a similar way to other shared experiences that become reference points in peer group memory. Such imagery might also serve to build trust within the group: if the images are taken and shared among a group, they may imply that no one who was present at the time of the offence will report to police, since the images may implicate everyone. These are only speculations, though they have some resonance in the visual communication literature regarding the function of social image taking and sharing generally. Indeed, for van House (2011), self-representation through making, showing, viewing and talking about images forms part of how we enact ourselves and contributes to the construction of social norms. Such motivations might also be extrapolated to the motivations of offenders who photograph and/or video their crimes. Photography is not merely an act of documenting and representing an experience, scene or event; it is itself an act of social and cultural production (Carney, 2010). Though early photography required perhaps greater, or more deliberative, curation and construction, the function of photography as a medium of communication and meaning-making is by no means lessened in digital society. Rather, it is an embedded feature of everyday life through which norms, values and practices are both produced and reproduced — as much for crime and injustice as for any other feature of society. Though familiar criminal motivations may underlie the new trend of taking and sharing images of crime, at the same time, it is difficult to ignore the banality of image-taking and sharing as a social and communicative practice of everyday life in general — one that is simply extended to everyday crimes.

Challenges and Implications

Cultural criminologies have long identified people's fascination with crime, criminality and the criminal spectacle (Ferrell & Sanders, 1995; Hayward, 2010; Jewkes, 2015). The literature has examined, for example, the popularity and impacts of crime news reporting (Chibnall, 2013; Palmer, 1998), crime fiction in popular culture (Gever, 2005; O'Brien, Tzanelli, Yar, & Penna, 2005) and crime evidence, photography and artefacts as 'artistic' exhibition (Biber, 2006; Carney, 2010). Has this fascination shifted as the digital camera has become embedded in everyday life? How have digital imagery as 'visual conversation' and social media networking combined with constructions of masculinity that celebrate men's physical and sexual violence? Though this chapter has focused foremost on the case study of criminal selfies in the context of sexual assault, the examples provided here raise broader challenges and carry implications for other crime imagery in digital society.

There may well be some positive implications of the visibility that crime selfies and other user-generated images of crime and injustice create. At a restorative level, there is the capacity to 'speak the truth' to harms and social injustices that are either poorly understood or denied. At the level of criminal procedure, there is capacity for images of sexual assault, for instance, to be used as evidence in criminal trials and secure convictions of perpetrators who might otherwise have gone unpunished. Yet, there may also be a need to consider the taking and distribution of images of a violent offence as an aggravating factor at sentencing in order to recognise the extended harm towards victims (Powell, 2010). As discussed earlier, it cannot be ignored that spectatorship is a key motivator of some assaults, particularly multiple perpetrator assaults (Allen, 2011). Further elaborating, Allen (2011, p. 841) argues that: 'drag races, dogfights, and gang rapes are audience-oriented crimes . . . Just as states have held spectators criminally liable in drag racing and dogfighting, so too should states extend spectator liability to spectators in gang rapes'. Indeed, several jurisdictions in the United States have passed Witness Responsibility statutes, creating a misdemeanour offence for a witness failing to report a sexual assault or homicide to police (Allen, 2011).

A further implication of criminal selfies in the 'digital superpublic' (Senft & Baym, 2015),is that viewers are endlessly invited to participate and reparticipate in extending the harm to the victim through consuming images of the violence perpetrated against them. As Powell and Henry (2016b) have identified in relation to sexual assault imagery, once an image is distributed online, for victim-survivors, the violence has no finish; there is no end point to the trauma. This feeling of perpetual revictimisation brings into sharp focus the importance of a 'right to be forgotten'. The endless circulation of images of harm may perpetuate an experience, even an identity, of being forever a victim. A related argument is poignantly made by digital technology scholar Tonia Sutherland (2017) in her article, *Making a Killing: On Race, Ritual, and (Re)Membering in Digital Culture*, where she discusses the empowerment/disempowerment nexus of images of victimisation and injustice towards black bodies. In particular, though Sutherland notes the important role of images as evidence of racial injustice and of 'bearing witness' to black suffering, she argues that 'in digital spaces these practices have been appropriated to reinforce systems of white supremacist power and racial inequality, re-inscribing structural and systemic racism' (2017, p. 33). When images of violence and injustice come to be misappropriated, as in the example of #Trayvoning discussed above, they cease to function as mediated witnessing and, instead, function as reproducers of social norms of inequality and a means of exerting power and control over marginalised communities.

Conclusion

The harms of the distribution of sexual assault images, then, extend beyond that experienced by each individual victim of violence. Collective harms are caused when images of sexual assault and other violent crimes are circulated in ways that minimise the harms and reinforce sexist, racist and other social norms of inequality. How might such representations of the original crime come to influence how the broader digital society feels and acts in response to such crimes? There may well appear to be an amplification of concern and a call towards social justice activism (as further discussed in

Chapter 8); but there is also an amplification of the systems of inequality that produce such violence in the first place (Moore & Singh, 2015).

To build further on the concept of the *digitised spectacle*, social media algorithms are designed to amplify popular and engaging content in order to hold audience attention. The algorithms are not designed to recognise harm — they do not discriminate between content that elicits a positive or negative response; any content which initially draws user attention is automatically and rapidly disseminated throughout the social network. The digitised spectacle is a *networked spectacle* at the same time as it is an *algorithmic spectacle*; an automated amplification of users' own fascination with violence and power. Yet, as Wood (2017) argues, such a process is not merely a mirror reflecting back to society its own values and norms through a series of 'likes', reposts and comments. Rather, there is 'algorithmic deviancy amplification' as more and more users are invited to witness, vicariously experience and/or revisit violent transgressions (Wood, 2017). In effect, the algorithms that actively push content into the view of human users form a core component of the power relations produced and reproduced throughout the network. While conventional cybercriminologies have considered the criminogenic function of online criminal networks of association, such analyses focus on associations between human actors within the network; there is little criminological engagement with non-human actants, namely the interaction of human and technical agency within online networks, in seeking to understand emerging structures, cultures and practices of crime (for exceptions, see Robert & Dufresne, 2015; Wood, 2017).

This chapter has explored the intersection of norms, technology and networks that promote the circulation of images of violent and sexual assault taken at the scene of the crime. It is our contention that such images cannot simply be understood as the actions of motivated offenders or as incidental documentation of crime. Rather, they should be understood as a cultural commodification of harm that is produced by operative gender and racial norms when channelled through the dominant practices of social networks. To take full account of practices of crime, criminality and justice in digital society, then, criminology is challenged to integrate analyses of the social and the technological; the cultural and the structural; the intangible and the experiential. Such is the project of an emerging digital criminology.

Recommended Further Reading

Dodge, A. (2016). Digitizing rape culture: Online sexual violence and the power of the digital photograph. *Crime, Media, Culture, 12*(1), 65–82.

Powell, A., & Henry, N. (2017). Chapter 3: Rape culture unveiled. In *Sexual Violence in a Digital Age* (pp. 79–116). London: Palgrave Macmillan.

Wood, M. A. (2017). Antisocial media and algorithmic deviancy amplification: Analysing the id of Facebook's technological unconscious. *Theoretical Criminology, 21*(2), 168–185.

References

Albury, K. (2015). Selfies, sexts and sneaky hats: Young people's understandings of gendered practices of self-representation. *International Journal of Communication, 9*(12), 1734–1745.

Allan, S., & Peters, C. (2015). The "Public Eye" or "Disaster Tourists" Investigating public perceptions of citizen smartphone imagery. *Digital Journalism, 3*(4), 477–494.

Allen, K. K. (2011). Guilt by (more than) association: The case for spectator liability in gang rapes. *Georgetown Law Journal, 99*(3), 837–867.

Andén-Papadopoulos, K. (2008). The Abu Ghraib torture photographs: News frames, visual culture, and the power of images. *Journalism*, *9*(1), 5–30.

Baker, K. (2013, September 16). Town Destroyed for What Two People Did: Dispatch from Steubenville. *Jezebel*, http://jezebel.com/a-town-destroyed-for-what-two-people-did-dispatch-fr-1298509440 (last accessed 29 November 2017).

Bates, L. (2014). #JadaPose: the online ridiculing of a teen victim is part of a sickening trend, *The Guardian*, www.theguardian.com/lifeandstyle/womens-blog/2014/jul/17/jadapose-online-ridiculing-rape-victims-sickening-trend (last accessed 29 November 2017).

BBC. (2016). Mum in Chewbacca mask shatters Facebook live record. Available at: www.bbc.com/news/blogs-trending-36348013 (last accessed 29 November 2017).

Biber, K. (2006). The spectre of crime: Photography, law and ethics. *Social Semiotics*, *16*(1), 133–149.

Brown, M. (2014). Visual criminology and carceral studies: Counter-images in the carceral age. *Theoretical Criminology*, *18*(2), 176–197.

Bucher, T. (2017). The algorithmic imaginary: Exploring the ordinary affects of Facebook algorithms. *Information, Communication & Society*, *20*(1), 30–44.

Bushman, B. J., Chandler, J., & Huesmann, L. R. (2009). Chapter 11: Do violent media numb our consciences? In W. Koops, D. Brugman, T. J. Ferguson, & A. F. Sanders (Eds.), *The development and structure of conscience* (p. 237). Hove: Psychology Press.

Butler, J. (1993). Endangered/endangering: Schematic racism and white paranoia. In Gooding-Williams, R. (Ed.) *Reading Rodney King/reading urban uprising* (pp. 15–22). New York: Routledge.

Butler, J. (2007). Torture and the Ethics of Photography. *Environment and Planning D: Society and Space*, *25*(6), 951–966.

Carney, P. (2010). Crime, punishment and the force of photographic spectacle. In K. Hayward & M. Presdee (Eds.) *Framing crime: Cultural criminology and the image* (pp. 17–35). London: Routledge.

Carrabine, E. (2011). The iconography of punishment: Execution prints and the death penalty. *The Howard Journal of Crime and Justice*, *50*(5), 452–464.

Carrabine, E. (2012). Just images: Aesthetics, ethics and visual criminology. *The British Journal of Criminology*, *52*(3), 463–489.

Carrabine, E. (2014). Seeing things: Violence, voyeurism and the camera. *Theoretical Criminology*, *18*(2), 134–158.

Chibnall, S. (Ed.). (2013). *Law-and-order news: An analysis of crime reporting in the British press* (Vol. 2). London: Routledge.

Connell, R. W. (1995). *Gender and power*. Standford: Standford University Press.

Couldry, N., Hepp, A., & Krotz, F. (Eds.). (2009). *Media events in a global age*. Abingdon: Routledge.

Crossley, P. (2017, May 17). When Facebook live streams a murder, who's responsible? *ABC News*. Available at: www.abc.net.au/news/2017-05-17/facebook-livestream-murder-suicide/8500586 (last accessed 29 November 2017).

Culp-Ressler, T. (2013, September 9) Is the next Steubenville rape case unfolding before our eyes? *Think Progress*. Available at: http://thinkprogress.org/health/2013/09/09/2590771/vanderbilt-rape-case/ (last accessed 29 November 2017)

Daly, K. (2014). Reconceptualizing sexual victimization and justice. In A. Pemberton, I. Vanfraechem, & M. F. Ndahinda (Eds.) *Justice for victims: Perspectives on rights, transition and reconciliation* (pp. 378–395). Abingdon: Routledge.

Dean, C. J. (2003). Empathy, pornography, and suffering. *Differences: A Journal of Feminist Cultural Studies*, *14*(1), 88–124.

Debord, G. (1967). *The Society of the Spectacle*. Donald Nicholson-Smith, trans. New York: Zone Books.

DeKeseredy, W. S., & Corsianos, M. (2015). *Violence against women in pornography*. New York: Routledge.

DeKeseredy, W. S., & Olsson, P. (2010). Adult pornography, male peer support, and violence against women: The contribution of the "Dark". In *Technology for facilitating humanity and combating social deviations: Inter-disciplinary perspectives: Interdisciplinary perspectives* (p. 34). New York: Information Science Reference.

DeKeseredy, W. S., & Schwartz, M. D. (Eds.). (2013). *Male peer support and violence against women: The history and verification of a theory*. Boston, MA: Northeastern University Press.

DeKeseredy, W. S., & Schwartz, M. D. (2016). Thinking sociologically about image-based sexual abuse: The contribution of male peer support theory. *Sexualization, Media, & Society, 2*(4), 2374623816684692.

Dreyfuss, E. (2017). Facebook streams a muder and now must face itself. *Wired Magazine*. Available at: www.wired.com/2017/04/facebook-live-murder-steve-stephens/ (last accessed 29 November 2017).

Ferrell, J., Hayward, K., Morrison, W., & Presdee, M. (Eds.). (2004). *Cultural criminology unleashed*. London: Routledge.

Ferrell, J., & Sanders, C. (Eds.). (1995). *Cultural criminology*. London: Glasshouse Press.

Flood, M. (2009). The harms of pornography exposure among children and young people. *Child Abuse Review, 18*(6), 384–400.

Franklin, K. (2013). Masculinity, status, and power: Implicit messages in Western media discourse on high-profile cases of multiple perpetrator rape. In M. A. Horvath, & J. Woodhams (Eds.), *Handbook on the study of multiple perpetrator rape: A multidisciplinary response to an international problem* (pp. 37–66). Abingdon: Routledge.

Frosh, P. (2015). The gestural image: The selfie, photography theory, and kinesthetic sociability. *International Journal of Communication, 9*(22), 1607–1628.

Gallardo, M. (2017, April 4). Details of Facebook Live sexual assault revealed in court, *ABC 7 Chicago*. Available at: http://abc7chicago.com/news/details-of-facebook-live-sexual-assault-revealed-in-court/1836376/ (last accessed 29 November 2017).

Gever, M. (2005). The spectacle of crime, digitized: CSI: Crime Scene Investigation and social anatomy. *European Journal of Cultural Studies, 8*(4), 445–463.

Gorin, V. (2015). Innovation(s) in photojournalism: Assessing visual content and the place of citizen photojournalism in Time's Lightbox photoblog. *Digital Journalism, 3*(4), 533–551.

Greer, C., & Reiner, R. (2015). Mediated Mayhem: Media, crime and criminal justice. In: M. Maguire, R. Morgan & R. Reiner (Eds.), *Oxford Handbook of Criminology* (pp. 245–278). Oxford: Oxford University Press

Guerrero, L., & Leonard, D. J. (2012). Playing dead: the trayvoning meme and the mocking of Black Death. *New Black Man*. Available at: www.newblackmaninexile.net/2012/05/playing-dead-trayvoning-meme-mocking-of.html (last accessed 29 November 2017).

Hayward, K. (Ed.). (2010) *Framing crime: Cultural criminology and the image*. Abingdon: Routledge.

Hern, A. (2017, January 6). Facebook Live is changing the world - but not in the way it hoped, *The Guardian*, www.theguardian.com/technology/2017/jan/05/facebook-live-social-media-live-streaming (last accessed 29 November 2017).

Hess, A. (2015). The selfie assemblage. *International Journal of Communication, 9*(2), 1629–1646.

Horvath, M., & Kelly, L. (2009). Multiple perpetrator rape: Naming an offence and initial research findings. *Journal of Sexual Aggression, 15*(1), 83–96.

Horvath, M., & Woodhams, J. (Eds.). (2013). *Handbook on the study of multiple perpetrator rape: A multidisciplinary response to an international problem* (Vol. 4). Abingdon: Routledge.

Jewkes, Y. (2015). *Media and crime*. London: Sage.

Katz, J. E., & Aakhus, M. (Eds.). (2002). *Perpetual contact: Mobile communication, private talk, public performance*. Cambridge: Cambridge University Press.

Katz, J. E., & Crocker, E. T. (2017). Chapter 4: Visual interpersonal communication in daily life. In A. S. Tellería (Ed.), *Between the public and private in mobile communication*. New York: Routledge.

Kellner, D. (2004). Media propaganda and spectacle in the war on Iraq: A critique of US broadcasting networks. *Cultural Studies? Critical Methodologies, 4*(3), 329–338.

Kellner, D. (2010). Media spectacle and media events: Some critical reflections. In N. Couldry, A. Hepp, F. Krotz (Eds.) *Media events in a global age* (pp. 76–91). Abingdon: Routledge.

Larcombe, W. (2011). Falling rape conviction rates: (Some) feminist aims and measures for rape law. *Feminist Legal Studies, 19*(1), 27–45.

Latour, B. (2005). *Reassembling the social: An introduction to actor-network-theory*. Oxford: Oxford University Press.

Latour, B. (1996). On actor-network theory: A few clarifications. *Soziale Welt*, 369–381.

Lee, R. L. (2016). Diagnosing the Selfie: Pathology or Parody? Networking the Spectacle in Late Capitalism. *Third Text*, *30*(3–4), 264–273.

Levy A (2013, August 5) Trial by Twitter. *The New Yorker*. Available at: www.newyorker.com/reporting/2013/08/05/130805fa_fact_levy (last accessed 29 November 2017).

Medew, J. (2007, November 6). Callous' teens escape jail for sex attack film. *The Age*. 12 June 2009. Available at: www.theage.com.au/news/national/callous-teens-escape-jail-for-sexattack-film/2007/11/05/1194117959942.html (last accessed 29 November 2017).

Mirzoeff, N. (2005). *Watching Babylon: The war in Iraq and global visual culture*. Abingdon: Routledge.

Moore, D., & Singh, R. (2015). Seeing crime: ANT, feminism and images of violence against women. In D. Robert & M. Dufresne (Eds.) *Actor-network theory and crime studies: Explorations in science and technology* (pp. 67–80). Abingdon: Routledge.

O'Brien, M., Tzanelli, R., Yar, M., & Penna, S. (2005). "The spectacle of fearsome acts": Crime in the melting P(l)ot in Gangs of New York. *Critical Criminology*, *13*(1), 17–35.

Ohio Court of Common Pleas. (2012) Transcript of proceedings, Court of Common Pleas, Jefferson County, Ohio, Juvenile Division. Probable cause hearing. Case number 2012-DL-138 and 2012-DL-139. Cases heard on Friday, 12 October, Honorable Tom Lipps presiding.

Oliver, K. (2001). *Witnessing: beyond recognition*. Minneapolis: University of Minnesota Press.

Oppel, R. (2013, March 17). Ohio teenagers guilty in rape trial that social media brought to light. *New York Times*. Available at: www.nytimes.com/2013/03/18/us/teenagers-found-guilty-in-rape-in-steubenville-ohio.html (last accessed 29 November 2017).

Palasinski, M. (2013). Turning assault into a "harmless prank"—teenage perspectives on happy slapping. *Journal of Interpersonal Violence*, *28*(9), 1909–1923.

Palmer, G. (1998). The new spectacle of crime. *Information Communication & Society*, *1*(4), 361–381.

Peelo, M. (2006). Framing homicide narratives in newspapers: Mediated witness and the construction of virtual victimhood. *Crime, Media, Culture*, *2*(2), 159–175.

Pink, S. (2011). Amateur photographic practice, collective representation and the constitution of place. *Visual Studies*, *26*(2), 92–101.

Powell, A. (2010). Configuring consent: Emerging technologies, unauthorized sexual images and sexual assault. *Australian & New Zealand Journal of Criminology*, *43*(1), 76–90.

Powell, A. (2015). Seeking rape justice: Formal and informal responses to sexual violence through technosocial counter-publics. *Theoretical Criminology*, *19*(4), 571–588.

Powell, A., & Henry, N. (2016a). Technology-facilitated sexual violence victimization: Results from an online survey of Australian adults. *Journal of Interpersonal Violence*. Advance online publication. doi: 10.1177/0886260516672055.

Powell, A., & Henry, N. (2016b). Policing technology-facilitated sexual violence against adult victims: Police and service sector perspectives. *Policing and Society*. Advance online publication. doi: 10.1080/10439463.2016.1154964.

Powell, A., & Henry, N. (2017). *Sexual violence in a digital age*. Basingstoke, UK: Palgrave Macmillan.

Powell, A., Henry, N., Henderson, E., & Flynn, A. (2013). The meanings of "sex" and "consent": History, discourse and impact of rape law reform in Victoria (Australia). *Griffith Law Review*, *22*(2), 456–480.

Reading, A. (2011). The London bombings: Mobile witnessing, mortal bodies and globital time. *Memory Studies*, *4*(3), 298–311.

Redden, M. (2016, August 15). 'It's victimization': push grows to charge onlookers who tape sexual assaults. *The Guardian*. Available at: www.theguardian.com/society/2016/aug/15/rape-prosecutions-onlookers-tape-sexual-assaults-legal-questions (last accessed 29 November 2017).

Rentschler, C. A. (2004). Witnessing: US citizenship and the vicarious experience of suffering. *Media, Culture & Society*, *26*(2), 296–304.

Robert, D., & Dufresne, M. (2015). *Actor-network theory and crime studies: Explorations in science and technology*. Abingdon: Routledge.

Sandberg, S., & Ugelvik, T. (2016). Why do offenders tape their crimes? Crime and punishment in the age of the selfie. *British Journal of Criminology*, *57*(5), 1023–1040.

Scharrer, E. (2008). Media exposure and sensitivity to violence in news reports: Evidence of desensitization? *Journalism & Mass Communication Quarterly*, *85*(2), 291–310.

Schwartz, M. D., & DeKeseredy, W. (1997). *Sexual assault on the college campus: The role of male peer support*. Thousand Oaks: Sage.

Senft, T. M., & Baym, N. K. (2015). Selfies introduction: What does the selfie say? Investigating a global phenomenon. *International Journal of Communication*, *9*(19), 1588–1606.

Shanks, M., & Svabo, C. (2014). Mobile-media photography: New modes of engagement. In M. Sandbye & J. Larsen, (Eds.). *Digital Snaps: The New Face of Photography* (pp. 227–246), London: I.B. Taurus.

Shifman, L. (2012). An anatomy of a YouTube meme. *New Media & Society*, *14*(2), 187–203.

Sills, S., Pickens, C., Beach, K., Jones, L., Calder-Dawe, O., Benton-Greig, P., & Gavey, N. (2016). Rape culture and social media: Young critics and a feminist counterpublic. *Feminist Media Studies*, *16*(6), 935–951.

Solon, O. (2017, April 26). Live and death: Facebook sorely needs a reality check about video. *The Guardian*. Available at: www.theguardian.com/technology/2017/apr/25/facebook-live-mark-zuckerberg-murder-video-thailand (last accessed 29 November 2017).

Surette, R. (2002). Self-reported copycat crime among a population of serious and violent juvenile offenders. *NCCD News*, *48*(1), 46–69.

Sutherland, T. (2017). Making a killing: On race, ritual, and (re)membering in digital culture. *Preservation, Digital Technology & Culture*, *46*(1), 32–40.

Tomsen, S. (2011). Felon fights: masculinity, spectacle and suffering. In *The Australian and New Zealand Critical Criminology Conference Proceedings 2010*. Sydney: Institute of Criminology, University of Sydney. Available at: https://ses.library.usyd.edu.au/handle/2123/7373 (last accessed 29 November 2017).

van House, N. A. (2011). Personal photography, digital technologies and the uses of the visual. *Visual Studies*, *26*(2), 125–134.

van House, N. A., Davis, M., Ames, M., Finn, M. & Viswanathan, V. (2005). The uses of personal networked digital imaging: An empirical study of cameraphone photos and sharing. In *CHI'05 extended abstracts on human factors in computing systems* (pp. 1853–1856). New York, NY: ACM. CHI '05 CHI 2005 Conference on Human Factors in Computing Systems, Portland, OR, USA — April 02–07, 2005.

van Krieken, K., Hoeken, H., & Sanders, J. (2015). From reader to mediated witness: The engaging effects of journalistic crime narratives. *Journalism & Mass Communication Quarterly*, *92*(3), 580–596.

Wang, R., Yang, F., & Haigh, M. M. (2017). Let me take a selfie: exploring the psychological effects of posting and viewing selfies and groupies on social media. *Telematics and Informatics*, *34*(4), 274–283.

Warfield, K. (2016). Making the cut: An agential realist examination of selfies and touch. *Social Media+ Society*, *2*(2), 1–10.

Waterhouse-Watson, D. (2014). 'You Posted What on Facebook?' Sport, Sex and the 'St Kilda Schoolgirl'. *Media International Australia*, *151*(1), 37–46.

Weiser, E. B. (2015). #Me: Narcissism and its facets as predictors of selfie-posting frequency. *Personality and Individual Differences*, *86*, 477–481.

Wellman, A., Reddington, F., & Clark, K. (2017). What's Trending: # SexualAssault: An Exploratory Study of Social Media Coverage of Teen Sexual Assaults. *Criminology, Criminal Justice Law & Society*, *18*(1), 88–105.

Williams, A. A., & Marquez, B. A. (2015). The lonely selfie king: Selfies and the conspicuous prosumption of gender and race. *International Journal of Communication*, *9*, 13.

Willett, R. (2009). In the frame: Mapping camcorder cultures. In D. Buckingham & R. Willett, (Eds.) *Video cultures: Media technology and everyday creativity* (pp. 1–22). Basingstoke: Palgrave Macmillan.

Wood, M. A. (2017). Antisocial media and algorithmic deviancy amplification: Analysing the id of Facebook's technological unconscious. *Theoretical Criminology*, *21*(2), 168–185.

Wood, M. A. (2018). 'I just wanna see someone get knocked the fuck out': Spectating affray on Facebook fight pages. *Crime, Media, Culture 14*, 23–40.

Woodhams, J., Cooke, C., Harkins, L., & Silva, T. D. (2012). Leadership in multiple perpetrator stranger rape. *Journal of Interpersonal Violence*, 27(4), 728–752.

Yar, M. (2012). Crime, media and the will-to-representation: Reconsidering relationships in the new media age. *Crime, Media, Culture*, 8(3), 245–260.

Young, A. (2007). Images in the aftermath of trauma: Responding to September 11th. *Crime, Media, Culture*, 3(1), 30–48.

Young, A. (2010). The Scene of the Crime. In Hayward, K. (Ed.) *Framing crime: Cultural criminology and the image* (pp. 83–97). London: Routledge.

Young, A. (2014). From object to encounter: Aesthetic politics and visual criminology. *Theoretical Criminology*, 18(2), 159–175.

Ziffer, D. (2006, October 26). YouTube yanks assault DVD. *The Age*. Available at: www.theage.com.au/news/national/youtube-yanks-assault-dvd/2006/10/26/1161749222232.html (last accessed 29 November 2017).

Zuckerberg, M. (2016). Today we're launching Facebook Live for everyone. public post. Available at: www.facebook.com/zuck/posts/10102764095821611 (last accessed 29 November 2017).

6

NETWORKED HATE

Racism, Misogyny and Violence

Introduction

The rally in the town of Charlottesville, Virginia, in mid-August 2017 was the moment when networks of hate materialised on the streets of America and were broadcast globally. The hate at Charlottesville was not singular. It was organised by a local blogger, Jason Kessler, under the banner of 'Unite the Right', so there were an array of groups and interests represented. Most visible were members of 'Identity Evropa', a white supremacist group opposed to multiculturalism and immigration, whose members wore white Oxford button-up shirts tucked into cream Khakis. They were led by Nathan Damigo, who rose to prominence when a video of him punching a woman in the face at the Berkeley right-wing rally went viral. Linked to this group is Richard Spencer, the head of the Policy Institute and prominent public figurehead of the white supremacist movement he has branded the 'alt-right' (Hawley, 2017; Niewert, 2017). Also amongst the rally were the Proud Boys, a male supremacist group whose members wore black Fred Perry polo shirts with yellow piping. This group emerged out of the 'negging' pickup artist trend that aims to seduce women with chauvinist insults thinly veiled as compliments and is led by co-founder of *Vice Magazine,* Gavin McInnes. Also a common sight were white shields bearing a black 'x', the symbol of the League of the South, which is a revanchist confederate movement in favour of southern secession. Often mistaken for police or paramilitary were the heavily armed, open carry militia-men, who align with two main groups: the Oath Keepers, who are ex-military or law enforcement; and the Three Percenters, who pledge to defend gun rights, if necessary using violence. Scattered amidst these groups were numerous other ad hoc movements, often designated by esoteric slogan T-shirts and varieties of neo-Nazi or Swastika flags. The white hoods of Klu Klux Klan were largely absent.

The visual distinctiveness of each of these groups is not accidental. The event had been some time in the planning and was designed to legitimise the movement and bring them further into mainstream discourse. The overwhelming majority were not from Charlottesville, which is a politically progressive university town, but hailed from all across the country. In spite of this spatial distance, there is clearly a strongly unified culture, ideology, rhetoric and aesthetic to all of these groups. To a certain degree, the Charlottesville rally seemed intended to replicate or counter the urban protest movements that characterised the Arab Spring occupation of the squares or the Black Lives Matter marches (discussed further in Chapter 8). While this was a 'real-world' rally, the common element giving rise to this coordination and unity among these white supremacist groups, and enabling them to assemble on the streets, is an extension of digital networks. It is — in this sense — the far-right face of the digital society.

While the rally was nominally to protest the removal of confederate statues, this was largely an excuse for the wider ideological goals of the groups. Indeed, rather than a protest in the tradition of political speech, the key features of the Charlottesville race rally were violence and suppression of public debate. Many protesters were visibly armed or threatening violence, denying basic liberties of speech and physical safety to the counter-protesters. The semblance of this rally as an exercise of free speech and debate over the removal of statues was quickly quashed; constitutional first amendment rights were cast in shadow by a particular reading of the second amendment, which allows for open carry of automatic weapons where states or cities allow it (Merelli, 2017). As a result, those who sought to exercise free speech or counter-protest the rally were not only intimidated but physically threatened. And the intimidation extended beyond the counter-protesters who sought to oppose the rally. Governor of Virgina Terry McAuliffe stated that the heavily armed militias 'had better equipment than our State Police had' (Stolberg, 2017, n.p.). This raises the enduring question: how hateful, intimidating and damaging do speech and political actions need to be before those privileged enough to push the limits of the first amendment have gone too far?

This chapter is not specifically about the far-right movement(s) in America, nor even about online racism in general. Rather, it seeks to explore the concept of networks of hate as an explanation of the wider, digitally mediated prejudice and inequality that enable events such as Charlottesville and many other instances of abuse, whether they be face-to-face on the streets, in the home or via digital communications. A digital criminological view of hate networks does not distinguish so readily between the 'online' and 'offline' categories but sees this overall phenomenon as thoroughly technosocial. For not only will offenders have lives shaped by technological and social interaction, so too will victims, responders, bystanders and the general public. This is the nature of the networks of hate in digital society.

So, in this chapter, we consider a number of ways in which hate networks manifest. We discuss hate crimes and hate speech, their usefulness and limits from a digital criminological perspective and how we can move forward to a wider, networked perspective on hate. The concept of hate networks is then elaborated in more detail, demonstrating how a technosocial understanding of hate is grounded in concepts of social and technological co-production, the wider systems of knowledge that underpin these practices and the role that institutions can play in enabling and/or regulating co-production of social norms. This discussion is driven by case studies that explore Islamophobia in the United Kingdom, algorithmic bias in American tech companies and toxic masculinity in the Australian defence force. Next, we explore the challenges and implications of networks of hate in relation to the tension between freedom of speech and hate speech, the need for algorithmic responses to hate networks and the complex nature of viral violent resistance to networked hate. These are examined through case studies that highlight the intersecting categories of race, class and gender in the contemporary digital society. Our focus in this chapter on racial, religious, gender and class manifestations of networked hate aims to highlight that technosociality interacts with existing social structures of inequality and disadvantage. It does not exist separate to these social processes but rather is produced by this context.

Hate in a Digital Society

The events at Charlottesville prompted widespread reaction right up to the highest levels. In the immediate aftermath of the rally, representatives of some of the most powerful institutions stood up and condemned the rally. Senior officers from the Army, Marines, Navy, Air Force and National Guard all took to Twitter to denounce racism, hate and intolerance (Dickstein, 2017). Prominent CEOs stepped down from President Trump's corporate advisory council and took to Twitter to air their concerns following the equivocal response to the violence by the White House (Weaver & Waters, 2017). An event such as this offers the opportunity not only to reflect on the broad structures of racism and patriarchy within society, and how these cultures of hate can be weaponised through digital technologies, but also on how it is understood legally and institutionally. Beyond the rhetorical condemnations that were in part — no doubt — intended to heal social wounds and manage public relations, how do the law, the government and society interpret and respond to hate? What are their limitations and what might a digital criminological analysis look like?

Hate Crimes and the Law

Hate crime laws represent the strongest state response to hate within society. Hate crimes in the United States are governed by both federal and state laws. At a federal level, laws governing crimes motivated by racism weren't introduced until 1968, following the assassination of Martin Luther King Jr (Lewis, 2014, p. 50; Streissguth, 2009, p. 288). The phrase 'hate crime' was not widely used before the mid-1980s (Jacobs & Potter, 1998, p. 3). The Federal Bureau of Investigation (FBI) defines a hate crime as a 'criminal offense committed against a person or property motivated in whole or in part by an offender's bias against a race, religion, disability, sexual orientation, ethnicity, gender or gender identity' (Federal Bureau of Investigation, 2017). According to American Professor of Sociology and Criminology Jack Levin (2007, p. 2048), the majority of these state laws focus primarily on race, ethnicity or religion. Thirty states include sexual orientation as a motivation for hate crime and 17 include gender identity (Movement Advancement Project, 2017). While there is evidence of hate crime on the basis of disability, there is little effective response compared to other categories (Levin, 2013). As of 2017, Arkansas, Georgia, Michigan, South Carolina and Wyoming still have no hate crime laws. Some states — Kentucky and Louisiana, for instance — took a different approach by introducing a 'Blue Lives Matter' law, making it a hate crime to attack a police officer or an emergency responder (Reinhard, 2017). While these hate crime laws exist at state and federal level, the legal avenues for redress in online-related crimes motivated by hate would be through a combination of other civil, criminal and civil rights laws (Citron, 2014, pp. 120–129).

The United States Department of Justice (DOJ) keeps detailed survey statistics on hate crimes, both reported and unreported, prosecuted and unprosecuted. According to their records, between 2004 and 2015, US residents experienced, on average, 250,000 hate crime victimisations a year, of which 42% were reported to police (Masucci & Langton, 2017, p. 1, 5). In terms of the perpetrator's motivation as perceived by the victim, 48% were motivated by race, 34% by gender, 22% by sexuality and 17% by religion (Masucci & Langton, 2017, p. 2). FBI statistics on local agency reporting, however, found a significantly smaller number of hate crimes: 5,850 in 2015 — an increase of 340 incidents from 2014, after two decades of steady decline (Federal Bureau of Investigation, 2016, p. 2). Of these, 57% were motivated by race, 21% by religion, 18% by sexuality and 2% by gender identity. It is worth noting that just over half of religiously motivated crimes were anti-Jewish and just under a quarter were anti-Muslim (Federal Bureau of Investigation, p. 3). Other statistics on hate crimes in 2015 and 2016 also suggest a recent upwards trend. The number of anti-Muslim hate crimes recorded by the Council on American–Islamic Relations (2017, p. 6) was 260 in 2016, an increase of 44% on the 180 recorded in 2015. But that was dwarfed by the 374% increase, from 38 hate crimes in 2014. Furthermore, in the ten days following the election of Donald Trump in November 2016, the Southern Poverty Law Centre (2017) documented 867 cases of bias-related harassment and intimidation, of which approximately a third targeted immigrants and a quarter African Americans. What is notable, and relevant to this book, is that hate crimes using the internet or other digital communications are not captured in the official statistics. As will be discussed further in this chapter, these statistics reflect only crimes in the traditional sense, where offender and victim are in the same physical time and place: they exclude the wider, digitally mediated phenomenon of hate.

In the UK, meanwhile, hate crime laws are solely federally based, making for a more consistent approach across its jurisdictions. The UK Crown Prosecution Service (CPS) (2017) defines hate crime as:

> any criminal offence which is perceived by the victim or any other person, to be motivated by hostility or prejudice based on a person's race or perceived race; religion or perceived religion; sexual orientation or perceived sexual orientation; disability or perceived disability and any crime motivated by hostility or prejudice against a person who is transgender or perceived to be transgender.

The CPS collect data on hate prosecutions and convictions, which show that there were 15,442 hate crime prosecutions undertaken in the 2015/16 reporting year, an increase of almost 5% from the previous year (Crown Prosecution Service, 2016, p. 3). There was an 83.2% overall conviction rate, and 33.2% had sentences increased due to the hate-based motivation (Crown Prosecution Service, 2016, p. 4). These data only record three categories of hate crime: race/religion motivations were the largest at 84%, homophobic/transphobic motivations represented 9.5% and disability motivations represented 6% (Crown Prosecution Service, 2016, pp. 4–5). The category that saw the greatest increase in prosecutions — 41% — was disability hate crimes, which have historically been under-reported (Crown Prosecution Service, p. 5; Sherry, 2013). Wider data on hate-motivated crimes that are not necessarily prosecuted as hate crimes are collected by the UK Home Office. In the 2016/17 reporting year, there were 80,393 crimes reported by police in which there was a hate motivation, an increase of 29% from the previous year, which is the largest increase since data collection began in 2011/12 (Home Office, 2017, p. 7). The Home Office captures data on five categories of hate crime, more closely resembling those of the US Department of Justice data. The largest category was race motivations, at 78% of all recorded hate crimes, while 11% were sexual orientation motivations, 7% were religious, 7% disability and 2% transgender (Crown Prosecution Service, 2016). Any attack due to the victim being a refugee or asylum seeker was included as a race-motivated hate crime (Crown Prosecution Service, 2016, p. 8). Unlike the US data, in 2016/17, the Home Office collected 'experimental statistics' specifically on *online* hate crime for the first time, which will be explored further in a later section.

While hate *crimes* tend to refer to a strict legal definition, hate *speech* is often used in a more general sense. Hate speech has many forms and degrees of severity. There are laws limiting speech in many instances, for example, holocaust denial is an offence in Israel, Germany and another 15 European countries. While the UK does not have laws against holocaust denial specifically, it has a broader set of laws that limit actions and speech that would fall under the category of hate or bias (Mason, 2015, pp. 62–63). A common critique, and an enduring challenge that legislative regulations against hate speech encounter, is the tension with free speech. This is especially pronounced in the United States, where free speech is enshrined in the first amendment and hate speech is not a criminal offence. American legal and civil rights scholar Frederick Lawrence (1992) interprets this to mean that the right to racist speech should be protected but, in the event it contributes to crimes such as vandalism or assault, the fact that it is motivated by bigotry means it should receive increased punishment. Towards this end, he suggests taking the idea of hate out of the legal framing altogether due to its lack of neutrality, referring instead to 'bias crimes' and 'racist speech'. Under current US laws, speech in all its forms is free, and the right to physical safety is protected by criminal law. But what about the harm done by hate speech — should this be covered by the law? Legal scholar Mari Matsuda suggests that there are three criteria that determine whether race-motivated hate speech can be prohibited without constituting undue censorship: first, it has a message of racial inferiority; second, it is directed against a historically oppressed group; and third, it is persecutory, hateful and degrading (Matsuda, 1993, p. 2357). This second criteria identified by Masuda is important to the discussion in this chapter as it highlights the need to understand the phenomenon of hate speech in broader social and criminological terms.

Beyond Hate 'Crime'

While hate crime laws represent the strongest state response to these harms, they don't capture the full extent of the phenomenon. Adopting different terminology will not, in and of itself, expand the conception of hate associated with the legal frame of reference. Legal philosopher Alexander Brown seeks to tackle this precise question, making the argument that hate speech is not just 'emotions, feelings, or attitudes of hate or hatred' (Brown, 2017, p. 466). He suggests that this commonly held assumption about personal beliefs is often the basis for suggesting that, so long as it is 'just' speech, the reflection of someone's belief, and does not escalate to physical assault or other crimes, it is not 'that' harmful. According to Brown, this misses the point because hate speech is both more and less than emotions, feelings and attitudes. It is less because one can say hateful things without the associated feelings, emotions and attitudes. And it is more because hate speech is more than those emotions, feelings or attitudes: it is also a wider structural form of harm connected, as Masuda suggested, to systems and histories of oppression. This leads Brown to two conclusions: first, that hate speech is a much wider phenomenon than is currently encompassed by the law; and, second, that it is not a singular concept but will mean different things and take on different forms depending on the context (Brown, 2017, p. 444).

If hate crimes refer to a narrow legal interpretation and hate speech finds itself in tension with free speech, is it helpful to use other terminology to describe the phenomenon? Various scholars have put forward terms but each, we believe, misses an important aspect as currently framed. Internet safety advocate Sue Scheff and journalist Melissa Schorr (Scheff & Schorr, 2017) approach the broad phenomenon of online hate from the perspectives of 'digital shaming' and 'cyberhumiliation'. Though these concepts capture elements of the motivations of offenders and the experience of victims, their work arguably overlooks the wider structural inequalities that enable the shaming; further, Scheff and Schorr tend to see resilience and self-help as solutions to these harms, which may help at an individual level but doesn't address the deeper causes. Howard Ehrlich (2009, p. 18), American sociologist and former director at the National Institute Against Prejudice and Violence at the University of Baltimore, suggests that 'hate' is an ineffective criminological, or indeed sociological, frame of reference to understand the problems of bigotry and prejudice, as it plays into the narrow legal definition of the phenomenon and also media sensationalism. Its usage is thus too narrow and not sufficiently analytic. As an example of the narrowness, he suggests that the early work on hate crimes by scholars such as Jack Levin and Jack McDevitt (1993) and Milton Kleg (1993) needed to develop a broader understanding of prejudice and discrimination, as well as trauma and victimisation, all of which are important parts of a criminological explanation. While Levin and colleagues (Levin & McDevitt, 2002; McDevitt, Levin & Bennett, 2002; Levin & Nolan, 2002) have certainly addressed this by expanding the scope of their research into the criminology of hate crimes, the point can be taken that it is important to supplement a narrow focus with one that is wider. Towards this end, Ehrlich (2009, p. 17) adopts the term 'ethnoviolence' to describe how group prejudice motivates actions intended to cause harm. However, the incidence of hate crimes, hate speech — and, for that matter, the wider structures that underpin hate culture — are now widely recognised as not only encompassing race and ethnicity but also other identity categories, such as religion, gender, sexuality, ability and age.

Another way of resolving the tension between free speech and hate speech on digital platforms is to employ informal social regulations that don't rely on the law (Gagliardone, Gal, Alves, & Martinez, 2015). One such approach is to adopt preventative policies and, where that fails, disciplinary measures to respond to hateful or other online practices that violate norms or standards within private organisations (Briendl & Kuellmer, 2013; Farrand & Carrapico, 2013; Wagner, 2013). This, however, can also come into tension with free speech, as will be shown. Communications scholars Matti Pohjonen and Sahana Udupa (2017) suggest that the hate speech versus free speech binary is too simplistic and tends to favour allowing speech rather than legally regulating it. Their suggestion is that the negative effects of hate in an online context can be treated as a complicating factor in the discourse of online risk, allowing it to be examined in more nuanced ways through a range of practices and policies. Another approach is to regulate digital media companies by changing the terms of use (Citron & Norton, 2011; Henry, 2009) and alter user behaviour on digital networking sites through algorithmic means (Agarwal & Sureka, 2016; Banks, 2010; Gitari, Zuping, Damien, & Long, 2015). While non-legal regulatory responses to digitally mediated cultures of hate will be explored further in this chapter, what can be taken from this discussion of hate crimes and hate speech is that, to the extent that relevant legal responses make compromises in order to protect free speech, there are a range of behaviours that are excluded from the scope of these laws that should be included in a criminological account.

The digital criminological approach proposed here seeks to understand hate at a broader level than the cases that are prosecutable under current laws. Rather, it seeks to expand the discussion of hate by broadening the discussion of how and why it emerges within society and, in particular, offer a technosocial account of how hate is implicated in a digitally mediated social order. According to critical criminologist Barbara Perry (2006, p. 155), hate crime has been under-theorised within the discipline, in spite of the fact that it lies at the intersection of a number of themes central to this field of inquiry, namely 'violence, victimization, race/ethnicity, gender, sexuality, and difference'. In previous studies, Perry has emphasised that hate crimes are 'usually directed towards already stigmatized and marginalized groups' (Perry, 2001, p. 10). This concern with the structural conditions of hate has since been developed, as well demonstrated in the conceptual discussion of networked hate, particularly in the UK context, by key scholars such as Neil Chakraborti and Jon Garland (Chakraborti, 2010, 2015, 2017; Chakraborti & Garland, 2009, 2012). From these studies, it is clear that both accounting for structures of inequality and disadvantage and paying attention to the intersection of cultures of hate and processes of digital mediation are vital to an understanding of hate from this broader digital criminological perspective. While the question of nomenclature for discussions of prejudice and bigotry is unlikely to be resolved here, in this book we will use 'networked hate' to articulate a technosocial account of hate in a digital society, a concept we examine below.

Networked Hate

Early in 1985, the Anti-Defamation League (ADL) released a report entitled *Computerized Networks of Hate*. It warned of two networks of hate that could be accessed by computer using a modem: the Aryan Nation Liberty Net, run by the grand dragon of the Texas Knights of the Klu Klux Klan, and Info International, run by one of the largest print publishers of neo-Nazi literature in the United States. Here, it can be seen that, like the term 'hate crime', the emergence of digitally mediated hate can be traced back to the mid-1980s (Akdeniz, 2009, pp. 8–9). Not only was this an early incidence of networked hate, it also highlighted emergent but enduring themes (Berlet & Mason, 2015). In announcing the report, the ADL press release stated that 'the danger lies not only in facilitating the spread of bigotry and anti-democratic propaganda but in its potential impact on impressionable young people, many of whom are computer users' (Anti-Defamation League, 1985, p. 2). While there may be a tone of moral panic in its concern over young people, it highlights the role that technology can play in constructing hate: it is not just a medium for transmitting information between those who already hold these views. The Aryan Nation Liberty Network maintained a public list of 'enemies', 'informers' and 'race traitors', including personal addresses and phone numbers, on its site, foreshadowing 'doxing' (making public someone's private personal information, particularly name, address and other contact details), a strategy that is used both by and against hate groups. The report also identified that the websites were designed to bypass a Canadian embargo against hate literature, demonstrating the ability of digitally networked hate to be global in its reach.

An insight into the contemporary state of networked hate can be seen in the UK Home Office records data on hate crimes with an online component. This is a recent initiative that adopts a smart collection methodology. Rather than dividing the offences into separate online and face-to-face crime categories, a flag can be applied to any crime where there is an online element (Home Office, 2017, p. 24). This means that a crime with an online element can be one that is committed directly in physical proximity to the victim or from afar, a conception of networked hate that will be advocated throughout this chapter. For the 2016/17 data, approximately half of the UK police forces reported on online hate crimes, so the results can only be treated as indicative of the general phenomenon. Within this data, online hate crimes were spread more evenly than 'real-world' crimes across the categories, with 63% racially motivated, 19% motivated by sexual orientation, 13% by disability, 12% by religion and 3% transgender (Home Office, 2017, p. 26). The most interesting part of the data for understanding networked hate is the distinction between the kind of offences that are flagged as having an online hate crime compared with the overall dataset on hate crimes. While criminal damage/arson and other offence categories are both relatively small for hate and online hate, there is significant divergence in the two main categories. Public order offences constitute the largest category of overall hate crime offences at 58%, whereas for hate crimes with an online element it is 13% (Home Office, 2017, p. 27). By far the largest category of offence for online crimes is violence against the person at 84%, whereas only 33% of the overall hate crimes are in this category (Home Office, 2017). Of the online hate crimes against the person, perhaps unsurprisingly, 92% were harassment offences. This suggests two things that may be related: first, that the kinds of hate crimes that are committed with an online element, and harassment in particular, are more likely to be perceived as targeting specific individuals; and second, more concerningly, that police and wider society do not yet see online hate crimes and harassment against individuals as a threat to wider public order.

Pew Research Centre offers some insight into the nature of networked hate in a United States context. The most recent report on online harassment (Pew Research Center, 2017, p. 3) highlighted in its broad finding that 41% of Americans had experienced, and 66% had witnessed, some kind of online harassment. Severe harassment was experienced by 18% of people, which was broken down into the categories of physical threats (10%), sustained harassment (7%), stalking (7%) and sexual harassment (6%) (Pew Research Center, 2017, p. 4). A total of 22% experienced less severe harassment, such as offensive name-calling (27%) and purposeful embarrassment (22%) (Pew Research Center, 2017, p. 4). Interestingly, public concern is more pronounced than these figures might suggest: 94% of the public are aware of the issue, and 62% consider it a major problem (Pew Research Center, 2017, p. 5). Online harassment of people aged 18–29 years is higher at 67%, with 41% having experienced severe harassment (Pew Research Center, 2017, p. 5). Women were more likely to see online harassment as a major problem (70%); this was even higher among women 18–29 (83%), compared to men overall (54%) and men aged 18–29 (55%) (Pew Research Center, 2017, p. 8). Notably, just over half of men favoured free speech (54%) over feeling safe online (46%), whereas nearly two thirds of women prioritised feeling safe (63%) over free speech online (36%) (Pew Research Center, 2017, p. 7). Harassment occurred most commonly via a single platform or website (82%), most commonly social media (58%), followed by comments sections (23%) (Pew Research Center, 2017, p. 23). Amongst those surveyed, 14% were targeted for their political view, 9% for physical appearance, 8% each for gender and race, 5% for religion and 3% for sexual orientation (Pew Research Center, 2017, p. 5). The data on public opinion about how to address online harassment is also interesting. Online services were identified by 79% of respondents as having a responsibility to intervene when harassment occurs (Pew Research Center, 2017, p. 6). The most effective response was considered by 35% to be policies and tools provided by online services and 31% favoured stronger online harassment laws. Regarding law enforcement, 43% thought that police did not take it seriously enough but only 8% viewed increased attention from law enforcement as the most effective solution (Pew Research Center, 2017).

Conceptualising Networked Hate

From the brief discussion so far, it is clear that technology, namely the systems, algorithms and databases of social media and other communications companies, plays a vital role in enabling networked hate. The nature of this relationship, however, is complex. Technology does not cause digitally mediated hate, but neither could it occur in the way it does without digital technology. The capabilities of technology and knowledge practices of society produce one another. Central to theorising the technosocial account of networked hate is an understanding of how social order and technological systems shape one another, generating new modes of human behaviour in digital society. A digital criminological approach to hate involves moving beyond the dichotomy of online hate and offline hate. This involves more than just ascribing a greater priority to online hate or bringing it alongside real-world hate. Treating these as separate categories perpetuates what sociologist and social media scholar Nathan Jurgenson (2011) describes as 'digital dualism', an online/offline dichotomy where real and virtual are positioned as separate realities (see Chapter 1). Events such as those in Charlottesville in 2017 highlight that, even when hate manifests as mass movements that are highly visible on the streets of cities, it is nevertheless, in many respects, a digitally produced and digitally mediated phenomenon. This section seeks to demonstrate that the nature of networked hate is a *technosocial* process, a digitally mediated phenomenon that results from ongoing cycles of social and technological co-production (Jasanoff, 2004a).

Co-production of Networked Hate

Four days after the London Bridge attack, London Mayor Sadiq Khan announced on Facebook that there had been a sharp increase in hate crimes and Islamophobic attacks (Mayor of London, 2017). According to data released by London City Hall, on the Monday following the weekend attack, there had been a 500% increase in Islamophobic attacks and a 40% increase in other racist incidents, the highest daily recorded level — exceeding previous spikes that had occurred following the murder of Lee Rigby in 2013, the Paris attacks in 2015 and the Manchester Arena bombing earlier in 2017 (London City Hall, 2017; Williams & Burnap, 2016). This is perhaps to be expected: attacks such as that on London Bridge quickly become mass-mediated events that affect wider society, generating a range of racialised effects, including hate crimes (Byers & Jones, 2007; Cameron, 2013; Hanes & Machin, 2014). While a heightened incidence of hate crimes may only be short term following these events, research on the 2011 London riots suggested that, even after initial reactions subside, something that triggers '*memory* of the riots exerts itself directly on ethnic prejudice' causing an increased sense of social distance between groups, similar to levels immediately after the riots (De Rooij, Goodwin, & Pickup, 2015, p. 381, emphasis in original). The authors also noted that the memory triggers used in the study 'were extremely weak compared to the nature of rhetoric that politicians or media might employ' (De Rooij et al., 2015, p. 381). Hate, in this sense, is shown to be not a one-off reaction but an enduring series of social effects.

While such 'reprisal' hate crimes occurred largely in the streets, there is a more extensive pattern of networked hate underpinning this phenomenon (Burnap et al., 2014). In their research into abuse experienced by British Muslims, criminologists Imran Awan and Irene Zempi (2017) identified not only that hate crimes peaked following events associated with terrorism or foreign threats but that victims' experience of 'virtual' and 'physical' was very similar, both in terms of causes – being a visibly identifiable Muslim – and effects – attacks that strike at the heart of the victim's identity. In an earlier paper, they detail the nature of Muslim visibility in both online and offline contexts where appearance was an important identifier, specifically the attire worn by women and beards worn by men (Awan & Zempi, 2016, p. 3). Physical proximity to mosques also played a role in face-to-face encounters, as did usernames in encounters on social media sites. The insight from findings such as these is that online abuse should be taken more seriously, given that it is more common than face-to-face abuse and experienced by victims as similarly harmful (Awan & Zempi, 2016; Awan & Zempi, 2017). While the authors suggest there is an affinity between online and offline anti-Muslim hatred, a technosocial approach takes this one step further, arguing that the online/offline or real/virtual binary is ineffective as an analytical frame of reference. For example, just as contemporary urban landscapes render mosques visible as sites for social prejudice and as places for assault to occur, so too do social media identities and practices render Muslims visibly 'other' online (Bugg & Gurran, 2011; Emmett, 2010). Awan and Zempi (2017, p. 377) describe how, once identified and subjected to Islamophobic hate, other users mimic these behaviours creating a 'cyber mob'. Technology is not just *revealing* pre-existing bigotry within society; rather, technology and society are shaping one another, coalescing in emerging cultures and practices that simultaneously *produce and reproduce* hate-based harms.

Which Knowledge, Whose Society?

Like many, Facebook CEO Zuckerberg (2017) took to social media to announce his concern about the events that had just transpired at Charlottesville:

> It is important that Facebook is a place where people with different views can share their ideas. Debate is part of a healthy society. But when someone tries to silence others or attacks them based on who they are or what they believe, that hurts us all and is unacceptable. There is no place for hate in our community.

Unlike most others who took to social media, he happened to own the platform in question and could do something to address the role Facebook plays in networks of hate. There are quite a few issues with his statement, but most relevant to this section is the implied neutrality of Facebook as a platform in facilitating the toxic debates he alluded to. Even to describe Facebook as a 'platform' and its role as a 'facilitator' is to understate the role it plays as a co-producer of the content and culture on its media platform. As Facebook COO (Chief Operating Officer) Sheryl Sandberg has stated more explicitly, 'at our heart we're a tech company; we hire engineers. We don't hire reporters, no one's a journalist, we don't cover the news' (quoted in Griffith, 2017). But Facebook's lack of neutrality can be seen, for example, when its services provided highly targeted advertising to a nominally unaligned, but nonetheless highly partisan and very non-transparent, lobbying organisation called Secure America Now. It is likely that undecided voters in the key swing states of Nevada and North Carolina saw videos in their Facebook feeds depicting Germany and France as overrun by an ISIS-style system of law and government; school children training for a caliphate; the Eiffel Tower topped with a crescent and the Mona Lisa largely obscured by a niqab (Elgin & Silver, 2017). This video was not just put out to everyone on the platform in a post. Facebook was paid to make sure the video reached very specific demographic sub-populations. This is not to suggest that the content was illegal, or to make an argument that it should be banned. It is to highlight that Facebook, by selling its advertising to all and sundry, is involving itself in the propagation of Islamophobic and anti-refugee content through its media services.

Codes and algorithms are not neutral, as sociologists and technologists such as Judy Wajcman (1991) have long identified. Alongside the software and hardware, there is at every stage of its operation a degree of human input that can influence its operation (Jasanoff, 2004b). The operation of codes and algorithms reflects the gender and race of the programmer, the personal biases of the programmers, the culture of the workplace, the strategies that shape design briefs, the normative values of the society, the spaces created by urban planning, the hierarchies of privilege, inequalities in the economy, crime and justice policies, the knowledges owned through intellectual property, the access to markets provided by trade deals and the (in)security created by national security (Carpenter, 2015; Edionwe, 2017; Tatman, 2016; Young, 2015). As Jasanoff said, it is vital to understand 'how knowledge finds, or acquires and holds legitimacy in particular social and political contexts. Global knowledge, almost by definition, is cut loose from all of that history of making legitimacy' (quoted in Turney, 1997). Indeed, at the most profound level, codes and algorithms also reflect the histories of lands and civilizations being taken from indigenous peoples, and of liberty and free labour taken through slavery and colonialism. This is not an abstract ethical principle. When Facebook wrongly deems Native American names to be 'fake' or Google Photos automatically tags African Americans as gorillas, the codes that allow this to happen stem from similar knowledge and assumptions that legitimated the violent histories of genocide and slavery (Guynn, 2015; Nicole, 2009). It is examples such as these that highlight that hate networks exist not only in the prejudiced actions of people but also in technosocial systems of bias and prejudice, involving complex interactions of human and non-human actants (Latour, 1996). Social and technological interactions always carry with them these kinds of affordances, and they should be part of the consideration when examining hate networks. To claim that technology is neutral is, in effect, an attempt to erase the social context of its users (Raine & Anderson, 2017).

In a 'post-truth' era where populism reigns and facts are hard to agree on, knowledge and information become as competing fronts in the culture wars of digital society. After each mass casualty event in countries such as the United States, UK and Australia, a deluge of breaking news, incomplete facts and speculative guesswork combine with deliberate misinformation on social media feeds and internet searches (Marwick & Lewis, 2017). This misinformation can take the form of automated bots circulating stories, 'cloaked' accounts trying to spread false information or simply regular users trying to spin the narrative for their own ends (Ben-Davis, & Matamoros-Fernández, 2016; Farkas, Schou, & Neumayer, 2017; Michael, 2017). This has also been a significant phenomenon during recent elections, potentially impacting outcomes (Ferrara, 2017; Howard & Kollanyi, 2016; Kollanyi, Howard, & Woolley, 2016). Communications scholar Adam Klein (2012) refers to these processes where misinformation is dispersed through digital platforms, social media and then out into the traditional media as a process of 'information laundering'. And it is not just rogue 'bad actors' corrupting discourse and creating a 'post-truth' world. The algorithms of a number of major digital media companies actively enable this process by directing misinformation to users who are likely to re-post, re-tweet or like the content. An unfortunately typical example of this can be seen in the immediate aftermath of the First Baptist Church mass shooting in Sutherland Springs, Texas. Far-right activists and pundits began speculating that the alleged shooter was linked with the left-wing antifascist network, AntiFA, which quickly led to it trending on Facebook and Twitter. This misinformation was given a further boost when Google searches for the suspect brought up links to these tweets at the top of its search (Lytvynenko, 2017; Madrigal, 2017). It is clear in this example how the algorithms and user practices of Twitter, Facebook and Google coalesce to spread misinformation. Furthermore, it is telling that, in an age of digital threats from 'bad actors', these massive digital media companies are not 'good actors' helping to solve the problem.

Role of Institutions

On 24 October 2017 a Facebook group, 'SNAFU – Situation Normal All Fucked Up', promoting cultures of child sex abuse, domestic violence and rape was shut down. The request for the group to be shut-down for violating community standards came from the Australian Defence Department, after an organisation, Victims of Abuse in the Australian Defence Force (ADF) Association, advised the Veterans Affairs Minister that serving members of the armed forces were active on the site (Australian Associated Press, 2016). The allegation was that, from their analysis of 8% (approximately 2400) of the SNAFU group's 30,000 'likes', there were 100 identifiable defence personnel. This event was another in a series of incidents in which the ADF had been criticised for a harmful and institutionalised sexist and racist subculture. In 2014, at least 20 members of the Australian armed forces were alleged to have been active on a racist Facebook group advocating racial violence that was maintained by the Australian Defence League, an organisation affiliated with the banned UK group the English Defence League (Hall, 2014). Meanwhile, in 2011 and 2012, the ADF again garnered controversy due to a series of high-profile cases where nude and/or sexual videos and photos of female staff members were taken and distributed non-consensually, as well as documented cases of extensive racist and sexist activities of defence force personnel on Facebook pages (Australian Associated Press, 2011; Cooper, 2012). As with these previous cases, the media coverage of the SNAFU Facebook group allegations focused on the transgressive nature of the content and the responsibility of individual members of the defence force, while nonetheless diminishing the seriousness of the incident by referring to the Facebook page as 'controversial' rather than potentially *criminal* under state and/or federal Australian laws. Once again, most discussions overlook the structures, both institutional and technological, that enable and perpetuate hate-based social norms.

There are, however, important wider issues related to the role of organisations such as the ADF in preventing networked hate. While digitally mediated abuse and hate within the ranks of the ADF have not come out of nowhere, neither have they occurred entirely with impunity. In 2015, a former soldier was given a 15-month suspended sentence for non-consensually filming and electronically circulating images of himself having sex with a woman (Australian Associated Press, 2015). When this case originally came to light in 2011, amidst a number of other instances where social media had been implicated in harm and abuse, it caused widespread outcry against cultures of misogyny within the armed forces (The Canberra Times, 2012; Wadham, 2011). In light of this, the ADF undertook to initiate a process of culture change within its organisation, commissioning a number of independent reviews (Australian Human Rights Commission, 2011, 2012; Department of Defence, 2011a), reports (Defence Abuse Response Taskforce, 2014; Rumble, McKean, & Pearce, 2011) and audits (Australian Human Rights Commission, 2013, 2014) into abuse, bullying and misogyny. Recognising the interface between its organisations and social media networks, it also developed an extensive report into social media use within its ranks (Department of Defence, 2011b). In an attempt to consolidate these findings, the *Pathways to Change* implementation strategy laid out 128 recommendations for pursuing cultural change, including seven that related to the use of social media (Department of Defence, 2012). The public face of the reform agenda, however, was defined by a Youtube video that went viral, in which Chief of the Army David Morrison responds directly to the incidence of 'image-based abuse'[1] (AustralianArmyHQ, 2013). With a cold fury, he condemns not only the primary offender but also those in the image-sharing network and, finally, anyone who does not support women in the military, saying 'if that does not suit you then get out'.

Large institutions are slow to change, but they wield significant influence on social norms. Institutional change in the military has been a generational process encountering many forms of internal and external resistance (Smith, 1984), and the inclusion of women is no different (Smith & McAllister, 1991). Key social control institutions are part of the process of social production: sociologist

Ben Wadham suggests this can be seen specifically in relation to race and gender in the way that 'the military reflects white Australian or Anglo-Australian male identities. These values are re-presented back to Australian society' (Wadham, 2013, p. 216). In a digitally mediated era, institutions of social control should equally be seen as part of a system of technosocial co-production. While there are certainly questions as to the long-term commitment of the military and the government, there is increasing civil and democratic control over the military (Lee-Koo, 2014; Wadham, 2016). The institutional reforms being pursued within the ADF mean that 'the institutional habitus of the white Australian male soldier is under scrutiny and in some ways erasure' (Wadham, Bridges, Mundkur, & Connor, 2016, p. 6). Changing norms within a system of co-production, however, is unlikely to always be positive and accommodating; it is more likely to be negative and reactionary in certain quarters. This was identified by Elizabeth Broderick, author of the independent Australian Human Rights Commission report, and then Sex Discrimination Commissioner in 2014, who suggested that 'significant progress' had been made but 'in all our discussions, our focus groups and the work we have been doing, we have heard talk of a backlash' (Australian Associated Press, 2014, n.p.). Broderick's teams had encountered anger, resentment and hostility in middle and junior levels of the organisation at what were seen as politically correct measures to promote women without merit. This backlash is common in processes of organisational change, but finding a public outlet in an enabling technosocial system such as Facebook can threaten to undermine long-term change, while also harming the wider public with which it interacts.

Challenges and Implications

This section deploys the concept of 'networked hate' in order to understand how social inequality and prejudice can be compounded by digital technologies. The circulation of hate by digital media and social institutions is a generative technosocial process. Digital mediations in a manner made possible by the coding of the software and the capacity of their hardware. Through these interactions, they not only shape each other by challenging and reinforcing social mores, often across geographical, legal and normative boundaries, they also shape the use of the software and future iterations of how it is coded. While this account offers a more comprehensive understanding of hate within society, it also raises some significant challenges for what is acceptable speech, what are acceptable collective responses to hate and how digital media companies ought to respond to harmful content they enable their users to produce.

One Person's Hate Speech is Another Person's Free Speech

In the Bay Area town of Albany, California, two teenage students filed suit in federal court on 13 May 2017, suing their principal and school area district for violating their right to free speech. Free speech, in this case, is in direct tension with the understanding of hate speech outlined earlier by Matsuda. Also alleged in their complaint was that they had been subjected to public shaming, violence and emotional abuse during a five-hour protest that occurred outside their school, which resulted from the 'racially hostile environment' created by school administrators (Tsai, 2017). This followed damages being sought on similar grounds by four other teenagers earlier in the month relating to the same events (Gafni, Lochner, & Kelly, 2017). All six allege they were singled out by the school at a restorative justice session where they were named as part of a group that produced and distributed racist Instagram posts. The school's actions were taken against these students after a number of students, all but one of whom were female students of colour, became aware of an Instagram image depicting them and their basketball coach with nooses around their necks alongside monkeys. The school took disciplinary action against 13 boys after they were found to have 'liked' and commented on the images. The majority were suspended, and the alleged creator of the image was expelled. The restorative justice hearing was held when some of the boys returned to school, at which time there was also a public protest outside the school. During the course of the day, two of the boys were assaulted, one suffering a broken nose (Esper, 2017). This, however, was not a one-off incident: prior to the Instagram post, the school had been the site of a number of racist actions, including students giving Nazi salutes to each other in the hallways (Matier & Ross, 2017).

These events sharply divided the school community and highlight the challenges of reconciling digitally mediated harm that occurs at a community level with a highly individualised conception of a right to free speech. Statements by the male students' attorney suggested that the disciplinary actions violated constitutionally protected freedoms: 'you have the right to be racist in this country, and you have the right not to be racist in this country. This turns the school into the Thought Police' (Gafni et al., 2017, n.p.). Responding to the free speech argument, the uncle of one of the students depicted in the image stated that 'free speech is a fundamental right, but it can't be at the expense of hurting someone' (Gafni et al., 2017). Indeed, a further problem with framing the issue solely as one of free speech is that it allows the harm to the students who had liked the Instagram post – the loss of liberty and assault that followed the school's disciplinary actions – to be part of the legal considerations; however, it draws focus away from the consequences of the initial harm to the students depicted in the post and caused by the act of liking and circulating the image. It also fails to appreciate the harmful nature of such images, as discussed in Chapter 5 of this book.

According to reporting, a key part of the students' case against the Albany school district revolved around what it means to 'like' a post (Esper, 2017). Is it considered to be a constitutionally protected form of free speech, or can it be considered an act occasioning harm to someone? While there may be a speech component to this, no clearer articulation of the harm experienced by the individual students and the wider student body can be found than that in a Youtube video made by Anika Mallard (2017), one of the students depicted in the images. In the video, students speak of the sadness, bewilderment and anger they felt when hearing about, seeing and knowing that the images were circulating in their community. While the incident highlights challenges of responding effectively to networked hate, we can also see how platforms can be used to support informal justice practices, a phenomenon that will be explored further in Chapter 7.

Ultimately, however, the case serves to illustrate that networks of hate represent more than a series of isolated incidents of harms directed at, and experienced by, individuals. Indeed, this singular and individualised framing, at least in part, causes such harms to be too easily passed off as 'speech'. Rather, following earlier work by critical criminologists Powell and Henry (2017), we take issue with the presumed 'harmlessness' of such 'communications'. When racism, dehumanisation and inferiorisation are normalised within a network (in this case, in both the school grounds and school communities on Instagram), the impacts are felt not only as individual harms but as *cumulative* and *collective* harms. Criminologist Gail Mason (2014, p. 76) suggests that, in responding to hate crimes, it is necessary to 'challenge the norms and moral boundaries that sustain racial, religious, sexual and other hierarchies of difference'. While she primarily focuses on the role of hate crime law in 'reconfiguring public perceptions of them [victims] as inferior, illegitimate or dangerous Others', it is the symbolic function of law that addresses the wider social prejudice (Mason, 2014, p. 76). While law may play a part in this symbolic role, it is facing, as civil rights activists Abraham Foxman and Christopher Wolf (2013, pp. 10–11) suggest in their book *Viral Hate*, the ever-proliferating online propaganda in which 'hate begets hate, and its widespread appearance makes it seem increasingly acceptable and normal'. Hate is a destructive social process long before it arises to the point of physical assault.

While responding to networks of hate through legal frameworks is likely to cause tension with free speech, what is clear is that there is a wider set of processes at play. This chapter does not pretend the constitutional issues raised by the first amendment and its individualistic interpretation of free speech, particularly as it relates to courtroom settings, can be resolved here. Rather, it seeks to shift the focus wider where possible to conceptualise the free speech versus hate speech contention as a structural social problem. More specifically, in an increasingly digitally mediated society, networked hate is treated as a technosocial problem, co-produced by structural inequalities intersecting with new communications platforms where the inequalities take on new, and often harmful, forms. There, cultures of hate can be adopted as social norms within both informal networks and formal institutions that are enabled by communications platforms. Addressing hate at this structural level is an issue of harm reduction and preventative culture change within institutions rather than a balance between free speech and harm.

Viral Violence as Digital Resistance?

On 25 August 2017, Instagram user 'colleendagg' posted the following statement:

> This is a young country, built on racism. Black people have been disenfranchised for over 250 years. The faster white people accept and validate the truth, the closer we'll come to a place of peace and understanding. Fighting racism is dependent on using my white privilege for the right reasons. There were 2 examples of white privilege in the video. The woman in the blue dress tried to use her white privilege on me, the fact that I'm white too must have slipped her mind. If you see it, say something. It's really that simple. Disclaimer; some people can't handle the truth. Stay ready.

This principled statement sought to recognise the violence of slavery and white supremacy and call for bystander intervention to prevent racism. It received over 13,000 likes and was widely shared both on the social media platform and across many news media platforms. The nature of her actions in the video she refers to, however, belie the clear moral position she adopts. Her call for the necessity of 'fighting racism' in this case was not merely metaphorical. Her privilege was not only of whiteness but also, in the case of this encounter, of class, gender normativity, physical strength and quite possibly a level of training in self-defence or combat sports.

The original video depicts two women arguing in the lobby of La Quinta Hotel on 22 August 2017. The younger women, Colleen Dagg, sits down on a couch and removes her high-heeled shoes, while the other women, Summer Cotts (who is not armed), says if she hits her with a shoe she will shoot her in the face, to which Dagg says if she lays a hand on her she will have to defend herself. Cotts then steps towards Dagg, grabbing her face and head, at which point Dagg responds, grabbing the woman's hair, throwing her to the ground, punching her hard in the face 10–15 times and dragging her around by the hair. Hotel staff members quickly intervene, separating the women. Cotts says that she is three months pregnant and wants to press charges for assault. Moments later, the Coral Springs police arrive and later charge Cotts with battery, presumably deeming the response by Dagg to be self-defence. Dagg declines to press charges and the police issue a notice to Cotts for disorderly conduct. This video was viewed over 1.5 million times in the first two days after it was posted and was reposted globally on tabloid news sites and video platforms. In a subsequent interview with the local Miami NBC6 news channel, Dagg says Cotts had made racist and stereotypical comments about a group of children who had spilled water on the floor. The almost universal framing of the story in news stories and social media sites was that Cotts deserved to be beaten for being racist and initiating the incident, even though the video does not capture the initial racist comments.

This video is a typical example of actions that are often celebrated as a kind of necessary informal justice against racism. The efficacy of this is extremely complex and hard to resolve, and the questions are ethical as well as legal ones. Is the physical violence justified? Is this justification on the basis of self-defence or as symbolic resistance to the structural violence of racism? Does the use of violent resistance play into the structural violence of patriarchy or pit the individuals against their class interests? More pragmatically, is it likely to be effective? Without knowing exactly what transpired, it is hard to explore these questions, let alone state a conclusion definitively. What can be said is that, as self-defence, the response was hardly proportional and could really only be understood as such in a state like Florida, where the use of deadly force in self-defence can be justified under the notorious 'stand your ground' laws, which were used to acquit George Zimmerman of the murder of Trayvon Martin. The basis on which it was being celebrated therefore seems to be as an instance of symbolic resistance or informal justice against structural racism. Again, this is hard to definitely answer without either having seen the entire event or being someone embedded in the social life of Florida. After all, tremendous injustice was done in the case of Trayvon Martin, and the structural violence of racism in that case seems hard to overstate. Does Cotts really embody all the privileges of whiteness? To some degree, it did seem like she was being ridiculed for seeming stupid or uneducated, as well as being racist, in which case there are issues of class privilege that perhaps she does not enjoy. While the example above, for the most part, didn't generate this level of debate, other, similar videos have been much more divisive.

Richard Spencer, the figurehead of the alt-right, was at the centre of a debate around whether it is acceptable to 'punch Nazis'. Spencer, however, was not so much a participant in the debate but the object case study. During an on-camera interview that occurred amidst the celebrations and protest of the Presidential inauguration in Washington DC, Richard Spencer was in the process of explaining the Pepe the Frog meme, which he was wearing as a lapel pin and which has been labelled by the Anti-Defamation League as a hate symbol. Mid-explanation, a masked protester suddenly enters from the left-hand side of the screen and punches Spencer in the face. At that point, the interview ends and Spencer walks away holding his jaw. This became a viral moment that itself spawned many memes and much debate. This event, however, was widely celebrated. Indeed, it quite arguably was a galvanising point for public concerns around the potential for violence by anti-fascist protest group AntiFA, with whom the masked assailant seemed likely to be associated. The ethics and efficacy of this event are again complex. While the attack was clearly not self-defence, Spencer at the time stood as one of the foremost symbols of white supremacy, although he disingenuously eschews the term. It would seem that, short of a pacifist position, symbolic counter-violence could be justified. The main issues are whether it compounds systemic violence and whether violent reprisals would render it strategically counterproductive. Spencer did subsequently say that he was scared to go out in public after the attack, although given the reach of his digital networks, it is not clear whether it blunts his ability to spread hate. These kinds of vigilantism and 'digilantism' will be explored in more detail in as the central focus of Chapter 7.

Algorithmic Responses to Networked Hate

The far-right protests in Charlottesville saw a scramble by a number of digital media companies to respond to hate content on their sites. Reddit, for example, announced a change to its rules governing content in late October 2017, leading to the banning of a number of discussion threads, known as subreddits, many among them of a right-wing political bent. In its statement, it suggested 'that the policy regarding "inciting" violence was too vague' and that 'any content that encourages, glorifies, incites, or calls for violence or physical harm against an individual or a group of people' would have action taken against it (Landoflobsters, 2017). Subreddits such as /r/Nazi, /r/killthejews, /r/far_right, /r/DylannRoofInnocent were quickly banned, but a number of others were allowed to continue, including /r/incels, which is often associated with advocating violence against women (Caffier, 2017; Tait, 2017) and /r/the_Donald, which is often associated with advocating racial and political violence (Feinberg, 2017; Oppenheim, 2017). If previous attempts are anything to go by, the effectiveness will be limited by a combination of backlash and hateful content moving to other parts of the site.

Nonetheless, this is the most significant attempt yet made to regulate the site, following a largely unsuccessful attempt in 2015 that generated a massive amount of backlash (Russell, 2015). CEO at the time, Ellen Pao, had sought to rein-in various harassing behaviours after a number of subreddits that had been used to circulate and profit from nude celebrity images obtained through a hack of iCloud servers generated increased public awareness of the wider hate culture on Reddit (Greenberg, 2014). This, however, was short-lived. After taking the step of banning five hate-based subreddits, including /r/fatpeoplehate, the site was flooded with body-shaming content that had previously been confined to the single subreddit. Pao was soon forced to resign, when the firing of a Reddit community manager caused a number of high-traffic subreddits to shut themselves to the public, effectively removing a large portion of the site from the open internet (Hern, 2015). In announcing her resignation, she stated 'in my eight months as Reddit's CEO, I've seen the good, the bad and the ugly on Reddit. The good has been off-the-wall inspiring, and the ugly made me doubt humanity' (Alba, 2015).

If, as sociologist Manuel Castells famously stated, 'the disgust became a network', then on Reddit the disgusting has become a network (Castells, 2011). This toxic masculinist culture did not occur in the absence of the technical affordances of Reddit's algorithms. According to communications scholar Adrienne Massanari (2017), it was key features of the site such as the 'karma' point system, the ease of account creation and the linking of material across subreddits that allowed harassment and abuse to become systemic (see also Burgess & Matamoros-Fernández, 2016; Higgin, 2013). Even where governance and policies might have provided limits, Media scholar Robert Topinka highlights how users adapt discourses and communication techniques on the site to 'cloak' hate and abuse against scrutiny in ways that make it also 'highly obvious and highly effective' (Topinka, 2017, p. 1). It is important, however, to note that Reddit is also home to many educational and supportive communities, such as /r/ExplainLikeIm5, where complex topics are explained to those looking to gain new understanding, /r/DepthHub, where topics are discussed in earnest and with rigor, or /r/

itookapicture, where users share amazing photos they took and explain the backstory. Many memes that have formed the backbone of popular culture originated on Reddit, including 'expanding brain', 'wheel stick', 'sad Keanu' and 'you had one job'. Reddit is also not alone in providing a home to abhorrent content: perhaps most notoriously, 4Chan provided a home for some of the most abusive, sustained harassment campaigns, particularly against women (Nagle, 2017). Similar content is extensive and pervasive on Youtube, Facebook, Twitter and Tumblr. The challenges faced by digital media platforms highlight the need for innovative approaches to regulating hate-based content.

There are more effective ways to respond to hate networks than responding to content that violates regulations or laws. As Spinello has suggested, there is both 'law and code' that can be used to control online activity deemed to be harmful (Spinello, 2014, p. 79). While enforcing the removal of content or pursuing legal remedies may have some deterrent effect on norms and behaviour, it is primarily responsive in nature. Code-based or algorithmic measures can function in a responsive or preventative manner (Reynolds, 2016). The process of identifying and removing content can be automated, or the actual user experience of software can be reshaped, changing the interaction between technology and society in a way that alters norms and values of online platforms, potentially without users even being aware of it. This approach is appealing to many tech companies facing mounting criticism of networked hate on their platforms because it represents a technical, software engineering solution to a social problem. This, however, is not a short cut — some measure of human judgement is likely to be required. Ultimately, we cannot simply code our way out of our own complex histories and ongoing practices of institutionalised bigotry and inequality.

Conclusion

On 21 August 2017, Alison Saunders, the UK's Director of Public Prosecutions, announced via an op-ed in the *Guardian* that the Crown Prosecution Service (CPS) would commit to 'treat online hate crimes as seriously as those committed face to face' (Saunders, 2017). Saunders contextualised specific spectacular public acts of violence such as Charlottesville alongside the broader challenge of 'a less visible frontline which is easily accessible to those in the UK who hold extreme views on race, religion, sexuality, gender and even disability' (Saunders, 2017). This reflects an increased urgency and priority being placed on online hate crime, as suggested by Awan and Zempi. What this chapter has sought to highlight is that this prioritisation should be accompanied by awareness that both 'online' and 'offline' hate crime are equally produced by digitally mediated networks of hate. What is more, it is likely that there is very little difference between the networks of hate producing face-to-face hate and those producing hate on digital media services. In digital society, networked hate is the result of technosocial co-production.

The CPS announcement followed the targeting of a number of UK politicians with extensive abuse on the basis of their gender, race or religion. Writing about her experiences of intimidation and abuse, Labour MP for Hackney North and Stoke Newington, Diane Abbott, details the following (Abbott, 2017, n.p.):

> I receive racist and sexist abuse online on a daily basis. I have had rape threats, death threats, and am referred to routinely as a bitch and/or nigger, and am sent horrible images on Twitter. The death threats include an EDL-affiliated account with the tag "burn Diane Abbott".

This harrowing account highlights how varied networks of hate converge and draws attention to the importance of an intersectional perspective to understand how even those who enjoy the privileges of elected office are still subject to the underlying structures of racism, sexism and inequality within society. This kind of hate, as has been shown throughout this chapter, is not limited to those in elected office, as these networks pervade so many aspects of modern life. Structural factors underpinning inequality and disadvantage are not benign, and neither is technology neutral; deeply rooted bias is reflected in technological affordances of digital communications and then further compounded as they are distributed throughout society.

It is vital to stress that networked hate cannot be dismissed as 'just online'. In June 2016, Labour MP for Batley and Spen, Jo Cox was brutally murdered by Thomas Mair, a man whose history included participation in banned far-right political parties, amassing a library of neo-Nazi literature and extensive online racist activity (Cobain, Parveen, & Taylor, 2016). While the most heinous crime occurred so openly on the street in the eyes of the public, his motivations and potential criminal activities span many mediums and networks, both open and closed, public and private. Similarly, many of the British MPs in the recent UK election were targeted not just via digital networks but also via phones, via post and at their homes (Grierson, 2017). The distinction between real/virtual and online/offline becomes ever less meaningful. More important to understanding networked hate is the role that intersecting cultures of white supremacy, toxic masculinity and other forms of bigoted privilege play in normalising these forms of violence.

The harm of this abuse is not just experienced at the level of the individual being victimised, it also has an effect on the wider society. So concerned were a number of MPs from across the political spectrum at the abuse they experienced, that they demanded the issue be addressed by Prime Minister Theresa May because of the threat it posed to participation in the political process (Mason, 2017). While there is no doubt that many threats detailed by MPs clearly rise to the level of convictable hate crime, there is also an implicit recognition that free speech may not be free for everyone if that speech is hate speech. While the UK is willing to take action against certain forms of hate speech, these protections in the United States are highly constrained and pose a major issue for safe participation in social and political discourse for many. In seeking to respond to the networks of hate, an additional pertinent issue raised in this chapter is whether legal avenues pursued by the CPS are likely to be effective in addressing the wider phenomenon. Given the many incidences of backlash when actions are taken against hate networks, it is conceivable that it may even be counterproductive, at least in the short term. More effective long-term change is likely to require broad cultural change, whether that be through informal justice or through formal organised movements, across society, its institutions and its technologies.

Note

1   While, colloquially, 'revenge pornography' has been widely used to refer to instances where a nude or sexual image of a person is distributed without their consent, a growing number of scholars advocate for alternative terms such as 'image-based sexual exploitation', 'image-based abuse' or 'image-based sexual abuse' on the grounds that these more accurately capture the nature of the harms experienced by victims (see DeKeseredy & Schwartz, 2016; Henry & Powell, 2016; McGlynn & Rackley, 2017; Powell & Henry, 2016, 2017).

Recommended Further Reading

Awan, I., & Zempi, I. (2017). 'I will blow your face off': Virtual and physical world anti-Muslim hate crime. *British Journal of Criminology, 57*(2), 362–380.

Massanari, A. (2017). #Gamergate and The Fappening: How Reddit's algorithm, governance, and culture support toxic technocultures. *New Media & Society, 19*(3), 329–346.

Topinka, R. J. (2017). Politically incorrect participatory media: Racist nationalism on r/ImGoingToHellForThis. *New, Media & Society,* Advance online publication. doi: 10.1177/1461444817712516.

Williams, M. L., & Burnap, P. (2016). Cyberhate on social media in the aftermath of Woolwich: A case study in computational criminology and big data. *British Journal of Criminology, 56*(2), 211–238.

References

Abbott, D. (2017). I fought racism and misogyny to become an MP. The fight is getting harder. Available at: www.theguardian.com/commentisfree/2017/feb/14/racism-misogyny-politics-online-abuse-minorities (last accessed 29 November 2017).

Agarwal, S., & Sureka, A. (2016). Spider and flies: Focussed crawling on Tumblr to detect hate promoting communities. Available at: https://arXiv.org/abs/1603.09164.

Akdeniz, Y. (2009). *Racism on the Internet.* Strasbourg: Council of Europe Publishing.

Alba, D. (2015). Ellen Pao steps down as CEO after Reddit Revolt. Available at: www.wired.com/2015/07/reddit-ceo-ellen-pao-steps-down-huffman-replacement/ (last accessed 29 November 2017).

Anti-Defamation League. (1985). Computerized networks of hate: An ADL fact finding report. Available at: www.archive.org/details/ComputerizedNetworksOfHate (last accessed 29 November 2017).

AustralianArmyHQ. (2013). Chief of Army Lieutenant General David Morrison message about unacceptable behaviour. Available at: www.youtube.com/watch?v=QaqpoeVgr8U (last accessed 29 November 2017).

Australian Associated Press. (2011). Australian defence force to investigate racist taunts by soldiers on Facebook. Available at: www.theaustralian.com.au/national-affairs/australian-defence-force-to-investigate-racist-taunts-by-soldiers-on-facebook/news-story/3bb345f7a85606ca6d469a275be9877b (last accessed 29 November 2017).

Australian Associated Press. (2014). Female ADF members facing backlash. Available at: www.sbs.com.au/news/article/2014/03/26/female-adf-members-facing-sexist-backlash (last accessed 29 November 2017).

Australian Associated Press. (2015). Former Australian soldier apologises for 'Jedi Council' pornography ring emails. Available at: www.theguardian.com/australia-news/2015/jun/07/former-australian-soldier-apologises-for-jedi-council-pornography-ring-emails (last accessed 29 November 2017).

Australian Associated Press. (2016). Facebook closes 'rape meme' page with ADF Troops Link. Available at: www.sbs.com.au/news/article/2017/10/24/facebook-closes-rape-meme-page-adf-troops-link (last accessed 29 November 2017).

Australian Human Rights Commission. (2011). Review into the treatment of women in the Australian defence force: Phase 2 report. Available at: http://defencereview.humanrights.gov.au/sites/default/files/ADFA_2011.pdf (last accessed 2 March 2018).

Australian Human Rights Commission. (2012). Review into the treatment of women in the Australian defence force: Phase 2 report. Available at: https://defencereview.humanrights.gov.au/sites/default/files/adf-complete.pdf (last accessed 2 March 2018).

Australian Human Rights Commission. (2013). Review into the treatment of women in the Australian defence force: Audit report. Available at: www.humanrights.gov.au/sites/default/files/document/publication/adfa-audit-report-2013.pdf (last accessed 29 November 2017).

Australian Human Rights Commission. (2014). Review into the treatment of women in the Australian defence force: Audit report. Available at: www.humanrights.gov.au/sites/default/files/document/publication/adf-audit-2014.pdf (last accessed 29 November 2017).

Awan, I., & Zempi, I. (2016). The affinity between online and offline anti-Muslim hate crime: Dynamics and impacts. *Aggression and Violent Behaviour, 27,* 1–8.

Awan, I., & Zempi, I. (2017). 'I will blow your face off': Virtual and physical world anti-Muslim hate crime. *British Journal of Criminology, 57*(2), 362–380.

Banks, J. (2010). Regulating hate speech online. *International Review of Law, Computers and Technology*, *24*(3), 233–239.

Ben-Davis, A., & Matamoros-Fernández, A. (2016). Hate speech and covert discrimination on social media: Monitoring the Facebook pages of extreme-right political parties in Spain. *International Journal of Communication*, *10*(7), 1167–1193.

Berlet, C., & Mason, C. (2015). Swastikas in cyberspace: How hate went online. In P. A. Simpson, & H. Druxes (Eds.), *Digital media strategies of far-right in Europe and the United States* (pp. 21–36). Lanham, MA: Lexington Books.

Briendl, Y., & Kuellmer, B. (2013). Internet content regulation in France and Germany: Regulatory paths, actor constellations, and policies. *Journal of Information Technology & Politics*, *10*(4), 369–388.

Brown, A. (2017). What is hate speech? Part 1: The myth of hate. *Law and Philosophy*, *36*(4), 419–468.

Bugg, L., & Gurran, N. (2011). Urban planning process and discourse in the refusal of Islamic schools in Sydney, Australia. *Australian Planner*, *48*(4), 281–291.

Burgess, J., & Matamoros-Fernández, A. (2016). Mapping sociocultural controversies across digital media platforms: One week of #Gamergate on Twitter, Youtube, and Tumblr. *Communication Research & Practice*, *2*(1), 79–96.

Burnap, P., Williams, M. L., Rana, O., Housely, W., Edwards, A., & Knight, V. (2014). Tweeting the terror: Modelling the social media reaction to the Woolwich terrorist attack. *Social Network Analysis and Mining*, *4*(2), 1–14.

Byers, B. D., & Jones, J. A. (2007). The impact of the terrorist attacks of 9/11 on anti-Islamic hate crime. *Journal of Ethnicity in Criminal Justice*, *5*(1), 43–56.

Caffier, J. (2017). Here are Reddit's Whiniest, most low-key toxic subreddits. Available at: www.vice.com/en_au/article/8xxymb/here-are-reddits-whiniest-most-low-key-toxic-subreddits (last accessed 29 November 2017).

Cameron, R. (2013). *Subjects of security: Domestic effects of foreign policy in the war on terror*. Basingstroke: Palgrave Macmillan.

Carpenter, J. (2015). Google's algorithm shows prestigious jobs ads to men, but not to women. Available at: www.independent.co.uk/life-style/gadgets-and-tech/news/googles-algorithm-shows-prestigious-job-ads-to-men-but-not-to-women-10372166.html (last accessed 29 November 2017).

Castells, M. (2011). The disgust becomes a network. Available at: www.adbusters.org/article/manuel-castells/ (last accessed 29 November 2017).

Chakraborti, N. (2010). Future developments for hate crime thinking: Who, what and why? In N. Charkraborti (Ed.), *Hate crime: Concepts, policy, future directions*. Collumpton, Devon: Willan Publishing.

Chakraborti, N. (2015). Rethinking hate crime: Fresh challenges for policy and practice. *Journal of Interpersonal Violence*, *30*(10), 1738–1754.

Chakraborti, N. (2017). Responding to hate crime: Escalating problems, continued failings. *Criminology and Criminal Justice*. Advance online publication. doi: 10.1177/1748895817736096

Chakraborti, N., & Garland, J. (2009). *Hate crime: Impact, causes and responses*. London: Sage.

Chakraborti, N., & Garland, J. (2012). Reconceptualizing hate crime victimization through the lens of vulnerability and 'difference'. *Theoretical Criminology*, *16*(4), 499–514.

Citron, D. K. (2014). *Hate crimes in cyberspace*. Cambridge, MA: Harvard University Press.

Citron, D. K., & Norton, H. (2011). Intermediaries and hate speech: Fostering digital citizenship for our information age. *Boston University Law Review*, *91*(4), 1435–1484.

Cobain, I., Parveen, N., & Taylor, M. (2016). The slow-burning hatred that led Thomas Mair to murder Jo Cox. Available at: www.theguardian.com/uk-news/2016/nov/23/thomas-mair-slow-burning-hatred-led-to-jo-cox-murder (last accessed 29 November 2017).

Cooper, H. (2012). Racism, sexism rife on ADF Facebook group. Available at: www.abc.net.au/news/2012-02-29/racism2c-sexism-rife-on-adf-facebook-group/3860736 (last accessed 29 November 2017).

Council on American–Islamic Relations. (2017). The empowerment of hate: Civil rights report 2017. Available at: www.islamophobia.org/images/2017CivilRightsReport/2017-Empowerment-of-Fear-Final.pdf (last accessed 29 November 2017).

Crown Prosecution Service. (2016). Hate crime report, 2014/15 and 2015/16. Available at: http://report-it.org. uk/files/hate_crime_report.pdf (last accessed 2 March 2018).

Crown Prosecution Service. (2017). Hate crimes and crimes against older people. Available at: www.cps.gov.uk/ publications/equality/hate_crime/index.html (last accessed 29 November 2017).

De Rooij, E. A., Goodwin, M. J., & Pickup, M. (2015). Threat, prejudice and the impact of the riots in London. *Social Science Research*, *51*, 369–383.

Defence Abuse Response Taskforce. (2014). Report on abuse at the Australian defence force academy. Available at: www.defenceabusetaskforce.gov.au/Reports/Documents/ReportonabuseatADFA.pdf (last accessed 29 November 2017).

DeKeseredy, W. S., & Schwartz, M. D. (2016). Thinking sociologically about image-based sexual abuse: The contribution of male peer support theory. *Sexualization, Media, & Society*, *2*(4), 2374623816684692.

Department of Defence. (2011a). Beyond compliance: Professionalism, trust and capability in the Australian profession of arms. Available at: www.defence.gov.au/pathwaytochange/docs/personalconductpersonnel/ Review%20of%20Personal%20Conduct%20of%20ADF%20Personnel_full%20report.pdf (last accessed 29 November 2017).

Department of Defence. (2011b). Review of social media and defence: Reviews into aspects of defence and Australian defence force culture. Available at: www.defence.gov.au/PathwayToChange/Docs/SocialMedia/ Review%20of%20Social%20Media%20and%20Defence%20Full%20report.pdf (last accessed 29 November 2017).

Department of Defence. (2012). Pathways to change: Evolving defence culture—A strategy for cultural change and reinforcement. Available at: www.defence.gov.au/PathwayToChange/Docs/120410%20Pathway%20 to%20Change%20-%20Evolving%20Defence%20Culture%20-%20web%20version.pdf (last accessed 29 November 2017).

Dickstein, C. (2017). Military chiefs denounce racism, hate after violence at Virginia white nationalist rally. Available at: www.stripes.com/military-chiefs-denounce-racism-hate-after-violence-at-virginia-white-nationalist-rally-1.483186 (last accessed 29 November 2017).

Edionwe, T. (2017). The fight against racist algorithms. Available at: www.theoutline.com/post/1571/the-fight-against-racist-algorithms (last accessed 29 November 2017).

Ehrlich, H. J. (2009). *Hates crimes & ethnoviolence: The history, current affairs and future of discrimination in America.* Boulder, CO: Westview Press.

Elgin, B., & Silver, V. (2017). Facebook and Google helped anti-refugee campaign in swing states. Available at: www.bloomberg.com/news/articles/2017-10-18/facebook-and-google-helped-anti-refugee-campaign-in-swing-states (last accessed 29 November 2017).

Emmett, C. (2010). The siting of churches and mosques as an indicator of Christian–Muslim relations. *Islam and Christian-Muslim Relations*, *20*(4), 451–476.

Esper, D. (2017). Albany high students go before judge. Available at: www.eastbaytimes.com/2017/08/02/ albany-high-student-lawsuits-go-before-judge/ (last accessed 29 November 2017).

Farkas, J., Schou, J., & Neumayer, C. (2017). Cloaked Facebook pages: Exploring fake Islamist propaganda in social media. *New Media & Society*, Advance online publication. doi: 10.1177/1461444817707759.

Farrand, B., & Carrapico, H. (2013). Networked governance and the regulation of expression on the Internet: The blurring of the role of public and private actors as content regulators. *Journal of Information Technology & Politics*, *10*(4), 357–368.

Federal Bureau of Investigation. (2016). Uniform crime report: Hate crime statistics, 2015. Available at: https:// ucr.fbi.gov/hate-crime/2015 (last accessed 2 March 2018).

Federal Bureau of Investigation. (2017). Hate crimes. Available at: www.fbi.gov/investigate/civil-rights/hate-crimes (last accessed 29 November 2017).

Feinberg, A. (2017). The alt-right can't disown Charlottesville. Available at: www.wired.com/story/alt-right-charlottesville-reddit-4chan/ (last accessed 29 November 2017).

Ferrara, E. (2017). Disinformation and social bot operations in the run up to the 2017 French presidential election. Available at: www.arxiv.org/pdf/1707.00086 (last accessed 29 November 2017).

Foxman, A., & Wolf, C. (2013). *Viral hate: Containing its spread on the Internet.* New York, NY: St Martin's Press.

Gafni, M., Lochner, T., & Kelly, G. (2017). Boys were subject to public shaming, violence following racist Instagram incident. Available at: www.mercurynews.com/2017/05/04/albany-boys-claim-they-were-subjected-to-public-shaming-violence-following-racist-instagram-incident/ (last accessed 29 November 2017).

Gagliardone, I., Gal, D., Alves, T., & Martinez, G. (2015). *Countering online hate speech.* Paris: United Nations Educational, Scientific and Cultural Organization.

Gitari, N. D., Zuping, Z., Damien, H., & Long, J. (2015). A Lexicon-based approach for hate speech detection. *International Journal for Multimedia and Ubiquitous Engineering, 10*(4), 215–230.

Greenberg, A. (2014). Hacked celeb pics made Reddit enough cash to run its servers for a month. Available at: www.wired.com/2014/09/celeb-pics-reddit-gold/ (last accessed 29 November 2017).

Grierson, J. (2017). Racism, misogyny, threats: Politicians who have suffered abuse. Available at: www.theguardian.com/politics/2017/jul/12/politicians-receive-racist-misogynistic-abuse-parliament-debate (last accessed 29 November 2017).

Griffith, E. (2017). Memo to Facebook: How to tell if you're a media company. Available at: www.wired.com/story/memo-to-facebook-how-to-tell-if-youre-a-media-company/ (last accessed 29 November 2017).

Guynn, J. (2015). Google photos labeled black people 'gorillas'. Available at: www.usatoday.com/story/tech/2015/07/01/google-apologizes-after-photos-identify-black-people-as-gorillas/29567465/ (last accessed 29 November 2017).

Hall, B. (2014). Navy probe as personnel are linked to racist Australian defence league. Available at: www.smh.com.au/national/navy-probe-as-personnel-are-linked-to-racist-australian-defence-league-20140125-31fre.html (last accessed 29 November 2017).

Hanes, E., & Machin, S. (2014). Hate crime in the wake of terror attacks: Evidence from 7/7 and 9/11. *Journal of Contemporary Criminal Justice, 30*(3), 246–267.

Hawley, G. (2017). *Making sense of the alt-right.* New York, NY: Columbia University Press.

Henry, J. (2009). Beyond free speech: Novel approaches to hate on the Internet in the United States. *Information & Communications Technology Law, 18*(2), 235–251.

Henry, N., & Powell, A. (2016). Sexual violence in the digital age: The scope and limits of criminal law. *Social & Legal Studies, 25*(4), 397–418.

Hern, A. (2015). Reddit revolts: Subforums shut down in protest over AMA co-ordinator sacking. Available at: www.theguardian.com/technology/2015/jul/03/reddit-ama-victoria-taylor-subforums-shut-down-protest-sacking (last accessed 29 November 2017).

Higgin, T. (2013). /b/lack up: What trolls can teach us about race. *Fibreculture Journal, 22*, 133–150.

Home Office. (2017). Hate crime, England and Wales, 2017/17. Available at: www.gov.uk/government/uploads/system/uploads/attachment_data/file/652136/hate-crime-1617-hosb1717.pdf (last accessed 29 November 2017).

Howard, P. N., & Kollanyi, B. (2016). Bots, #StrongerIn, and #Brexit: Computational propaganda during the UK-EU referendum. Available at: www.arxiv.org/abs/1606.06356 (last accessed 29 November 2017).

Jacobs, J. B., & Potter, K. (1998). *Hate crimes: Criminal law and identity politics.* Oxford: Oxford University Press.

Jasanoff, S. (2004a). The idiom of co-production. In S. Jasanoff (Ed.), *States of knowledge: The co-production of science and social order* (pp. 1–12). London: Routledge.

Jasanoff, S. (2004b). Ordering society, ordering society. In S. Jasanoff (Ed.), *States of knowledge: The co-production of science and social order* (pp. 13–45). London: Routledge.

Jurgenson, N. (2011). Digital dualism and the fallacy of web objectivity. Available at: www.thesocietypages.org/cyborgology/2011/09/13/digital-dualism-and-the-fallacy-of-web-objectivity/ (last accessed 29 November 2017).

Kleg, M. (1993). *Hate prejudice and racism.* Albany, NY: State University of New York Press.

Klein, A. (2012). Slipping racism into the mainstream: A theory of information laundering. *Communication Theory, 22*(4), 427–448.

Kollanyi, B., Howard, P. N., & Woolley, C. (2016). Bots and automation over Twitter during the first US presidential debate. Available at: www.assets.documentcloud.org/documents/3144967/Trump-Clinton-Bots-Data.pdf (last accessed 29 November 2017).

Landoflobsters. (2017). Update on site-wide rules regarding violent content. Available at: www.reddit.com/r/modnews/comments/78p7bz/update_on_sitewide_rules_regarding_violent_content/ (last accessed 29 November 2017).

Latour, B. (1996). On actor-network theory: A few clarifications. *Soziale Welt*, *74*(4), 369–381.

Lawrence, F. M. (1992). Resolving the hate crimes/hate speech paradox: Punishing bias crimes and protecting racist speech. *Notre Dame Law Review*, *68*(4), 673–722.

Lee-Koo, K. (2014). Implementing Australia's National Action Plan on United Nations Security Council Resolution 1325. *Australian Journal of International Affairs*, *68*(3), 300–313.

Levin, J. (2007). Hate crimes. In G. Ritzer (Ed.), *The Blackwell encyclopedia of sociology* (pp. 2048–2050). Malden, MA: Blackwell.

Levin, J. (2013). Disablist violence in the US: Unacknowledged hate crime. In A. Roulstone, & H. Mason-Bish (Eds.), *Disability, hate crime & violence*. Abingdon, Oxon: Routledge.

Levin, J., & McDevitt, J. (1993). *Hate crimes: The rising tide of bigotry and bloodshed*. New York, NY: Plenum Press.

Levin, J., & McDevitt, J. (2002). *Hate crimes revisited: America's war on those who are different*. Boulder, CO: Westview Press.

Levin, J., & Nolan, J. (2002). *The violence of hate: Confronting racism, anti-semitism and other forms of bigotry*. Boston, MA: Allyn & Bacon.

Lewis, C. S. (2014). *Tough on hate?: The cultural politics of hate crimes*. New Brunswick, NJ: Rutgers University Press.

London City Hall. (2017). Mayor: Zero tolerance as hate crime spikes after London Bridge attack. Available at: www.london.gov.uk/press-releases/mayoral/zero-tolerance-of-hate-crime-after-borough-attack (last accessed 29 November 2017).

Lytvynenko, J. (2017). Here's how a false conspiracy theory about the Texas shooter being antifa went viral. Available at: www.buzzfeed.com/janelytvynenko/how-a-false-conspiracy-theory-about-the-texas-shooter-being?utm_term=.mfQo4ymyo#.hwxkJ9Q9k (last accessed 29 November 2017).

Madrigal, A. (2017). Google's mass shooting misinformation problem. Available at: www.theatlantic.com/technology/archive/2017/11/googles-mass-shooting-misinformation-problem/545024/ (last accessed 29 November 2017).

Mallard, A. (2017). We are NOT afraid. Available at: www.youtube.com/watch?v=wv3h3yDsfa4 (last accessed 29 November 2017).

Marwick, A., & Lewis, R. (2017). *Media manipulation and disinformation online*. New York, NY: Data & Society Research Institute. Available at: www.centerformediajustice.org/wp-content/uploads/2017/07/DataAndSociety_MediaManipulationAndDisinformationOnline.pdf (last accessed 29 November 2017).

Mason, G. (2014). The symbolic purpose of hate crime law: Ideal victims and emotion. *Theoretical Criminology*, *18*(1), 75–92.

Mason, G. (2015). Legislating against hate. In N. Hall, A. Corb, P. Giannasi, & J. G. D. Greive (Eds.), *The Routledge international handbook on hate crime* (pp. 59–68). Abingdon, Oxon: Routledge.

Mason, R. (2017). No 10 to investigate abuse of candidates in election campaign. Available at: www.theguardian.com/politics/2017/jul/04/no-10-to-investigate-abuse-of-candidates-in-election-campaign (last accessed 29 November 2017).

Massanari, A. (2017). #Gamergate and the fappening: How Reddit's algorithm, governance, and culture support toxic technocultures. *New Media & Society*, *19*(3), 329–346.

Masucci, M., & Langton, L. (2017). Hate crime victimization, 2004–2015. Available at: www.bjs.gov/content/pub/pdf/hcv0415.pdf (last accessed 29 November 2017).

Matier, P., & Ross, A. (2017). Second hate incident at Albany High: Students giving Nazi salutes. Available at: www.sfchronicle.com/bayarea/article/Second-hate-incident-at-Albany-High-Students-11034762.php (last accessed 29 November 2017).

Matsuda, M. J. (1993). Public response to hate speech: Considering the victim's story. *Michigan Law Review*, *87*(8), 2320–2381.

Mayor of London. (2017). Posts. Available at: www.facebook.com/MayorofLondon/posts/475492676130228 (last accessed 29 November 2017).

McDevitt, J., Levin, J., & Bennett, S. (2002). Hate crime offenders: An expanded typology. *Journal of Social Issues*, *58*(2), 303–317.

McGlynn, C., & Rackley, E. (2017). Image-based sexual abuse. *Oxford Journal of Legal Studies*, *37*(3), 534–561.

Merelli, A. (2017). How the American right co-opted the idea of free speech. Available at: www.qz.com/1055351/how-the-american-right-co-opted-the-idea-of-free-speech/ (last accessed 29 November 2017).

Michael, K. (2017). Bots trending now: Disinformation and calculated manipulation of the masses. *IEEE Technology and Society Magazine*, *36*(2), 6–11.

Movement Advancement Project. (2017). Hate crime laws. Available at: www.lgbtmap.org/img/maps/citations-hate-crime.pdf (last accessed 29 November 2017).

Nagle, A. (2017). *Kill all normies: Online culture wars from 4chan and Tumblr to Trump and the alt-right*. Winchester: Zero Books.

Nicole, K. (2009). Is Facebook blocking native American names? Available at: www.adweek.com/digital/facebook-blocks-native-americans/ (last accessed 2 March 2018)

Niewert, D. (2017). *Alt-America: The rise of the radical right in the age of Trump*. New York, NY: Verso.

Oppenheim, M. (2017). Milo Yiannopoulos intern accused of killing his dad after he called him a Nazi. Available at: www.independent.co.uk/news/world/americas/milo-yiannopoulos-intern-lane-davis-kill-father-call-nazi-accused-samish-island-alt-right-a8021011.html (last accessed 29 November 2017).

Perry, B. (2001). *In the name of hate: Understanding hate crimes*. Abingdon, Oxon: Routledge.

Perry, B. (2006). Missing pieces: The paucity of hate crime scholarship. In W. S. DeKersedy, & B. Perry (Eds.), *Advancing critical criminology: Theory and application*. Lanham, MD: Lexington Books.

Pew Research Center. (2017). Online harassment 2017. Available at: www.assets.pewresearch.org/wp-content/uploads/sites/14/2017/07/10151519/PI_2017.07.11_Online-Harassment_FINAL.pdf (last accessed 29 November 2017).

Pohjonen, M., & Udupa, S. (2017). Extreme speech online: An anthropological critique of hate speech debates. *International Journal of Communication*, *11*, 1173–1191.

Powell, A., & Henry, N. (2016). Technology-facilitated sexual violence victimization: Results from an online survey of Australian adults. *Journal of Interpersonal Violence*, Advance online publication. doi: 10.1177/0886260516672055.

Powell, A., & Henry, N. (2017). *Sexual violence in a digital age*. London: Palgrave Macmillan.

Raine, L., & Anderson, J. (2017). Code-dependent: Pros and cons of the algorithm age. Available at: www.pewinternet.org/2017/02/08/theme-5-algorithmic-categorizations-deepen-divides/ (last accessed 29 November 2017).

Reinhard, B. (2017). Kentucky law makes it a hate crime to attack a police officer. Available at: www.wsj.com/articles/kentucky-law-makes-it-a-hate-crime-to-attack-a-police-officer-1490209097 (last accessed 29 November 2017).

Reynolds, M. (2016). Yahoo's anti-abuse AI can hunt out even the most devious online trolls. Available at: www.wired.co.uk/article/yahoo-online-abuse-algorithm (last accessed 29 November 2017).

Rumble, G. A., McKean, M., & Pearce, D. (2011). Report of the review of allegations of sexual and other abuse in defence: Facing the problems of the past. Available at: www.defence.gov.au/pathwaytochange/Docs/DLAPiper/Volume1.pdf (last accessed 29 November 2017).

Russell, J. (2015). Reddit bans five harassing subreddits, its trolls respond exactly as you'd expect. Available at: www.techcrunch.com/2015/06/11/quelle-surprise/ (last accessed 29 November 2017).

Saunders, A. (2017). Hate is hate. Online abusers must be dealt with harshly. Available at: www.theguardian.com/commentisfree/2017/aug/20/hate-crimes-online-abusers-prosecutors-serious-crackdown-internet-face-to-face (last accessed 29 November 2017).

Scheff, S., & Schorr, M. (2017). *Shame nation: The global epidemic of online hate*. Naperville, IL: Source Books.

Sherry, M. (2013). International perspectives on disability hate crime. In A. Roulstone, & H. Mason-Bish (Eds.), *Disability, hate crime & violence*. Abingdon: Routledge.

Smith, H. (1984). Educating the guardians: The politics of the Australian defence force academy. *Australian Journal of Political Science*, *19*(1), 25–35.

Smith, H., & McAllister, I. (1991). The changing military profession: Integrating women in the Australian defence force. *Journal of Sociology*, *27*(3), 369–391.

Southern Poverty Law Centre. (2017). Ten days after: Harassment and intimidation in the aftermath of the election. Available at: www.splcenter.org/20161129/ten-days-after-harassment-and-intimidation-aftermath-election (last accessed 29 November 2017).

Spinello, R. A. (2014). *Cyberethics: Morality and law in cyberspace* (5th ed.). Burlingon, MA: Jones & Bartlett Learning.

Stolberg, S. G. (2017). Hurt and angry, Charlottesville tries to regroup from violence. Available at: www.nytimes.com/2017/08/13/us/charlottesville-protests-white-nationalists.html (last accessed 29 November 2017).

Streissguth, T. (2009). *Hate crimes* (revised ed.). New York, NY: Infobase Publishing.

Tait, A. (2017). Spitting out the red pill: Former misogynists reveal how they were radicalised online. Available at: www.newstatesman.com/science-tech/internet/2017/02/reddit-the-red-pill-interview-how-misogyny-spreads-online (last accessed 29 November 2017).

Tatman, R. (2016). Google's speech recognition has a gender bias. Available at: www.makingnoiseandhearingthings.com/2016/07/12/googles-speech-recognition-has-a-gender-bias/ (last accessed 29 November 2017).

The Canberra Times. (2012). Editorial: Our military has tarnished itself. Available at: www.smh.com.au/federal-politics/editorial/our-military-has-tarnished-itself-20120711-21wkj.html (last accessed 29 November 2017).

Topinka, R. J. (2017). Politically incorrect participatory media: Racist nationalism on r/ImGoingToHellForThis. *New, Media & Society*, Advance online publication. doi: 10.1177/1461444817712516.

Tsai, J. (2017). Online racism: Two more students sue over public shaming. Available at: www.eastbaytimes.com/2017/05/13/online-racism-two-more-albany-high-students-sue-over-public-shaming/ (last accessed 29 November 2017).

Turney, J. (1997). Can science studies save the world? Available at: www.timeshighereducation.com/features/can-science-studies-save-the-world/103349.article (last accessed 29 November 2017).

Wadham, B. (2011). Dark side of mateship in Australia military ranks. Available at: www.crikey.com.au/2011/04/06/the-dark-side-of-mateship-in-australian-military-ranks/ (last accessed 29 November 2017).

Wadham, B. (2013). Brotherhood: Homosociality, totality and military subjectivity. *Australian Feminist Studies*, *28*(76), 212–235.

Wadham, B. (2016). The minister, the Commandant and the cadets: Scandal and the mediation of Australian civil-military relations. *Journal Sociology*, *52*(3), 551–568.

Wadham, B., Bridges, D., Mundkur, A., & Connor, J. (2016). 'War-fighting and left-wing agendas': Gender and change in the Australia defence force. *Critical Military Studies*, Advance online publication. doi: 10.1080/23337486.2016.1268371.

Wagner, B. (2013). Governing internet expression: How public and private regulation shape expression governance. *Journal of Information Technology & Politics*, *10*(4), 389–403.

Wajcman, J. (1991). *Feminism confronts technology*. University Park, PA: Penn State Press.

Weaver, C., & Waters, R. (2017). Business leaders abandon Donald Trump over Charlottesville. Available at: www.ft.com/content/2cb0f04c-80fe-11e7-94e2-c5b903247afd?mhq5j=e6 (last accessed 29 November 2017).

Williams, M. L., & Burnap, P. (2016). Cyberhate on social media in the aftermath of Woolwich: A case study in computational criminology and big data. *British Journal of Criminology*, *56*(2), 211–238.

Young, L. J. (2015). Computer scientists find bias in algorithms. Available at: www.spectrum.ieee.org/tech-talk/computing/software/computer-scientists-find-bias-in-algorithms (last accessed 29 November 2017).

Zuckerberg, M. (2017). Posts. Available at: www.facebook.com/zuck/posts/10103969849282011 (last accessed 29 November 2017).

7

INFORMAL JUSTICE

Digilantism, Victim Participation and Recognition

Introduction

British woman Caroline Way, when she was 41, suffered a broken jaw, a cracked eye socket and two black eyes as a result of her partner's horrific domestic violence (Younan, 2017). On 16 March 2014, Caroline took an initial selfie of her face, bruised and swollen, as she lay in a hospital bed, having been admitted for treatment. She then continued to take a selfie every day throughout her six-week physical recovery. And, in April 2017, three years after the assault, Caroline decided to share her selfie journey of recovery: posting the images publicly on Facebook for everyone to see (McLaughlin, 2017). Accompanying the Facebook post, she wrote:

> . . . this isn't going to be a comfortable thing for people to see . . . I used to take a picture of my face every day just to see it changing and how I was getting better . . . I became a selfie queen . . . I found it so therapeutic . . . This was a way of telling myself that because I could see my physical scars retreating, I knew my mental ones would too . . . I'm posting this after 3 years as I don't want any girls to have to have their faces rebuilt and their whole lives dictated by abuse. I'm trying really hard not to let my past dictate my future, but it sometimes feels like it does. Like it, ignore it I don't care, but don't let yourself be stuck in a relationship that turns bad and the end result is this . . .

Intimate partner violence is remarkably common, particularly against women. In the UK, according to the Crime Survey for England and Wales (CSEW), in the 12 months preceding the survey, approximately 8% of women and 4% of men reported experiencing domestic violence (National Office of Statistics, 2016b). Intimate partner violence represents a third of all physical assaults recorded by UK police, and women are far more likely to be killed by their partners than men: of all murders, 44% of female victims compared with 6% of male victims were killed by an intimate partner or ex-partner (National Office of Statistics, 2016a, 2016b). Intimate partner violence is estimated to affect one in four British women (25%) in their lifetime; on average, two women are murdered by a partner or ex-partner every week (National Office of Statistics, 2016a).

Worldwide prevalence rates vary, though overall, 35% of women have experienced either physical and/or sexual intimate partner violence or non-partner sexual violence at some stage in their lifetime (World Health Organization, 2013). In most countries across the world, such violence is rarely reported to police; and, when it is, it is still often difficult for victims to receive a just response. Perhaps this is why some victims have turned to online communities to share their experience of victimisation and seek some acknowledgement of the wrong that has been done.

This chapter is concerned with vigilantism in a technosocial context, whereby citizens take justice into their own hands (Vander Ende, 2014). Rather than merely following crime in real time via social media (as discussed in Chapter 4), vigilantes could instead be described as seeking 'informal justice': a recognition outside of the formal criminal justice processes operated by the state (Fileborn, 2014; Powell, 2015a, 2015b). In other words, informal justice refers to actions that might be pursued by, or on behalf of, victims and victim-survivors in civil society, such as through personal networks, religious and other community forums and online spaces, rather than through the formal police, court and prison systems. There are many such examples in the context of digital society. Victim-survivors of violence, including intimate partner violence, sexual violence and sexual harassment, feature foremost in the sparse, though rapidly emerging, research literature. And related examples include both the public naming and shaming of suspected and/or convicted offenders and democratically-motivated 'hacktivism'. In this chapter, we explore key examples and, in doing so, consider what it means to seek 'informal justice' and to engage in new forms of vigilantism in digital society. Finally, we consider the outcomes of these emerging forms of justice-seeking, both in terms of the experiences of individuals and the broader implications for crime and justice in digital society.

Vigilantism in Digital Society

Vigilantism is a contested concept within criminology, and indeed social sciences more broadly; making it difficult to define (Moncada, 2017; Pratten & Sen, 2007; Warren, 2009). This may be because there are many different types of vigilante actors, with a range of different motivations, engaging in different strategies with vastly different outcomes. Vigilantes may act in loosely coordinated and/or quickly emerging groups (such as crowds and mobs) or in highly organised and sustained collectives (Phillips, 2017). In light of such conceptual vagueness, it is important to first briefly define and further understand vigilantism itself, before specifically examining how it is changing in a digital age.

Understanding Vigilantism

Political scientist Eduardo Moncada (2017, p. 408) provides a comprehensive discussion before establishing a baseline definition of vigilantism, which he describes as: '*the collective use or threat of extra-legal violence in response to an alleged criminal act*' (emphasis in original). Moncada's definition then distills three key features of vigilantism: it is *collective*, it involves either the threat or actual use of *violence* and it occurs in response to an *alleged crime* which could be punishable by the state. It is very similar to criminologist Les Johnston's root definition: a 'social movement giving rise to premeditated acts of force — or threatened force — by autonomous citizens' (Johnston, 1996, p. 232). Indeed, like his earlier efforts to 'establish vigilantism as a criminological concept' (Johnston, 1996, p. 221), the definition excludes individuals who act alone (which might be better understood as revenge or retribution); it excludes non-violent modes of response (such as public naming and shaming) or harms that occur either outside of the territorially bounded state or are not legislated as crimes (such as some non-criminal harms, including sexual harassment). Though the definition is narrow, Moncada argues that, from this shared definitional platform, researchers may vary the concept to define and examine *different varieties of vigilantism*. These varieties might further narrow, or indeed expand upon, any or each of the three key features; but, he suggests, researchers ought to do so explicitly in order to maintain conceptual clarity and the possibility of comparative analyses across studies. He provides numerous examples of such concept variation, such as 'racial vigilantism', which substitutes the justification for vigilantism being an alleged violation of the criminal law with a perceived deserved punishment on the basis of race (Moncada, 2017).

Few studies have conceptually examined the causes and motivations of vigilantism. Among the available scholarly arguments as to why vigilantism occurs is that it is in reaction to actual or perceived state inaction in response to crime (Phillips, 2017; Silke, 2001). Such state inaction may arise in vastly different contexts globally, including during times of civil unrest, wartime violence, postcolonial conflict, dictatorships and inequalities between those in state power and some sectors of the community. Some scholars further describe the explanations of vigilantism as lying in socio-cultural or normative factors, noting that a local area's past history of vigilantism during wartime violence or civil unrest may shape the likelihood of future citizens' engaging in a repertoire of vigilante behaviours (Bateson, 2012, 2013; Phillips, 2017). Likewise, in some contexts, vigilantism occurs in a context of both structural and values-based contests over power, such as those between traditional indigenous justice customs and colonial legal systems (Handy, 2004; Schia & de Carvalho, 2015) or between groups seeking to hold onto power and those who seek social and political change. For example, vigilantism has a long history in the United States, in particular, some citizens' efforts to maintain the dual systems of slavery and racial inequality through lynchings and other violent extrajudicial 'punishment' of African Americans (Moncada, 2017), notably cemented through vigilante organisations such as the Klu Klux Klan (Hadden, 2001).

Meanwhile, in the UK, criminological concerns with vigilantism have largely focused on citizen-led organisations and riots that have arisen in response to community fears of child sex offending (Williams & Thompson, 2004a, 2004b). The Paulsgrove (Portsmith, UK) housing estate riots in August 2001 are among the more commonly cited case studies in the criminological literature on vigilantism (Evans, 2003; Marsh & Melville, 2011; McDonald, 2014; Silke, 2001; Williams & Thompson, 2004a, 2004b). Eight-year-old Sarah Payne was abducted while playing hide-and-seek in a field with her siblings, and then indecently assaulted and murdered. The investigation and 2001 trial later sentenced to life in prison 41-year-old Roy Whiting, who had previously been convicted for the abduction and indecent assault of a child. The case was widely reported in the British media and resulted in a campaign for 'Sarah's Law', which sought to make information about convicted child sexual offenders public.[1] The national tabloid newspaper *News of the World* actively drove the campaign, including publishing the identities and photographs of convicted sexual offenders (Evans, 2003). Among those named and shamed by the *News of the World* was a Paulsgrove resident who had several prior convictions for sexual assault of children. According to media reports, up to 300 Paulsgrove residents protested the presence of these offenders in their estate through weeks of violent rioting that resulted in smashed windows, burgled houses, cars set on fire, petrol bombs, chanting and slogans such as, 'Don't house them — hang them'. The riots forced targeted residents to flee in fear of their safety, including some who had been incorrectly named as having a sexual offending history (McCartney, 2000). The case arguably provides an archetypal example of vigilante or mob 'justice' and also usefully illustrates the harms that can arise from a combination of 'moral panics' (Hall,

Critcher, Jefferson, Clarke, & Roberts, 2013), fear of crime (Altheide, 1997), crime news media reporting (Chibnall, 2013; Greer, 2010) and penal populism (Newburn & Jones, 2005; Pratt, 2007); concepts which are themselves widely discussed within criminology globally.

Yet, British criminologist Jessica Evans (2003) provides a further conceptualisation of vigilantism that draws on the Paulsgrove case but offers what she describes as a more subtle understanding, taking into account contemporary politics of active citizenship and 'responsibilisation'. As criminologists have routinely noted, crime prevention and control rhetoric has, over the last 40 years, sought to reduce expectations from the community of the capacity of the state and its agents to effectively curb crime and instead increasingly 'responsibilised' citizens for protecting themselves and their property (Garland, 1996; O'Malley, 1992). The responsibilisation of citizens for crime prevention and control reflects a broader neo-liberal turn in which the 'post-Keynesian state seeks to shift responsibility onto the private sector, the voluntary sector, communities and individuals . . . to provide solutions to problems previously thought to be the exclusive responsibility of centralized authorities' (Evans, 2003, p. 167). At the same time, government crime policies, to which we might add mass media and social media cultures, have inaugurated a 'renewal of vigilance' in which citizens are called on to be 'awake' or 'observant' in relation to the risks of crime (Evans, 2003, p. 165). It is this political context, suggests Evans, that has resulted in 'the collapse of a meaningful distinction between vigilance and vigilantism' (Evans, 2003, p. 165). In simple terms, the more we are called on to be vigilant about the risks of crime, and the more we are 'responsibilised' for crime prevention and control, the greater the slippage towards taking matters into our own hands (Chang, Zhong, & Grabosky, 2018).

Political scholar Brian Phillips has alternately theorised vigilantism as a 'type of political participation' (Phillips, 2017, p. 1359). Writing of citizen-led and organised vigilante groups in Mexico, he argues that such groups are formed and used by poorer citizens, who experience economic disadvantage with an associated security gap, such that they feel 'relatively insecure compared with wealthier neighbours, who have greater access to private and public security' (Phillips, 2017, p. 1359). By this characterisation, vigilantism may, in some instances, be understood as part of a repertoire of political 'tools of the weak'. Similarly, women's vigilante groups, such as the Gulabi Gang of India who mete violent justice on husbands who beat their wives (Sen, 2012; Sundar, 2010), or women of Juarez, Mexico, who have taken justice into their own hands after hundreds of girls and women continue to be raped and murdered with little state action in response (Carrington, 2014; Roberts, 2016), might be understood through the frame of legitimate political participation. As Atreyee Sen argues, such vigilantism by otherwise disempowered women 'procures a legitimate space when viewed and examined through the model of ethical violence, and related to understandings of the proportionate punishment for crimes against women' (Sen, 2012, p. 3).

Together, what this limited international literature suggests is that there are contexts — arguably social justice contexts of inequality of marginalised and/or exploited groups — in which vigilantism might be viewed as justifiable, even legitimate. Yet, as Phillips (2017) and others warn, vigilantism can also result in serious human rights violations, persecution and an escalation of violence, bigotry and hate-crime (McDonald, 2014).

Digital Vigilantism

Given the contested nature of vigilantism in general, it is hardly surprising that there is no commonly accepted definition of digital vigilantism — 'digilantism' (or 'cyber-vigilantism', see Smallridge et al.,

2016). Many acts of digilantism might well blur or exceed the boundaries instituted by those seeking to confine the concept of vigilantism. Of the core elements discussed by both Johnston (1996) and Moncada (2017), digilantism might well be (i) *collective* and to some extent premeditated, even organised; and it may also be (ii) enacted by autonomous citizens or at least individuals acting in their *private* capacity. However, not all collective actions popularly understood as digilantism necessarily involve (iii) the use, or threat of, *physical violence* or acts of force; and nor are all infractions that attract the response of digilantes necessarily *criminal*. Indeed, as sociologist and communications scholar Daniel Trottier (2017) has observed, many acts of digital vigilantism involve a kind of 'weaponised visibility' in which targets are variously named and shamed, doxed (their private identity information publicly revealed) and/or harassed by the collective in response to a perceived social infraction — rather than necessarily a criminal one. This has been the case in a number of high profile instances including: #Gamergate (in which women programmers were subjected to a campaign of harassment after criticising sexism in game development, Massanari, 2017), #DongleGate (in which a male tech conference attendee was fired after being exposed online for making sexist jokes, Ingraham & Reeves, 2016), 'Dog Shit Girl' (in which a woman received online abuse after a video of her on a subway train with her dog while it defecated on the floor went viral, Solove, 2007), the 'Wheelie Bin Cat Lady' (who received death threats online after a video of her pushing a cat into a garbage bin was widely circulated, Jones, 2016) and for 30-year-old American woman Justine Sacco.

Justine Sacco worked in corporate communications and had a small following of 170 friends and family on Twitter. As she was travelling between New York and Cape Town in December, 2013, for family holidays, Justine sent off a series of (in hindsight) poorly formed 'joke' tweets. In a later article for the *New York Times* titled 'How One Stupid Tweet Blew Up Justine Sacco's Life', Ronson (2015a) described a series of tweets Justine had made as she travelled:

> 'Weird German Dude: You're in First Class. It's 2014. Get some deodorant.' — Inner monologue as I inhale BO. Thank God for pharmaceuticals.
>
> Chilly — cucumber sandwiches — bad teeth. Back in London!
>
> Going to Africa. Hope I don't get AIDS. Just kidding. I'm white!

It was this last tweet, posted not long before she boarded an 11-hour flight to Cape Town, that would attract a campaign of digital shaming with very real corporeal effects. Justine reported her motivation for the joke as making fun of the 'bubble' that many Americans live in, never thinking about their own privilege or issues that disproportionately impact the developing world; she later said that she never thought anyone would take the tweet literally (Ronson, 2015b). Yet, by the time Justine's flight landed, an online mob had formed and the hashtag #HasJustineLandedYet was trending number one worldwide on Twitter. The mob was calling for justice in response to the social infraction described variously as 'outrageous', 'offensive' and 'racist ignorance'. Twitterers called for Justine to be fired from her job, and one user photographed her at Cape Town international airport, sharing the image with the crowd to announce that she had indeed arrived. Ronson describes how such examples of collective fury can feel righteous, 'as if justice were being democratized' (Ronson, 2015a, 2015b, n.p.), and yet sometimes the 'punishment simply didn't fit the crime'. For Justine Sacco, that punishment meant being personally and professionally shamed, fired from her job, struggling to find replacement work and feeling herself unable to date since 'we Google everyone we might date' (Ronson, 2015a, 2015b, n.p.).

Such crowdsourced justice-seeking can be found across the globe. In China, online investigations by everyday citizens have been described as the 'human flesh search', a literal translation from the Chinese *rénròu sōusuŏ* (Chang & Leung, 2015; Chang et al., 2018) referring to vigilantism conducted via an online forum. According to information technology researchers Rui Chen and Sushil Sharma (2011, pp. 51–52) the 'Human flesh search emerged in 2001 at Mop.com, a popular Chinese forum, in the format of online question and answer (Q&A) . . . [it] matured in 2006 when it became available to the general public and targeted serious social topics'. The human flesh search further 'involves mediated search processes whereby online participants collectively find demographic and geographic information about deviant individuals, often with the shared intention to expose, shame, and punish them to reinstate legal justice or public morality' (Cheong & Gong, 2010, p. 472). Among the first examples discussed in the scholarly literature is a crowdsourced investigation that occurred in 2006 of a woman perpetrating animal cruelty in a 'crush video'[2] (Cheong & Gong, 2010; Cheung, 2009; Nhan, Huey, & Broll, 2017). According to media reports, it took just six days for online citizens to identify and track down the woman, resulting in her public naming and shaming, as well as identification of her employer; after which she was fired from her job (Downey, 2010).

Cases such as those discussed here serve as a reminder that 'online' mobs have very real effects: emotional and psychological impacts on the target, social impacts through damage to one's reputation among family, friendship and/or dating circles, as well as economic and career impacts through lost employment. Though the use of force may not be the physical violence required by pre-digital, narrow definitions of vigilantism, it is difficult to deny the potential for very real harms as a result of online responses to a social infraction. And digilantism can have embodied effects in other ways, including physical violence.

In another case from China, a human flesh search went terribly wrong, resulting in an unsuspecting public actively assisting a man to locate and subsequently murder his ex-girlfriend. According to media reports, 20-year-old university student Zhou Chunmei had first met her boyfriend Lin Ming in 2004; yet, when Zhou received entry to university, she broke off the romance and, according to Lin, 'disappeared' in October 2008, having cut off all communication with him (Sichuan Online, 2009). In an effort to find her, Lin posted a callout online to assist him in tracking down his lost love. Lin claimed that he had financially supported her and had been cruelly used and rejected by her, but that he was now terminally ill with cancer and it was his last dying wish to reconcile with Zhou (Cheung, 2009; Liang & Lu, 2010). Lin's story was met with moral outrage by an online community of internet citizens, who labelled Zhou as 'ungrateful' and collectively identified and shared various information about her, including photos of her, her contact information and her university dormitory room number (Cheung, 2009). On the basis of this assistance from a broader public, Lin found Zhou and visited her at her dormitory, where he subsequently stabbed and killed her. In effect, one man's stalking and domestic homicide had been not so much assisted as made possible through crowdsourcing the location of his ex-girlfriend. Though cases such as these present the negative and dangerous side of digilantism as mob justice gone wrong, there are other examples of positive outcomes of vigilantes in digital society.

Democratic Digilantism and 'Hacktivism'

According to communication and media scholars Li Gao and James Stanyer (2014, p. 816), China's human flesh search engine is 'more than merely the online bullying of individuals by online vigilantes, it can also take on a political dimension'. In a study of eight cases occurring between 2007 and 2009, Gao and Stanyer (2014) identify Chinese digilantism directed at the identification and penalisation of state officials engaged in corruption. One such case occurred in December 2008, when documents pertaining to the travel expense claims of government officials were accidentally left on a subway train in Shanghai and were found by a citizen who anonymously posted them online. The documents provided some evidence that, during work trips to the United States and Canada, the government employees had spent public funds on visiting major tourist attractions. Citizens got to work discussing the alleged corruption online, and further identifying the details of the government officials named in the documents. Under growing public pressure, local government authorities dismissed the two identified employees and launched inquiries into the departments responsible for the trips (Gao & Stanyer, 2014). Such examples of politically oriented digilantism from non-democratic settings, such as China, are particularly important for a globally oriented digital criminology.

While research literature emerging from Western democracies tends to foreground negative instances of both vigilantism and digilantism, research discussing non-democratic states often high-lights the important role that the internet can play in fostering digilantism that serves democratic ends (Cheong & Gong, 2010; Gao & Stanyer, 2014; Qiu, Lin, Chiu, & Liu, 2015; Tang & Sampson, 2012). China is home to the largest online population in the world, with over 730 million internet users as of March 2017, followed at a distant second by India (460 million) and third the United States (280 million, see China Internet Network Information Center, 2017; Statistica, 2017). Many researchers have identified internet participation as particularly important in China in light of government bans on spontaneous and unauthorised public demonstration, as well as restrictive censorship of the conventional news media: 'the internet provides people with an alternative channel via which they can relatively safely express opinions and articulate problems' (Tang & Sampson, 2012, p. 459). As such, online discussion and digilantism can be a means for civic participation directed towards politically-motivated purposes (Cheong & Gong, 2010). Indeed, Gao and Stanyer's (2014, p. 825) study of Chinese digilantism suggested that a 'key trigger is the lack of alternative means for holding corrupt officials to account or questioning official claims'.

Contemporary Russia, meanwhile, has been described by some scholars as a 'semi-authoritarian political environment' or 'hybrid regime . . . that can neither be regarded as classic authoritarian nor as fully-fledged democratic' (Toepfl, 2011, p. 1302; see also Denisova, 2017; Koesel & Bunce, 2012). Elections are held regularly but serious questions have been raised as to their legitimacy and competitiveness, and restrictions on civil and political liberties — such as freedom of association and an independent media — have tightened under the leadership of current president Vladimir Putin (Denisova, 2017; Toepfl, 2011). Corruption among government, police and legal officials is also reportedly systemic (Petrov, Lipman, & Hale, 2014), with alleged police violence, even murder, of Russian citizens (Toepfl, 2011). For example, Toepfl (2011) describes a 2010 incident referred to as *Zhivoy Shchit* or 'living shield', in which several drivers were stopped by police and ordered to park their vehicles crosswise to the road. A few minutes later, a car rushed through the line of cars at high speed, endangering the drivers — who had all remained in their vehicles, as instructed — and making apparent the police officers' deliberate use of the citizens and their cars as a human roadblock. This particular incident came to the attention of Russian citizens via YouTube, as one of the victims, 29-year-old Stanislav Sutyagin, uploaded a self-recorded video detailing what had happened shortly afterwards. Stanislav's testimony was shared and discussed on blogging sites and alternative news media, while also being reported in the mainstream, state-sanctioned media. Reportedly, the YouTube testimony and subsequent pressure from alternative and social media contributed to the government calling for an investigation into the incident, and the dismissal of the police officer in charge of the operation (Toepfl, 2011). Citizen-captured video of ballot-stuffing and claims of electoral fraud were also shared via social media and blogging platforms leading up to the Russian election protests in December 2011 through 2012 and into 2013 (Denisova, 2017; Koltsova & Shcherbak, 2015; Reuter & Szakonyi, 2015; Smyth & Oates, 2015).

In a semi-authoritarian regime, social media and other digital platforms can provide a mechanism for resistive 'truth-telling' in an otherwise state-controlled media environment. Indeed, a growing body of scholarship has theorised social media activism through Nancy Fraser's (1990, 2014) concept of 'subaltern counterpublic' spaces (Fileborn, 2014; Kasra, 2017; Powell, 2015a, 2015b). In critique of Jurgen Habermas' notion of a singular public sphere of communicative action, Fraser (1990) has argued that subordinated social groups form their own parallel public spheres, in which culturally and discursively marginalised or silenced groups engage in resistant and/or critical speech that is ordinarily delegitimised and excluded from the public sphere. Fraser describes the emancipatory potential of these counterpublics which, she says, are not separatist enclaves but rather 'aspire to disseminate one's discourse into ever-widening arenas' (Fraser, 1990, p. 67). As such, social networking sites and other online platforms may be understood as 'networked publics' (Boyd & Marwick, 2011; Renninger, 2015) that provide various opportunities for both public and counterpublic communications that may be ultimately democratising. Nonetheless, it is important not to overstate the capacities of democratic digilantism to result in substantive change: in the Chinese and Russian case studies discussed above, citizen justice-seeking appears to have resulted in state authorities taking action against the individual and low-level officials or officers involved, while the institutionalisation of corruption and/or state violence remain unresolved.

To return to a Western context, among the most well-known examples of democratically motivated digilantism are a series of disclosures of private documents by online whistleblowing platform WikiLeaks. Established in 2006, WikiLeaks provides a mechanism for the anonymous submission and publication of information that has been censored or not otherwise made publicly available by state authorities and/or private agencies. Its founder, Julian Assange, has argued that open and transparent government is fundamental to democracy and, indeed, the values of freedom and justice: 'It is not our goal to achieve a more transparent society; it's our goal to achieve a more just society' (cited in Crovitz, 2010). In the now infamous 2010 disclosures of US war documents, WikiLeaks published (among many other things) classified video footage taken by US soldiers from a helicopter over a controversial 2007 airstrike in Baghdad. The strike had resulted in the killing of two journalists and several Iraqi civilians (WikiLeaks, 2010). More recently, WikiLeaks participated in the public disclosure of thousands of emails from Democratic National Committee servers during the 2016 US election campaign (WikiLeaks, 2016). According to some scholars, WikiLeaks is an example of the 'new digital culture of disclosure' (Brevini, 2017, p. 9) or, indeed, a 'new politics of truth' (Munro, 2017, p. 520). As discussed in Chapter 1 of this book, contemporary Western democracies have been experiencing a crisis of 'truth', in which the catch-cry that much of mainstream media reporting is 'fake news' and mistrust of traditional sources of authority (Mueller, Carter, & Whittle, 2015) have opened the gates to a stream of news that really is fake, coalescing in claims that we now live in a 'post-truth' world (Glasser, 2016).

This distrust of all sources of information is used as a political device that undermines democracy: such 'politics of truth' have arguably taken on heightened significance during the Trump administration, building on a sense that 'we are living in a time of radical uncertainty about the "official" version of the truth' (Sifry, 2011, p. 16). The practice of 'radical transparency' (Pieterse, 2012) offered by platforms such as WikiLeaks is arguably both symptomatic and reproductive of a wider public distrust of government, mainstream media and other traditional sources of information. For some scholars, such as Iain Munro (2017), contemporary politics of truth reflect French philosopher Michel Foucault's (1987, p. 127) concept of 'games of truth' or the 'ensemble of rules for the production of truth'. Taking as given that all claims to truth reflect contested practices of power and resistance, in the context of digital society new practices of contestation have emerged, powered by digital platforms that enable citizens to play, in Foucault's terms, the 'same game differently' (Foucault, 1987) and to undermine the rules governing which 'truths' are deemed to be valid.

A further and final case study that might be understood within the frame of democratic digilantism is a series of operations (or 'ops') conducted by members of the nebulous and amorphous network of hackers known as 'Anonymous'. Though the media often refer to Anonymous or (Anons) as a 'group' or 'collective' of hackers, the network 'lacks the cohesion and continuity usually associated with groups or collectives' (Uitermark, 2017, p. 403). Indeed, in the absence of a uniting ideology or a sustained set of goals or values, Anonymous may be better understood as a loose 'swarm' (Wiedemann, 2014, p. 322) of digilantes than as a social movement or organisation for digital activism (discussed further in Chapter 8).

Various operations conducted by Anons at different times and in different parts of the world have also been variously framed as digilantism, hacktivism and even cyber-terrorism. In 2013, for instance, in response to a failed police investigation into the Steubenville, Ohio (USA) rape case (discussed in Chapter 5), members of Anonymous famously took justice into their own hands. Under the banners of #OpSteubenville and #OpRedRoll, they hacked into the high school servers and students' e-mail accounts — retrieving photographic evidence of the rape, as well as personal data of the students allegedly involved. Anons then threatened to release the personal data if the individuals did not come forward to police. In another video, the computer-synthesised voice of a hooded figure in a Guy Fawkes mask read out the names of students who were suspected of having been either directly or indirectly involved — alongside a slideshow of screenshots from Twitter and a photograph of the unconscious victim from Instagram. These operations drew further attention to the case, first online and subsequently in the mainstream media, reportedly placing pressure on local law enforcement to step up their investigations of the rape itself and to extend their investigations to its cover-up (Powell, 2015b; Woods, 2014). Insofar as these Anonymous operations were directed at the alleged individual perpetrators (and non-state actors) of a domestic criminal offence, 'digilantism' would indeed appear to be the most apt descriptor.

Yet, in the 2010 operation '#titstorm', a group of Anons flooded the website of Australia's Parliament House, as well as parliamentary email addresses, with pornographic material in a Distributed Denial of Service (DDoS) attack that resulted in lapses in access to several government sites and systems (Hardy, 2010). The attack was staged as a protest against an Australian Government plan to introduce internet filtering that would restrict access to illegal pornographic content such as child abuse material. Under Australian anti-child abuse material legislation, simulated pornography involving child-like characters (such as in animated or computer-generated content) as well as pornography featuring models who appear to be under age are treated in the same way as pornographic content that features real child victims of abuse. As part of a broader campaign supporting internet freedom, some Anons took issue with the proposed internet filter, sending animated pornography as well as images of 'small breasted women' (who, in some instances, may appear to be underage) as part of the DDOS attack. In a statement released to the media (Moses, 2010), Anonymous members said of their motivation for the attack:

> The Australian government will learn that one does not mess with our porn. No one messes with our access to perfectly legal (or illegal) content for any reason.

While the attack caused some (limited) disruption, and also involved the hacking and defacement of a government website (some of the pornographic material was plastered across the Prime Minister's official homepage), operation #titstorm could be appropriately labelled 'hacktivism' — 'similar to certain forms of real-world protest actions, such as vandalism and destruction of private property in furtherance of a political agenda' (Holt, 2012, p. 340). Following the attack, 19-year-old Steve Slayo was charged with 'causing unauthorised impairment of electronic communication to or from a Commonwealth computer', facing a potential maximum penalty of 10 years imprisonment. Instead, Slayo received a fine and a good behaviour order — a representative from the Australian Federal Police high tech crime investigations unit reportedly said that the penalty in the case did not reflect the severity of the threat that such cyberattacks represent (Pauli, 2011).

Since operation #titstorm, legal scholars, both in Australia and internationally, have criticised the lack of distinction in existing legislation between serious computer offences, including cyber-terrorism, on the one hand and instances of hacktivism that might more appropriately be considered legitimate forms of protest in a digital democracy (Clough, 2010; Hardy, 2010; Holt, 2012; O'Malley, 2013). Indeed, as discussed in Chapter 3 of this book, governments are increasingly responding to computer crimes and online incursions through a securitised, militarised frame of reference: the lines between cybercrime, cyber-war, cyber-terrorism and, arguably, cyber*activism* are legislatively blurred. Yet, of particular interest here is that, though some Anonymous ops have famously been targeted towards exposing evidence of individual crimes, others supported a broader political cause (such as a free and open internet), which also illustrates the blurring or conceptual vagueness between digilantism, on the one hand, and digital activism, on the other.

Digilantism as an Extended Form of Vigilantism

While a conventional criminological concept of vigilantism might distinguish it from the actions of either individuals or groups using non-physical force in response to actions that are not necessarily criminal, when considering informal justice, digilantism and digital activism alongside each other in this way, the definitional ambiguity and slippage between these concepts becomes more apparent. Individual victims seeking cultural recognition for a harm done to them, for instance, may soon be joined online by others seeking to identify and shame the alleged perpetrator online. Furthermore, citizens acting collectively in response to a specific criminal or social infraction may, in turn, become involved in broader action in response to systemic infractions of that type (or others). As such, though we support Moncada's (2017) call for conceptual clarity in criminological investigations of vigilantism, in the context of digital society, rigid adherence to what counts as a *criminal* infraction, and to what counts as *force*, is increasingly difficult to sustain.

For example, as discussed in Chapter 3 of this book, in digital society, the role of the sovereign state as the defining structure for crime and justice is arguably shrinking. Behaviours that are criminal in one jurisdiction may not be in another; and actions by, or against, a citizen may be conducted across global networks or in another jurisdiction entirely. The 'policing' of social and cultural normative infractions grows in importance in the overall function and (largely corporate) regulation of a global, networked, civil society. In this context, digilantism may have greater salience in instances of supranational and/or non-criminal harms, where a formal criminal justice response is not readily available. However, what we ultimately argue here is that — in combination with broader socio-political factors such as responsibilisation, discussed earlier — digilantism and related forms of citizen-participatory or informal justice are increasingly embedded in the technosocial practices of a digital society; and across both local and global networks. As such, while it is important for criminologists studying digilantism to identify the nature of the infraction under investigation, we do not advocate for a narrow conceptualisation that would exclude non-criminal infractions from the scope of study either of vigilantism or of digital criminology.

Moreover, it is not our intention in laying out this conceptual discussion to suggest that digilantism can be readily distinguished from vigilantism on the basis that the former results in non-physical harms or does not include the threat, or use, of force. Such an approach to digital vigilantism is undesirable within a digital criminological approach: first, because it reinstitutes a virtual/real dichotomy that is no longer viable in understanding digital society; and, second, because it suggests that the threat or use of force in digilantism is less physical. In some cases, there may be an overlap between digilante strategies such as doxing, harassment and shaming, and the physical 'use of force' that criminologists have typically required for acts to be defined as 'vigilantism' (Johnston, 1996; Moncada, 2017, as discussed earlier). Certainly, as our discussion here has identified, some instances of digilantism have resulted in physical assaults, even murders; at which point, they more clearly align with definitions of traditional vigilantism. Nonetheless, many other examples of digilantism result in affectual, social and economic harms that are experienced, not by an avatar in 'cyberspace, but by an embodied individual as they move about their everyday life. More particularly, threats to one's safety, whether delivered through digital communication or other means, can have corporeal effects on one's freedom of movement and participation. Here, we are informed by emerging research within criminology that likewise seeks to recognise the embodied harms that may result from technosocial practices of violence, harassment or abuse (Powell, 2015a).

To return to the examples discussed at the start of this chapter, online disclosures and truth-telling by victim-survivors of intimate partner and/or sexual violence present insightful case studies through which to further explore tensions and ambiguities in informal justice-seeking in digital society. In particular, in contrast to some of the more pessimistic examples in the preceding discussion, there is arguably a very real potential for some forms of digilantism to represent genuine strategies of informal justice-seeking at individual levels, as well as contributing to broader social justice activist agendas.

Feminist Digilantism and Informal Justice

Victim-survivors of sexual and domestic violence, harassment and gender-based hate speech are describing the nature of the violations they've experienced across a range of platforms and in varying ways. As several Australian criminologists identify, such personal disclosures of interpersonal violence in online spaces can in themselves serve as a form of informal justice for victim-survivors (Fileborn, 2014; Loney-Howes, 2015; O'Neill, 2018; Powell, 2015a, 2015b); and sometimes further result in the naming and shaming of perpetrators more commonly associated with digilantism.

DIY Justice Online

Women are increasingly fighting back in response to sexist harassment and gendered hate that they receive online all too frequently. Described by some scholars as a kind of 'feminist digilantism' or 'DIY justice online' (Jane, 2016, p. 287), women are drawing on their social networks to name and shame the perpetrators of these gender-based harms. For example, in November 2015, Australian journalist and outspoken feminist activist Clementine Ford named and shamed hotel supervisor Michael Nolan for his offensive comments on her Facebook page. Ford's 'feminist digilantism' resulted in the hotel chain terminating Nolan's employment. In another example, women frustrated by the lack of action taken against harassers sending unsolicited 'dick pics' via social media giant Facebook started a petition calling for a ban on sexual images being sent through the platform's instant messenger service (Gordon, 2016). Meanwhile, in 2016, a London woman sent a barrage of dick pics she found online to the man who had sent her his own unsolicited image; reportedly, and ironically, receiving these left him feeling disgusted and enraged (Rusciano, 2016).

In an interview at the launch of her book, *Fight Like a Girl*, Clementine Ford (2016) explains why it is important for women to fight back in the face of online abuse:

> Women are trained from early on to figuratively and literally avoid taking up too much room, but we need to do the opposite of that now, and to figure out how to take up as much room as possible … it's your space as well, and you're entitled to be there. We are all entitled to take up space.

In some instances then, the naming and shaming of perpetrators of the social infractions of sexism, online harassment and/or gendered hate might be understood as a legitimate 'type of political participation' (Phillips, 2017, p. 1359), as discussed earlier in this chapter. In this way, digilantism can be seen as a 'tool of the weak'; deployed to challenge systemic structures of gender inequality in a context where no formal recourse is available.

Survivor Selfies and Hashtag Disclosures

Some individual victim-survivors — such as Caroline Way, discussed at the start of this chapter — are turning to visual communication to disclose domestic and sexual violence in particular. Perhaps the most well-known example of such 'survivor selfies' (Ferreday, 2017; Wood, Rose, & Thompson, 2018) is the photographic activist endeavour, *Project Unbreakable*. Created in October 2011 by then 19-year-old photographer Grace Brown, the project began with Brown's photographs of victim-survivors, mostly people she knew, holding posters with handwritten quotes from the words spoken to them by their attackers (Malone, 2012). In the beginning, most held the posters in front of their faces, contributing anonymously. Now there are thousands of photographs, some taken by Brown as she travels around the United States continuing her project; many, however, are images taken and submitted by victim-survivors, often revealing their identities, standing with expressions of defiance and strength. The project began as a way of raising awareness of sexual assault but, as the Tumblr site describes, it also 'provides a way of healing for violence survivors'.

The posters in *Project Unbreakable* do not name perpetrators, though some identify the victim-perpetrator relationship as a sibling, an uncle, a neighbour, a family friend, an employer, an ex-boyfriend and so on. As such, the truth telling in these victim-survivor photo captions is arguably not about vigilantism, but rather about healing, and even redress, through the public disclosure of the wrong and its acknowledgement by an online community of supporters (O'Neill, 2018; Powell, 2015a, 2015b). Indeed, in a book chapter titled *Like a Stone in Your Stomach: Articulating the Unspeakable in Rape Victim-Survivors' Activist Selfies*, feminist sociologist Debra Ferreday unpacks the affective politics of these powerful, visual, disclosures. Ferreday (2017) recognises that the survivor testimonies call to others to bear witness to the extent of rape and sexual violence, while also doing justice to each individual account and making whole the 'fragmented hidden community of the walking wounded' (p. 129). Furthermore, drawing on technology researchers Theresa Senft and Nancy Baym (2015, discussed in Chapter 5), Ferreday argues that these survivor selfies are not only *representations* of violence; rather, they constitute technosocial practices that 'function as a site of resistance' (p. 129) in which trauma that is most often 'privatised, individualised and made unspeakable' is 'transformed into the basis of collective action and mutual support' (p. 133).

Meanwhile, 'hashtag testimonials', a subset of hashtag activism (discussed further in Chapter 8), are also increasingly a forum for victims of sexual violence and harassment to share their experiences for collective action and mutual support. These testimonials produce powerful, and all-too-familiar, narratives of the impacts of violence, of perpetrator tactics and of the often long aftermath of recovery from abuse. For example, millions of 140-character testimonies of sexual violence victimisation have been shared online via hashtags such as: #metoo #rapedneverreported, #whenIwas, #yesallwomen, #whyIstayed and #notokay (BBC, 2016; Clifton, 2014; Telegraph, 2016). Many of these first-hand accounts are by victim-survivors who are disclosing their experiences of abuse for the first time. These are just some of the examples that have gained the attention of feminist and mainstream media. Online searches present many other such examples of victim-survivors pursuing an alternative and informal justice, not all of which 'go viral'. While, in the instances described above, victim-survivors often overtly identify themselves and their rapists and/or harassers, many more accounts of sexual violence are shared online, in Tumblr blogs, on forums such as Reddit and in closed online communities, without naming and shaming perpetrators and where the identity of the victim often remains anonymous (O'Neill, 2018; Powell, 2015a, 2015b).

While victim-survivor testimonies can certainly be framed as a form of digital or online activism, they are not always so. As noted above, in many instances, a victim-survivor may disclose their experience in a private or semi-private forum and in a way that primarily seeks to meet their personal needs — whether therapeutic or justice-seeking. In others, the gap between individual disclosure and act of collective political resistance is lessened, even nonexistent. In hashtag testimonials, for example, the personal is made very publicly political. Yet, as suggested by Ferreday (2017) and others (Fileborn, 2014; O'Neill, 2018), the power of these disclosures and testimonials is far greater than the recognition (discussed further below) that might be offered to individual women who share their experiences. There is also a collective impact of such campaigns, which expose the sheer enormity of the problem and draw attention to it in more traditional media and political forums. Moreover, when perpetrators and harassers are publicly named and shamed, attention is drawn not just to the individual acts of some men, but to the structures of society that tolerate men's violence against women more generally. As such, the diversity of these practices and their effects is perhaps not fully captured by either the concepts of 'digilantism' or 'digital activism', as they also constitute a kind of informal justice-seeking.

Seeking Informal Justice Through Recognition

Victims of domestic and sexual violence have often been disbelieved, and their experiences minimised or even denied. Indeed, despite the promise that justice will follow one's 'day in court', the criminal justice system has routinely failed victim-survivors of 'private' forms of violence: very few cases of sexual and domestic assault result in criminal convictions (Daly & Bouhours, 2010; Kelly et al., 2005; Lievore, 2005). Some scholars have gone further to argue that the very format of the hearing offered by the criminal justice system is antithetical to the justice needs of victim-survivors (Clark, 2010; Daly, 2014; Herman, 2005). For instance, as Haley Clark identifies, victim-survivors' justice needs include: *participation, voice, control, validation* and *vindication* (Clark, 2010; Daly, 2014, emphasis added) at the same time as criminal justice processes sideline, silence, disempower and doubt accounts of private victimisation. Testifying to one's experience of domestic violence or sexual assault in online counterpublics, where victim-survivors can have control over the extent and nature of their participation, tell their account in their own voice and receive validation, even vindication, by a community of peers who understand the nature of such violence, is potentially a powerful mechanism for seeking justice informally (Fileborn, 2014; Loney-Howes, 2015; O'Neill, 2018; Powell, 2015a, 2015b).

Telling one's story is furthermore commonly held as crucial not only for an individual's psychological recovery from trauma (Brison, 2002; Harvey, 2000), but for the collective recognition and action that is promised when others 'bear witness' to victim-survivors' experiences (Henry, 2010; Rosenberg, 1996; Solinger et al., 2010; Todorova, 2011). In a criminal trial, the jury are tasked with being impartial observers and ultimately to decide on the veracity of the evidence and the truthfulness of victim accounts. In the people's court of online counterpublics, however, victim-survivors engage in an alternate format of 'truth-telling'. In this public narrative, as we will discuss further, audiences are invited to validate accounts of violent victimisation, and to responsibilise perpetrators, and society more broadly, to correct the harms. The capacity to narrate one's experience of violence online, and share this with a community of one's peers, serves not only to fulfil some of the justice needs of individual victim-survivors but arguably also helps correct the collective injustice of *misrecognition* (Fraser, 2007, 2009).

In her threefold conceptualisation of justice, Fraser (2009) describes the injustices of *maldistribution* (unequal distribution of economic resources), *misrepresentation* (disparity in political participation) and *misrecognition* (institutionalised patterns of unequal cultural value). Indeed, Fraser further describes the injustices of *gender misrecognition*, in particular, as constituting pervasive, cultural, gender-specific practices of status subordination that result in women's:

> … sexual harassment, sexual assault and domestic violence; trivializing, objectifying and demeaning stereotypical depictions in the media; disparagement in everyday life; exclusion or marginalization in public spheres and deliberative bodies; and denial of the full rights and equal protections of citizenship.
>
> (Fraser, 2007, p. 26)

By Fraser's account, rape and, indeed, sexual violence and harassment more broadly are injustices grounded in cultural, discursive or status inequality, in which women are routinely devalued, depreciated and disrespected. Correcting such injustices requires a feminist politics of recognition, aimed at overcoming women's status subordination by examining and dismantling the 'institutionalized patterns of cultural value [that] constitute women as inferior, excluded, wholly other, or simply invisible' (Fraser, 2007, p. 31). Sharing one's victimisation account with a community of online peers may provide much needed acknowledgement and validation of the harm experienced. Indeed, the blurring of public and private space associated with a digital society has further enabled these otherwise 'private' harms to become increasingly public knowledge (as also discussed in Chapter 5).

Yet, practices garnering greater *visibility* of sexual, domestic and other violences do not guarantee *recognition* of the wrongs committed. Nor do they necessarily guarantee 'justice,' informal or otherwise, in response. Indeed, there are multiple influences underscoring the diverse social and cultural practices of justice, discussed throughout this chapter, that are emerging in the context of digital society.

Technosocial Practices of Informal Justice

Throughout this book, several key features of digital society and their associated socio-technical theories have been brought to bear on contemporary issues of crime and justice. Of particular relevance to the concerns of this chapter are shifts in spatiality, temporality and algorithmic sociality.

Digilantism and informal justice-seeking practices have arguably proliferated in a context of substantial *spatial shifts* that are characteristic of digital society. This is not to suggest that the justice practices described here are occurring in a digital space that is distinct from more material spaces. Indeed, a key thread woven throughout this book is the challenge of examining crime and justice through a more technosocial lens that avoids such online/offline dichotomies. Rather, as initially discussed in Chapter 3, there has been a reconfiguration of spatial arrangements in digital society, and this understanding serves to contextualise the technosocial justice practices discussed here. Drawing on sociologist Manuel Castells (1996a), the meaning of space has altered in digital society, such that distant places have become more interconnected, and along with this connection is a changed temporal experience of space as spontaneously and instantaneously traversable. Castells (1996a, p. 13) described this new spatial structure as the 'space of flows', which 'means that the material arrangements allow for simultaneity of social practices without territorial contiguity'. For Castells, this space of flows is constituted not only by technological infrastructure but also by economic, socio-cultural and political networks of interaction or 'dominant activities' (such as financial markets, corporations, media, sports and global criminal economies), each of which operates within the model of the space of flows, though with its own specificity. In a further essay, Castells' (1999, p. 297) also noted the insertion of 'influence and pressure of the grassroots' in ways that 'may alter the cultural and political dynamics of our societies and ultimately, may alter the space of flows itself'. The potential for these spatial shifts to alter cultural and political dynamics was acknowledged by Fraser in her reframing of justice in the context of information networks, global media and 'cyber' technologies. Fraser (2008, p. 23) observed, paraphrasing Castells, that 'the forces that perpetrate injustice belong not to the "space of places," but to the "space of flows"'. Fraser (2008) further observed the implication of this spatial shift in injustices:

> Not locatable within the jurisdiction of any actual or conceivable territorial state, they cannot be made answerable to claims of justice that are framed in terms of the state-territorial principle (p. 23).

These shifts clearly have direct bearing on individuals' practices of justice-seeking in response to harms that have no direct state-territorial pathway to formal justice. In digital society, this may include harms that occur across state jurisdictional boundaries (which are notoriously difficult to police and prosecute, as discussed in Chapter 3), as well as emerging harms that have no legal status as either a crime or civil infraction (such as some forms of gender- or race-based hate, as discussed in Chapter 6). Yet, more than this, the logic of the space of flows has arguably extended to techno-social practices of informal justice-seeking, even in some instances, where formal criminal justice processes might be readily available as a potential response. This suggests that the technosocial practices of informal justice-seeking are adapting across different networks of interaction, such that they form part of an accepted socio-cultural milieu.

In addition to shifts in spatiality, citizen engagement with technosocial practices of informal justice is arguably further cultivated by *temporal* shifts, in particular those enabling the viral spread of digilante activities or content. Globally networked digital citizens experience, and increasingly demand, rapidity — even immediacy — of information and communications. Indeed, according to Castells (1996b, p. 463), the shifting 'space of flows' is associated with an experience of 'timeless time' in which 'linear, irreversible, measurable, predictable time is being shattered in the network society.' It is not only that a global economy and media cycle have, in effect, compressed time by operating around the clock. Rather, Castells seeks to capture in the concept of 'timeless time' a 'mixing of tenses to create a *forever universe*, not self-expanding but self-maintaining, not cyclical but random, not recursive but incursive' (Castells, 1996b, p. 464, emphasis added). 'Timeless time' and a 'forever universe' have particular implications for engagements with digilantism and informal justice. To return to the case of Justine Sacco discussed earlier, for instance, first, her social infraction had garnered global wrath within mere hours of her 140-character solecism on Twitter; and, second, due to the permanence that is characteristic of digital society, social and other norm violations exist in the 'forever universe'; meaning that repercussions may continue to occur, or reignite, months and even years after the original offence.

There are additional logics that amplify the experience of timeless time in digital society. Contemporary internet 'wisdom' suggests that hate spreads faster than love online; a colloquialism that is not far from the evidence gathered by social researchers. Indeed, one of the predictors of *virality* (the rapid and 'infectious' spread of content online, discussed in Chapter 2) is the presence of 'activation' or high-arousal emotions such as awe, amusement, anxiety and anger, as opposed to low-arousal emotions such as sadness (Berger & Milkman, 2012; Guadagno, Rempala, Murphy, & Okdie, 2013). Moreover, researchers have found that positive content is often shared to foster in-group connection and solidarity, while negative and hostile content towards out-groups is similarly shared rapidly due to its solidarity-building function within the social network (Peters & Kashima, 2007). Criminologists and socio-legal scholars have likewise long identified that collective moral outrage in response to crimes plays an important function in maintaining social solidarity (Freiberg, 2001; Durkheim in Giddens, 1972; Sutton, 2000). It is in this context, not surprisingly, that shared outrage in response to a criminal or social infraction through a social network would 'go viral', contributing to shaming and other responses by individual digilantes. Yet, additionally, and to apply concepts from Actor Network Theory (ANT, also discussed in Chapters 2, 5 and 6), such affective triggers for human action are further amplified through their interaction with non-human actants in technosocial systems. Specifically, and as identified by technology scholar Shoshana Zuboff (2015, p. 82), interactions in digital society are cooperatively shaped by 'a new kind of invisible hand'. By this, she refers to the deliberate deployment of algorithms designed not only to *gather* information about us, but to maximise our *participation* in profit-driven social networks; virality is ultimately good for business. It is this logic of 'algorithmic sociality' (discussed in Chapter 2) that fundamentally enables a kind of 'viral justice' (Wood, Rose, & Thompson, 2018). The pleasure of piling on the digilante bandwagon, or 'digital pillory' (further discussed below), is commodified by the market-driven interests of our corporate sovereigns, whose algorithms further enable the rapid spread of derision and shaming through the network. Moreover, these combine with affective logics to suggest that anger in response to a violation of criminal or social norm may be more likely to 'go viral' than, for example, sadness or empathy in response to an individual disclosure of victimisation.

Yet, in addition to these key logics or characteristics, there is also an inherent multiplicity, multiconnectivity and heterogeneity to the practices of informal justice and digilantism discussed here. Such practices resist typological demarcations, as they shift in target, nature, and context; sometimes starting as an individual's disclosure of victimisation, sometimes morphing into a loose swarm of digilante activity and sometimes further aligning with a broader set of political motivations or social justice goals. In some instances, these practices spread amorphously and multidirectionally, without always an apparent core goal or direction. As such, practices of informal or non-state sanctioned justice-seeking in digital society are not only technosocial but characteristically rhizomatic.

Rhizomatic Justice

Several scholars have described contemporary digital activism and social movements as 'multiplicitous', 'horizontal', 'leaderless' and 'rhizomatic' (Funke, 2014; Kasra, 2017; Lim, 2017; Powell, 2013). Indeed, as Joanne Lim (2017, p. 211) describes of digital activism among Malaysian youth: 'When observing the rhizomatic behaviour of online activism, it is apparent that social media nodes often spread with no direction, with no beginning and no end'. Drawing on French philosopher Gilles Deleuze and his collaborator Felix Guattari's (1980) concept of the rhizome, such scholars seek to emphasise the non-hierarchical, asymmetrical and heterogeneous structures of activism in digital society, in which there are 'multiple entranceways and exits' (Deleuze & Guattari, 1980, p. 21). According to social movement research Peter Funke (2014, p. 29): 'This rhizomatic logic is able to accommodate the considerable diversity and the multiplicity of struggles and possible futures, bringing about amorphous sets of associated and loosely linked organizations, groups and movements . . .'.

In a similar vein, the multiple meanings, cultures and practices of informal justice described here can be understood as forming a complex sociotechnical system that, like other forms of contemporary activism, is increasingly rhizomatic. To elaborate on the metaphor, we further draw on education scholar Noel Gough's (2004) associated concept 'rhizomANTic' (sometimes 'rhizomantic'), which embeds an explicit attention to the interaction of human and non-human 'actants' (see also Latour, 1996) in the practices of technosocial justice discussed here. Gough's neologism is a reminder of the relevance of Actor Network Theory (ANT) when examining the multiplicity and heterogeneity of digital society. Though ANT, as a conceptual enterprise, is directed at understanding the essence of society and nature, not as categories and binaries (such as human/non-human, agency/structure, distant/far, materiality/sociality) but as a complex collection of activities and relationships; Latour (1996) has taken care to correct the common misperception of ANT as the study of technological networks specifically. Rather, in the same way that the rhizome is both a metaphor for broader relations within society and one which assists in conceptualising certain practices within digital society, the 'actor-networks' of ANT represent both broader processes and relations as well as holding particular relevance for the human–technological interactions. Such concepts are particularly apt for shifting our thinking on informal justice, digilantism and even digital activism (discussed further in Chapter 8) as interrelated assemblages of sociotechnical cultures, relations and practices that seek to make a difference in the world and yet are 'dynamic, heterogeneous, and nondichotomous' (O'Riley, 2003, p. 27). Furthermore, as is captured by our earlier discussion of 'algorithmic sociality', there are multiple interconnections between humans and other humans, humans and non-humans, as well as non-humans and non-humans, throughout these assemblages. To consider digilantism as 'rhizomantic' justice is to go, in science and technology scholars Christopher Gad and Casper Bruun Jensen's (2010, p. 55) terms, '"beyond ANT," without leaving it entirely behind' (see also Law & Hassard, 1999).

Challenges and Implications

Ultimately, digilantism and informal justice-seeking can be understood as technosocial practices that occur within a set of complex and rhizomatic (or perhaps 'rhizomANTic') assemblages of humans, non-humans, cultures, relations and systems. What the discussion developed here suggests is that, as practices, digilantism and informal justice-seeking can have varied motivations, individual impacts and wider effects. Some of these may be oriented towards the goals of enhancing democracy or challenging structures of inequality. At the same time, these 'justice' practices may sometimes contribute to furthering bigotry and/or result in outcomes and effects that far outweigh the original infraction, or cross over into the exercise of extra-judicial physical violence.

What is clear is that, while many of the examples provided in this chapter are more optimistic and positive in their orientation to digilantism and informal justice, there are simultaneously very real challenges and potentially negative implications of such technosocial practices. Indeed, emerging criminological and socio-legal research has already identified the risks associated with 'trial by social media' and the violations of due process and offenders' rights that may result when Twitter and Facebook enter into criminal justice agency processes (Bartels & Lee, 2013; Ellis & McGovern, 2016; Johnston et al., 2013; Krawitz, 2012; Lee & McGovern, 2013; Milivojevic & McGovern, 2014; Powell, Overington, & Hamilton, 2017). Moreover, and as was discussed in Chapter 4 in relation to Redditors' 'armchair investigation' of the Boston bombings, sometimes digilantes get it wrong, resulting in harassment and abuse directed towards 'innocent victims' — individuals wholly unrelated to the incident and the intended target (Chang et al., 2018). Yet, regardless of whether digilantism is directed at the 'right' target, there are also very real dilemmas regarding the potential for serious harms that may be enacted against individuals who find themselves at the mercy of the crowd.

Among the key risks or challenges of digilantism is that of disproportionate 'punishments' (Kosseff, 2016). Indeed, as media scholars Kristy Hess and Lisa Waller (2014) identify, the interaction between social and mainstream news media has the effect of intensifying the 'digital pillory' such that minor criminal or social infractions by 'ordinary' individuals can attract very serious outcomes. They draw on several case studies to illustrate their argument, including one of a 44-year-old Australian woman who was caught on mobile video, urinating on a seat in a public stadium while watching a football match. The video was posted on YouTube and subsequently went viral. However, it was the mainstream news media who amplified the public shaming and humiliation of the woman by continuing to report updates on her case as she appeared in the Magistrates' Court, fined $100 with no conviction recorded for the minor offence of public urination. Yet, according to court reports, the woman had suffered clinical depression as a result of the public attention to her case, with the impacts also felt by her family and friends (Hess & Waller, 2014). Similarly, criminologist Steven Kohm (2009) has problematised:

> the way shame and humiliation in criminal justice have become increasingly commodified, enacted, and experienced through hybrid forms of mass media that blur the boundaries of reality and entertainment (p. 188).

The capacity for the interactive effects of social and mainstream news media to amplify public sentiment in relation to crime and justice is increasingly of concern for criminologists. As Australian criminologists Sanja Milivojevic and Alyce McGovern (2014) have identified, although social media provide an opportunity for citizens to interrupt the traditional agenda-setting role of the news media, there are also troubling trends through which social and news media combine to 'stir the attention . . . of policy makers' (p. 34) and expand both fear and punitiveness towards crime. In their analysis, social media technologies have the capacity both to positively disrupt and to negatively reinforce crime politics — which may, in turn, be co-opted by politicians seeking to appease a public seeking meaning through responses to crime.

Finally, in much of the discussion here, technology has largely been framed as a tool that can facilitate the divergent and marginalised discourses of resistive politics to flourish. Yet, as discussed in Chapter 3, it is simultaneously the case in digital society that many of these counterpublics exist within privately owned spaces; ultimately subject to the censorship, regulation, market agendas and 'invisible hands' of the new 'corporate sovereigns', rather than operating as an entirely democratic online agora. Furthermore, and as already noted, it is important not to overstate the capacities of democratic digilantism to result in substantive social and structural change; in some instances, challenging autocratic or 'hybrid' democratic regimes has resulted in either penalisation of the digilantes involved or, where actions are taken by the state, they remain against lower-level officials and do not necessarily represent a fundamental threat to the institutionalisation of corruption and/or state violence.

Conclusion

The rapid uptake of communication technologies and user-generated content has enabled online modes of informal justice-seeking and vigilantism to be produced more quickly than ever before and communicated to a wide globally networked public, in particular via media and policy audiences (see Chapters 1 and 2). As such, while citizen participation in justice-seeking and/or vigilantism is not a *new* practice, it is now considerably extended, both in scope and in global reach, as digital platforms 'now enable vastly more users to experiment with a wider and seemingly more varied range of collaborative creative activities' (Harrison & Barthel, 2009, p. 174). As the discussion above suggests, there are several instances of digilantism gone very wrong and many of punishments that are arguably excessive in both scope and reach relative to the social 'crimes' committed. Yet, in other examples, digilantism could be described as a legitimate exercise of democratic freedom, as well as a legitimate strategy in the pursuit of informal justice. Indeed, there is arguably an overlap between digilantism and digital activism — with both drawing in similar ways on 'liberation technologies' from 'hacking to whistleblowing, leaking and "clicktivism"'(Pieterse, 2012, p. 1910).

In other words, while the activities of digilantes may be in response to a specific case of injustice, in some instances, they may also be united in pursuit of a broader political or social justice goal. It is to these cultures and practices of crime and social justice activism in digital society that we turn in the following, and final, of our substantive chapters.

Notes

1   In 2011, the child sex offender disclosure scheme (CSOD) was implemented across police forces in England, Wales and later in Scotland. The scheme is not a public disclosure scheme, but rather allows people who care for children to apply to police for information on whether someone has a prior record for child sexual offences (see Kemshall & Weaver, 2012; Kemshall, Wood, & Westwood, 2010; Manson, 2015).
2   Crush videos, or 'animal snuff films', refer to the recorded abuse and/or killing of small animals, typically under a woman's stiletto or high heel, in a manner stylised on violent, fetish, pornography (Anclien, 2009; Beerworth, 2010).

Recommended Further Reading

Kasra, M. (2017). Vigilantism, public shaming, and social media hegemony: The role of digital-networked images in humiliation and sociopolitical control. *The Communication Review, 20*(3), 172–188.
Powell, A. (2015). Seeking rape justice: Formal and informal responses to sexual violence through technosocial counter-publics. *Theoretical criminology, 19*(4), 571–588.
Trottier, D. (2017). Digital vigilantism as weaponisation of visibility. *Philosophy & Technology, 30*(1), 55–72.

References

Altheide, D. L. (1997). The news media, the problem frame, and the production of fear. *The Sociological Quarterly, 38*(4), 647–668.
Anclien, J. J. (2009). Crush videos and the case for criminalizing criminal depictions. *University of Memphis Law Review, 40*, 1.
Bartels, L., & Lee, J. (2013). Jurors using social media in our courts: Challenges and responses. *Journal of Judicial Administration, 23*, 35.
Bateson, R. (2012). Crime victimization and political participation. *American Political Science Review, 106*(3), 570–587.
Bateson, R. A. (2013). *Order and violence in postwar Guatemala.* New Haven, CT: Yale University.
BBC. (2016, October 9). #NotOkay: Trump tape prompts outpouring of sex assault stories, BBC News, US and Canada, www.bbc.com/news/37603217 (last accessed 29 November 2017).
Beerworth, A. A. (2010). United States v. Stevens: A proposal for criminalizing crush videos under current free speech doctrine. *Vermont Law Review, 35*, 901.
Berger, J., & Milkman, K. L. (2012). What makes online content viral? *Journal of Marketing Research, 49*(2), 192–205.
Boyd, D., & Marwick, A. E. (2011). Social Privacy in Networked Publics: Teens' Attitudes, Practices, and Strategies (SSRN Scholarly Paper No. ID 1925128). *Rochester, NY: Social Science Research Network.* Available at: https://papers.ssrn.com/sol3/papers.cfm?abstract_id=1925128 (last accessed 29 November 2017).
Brevini, B. (2017). WikiLeaks: Between disclosure and whistle-blowing in digital times. *Sociology Compass, 11*(3), 1–11.
Brison, S. J. (2002). *Aftermath: Violence and the Remaking of a Self.* Princeton, NJ: Princeton University Press.
Carrington, K. (2014). *Feminism and Global Justice.* London: Routledge.
Castells, M. (1996a). An introduction to the information age. *City, 2*(7), 6–16.
Castells, M. (1996b). The edge of forever: Timeless time. In *The rise of the network society* (Vol. 1, 2nd ed., pp. 460–499). New Jersey: Blackwell.
Castells, M. (1999). Grassrooting the space of flows. *Urban Geography, 20*(4), 294–302.

Chang, L. Y., & Leung, A. K. (2015). An introduction to cyber crowdsourcing (human flesh search) in the Greater China region. In R. G. Smith, R. Cheung, & L. Y. C. Lau (Eds.) *Cybercrime risks and responses* (pp. 240–252). Basingstoke: Palgrave Macmillan.

Chang, L. Y., Zhong, L. Y., & Grabosky, P. N. (2018). Citizen co-production of cyber security: Self-help, vigilantes, and cybercrime. *Regulation & Governance*, *12*(1), 101–114.

Chen, R., & Sharma, S. K. (2011). Human flesh search—Facts and Issues. *Journal of Information Privacy and Security*, *7*(1), 50–71.

Cheong, P. H., & Gong, J. (2010). Cyber vigilantism, transmedia collective intelligence, and civic participation. *Chinese Journal of Communication*, *3*(4), 471–487.

Cheung, A. S. (2009). China Internet going wild: Cyber-hunting versus privacy protection. *Computer Law & Security Review*, *25*(3), 275–279.

Chibnall, S. (Ed.). (2013). *Law-and-order news: An analysis of crime reporting in the British press* (Vol. 2). Abingdon: Routledge.

China Internet Network Information Center. (2017, January). *The 39th statistical report on internet development in China*. Beijing: China Internet Network Information Center. Available at: www.cnidp.cn (last accessed 29 November 2017).

Clark, H. (2010). 'What Is the Justice System Willing to Offer?': Understanding Sexual Assault Victim/Survivors' Criminal Justice Needs. *Family Matters*, (85), 28.

Clifton, D. (2014, October 31). '19 #BeenRapedNeverReported Tweets That Everyone Needs to See,' *Mic.com*, https://mic.com/articles/102918/19-been-raped-never-reported-tweets-that-everyone-needs-to-see (last accessed 29 November 2017).

Clough, J. (2010). *Principles of cybercrime*. Melbourne: Cambridge University Press.

Crovitz, L. (2010, December 6). Julian Assange, informational anarchist. *Wall Street Journal*. Available at: www.wsj.com/articles/SB10001424052748703989000457565313548361870 (last accessed 29 November 2017).

Daly, K., & Bouhours, B. (2010). Rape and attrition in the legal process: A comparative analysis of five countries. *Crime and Justice*, *39*(1), 565–650.

Deleuze, G., & Guattari, F. (1980). *A thousand plateaus: Capitalism and schizophrenia*. Paris: Minuit.

Denisova, A. (2017). Democracy, protest and public sphere in Russia after the 2011–2012 anti-government protests: Digital media at stake. *Media, Culture & Society*, *39*(7), 976–994.

Daly, K. (2014). Reconceptualizing sexual victimization and justice. In I. Vanfraechem, A. Pemberton, & F. M. Ndahinda, (Eds.) *Justice for victims: Perspectives on rights, transition and reconciliation* (pp. 378–395). Abingdon: Routledge.

Downey, T. (2010), China's cyberposse. *The New York Times*. Available online at www.nytimes.com/2010/03/07/magazine/07Human-t.html?pagewanted=all&_r=0 (last accessed 29 November 2017).

Ellis, J., & McGovern, A. (2016). The end of symbiosis? Australia police–media relations in the digital age. *Policing and Society*, *26*(8), 944–962.

Evans, J. (2003). Vigilance and vigilantes: Thinking psychoanalytically about anti-paedophile action. *Theoretical Criminology*, *7*(2), 163–189.

Ferreday, D. (2017). Like a stone in your stomach: Articulating the unspeakable in rape victim-survivors' activist selfies. In A. Kuntsman (Ed.) *Selfie citizenship* (pp. 127–136). New York: Springer.

Fileborn, B. (2014). Online activism and street harassment: Digital justice or shouting into the ether? *Griffith Journal of Law & Human Dignity*, *2*(1), 32–51.

Ford, C. (2016). *Fight like a girl*. Melbourne: Allen & Unwin.

Foucault, M. (1987). The ethic of care for the self as a practice of freedom: An interview with Michel Foucault on January 20, 1984 in the final foucault: Studies on Michel Foucault's last works. *Philosophy & Social Criticism*, *12*(2–3), 112–131.

Fraser, N. (1990). Rethinking the public sphere: A contribution to the critique of actually existing democracy. *Social Text*, (25/26), 56–80.

Fraser, N. (2007). Feminist politics in the age of recognition: A two-dimensional approach to gender justice. *Studies in Social Justice*, *1*(1), 23.

Fraser, N. (2008). Abnormal justice. *Critical Inquiry, 34*(3), 393–422.

Fraser, N. (2009). *Scales of justice: Reimagining political space in a globalizing world*. New York: Columbia University Press.

Fraser, N. (2014). 'Publicity, Subjection, Critique: A Reply to my Critics'. In K. Nash (Ed.). *Transnationalizing the public sphere*. Cambridge: Polity Press.

Freiberg, A. (2001). Affective versus effective justice: Instrumentalism and emotionalism in criminal justice. *Punishment & Society, 3*(2), 265–278.

Funke, P. N. (2014). Building rhizomatic social movements? Movement-building relays during the current epoch of contention. *Studies in Social Justice, 8*(1), 27.

Gad, C., & Jensen, C. B. (2010). On the consequences of post-ANT. *Science, Technology, & Human Values, 35*(1), 55–80.

Gao, L., & Stanyer, J. (2014). Hunting corrupt officials online: the human flesh search engine and the search for justice in China. *Information, Communication & Society, 17*(7), 814–829.

Garland, D. (1996). THE LIMITS OF THE SOVEREIGN STATE: Strategies of Crime Control in Contemporary Society. *The British Journal of Criminology, 36*(4), 445–471.

Giddens, A. (1972). *Emile Durkheim: Selected writings*. Cambridge: Cambridge University Press.

Glasser, S. B. (2016). *Covering politics in a "Post-Truth" America*. Washington, DC: Brookings Institution Press.

Gordon, L. (2016, June 16). For every woman who receives an unsolicited dick pic: Take notes. *Revelist*. Available at: www.revelist.com/viral/dick-pic-response/3056

Gough, N. (2004). RhizomANTically becoming-cyborg: Performing posthuman pedagogies. *Educational Philosophy and Theory, 36*(3), 253–265.

Greer, C. (2010). News media criminology. In E. McLaughlin, & T. Newburn (Eds.), *The SAGE handbook of criminological theory* (pp. 490–513). London: Sage Publications.

Guadagno, R. E., Rempala, D. M., Murphy, S., & Okdie, B. M. (2013). What makes a video go viral? An analysis of emotional contagion and Internet memes. *Computers in Human Behavior, 29*(6), 2312–2319.

Hadden, S. E. (2001). *Slave patrols: Law and violence in Virginia and the Carolinas*. Cambridge: Harvard University Press.

Hall, S., Critcher, C., Jefferson, T., Clarke, J., & Roberts, B. (2013). *Policing the crisis: Mugging, the state and law and order*. Basingstoke: Palgrave Macmillan.

Handy, J. (2004). Chicken thieves, witches, and judges: Vigilante justice and customary law in Guatemala. *Journal of Latin American Studies, 36*(3), 533–561.

Hardy, K. (2010). Operation Titstorm: Hacktivism or Cyberterrorism. *UNSW Law Journal, 33*(2), 474.

Harrison, T. M., & Barthel, B. (2009). Wielding new media in Web 2.0: exploring the history of engagement with the collaborative construction of media products. *New Media & Society, 11*(1–2), 155–178.

Harvey, M. R. (2000). In the aftermath of sexual abuse: Making and remaking meaning in narratives of trauma and recovery. *Narrative Inquiry, 10*(2), 291–311.

Henry, N. (2010). The impossibility of bearing witness: Wartime rape and the promise of justice. *Violence Against Women, 16*(10), 1098–1119.

Herman, J. L. (2005). Justice from the victim's perspective. *Violence Against Women, 11*(5), 571–602.

Hess, K., & Waller, L. (2014). The digital pillory: Media shaming of 'ordinary' people for minor crimes. *Continuum, 28*(1), 101–111.

Holt, T. J. (2012). Exploring the intersections of technology, crime, and terror. *Terrorism and Political Violence, 24*(2), 337–354.

Ingraham, C., & Reeves, J. (2016). New media, new panics. *Critical Studies in Media Communication, 33*(5), 455–467.

Jane, E. (2016). Online misogyny and feminist digilantism. *Continuum, 30*(3), 284–297.

Johnston, L. (1996). What is vigilantism? *The British Journal of Criminology, 36*(2), 220–236.

Johnston, J., Keyzer, P., Holland, G., Pearson, M. L., Rodrick, S., & Wallace, A. (2013). *Juries and social media: a report prepared for the Victorian Department of Justice*. Melbourne: Standing Council on Law and Justice.

Jones, M. L. (2016). *Ctrl+ Z: The right to be forgotten*. New York: New York University Press.

Kasra, M. (2017). Vigilantism, public shaming, and social media hegemony: The role of digital-networked images in humiliation and sociopolitical control. *The Communication Review, 20*(3), 172–188.

Kelly, L., Lovett, J., & Regan, L. (2005). *A gap or a chasm? Attrition in reported rape cases.* London: Child and Woman Abuse Studies Unit, London Metropolitan University and Home Office Research, Development and Statistics Directorate.

Kemshall, H., & Weaver, E. (2012). The sex offender public disclosure pilots in England and Scotland: Lessons for 'marketing strategies' and risk communication with the public. *Criminology and Criminal Justice, 12*(5), 549–565.

Kemshall, H., Wood, J., & Westwood, S. (2010). *Child sex offender review (CSOR) public disclosure pilots: A process evaluation.* London: Home Office.

Koesel, K. J., & Bunce, V. J. (2012). Putin, popular protests, and political trajectories in Russia: A comparative perspective. *Post-Soviet Affairs, 28*(4), 403–423.

Kohm, S. A. (2009). Naming, shaming and criminal justice: Mass-mediated humiliation as entertainment and punishment. *Crime, Media, Culture, 5*(2), 188–205.

Koltsova, O., & Shcherbak, A. (2015). 'LiveJournal Libra!': The political blogosphere and voting preferences in Russia in 2011–2012. *New Media & Society, 17*(10), 1715–1732.

Kosseff, J. (2016). The hazards of cyber-vigilantism. *Computer Law & Security Review, 32*(4), 642–649.

Krawitz, M. (2012, November 16). *Guilty as tweeted: Jurors using social media inappropriately during the trial process.* UWA Faculty of Law Research Paper No. 2012–02. Available at: https://ssrn.com/abstract=2176634 (last accessed 29 November 2017).

Latour, B. (1996). On actor-network theory: A few clarifications. *Soziale Welt, 47*(4), 369–381.

Law, J., & Hassard, J. (1999). *Actor network theory and after.* London: Blackwell/Wiley.

Lee, M., & McGovern, A. (2013). *Policing and media: public relations, simulations and communications.* London: Routledge.

Liang, B., & Lu, H. (2010). Internet development, censorship, and cyber crimes in China. *Journal of Contemporary Criminal Justice, 26*(1), 103–120.

Lievore, D. (2005). *Prosecutorial decisions in adult sexual assault cases.* Canberra: Australian Institute of Criminology.

Lim, J. B. (2017). Engendering civil resistance: Social media and mob tactics in Malaysia. *International Journal of Cultural Studies, 20*(2), 209–227.

Loney-Howes, R. (2015). Beyond the spectacle of suffering: Representations of rape in online anti-rape activism. *Outskirts, 33*(1), 1–17.

Malone, L. (2012, March 13). Project unbreakable: From Victim to Victor. *Sydney Morning Herald.*

Manson, W. (2015). "Keeping children safe": The child sex offender disclosure scheme in Scotland. *Journal of Sexual Aggression, 21*(1), 43–55.

Marsh, I., & Melville, G. (2011). Moral panics and the British media–a look at some contemporary 'folk devils'. *Internet Journal of Criminology, 1*(1), 1–21.

Massanari, A. (2017). #Gamergate and the fappening: How Reddit's algorithm, governance, and culture support toxic technocultures. *New Media & Society, 19*(3), 329–346.

McCartney, J. (2000, August 13). The Mob Rules, OK, *The Telegraph.* Available at: www.telegraph.co.uk/news/uknews/1352586/The-mob-rules-OK.html (last accessed 29 November 2017).

McDonald, D. (2014). The politics of hate crime: Neoliberal vigilance, vigilantism and the question of paedophilia. *International Journal for Crime, Justice and Social Democracy, 3*(1), 68–80.

McLaughlin, K. (2017, April 30). Girlfriend who was battered and throttled by her ex shares daily selfie documenting her recovery. *Daily Mail.* Available at: www.dailymail.co.uk/news/article-4459826/Domestic-violence-victim-shares-selfies-recovery.html (last accessed 29 November 2017).

Milivojevic, S., & McGovern, A. (2014). The death of Jill Meagher: Crime and punishment on social media. *International Journal for Crime, Justice and Social Democracy, 3*(3), 22–39.

Moncada, E. (2017). Varieties of vigilantism: Conceptual discord, meaning and strategies. *Global Crime, 18*(4), 403–423.

Moses, A. (2010, February 10). Operation Titstorm: Hackers bring down government websites. *The Age.* Available at: www.theage.com.au/technology/technology-news/operation-titstorm-hackers-bring-down-government-websites-20100209-nqku (last accessed 29 November 2017).

Mueller, F., Carter, C., & Whittle, A. (2015). Can audit (still) be trusted? *Organization Studies, 36*(9), 1171–1203.

Munro, I. (2017). Whistle-blowing and the politics of truth: Mobilizing 'truth games' in the WikiLeaks case. *Human Relations, 70*(5), 519–543.

National Office of Statistics. (2016a). *Focus on violent crime and sexual offences: Year ending March 2015*. London: HM Government.

National Office of Statistics. (2016b). *Domestic abuse in England and Wales: Year ending March 2016*. London: HM Government.

Newburn, T., & Jones, T. (2005). Symbolic politics and penal populism: The long shadow of Willie Horton. *Crime, Media, Culture, 1*(1), 72–87.

Nhan, J., Huey, L., & Broll, R. (2017). Digilantism: An analysis of crowdsourcing and the Boston marathon bombings. *The British Journal of Criminology, 57*(2), 341–361.

O'Malley, P. (1992). Risk, power and crime prevention. *Economy and Society, 21*(3), 252–275.

O'Malley, G. (2013). Hacktivism: Cyber Activism or Cyber Crime. *Trinity College Law Review, 16*, 137–160.

O'Neill, T. (2018). 'Today I Speak': Exploring how victim-survivors use reddit. *International Journal for Crime, Justice and Social Democracy, 7*(1), 44–59.

O'Riley, P. A. (2003). *Technology, culture, and socioeconomics: A Rhizoanalysis of educational discourses*. New York: Peter Lang.

Pauli, D. (2011, March 4). Anonymous DDoS charges too weak: AFP. *ZDnet*. Available at: www.zdnet.com/article/anonymous-ddos-charges-too-weak-afp/

Peters, K., & Kashima, Y. (2007). From social talk to social action: Shaping the social triad with emotion sharing. *Journal of Personality and Social Psychology, 93*, 780–797.

Petrov, N., Lipman, M., & Hale, H. E. (2014). Three dilemmas of hybrid regime governance: Russia from Putin to Putin. *Post-Soviet Affairs, 30*(1): 1–26.

Phillips, B. J. (2017). Inequality and the Emergence of Vigilante Organizations: the Case of Mexican Auto-defensas. *Comparative Political Studies, 50*(10), 1358–1389.

Pieterse, J. N. (2012). Leaking Superpower: WikiLeaks and the contradictions of democracy. *Third World Quarterly, 33*(10), 1909–1924.

Powell, A. (2013). Argument-by-technology: How technical activism contributes to internet governance. In I. Brown (Ed.), *Research handbook on governance of the internet* (pp. 198–220). Cheltenham, UK: Edward Elgar.

Powell, A. (2015a). Seeking informal justice online. In A. Powell, N. Henry, & A. Flynn (Eds.), *Rape justice: Beyond the criminal law* (pp. 218–237). Basingstoke, UK: Palgrave Macmillan.

Powell, A. (2015b). Seeking rape justice: Formal and informal responses to sexual violence through technosocial counter-publics. *Theoretical Criminology, 19*(4), 571–588.

Powell, A., Overington, C., & Hamilton, G. (2017). Following #JillMeagher: Collective meaning-making in response to crime events via social media. *Crime, Media, Culture*. Advance online publication. doi: 10.1177/1741659017721276.

Pratt, J. (2007). *Penal populism*. London: Routledge.

Pratten, D., & Sen, A. (2007). Global vigilantes: Perspectives on justice and violence. In D. Pratten, & A. Sen (Eds.) *Global Vigilantes: Anthropological Perspectives on Justice and Violence*. London: Hurst.

Qiu, L., Lin, H., Chiu, C.Y., & Liu, P. (2015). Online collective behaviors in China: Dimensions and motivations. *Analyses of Social Issues and Public Policy, 15*(1), 44–68.

Renninger, B. J. (2015). "Where I can be myself… where I can speak my mind": Networked counterpublics in a polymedia environment. *New Media & Society, 17*(9), 1513–1529.

Reuter, O. J., & Szakonyi, D. (2015). Online social media and political awareness in authoritarian regimes. *British Journal of Political Science, 45*(1), 29–51.

Roberts, M. A. (2016). "We the women of Juárez are strong": a rhetorical analysis of Diana, the huntress of bus drivers. Available at: https://ir.ua.edu/handle/123456789/2648 (last accessed 29 November 2017).

Ronson, J. (2015a, February 12). How one stupid tweet blew up Justine Sacco's life. *New York Times*.

Ronson, J. (2015b). *So you've been publicly shamed*. New York: Riverhead Books.

Rosenberg, D. (1996). Individual Justice and Collectivizing Risk-Based Claims in Mass-Exposure Cases. *New York University Law Review, 71*, 210–257.

Rusciano, E. (2016, June). *If someone sends you a picture of their penis is it okay to publicly shame them?* Available at: www.News.com.au

Schia, N., & de Carvalho, B. (2015). Reforms, Customs and Resilience: Justice for Sexual and Gender-Based Violence in Liberia. In A. Powell, N. Henry, & A. Flynn (Eds.), *Rape justice: Beyond the criminal law* (pp. 143–159). Basingstoke, UK: Palgrave Macmillan.

Senft, T. M., & Baym, N. K. (2015). Selfies introduction ~ What does the selfie say? Investigating a global phenomenon. *International Journal of Communication, 9*(19), 1588–1606.

Sen, A. (2012). Women's Vigilantism in India: A case study of the pink sari gang. *Online Encyclopedia of Mass Violence.* Available at: www.massviolence.org/women-s-vigilantism-in-india-a-case-study-of-the-pink-sari (last accessed 29 November 2017).

Sichuan Online. (2009, February 25). *Sichuan girl killed by ex-boyfriend "human" became an accomplice.* Available at: http://news.sohu.com/20090225/n262452158.shtml (in Chinese, accessed by Google translate) (last accessed 9 March 2018).

Sifry, M. (2011). *WikiLeaks and the age of transparency.* Berkley, CA: Counterpoint.

Silke, A. (2001). Dealing with vigilantism: Issues and lessons for the police. *The Police Journal, 74*(2), 120–133.

Smallridge, J., Wagner, P., & Crowl, J. N. (2016). Understanding cyber-vigilantism: A conceptual framework. *Journal of Theoretical & Philosophical Criminology, 8*(1), 57.

Smyth, R., & Oates, S. (2015). Mind the gaps: Media use and mass action in Russia. *Europe-Asia Studies, 67*(2), 285–305.

Solinger, R., Fox, M., & Irani, K. (Eds.). (2010). *Telling stories to change the world: Global voices on the power of narrative to build community and make social justice claims.* New York: Routledge.

Solove, D. J. (2007). *The future of reputation: Gossip, rumor, and privacy on the Internet.* New Haven: Yale University Press.

Statistica. (2017). *Countries with the highest number of internet users 2017.* Available at: www.statista.com/statistics/262966/number-of-internet-users-in-selected-countries/ (last accessed 29 November 2017).

Sundar, N. (2010). Vigilantism, Culpability and Moral Dilemmas. *Critique of Anthropology, 30*(1), 113–121.

Sutton, A. (2000). Crime prevention: A viable alternative to the justice system? In D. Chappell, & P. Wilson (Eds.), *Crime and the criminal justice system in Australia: 2000 and beyond* (pp. 316–331). Australia: Butterworths.

Tang, L., & Sampson, H. (2012). The interaction between mass media and the internet in non-democratic states: The case of China. *Media, Culture & Society, 34*(4), 457–471.

Telegraph. (2016, April 19). #WhenIWas: Women are sharing stories on Twitter about being sexually harassed as children. Available at: www.telegraph.co.uk/women/life/wheniwas-women-are-sharing-stories-on-twitter-about-being-sexual/ (last accessed 29 November 2017).

Todorova, T. (2011). 'Giving memory a future': confronting the legacy of mass rape in post-conflict Bosnia-Herzegovina. *Journal of International Women's Studies, 12*(2), 3.

Toepfl, F. (2011). Managing public outrage: Power, scandal, and new media in contemporary Russia. *New Media & Society, 13*(8), 1301–1319.

Trottier, D. (2017). Digital vigilantism as weaponisation of visibility. *Philosophy & Technology, 30*(1), 55–72

Uitermark, J. (2017). Complex contention: Analyzing power dynamics within anonymous. *Social Movement Studies, 16*(4), 403–417.

Vander Ende, J. (2014). Vigilantism. In G. Bruinsma, & D. Weisburd (Eds.) *The encyclopedia of criminology and criminal justice.* New York: Springer.

Warren, I. (2009, December). *Vigilantism, the press and signal crimes 2006–2007.* Paper presented at the Australia & New Zealand Critical Criminology Conference 2009, Melbourne.

Wiedemann, C. (2014). Between swarm, network, and multitude: Anonymous and the infrastructures of the common. *Distinktion: Scandinavian Journal of Social Theory, 15*(3), 309–326.

WikiLeaks. (2010). *Collateral murder.* Available at: https://collateralmurder.wikileaks.org/ (last accessed 29 November 2017)

WikiLeaks. (2016). *Hillary Clinton Email Archive.* Available at: https://wikileaks.org/clinton-emails/ (last accessed 29 November 2017).

Williams, A., & Thompson, B. (2004a). Vigilance or vigilantes: The Paulsgrove riots and policing paedophiles in the community part 1: The long slow fuse. *The Police Journal, 77*(2), 99–119.

Williams, A., & Thompson, B. (2004b). Vigilance or vigilantes: The Paulsgrove riots and policing paedophiles in the community part II: The lessons of paulsgrove. *The Police Journal, 77*(3), 193–205.

Wood, M., Rose, E., & Thompson, C. (2018). Viral justice? Online justice-seeking, intimate partner violence and affective contagion. *Theoretical Criminology.* Advance online publication. doi:10.1177/1362480617750507.

Woods, H. S. (2014). Anonymous, Steubenville, and the politics of visibility: Questions of virality and exposure in the case of #OPRollRedRoll and #OccupySteubenville. *Feminist Media Studies, 14*(6), 1096–1098.

World Health Organization. (2013). *Global and regional estimates of violence against women: Prevalence and health effects of intimate partner violence and non-partner sexual violence.* Geneva: World Health Organization.

Younan, C. (2017, September 19). "I found it so therapeutic": Woman takes regular selfies to help her overcome brutal attack. *The Daily Star.* Available at: www.dailystar.co.uk/news/latest-news/610180/Woman-selfie-brutal-attack-ex-boyfriend-pictures (last accessed 29 November 2017).

Zuboff, S. (2015). Big other: surveillance capitalism and the prospects of an information civilization. *Journal of Information Technology, 30*(1), 75–89.

8

MORE THAN A HASHTAG

Crime and Social Justice Activism

Introduction

December 2010 marked the beginning of a series of pro-democracy demonstrations in Tunisia that spread throughout North Africa and the Middle East during 2011, garnering worldwide news media and scholarly attention. Hundreds of thousands of citizens took to the streets to march in the name of political reform; they caused the end of several dictatorships. The 'Arab Spring' resulted in the toppling of President Ben Ali in Tunisia and Hosni Mubarak in Egypt, both of whom had ruled their respective countries for almost 30 years. Revolutionary rioting spread to neighbouring countries including Libya, Yemen, Syria and Bahrain. Globally, news media audiences became enthralled with the role that social media had apparently played in the pro-democracy uprisings. Since the 2000s, internet access and mobile phone uptake have enabled a culture of digital activism in Egypt and its neighbours (Khondker, 2011). In an authoritarian regime where the government controls media outlets and quashes open public debate, online blogs, forums, Facebook pages and Twitter provided networked 'spaces of flow' where disenfranchised and angry citizens could build momentum towards political reform (Howard & Hussain, 2011). Like many activist movements, though fed by an undercurrent of injustice and marginalisation, in Egypt matters escalated in response to a triggering incident. A 28-year-old man, Khaled Mohamed Saeed, was brutally bashed and killed by Egyptian police. When visiting his body in the morgue, Saeed's brother took photographs on his mobile phone (Howard & Hussain, 2011); images that later went viral. Upon discovering the images, a local activist and computer engineer, Wael Ghonim (Ghonim, 2015), set up a Facebook page in memory of Saeed, which would become a rallying point for thousands of citizens desperate to see change, while on Twitter the rhetoric continued using the hashtag #weareallkhaledsaid. Images of the subsequent mass demonstrations and ongoing police brutality were captured and shared by protestors; they were further distributed, and their effect amplified, by a global network of 'mediated witnesses' (Peelo, 2006 and discussed in Chapter 4).

Though the Arab Spring has featured repeatedly in research as an example of the democratising effect of technologies, almost eight years later the role of social media in supporting social change seems less certain. Worldwide, from #Occupy, to #BringBackOurGirls, to #JeSuisCharlie, to #YesAllWomen, to #Resist, to #UmbrellaRevolution, 'hashtag activism' emerges from various incidents supporting a range of movements, with widely divergent effects. While it has become common to disparage hashtag activism as 'clicktivism' or 'slacktivism', much research across media, communications, politics and international studies suggests that significant impacts can be felt from these contemporary activist networks, though they simultaneously suggest caution. Criminology, meanwhile, has been slow to engage with activist movements or how they might be shifting as a result of greater integration with social media and other digital platforms. Potentially, this is in part a reflection of criminology's conventionally narrow frame of reference in domestically legislated crimes (as discussed in Chapter 3). However, in the context of digital society, and in light of associated challenges to nation states, a global and critical criminological orientation ought rightly to be concerned with harms beyond those legislated by the state. In recent years, there are many examples of social movements that have arisen in response to local criminal harms, but which have extended to involve nationwide and even global technosocial activist repertoires. One such exemplar that we suggest should engage the digital criminological imagination is #BlackLivesMatter. This chapter discusses the emergence of new methods of activism, and the reconfiguration of old ones, through an exploration of this key crime and social justice movement that, though emerging foremost in the United States, carries relevance elsewhere across the globe.

#BlackLivesMatter

The Killing of Trayvon Martin

In Sanford, Florida, on 26 February 2012, George Zimmerman fatally shot 17-year-old Trayvon Martin. Martin, an African-American teen, was walking along the street that Sunday night, carrying snacks and a can of iced tea that he had purchased at the local convenience store (see also Chapter 5). It was early in the evening as he made his way home towards his father's residence, talking with his girlfriend on his mobile phone; at what phone records later confirmed was 7:12 pm. Meanwhile, Zimmerman, a 28-year-old, white-Hispanic neighbourhood watch volunteer, saw Martin walking the streets and proceeded to follow him from his car, calling 911 to report 'a real suspicious guy' who 'looks like he's up to no good'. According to media reports of the 911 call recording, the responding dispatcher told Zimmerman that they did not need him to continue following the man he'd seen (Botelho, 2012; Ramaswamy, 2017); but Zimmerman ignored the request. Shortly after, an altercation between Zimmerman and Martin was heard by neighbours, as well as a gunshot. By the time emergency services and police arrived, and attempted to revive Martin, it was too late; he was declared dead at 7:30 pm (Ramaswamy, 2017). Martin had been unarmed; the shot came from Zimmerman's 9 mm semi-automatic hand gun.

The manner of Trayvon's death itself was controversial for the apparent racial profiling element. Though he later claimed the killing was in self-defence, Zimmerman offered no substantive cause for the suspicions that Trayvon was 'up to no good' which led to him pursue the young man in the first place. Yet, it was the subsequent police and criminal justice system response that turned the case into national news and part of a wider movement. It was 44 days before police arrested Zimmerman, and in July 2013, he was found not guilty of second degree murder (Ramaswamy, 2017). Lawrence

Bobo (2015), Professor of Sociology in the Department of African and African American Studies at Harvard University, described it as follows:

> The murder of Trayvon Martin was a tragedy. The acquittal of George Zimmerman on murder charges was an unspeakable national shame and travesty . . . the second murder of Trayvon Martin . . . Both murders of Trayvon Martin are of a piece with deep problems of discrimination, racism, and class bias woven into the fabric of our criminal justice system and of the American social order writ large (p. xi).

The not guilty verdict in Zimmerman's case sparked riots, first locally in Florida and eventually nationally across the United States. For many, the killing of Trayvon Martin, and the 'second murder' by the criminal justice system, 'epitomised the truth that the system black Americans had been told to trust was never structured to deliver justice to them' (Lowery, 2017, n.p.). Twitter hashtags such as #RipTrayvonMartin, #Blackout4Trayvon and #JusticeForTrayvon demonstrated widespread outrage at Florida's legal system and its inadequacies in response to Martin's death. The extent of this public outrage was palpable; approximately five million tweets were made in response to Zimmerman's acquittal in the day following the court's decision (Jurkowitz & Vogt, 2013).

Among the posts widely reported and discussed in mainstream and social media in response to the tragedy and injustice of Trayvon's case, was a Facebook post by 31-year-old activist Alicia Garza, titled 'a love letter to black people'. The day of the Zimmerman verdict, 13 July 2013, Alicia wrote:

> The sad part is, there's a section of America who is cheering and celebrating right now. and that makes me sick to my stomach. We GOTTA get it together y'all . . . stop saying we are not surprised. that's a damn shame in itself. I continue to be surprised at how little Black lives matter. And I will continue that. stop giving up on black life.
>
> Black people. I love you. I love us. Our lives matter.

From her initial Facebook post, Alicia Garza was soon joined by her friends and fellow activists Patrisse Cullors and Opal Tometi, who shared the post with the hashtag #BlackLivesMatter and set up Tumblr and Twitter accounts under the same banner (Garza, 2014; Lowery, 2017). Garza has since described #BlackLivesMatter as a call to action against the anti-Black racism that is endemic in the United States and a response to the profound injustice of Trayvon's case, in which he was 'post-humously placed on trial for his own murder' while his 'killer, George Zimmerman, was not held accountable for the crime he committed' (Garza, 2014, n.p.). The three women spread the word throughout their social networks, asking friends to share their own stories about how #BlackLivesMatter via the Tumblr and Twitter accounts they had created (Langford & Speight, 2015).

From Incidents to Protests

The practical function of hashtags is to connect otherwise disparate social media posts in order to form meaningful threads or 'conversations' and allow users within a dispersed network to easily locate related content. In effect, hashtags make for readily 'searchable talk' (Zappavigna, 2015). It was in 2007 that Twitter user Chris Messina proposed this innovative solution for organising, filtering and contextualising Twitter information. His tweet "how do you feel about using # (pound) for groups. As in #barcamp [msg]?" (Messina, 2007) is marked as the creation of the hashtag that has come to define key workings of Twitter and other social media platforms (notably Instagram and Facebook). Initially an informal practice, the hashtag is an extension of an early internet convention in Internet Relay Chat (IRC) that distinguished public channels of conversation from private local servers within online networks. Functionally, when used on Twitter, terms starting with a hash symbol (#) are formatted by the platform as clickable and searchable text that is then able to be read in sequential order by any user seeking tweets containing the same #hashtag (Tonkin, Pfeiffer, & Tourte, 2012, p. 50). The hashtag plays an important function in enabling communal response to information by labelling content using themes and interests that are organised and aligned with similar voices (Zappavigna, 2012, p. 1). When used on social media platforms, the hashtag convention allows users' online participation to be easily discovered by other members of the network (Chang, 2010), enabling the formation of public conversations that may also evolve into ad hoc topical communities (Bruns, Highfield, & Lind, 2012). As such, hashtags have extended beyond their pragmatic use for text searchability and have come both to exhibit relational functions (through the rapid formation of discursive communities) and to mark processes of meaning-making within public and counterpublic spaces (Scott, 2015; Zappavigna, 2012). In using a hashtag, social media users often simultaneously signify the most important affectual or experiential component of their posted content (Scott, 2015).

According to Twitter, though #BlackLivesMatter first appeared on the platform in July 2013, it was in late 2014 that the hashtag reached its first substantial peak. Throughout the second half of 2013, it had appeared on Twitter 5106 times, or approximately 30 times a day (Pew Research Center, 2016), perhaps demonstrating the hashtag's initial spread through the social networks of Garza, Cullors and Tometi. But the national, and indeed global, uptake of the #BlackLivesMatter hashtag accelerated greatly in August 2014 when 18-year-old African-American teenager Michael Brown was fatally shot by a white police officer, Darren Wilson, in Ferguson, Missouri.

On Saturday 9 August 2014, unarmed teenager Michael Brown was fatally shot by police officer Darren Wilson in Ferguson. Brown had earlier stolen a box of cigarillo's from a local convenience store and was walking home with a friend, Dorian Johnson, when Officer Wilson stopped his car to question the two young men (Buchanan et al., 2017). Although accounts of the subsequent events differ, it is clear that Brown and Wilson were involved in an altercation and that Wilson fired two shots at Brown as he fled the scene (Buchanan et al., 2017). As Wilson pursued Brown, the officer fired again: this time the fatal shots that killed Brown, approximately 45 meters from the initial confrontation at the police car (Buchanan et al., 2017). In the media attention and legal cases that followed, critical information about these events became clearer through investigations harnessing the videos and images documenting these incidents. From the CCTV footage in the convenience store showing Brown shop-lifting through to the videos recorded by locals on their mobile phones of Brown lying face down in the street, these images were then shared amongst neighbours, friends and the news media, circulating news of the incident in Ferguson beyond the local community (Bosman & Goldstein, 2014).

Brown's death resonated through social media, raising public consciousness of the issue of racial injustice and police violence in the United States. Indeed, it was a tweet from an eye-witness that raised crucial awareness of Brown's death and countered the official narrative being put forward by police and early media reports. In the immediate aftermath of Brown's shooting, Twitter user @TheePharoah posted 'I JUST SAW SOMEONE DIE OMFG', later uploading an image of a police officer standing over Brown's dead body lying in the street (Ries, 2014). Although an early official response claimed the confrontation occurred because Brown was blocking traffic, eye-witness @TheePharoah had already claimed it had happened for 'no reason! He was running!'.

The killing of Michael Brown followed several widely reported extrajudicial killings of African Americans, including 12-year-old Tamir Rice, 43-year-old Eric Garner, 25-year-old Freddie Gray and 22-year-old Oscar Grant; arguably adding to the momentum of protests that occurred both online and in the streets of Ferguson (Bonilla & Rosa, 2015; Freelon, McIlwain, & Clark, 2016). Tamir Rice, for instance, was killed on 22 November 2014 by police who had been called to a park in Cleveland in response to eye-witness reports that a juvenile was playing in the park with what might have been a fake gun. The 911 dispatcher failed to relay to police that the incident might involve a child and that the gun might be fake. CCTV footage from across the street shows a police car pulling up to the gazebo where Tamir was sitting alone and police firing on him seconds after arriving. It was later confirmed that Tamir had, in fact, been playing with a pellet gun (Ali, 2017; Embrick, 2015; Richardson, 2014). Meanwhile, on 17 July 2014, Eric Garner, a 43-year-old man, was killed by police in Staten Island (New York) after being stopped for selling untaxed cigarettes. The police who arrested him in a local park applied a chokehold and wrestled him to the ground, compressing his chest. Recorded on mobile phone by a local bystander, a video later circulated which clearly showed police applying a chokehold, while Garner gasped for breath, saying 'I can't breathe'. An autopsy report would later identify the choking and compression by police, and the lack of timely medical assistance, as the cause of Garner's death (see Baker, Goodman, & Mueller, 2015; Embrick, 2015; Richardson, 2014). Freddie Gray, a 25-year-old man, died in Baltimore on 19 April 2015, a week after police mistreatment during his arrest on April 12, which left him with severe injuries to his larynx, three broken vertebrae and spinal injuries; which were later reported as being 80% severed through his neck (see Embrick, 2015). Mobile phone video from a bystander shows the arrest of Gray, which according to state prosecutors in the case against the police officers involved, had no just grounds; media reports described the police as arresting Gray for 'running while Black' (BBC, 2016). And, on 1 January 2009, Oscar Grant, a 22-year-old man, was fatally shot by a transit police officer in Oakland, California. Two officers had restrained the unarmed man on suspicion of an earlier physical altercation reported on the train, forcing him to lie face down on the ground, when one drew his pistol and shot Grant in the back. Several commuters recorded video on their mobile phones, which captured the fatal shooting and provided evidence of police misuse of force (Associated Press, 2014). The centrality and importance of Twitter to the movements in response to these deaths arguably contributed to #Ferguson becoming the most used social-issue hashtag in the 10-year history of the platform (Anderson & Hitlin, 2016).

Unlike the killing of Trayvon Martin, the response to Michael Brown's death in Ferguson and on social media was immediate, clear and focused. According to media scholar Deen Freelon, Charlton McIlwain and Meredith Clark (2016), 25 November, the day the decision not to indict Darren Wilson for Michael Brown's death came down, is the day #BlackLivesMatter went mainstream. What started as a community response to a local man's death became the centre of a nationwide movement that was marked by demonstrations and violent clashes in the town. Initially an 'impromptu gathering', the community response escalated into 'sustained protest marked by daily demonstrations and violent confrontations with highly armed local police — all of which were documented in detail across social media platforms like Twitter, Instagram, YouTube, and Vine' (Bonilla & Rosa, 2015). The rapid uptake of #Ferguson and #BlackLivesMatter offers further insight into the interaction of street-based resistance and online activism (Pew Research Center, 2016). Freelon and colleagues (2016) further note that, while several hashtags were in use throughout the #Ferguson protests, including #handsupdontshoot #michaelbrown #darrenwilson #justiceformichael, it is significant that #BlackLivesMatter came to the fore, as the hashtag explicitly frames the individual incident in broader socio-structural terms. In short, #BlackLivesMatter makes visible the racial inequality that underlies not only Trayvon Martin and Michael Brown's deaths, but the systemic injustice of multiple killings of African-American men and women (Freelon et al., 2016).

From Protests to a (Global) Social Movement

#BlackLivesMatter offers a clear example of the technosocial practices of activism 'both online and in the streets' through a decentralised network that does not control, but rather informs and facilitates messaging and protest activities (Freelon, McIlwain, & Clark, 2018). Within this opportunity comes an increased array of audience, participants and narrative to be aligned with the broad scope of the movement. American historian Russell Rickford (2016) acknowledges the diversity of those involved in the movements, explaining that:

> Black Lives Matter is youthful, though it has reenergized older activists who are eager to connect with a new generation of organizers. It arises from an organic black protest tradition, while drawing impassioned participants of all colors. Its leadership departs sharply from the model of the singular, charismatic clergyman or politician. Founded by black women, two of whom are queer, the movement has galvanized an array of grassroots activists in multiple communities. Few are full-time organizers, though many have had encounters with racialized policing or otherwise are personally affected by mass incarceration. Many are also feminist, LGBTQ, working-class or low-income, social media savvy, and streetwise. Like other members of the movement, they are waging an unpretentious, democratic, militant crusade, determined to remain autonomous both from the American political establishment and from old guard leaders, such as Jesse Jackson and Al Sharpton, seen as more invested in punditry than in popular struggle (p. 35).

It is because of this diversity and broad aims that the founders describe #BlackLivesMatter as a human rights movement battling for civil, social, political, legal, economic and cultural rights (Tometi & Lenoir, 2015). #BlackLivesMatter has aimed to distinguish its tactics and its philosophy from those of the earlier civil rights movement (Cobb, 2016). Importantly, the founders of the movement promote voices of the 'queer, trans, migrant, formerly incarcerated, disabled and all of us who find ourselves unapologetic about our complexity' to champion the scope of a human rights agenda (Tometi & Lenoir, 2015). In order to achieve these aims, technologies have been central to engaging a broad audience across various fields of everyday political and social life (Campbell, 2018). Importantly, where these technologies succeed is by raising awareness of 'alleged, widespread police wrongdoing that might have otherwise gone unnoticed' to those 'who are less likely to experience frequent, direct police contact' (Hockin & Brunson, 2016, p. 2).

The distinction between #BlackLivesMatter and the traditional gatekeepers of the civil rights movements demonstrates the potentially disruptive effect of digital technologies on protests and counter-movements. Moreover, the disparate groups organising the new movement were enabled by digital technologies to form coherent activist strategies and physical protests. In Ferguson, organisers, activists, citizen-journalists and the public were able to use specific hashtags (#Ferguson, #BlackLivesMatter) to promote the issue of police violence and racism in America (Jackson & Foucault Welles, 2016). The success of this use of technology by activists to educate the public, amplify marginalised voices and advocate structural police reform has been phenomenal (Freelon et al., 2016). These hashtags not only highlighted the issue to a broader social media audience but also allowed activists to advance their cause by further 'occupying' discourse in physical spaces such as 'highways, intersections, sporting events, retail stores, malls, campaign events, police stations, and municipal buildings' (Rickford, 2016, pp. 35).

In addition to employing digital technologies to raise awareness, #BlackLivesMatter activists were able to organise directly via social media and other internet platforms. Activists communicated via different platforms to build relationships, create a sense of community and mobilise. Digital media researcher Perri Campbell (2018) offers some insight into the methods used by activists, detailing how Google Hangouts offered one mode of communication for sharing information. The platform provided members with a sense of immediacy and connection to the movement due to its low threshold of engagement by allowing asynchronous communication, combined with its data-rich content (allowing links and videos) across platform members (Campbell, 2018). While #BlackLivesMatter activists' embrace of such technologies has been central to their success, it has not been unique. Social media and communications platforms have become central to justice and democracy movements around the world by focusing on the 'processes of social media', enabling them to mobilise or remain 'on social media as a tool for sharing information in general' (Cox, 2017, p. 1849).

A significant element in the use of hashtag activism was the rise of solidarity with protesters in response to the events in Ferguson. Jelani Ince, Fabio Rohas, and Clayton Davis (2017) argue that 'as Ferguson became prominently featured in national discourse, it likely encouraged social media users to express their concern' and solidarity with the movement. Similarly, sociologist Stephen Barnard (2017) contends that, as militarised police forces teargassed and arrested protestors, the protestors gained sympathetic responses from many news outlets, which helped expand the online mobilisation of the movement. While great attention has been placed on the online actions of hashtag activists, social media activism also expanded the mobilisation of other forms of activism around the country. Aside from the traditional protests in Ferguson and rallies around the country, #BlackLivesMatter enables forms of disruptive techniques such 'die-ins' and 'teach-ins' that aim to highlight routine attacks on black lives to audiences that may be blind to their occurrence (Rickford, 2016).

Die-ins represent a form of visual activism in which participants simulate being dead — for example, by crowding into a space and then lying still on the floor (Klein, 2014; Mirzoeff, 2015). In solidarity with #BlackLivesMatter protesters, die-in participants have created street theatre in public places, such as a participant yelling 'I can't breathe' (referencing Eric Garner) or activists lying in public for four-and-a-half minutes, which is a symbolic reference to the four-and-a-half hours Michael Brown's body lay in the street before being removed by state officials (Mirzoeff, 2015). During a die-in, participants are often filmed or live-streamed to share the experience with others (Mirzoeff, 2015). Teach-ins were also created in solidarity with the broader movement, with the aim to inform, inspire and mobilise community members to force social change and combat institutional racism (Aloi, 2015). They approach activism organisation and mobilisation by actively engaging in local education spaces, further harnessing and disseminating the energy of the online protest movement (Aloi, 2015).

The activities of #BlackLivesMatter extend beyond online messaging and rhetoric — though this may be how a vast majority engage with the movement globally — to mobilising large groups both locally and globally (Freelon et al., 2016). In this way, it is like other social movements, such as Occupy or protests in the Arab Spring. #BlackLivesMatter shares other similarities with them, in that all three global movements evolved from a local, digitally enabled protest. Just as Occupy started as 'Occupy Wall Street', then diversified into online space and physical locations around the world, so too #BlackLivesMatter has extended beyond police–citizen interaction in the United States to illuminate ways that 'practices of white supremacy continue to constrain Black lives' around the world (Ray, Brown, & Laybourn, 2017, p. 1795). The 'globalisation' of #BlackLivesMatter occurred as the message spread into public consciousness through hashtag activism, advocacy and protests against racial injustices throughout the United States and in other countries (Ince et al., 2017). At first, many of these aligned with the Ferguson protests: close to 900 #BlackLivesMatter global marches, protests and demonstrations took place between July 2014 and June 2015 (Langford & Speight, 2015, p. 80). Since then, there has been a proliferation of #BlackLivesMatter support globally, with local 'chapters' adopting and reframing the cause for local issues and problems. For example, a #BlackLivesMatter chapter has emerged in Australia in response to police brutality and Black deaths in custody. The Australian movement acts in solidarity with its American counterpart but focuses on the experiences of Indigenous Australians, the colonial history of Australian settlement and the lack of government response to these issues (Higgins & Brennan, 2017; Huggins, 2017).

#SayHerName: Black Women's Lives Matter

It is important to remember that, while the deaths of some unarmed black men and boys at the hands of police have made national and global headlines, many more extra-judicial and unjust killings occur each year in the United States alone. According to media reports, for instance, more than 80 black women have been killed in contact with the police since 2013, and the number continues to grow. The tragic deaths of black women such as Natasha McKenna, Tanisha Anderson, Yvette Smith, Michelle Cusseaux, Aura Rosser, Kayla Moore, Shelly Frey, Rekia Boyd, Miriam Carey and Maya Hall, among many others, simply do not garner the same media and public attention. Yet, for Columbia University law professor Kimberlé Williams Crenshaw, the hashtags #SayHerName and #BlackWomenMatter serve to build understanding, as well as critique state violence against black women, which is often justified in mainstream discourse in similar ways to violence against black men (Crenshaw & Ritchie, 2015; Khaleeli, 2016). As further described by Associate Director of the African American Policy Forum, Rachel Gilmer:

> When we wear the hoodie, we know that we're embodying Trayvon. When we hold our hands up, we know we're doing what Mike Brown did in the moments before he was killed. When we say 'I can't breathe,' we're embodying Eric Garner's final words . . . We haven't been able to do the same thing for black women and girls. We haven't carried their same stories in the same way.

(quoted in Workneh, 2015, n.p.)

Crenshaw (1989, 1991) herself is, of course, well known as founding the concept of intersectionality, which denotes the multiple ways in which race and gender interact to shape black women's experiences of violence, discrimination and inequality in public and private life. In seeking to centre attention on the lives of black women and their experiences of state violence through the #SayHerName campaign, Crenshaw and her fellow activists are explicitly engaging in an intersectional activist mobilisation.

There are very few researchers of digital activism who have similarly engaged in an explicit intersectional analysis. Yet, already, a handful of studies have sought to examine #SayHerName as a unique example of contemporary social media activism that makes visible the frequently invisible lives of black cis-gender and transgender women lost to police violence (Baylor, 2016; Brown, Ray, Summers, & Fraistat, 2017; McMurtry-Chubb, 2015; Towns, 2016; Williams, 2016). Moreover, as Crenshaw has described, many of the police killings of black women can be seen not only through lenses of racism and sexism, but also further multiple vulnerabilities of mental illness, disability, sexuality and gender-identity (Khaleeli, 2016). In short, police violence affects more than just straight cis-gender black men (Brown et al., 2017; Crenshaw & Ritchie, 2015). Intersectionality is more than a framework for making visible the multiple dimensions of inequality that shape experiences of injustice: there are also particularities to these experiences that cannot be fully understood through one dimension in isolation. For example, for black women, there is a continuum of state violence beyond lethal force and physical assaults — sexual assault and harassment are common among complaints of police abuse (Crenshaw cited in Khaleeli, 2016). Then there are the intersections of police lethal force against black women and men's violence against women in the home. Indeed, according to *The Guardian*'s 2015 to 2016 campaign 'The Counted', which documents police killings in the United States, at least two women[1] died as a result of police attending domestic violence incidents where the police had been called to protect them. While the lack of due attention in mainstream media reporting and public discourse in response to such examples may well be a result of the combination of racism with sexism, there also appears to be a further difference between black men's and black women's deaths: women's deaths may well be less *public*. That is, many instances of police violence against women have reportedly occurred in custody rather than in the streets. In other words, while the deaths of men in public space have been captured by bystanders on mobile phones and the images subsequently widely distributed via social media, state violence against women — like much of men's violence against women — may be more likely to occur away from view.

Alicia Garza, one of the women who founded #BlackLivesMatter, has likewise observed the erasure of women not only in public discourses of police violence but in the movement itself. 'Perhaps if we were the charismatic Black men,' she writes, 'it would have been a different story, but being Black queer women in this society (and apparently within these movements) tends to equal invisibility and non-relevancy' (Garza, 2014, p. 2). The intersectionality of racism, sexism and heterosexism (or 'heteropatriarchy', as Garza has described it) appears all too palpable in the ways that #BlackLivesMatter has come to be associated largely with straight cis-black men (Garza, 2014). Yet, for Garza:

> Black Lives Matter is a unique contribution that goes beyond extrajudicial killings of Black people by police and vigilantes . . . Black Lives Matter affirms the lives of Black queer and trans folks, disabled folks, Black-undocumented folks, folks with records, women and all Black lives along the gender spectrum. It centers those that have been marginalized within Black liberation movements. It is a tactic to (re)build the Black liberation movement (p. 2).

Conceptualising Justice Activism in Digital Society

Where the founders of #BlackLivesMatter may contest the way the movement has grown and been adapted by others, the integration of technology in its founding and the reach of its ongoing activities mark it clearly as a contemporary social movement that exemplifies key features of digital society. For sociologist Mario Diani (1992, p. 13), social movements themselves could be defined as 'networks of informal interaction between a plurality of individuals, groups and organisations, engaged in a political or cultural conflict on the basis of a shared collective identity'. Diani conceptualised social movements in a pre-internet era where the physical location and the limits of communication technology constrained the potential of shared collective identity. While social movements generally have been understood as the symbolic 'unmasking' of power by offering new perceptions of the world (Melucci, 1989, p. 75), in digital society it is apparent that such 'unmaskings' are now made with the assistance and integration of digital tools and media platforms (Tilly & Wood, 2015).

As online activism emerged as a point of scholarly enquiry during the early 2000s, the internet was viewed mainly as a means of extending traditional activist techniques (Castells, 2001; Juris, 2005; Rolfe, 2005; Vegh, 2003). Key to this understanding was the work of Sandor Vegh, who identified the internet-based and enhanced work of activists who took 'advantage of the technologies and techniques offered by the Internet to achieve their goals' (2003, p. 71). Vegh also identified that, at the time, online activism could be categorised in three ways: awareness/advocacy, organisation/mobilisation and action/reaction. Arguably, these categories provide a limited perspective on the many potentials for digital technologies in social movements, restricting them to tools that supplement traditional activist repertoires. For example, online boycotts, virtual sit-ins or disruption to websites, email petitions and communication tools for organising activist meetings were commonly discussed as 'online modes' of resistance (Postmes & Brunsting, 2002); all of which are modifications or extensions of existing, pre-digital actions. However, as digital technologies have become closer to ubiquitous, challenging a clear demarcation between online and offline, technology has emerged not merely as an extension to the 'action repertoires' of activists, but rather as central to the success of social movements. In the remainder of this section, we discuss the intersection of digital media, communications and networks with the cultural, political and affective logics of contemporary activism. In doing so, we engage with concepts that seek to embed a technosocial perspective on social movements in digital society.

Social Movements in Networks and Counterpublics

Among the foremost features of social movements in digital society is the flow of information, participation and collectivism in both local and global networks. Manuel Castells (1997) famously foretold the substantial disruption that the internet would have on activism through his concept of the 'networked social movement'. For Castells, the potential of networked social movements lay in their function as 'decentered form[s] of organisation and intervention' that both mirror and counteract the logic of domination in the information society (1997, p. 362). Networked social movements are enhanced by 'speed, flexibility, and global reach of information flows' that provide the infrastructure for the operation of network-based organisational and social forms of resistance, protest and activism (Juris, 2004, p. 347). This 'space of flows' (also discussed in Chapters 3 and 7) allows social movements to operate across what were previously locally-based restrictions of time, space and physical place. Yet, networked social movements are not only remarkable for their connections across global online networks; Castells (1997) suggested that they also represent a new organisational structure. Where old movements were restricted and hierarchical with a *vertical leadership structure*, networked social movements embody more *horizontal participative structures* that emphasise self-management, connectedness and 'decentralized coordination based on autonomy and diversity' (Juris, 2004, pp. 355).

Operationally, networked social movements differ from the traditions of protest and rebellion in the pre-digital era. Exploring the impact of democracy movements around the world, in 2012, Castells identified a common, decentralised, autonomous or leaderless structure that is also able to coordinate and deliberate across networks, rather than originating in an identifiable core (p. 224). He argues that the more interactive and self-configurable the communication, the less hierarchical the organisation and the participatory movement (2012, p. 15). Rather than considering technology as a supplement or tool for change, networked social movements are embedded with technology in a way that allows individual experiences to be linked with each other, encouraging action and emotional connection to those who engage with the same sentiment (Castells, 2012). Political scientists W. Lance Bennett and Alexandra Segerberg (2012) expand on the relationship between movements and the individual, identifying personalised politics as a key affordance in the digital age. They argue that contemporary social movements can include citizens with flexible associations, who have common goals and ideals but act independently (Bennett & Segerberg, 2012, pp. 5–6). This individualisation of political participation allows movements to network complementary individual efforts of activists and to form aggregated power through collective action. Juris (2008, 2012) clarified that digital technologies encompass both the logic of networking, which allows for the diversity of actors within the collective, and a 'logic of aggregation', which enables and encourages mobilisation in physical space. For Castells (2012), the emergent networks of digital space allow for movements to better engage in face-to-face activism. Thus, networked social movements are essentially technosocial in nature: offering sites of activism, protest and resistance that pursue their cause wherever opportunity can be found — online, offline and in combination.

Networked social movements arguably also demonstrate the 'democratising force' of social and participatory media, particularly the enhanced capacity for marginalised and disempowered groups, whose voices are often unheard in traditional media and public discourse, to be represented. Indeed, as discussed in Chapters 2 and 5, user-generated and participatory media have often been described as promoting greater democratic participation in public life (Loader & Mercea, 2011; Papacharissi, 2015; Yar, 2012). Furthermore, rather than representing a singular 'public', social media may be better described as 'networked publics' (Boyd, 2008) that also provide various opportunities for 'counterpublic' communications (Fraser, 1990). In response to mainstream narratives of crime and justice, activists can deploy hashtags, images and other distributed messages to further legitimise their position, to foster a greater sense of community within marginalised groups and to further extend their reach to a broader audience. Rather than being a movement that is 'joined', counterpublics retain fluid boundaries through which individuals seek the validation and extension of other people's existing viewpoints and their circulation of messages within the collective (Warner, 2002). For example, #BlackLivesMatter and #Ferguson exist as counterpublics that can be understood as mobilising both individual and collective responses to injustice (Bonilla & Rosa, 2015). By embracing online space, outsiders who identify with the message being conveyed can choose to add their voice to the dissent distributed within these counterpublics, in turn amplifying their scale and reach (Clark, 2016, p. 236).

New Repertoires of Collective Action

In addition to operating with different structures and in different spaces, digital technologies have arguably shifted contemporary 'repertoires of collective action' (Tilly, 1977; Van Laer & Van Aelst, 2009, 2010). According to social movement theorist Charles Tilly (1977, 1986, 1993), it is possible to chart changes over time and place in the 'ways that people act together in pursuit of shared interests — changes in repertoires of collective action' (1993, p. 253). Such repertoires, it is widely recognised, are subject to various external limitations; in some jurisdictions, for example, there are legal restrictions on protest, including gatherings in public spaces and propaganda against the state (Ennis, 1987). Additionally, many potential social movements face limits on resource mobilisation; for some groups or communities, their very socio-economic structural position may mean there are very few financial resources to support collective action (Ennis, 1987). Within this context, collective action has always operated within structural 'fields of choice' regarding the strategies for activism (Ennis, 1987). However, these fields have considerably shifted, opening up new, more widely accessible, repertoires of collective action in digital society.

Prior to the digital age, activist use of media and technology had been limited to the 'strategic repertoire' social movements. This repertoire was restricted to working through print (newspapers, posters, pamphlets, leaflets, direct mail), radio, television and other creative methods (Atton, 2003) and the audiences these afforded. The distribution of flyers, posters and other printed documents was central to promoting activist organisations and notifying people of upcoming meetings or protests. The news media, in particular, played a crucial role in disseminating and creating awareness surrounding social issues. Yet, according to communications scholar R. Kelly Garrett (2006), the introduction of digital technologies to these repertoires provided greater flexibility to the manner in which movements are mobilised, organised and the extent to which participation within them is defined. Indeed, repertoires of strategising and mobilising have shifted and merged with expansion of technology ranging from the use of blogs, online petitions, social media, digital imagery and live streaming video amongst others (Bennett, 2003; Lim, 2012). Such tools can be understood as feeding information throughout activist networks and, in effect, expanding and amplifying the 'old' repertoires of collective action (Lim, 2012).

What such practices highlight are key features of technosociality in digital society, which is exemplified by our perpetual contact with mobile and internet-connected devices, as well as the demand for instantaneity and increased scale of communicative interactions (discussed in Chapters 1 and 2). These, when discussed in terms of social movements, have transformed the nature of 'the role of communication media in politics, making media skills, persuasion, and socialisation fundamental to contemporary contention' (Kelly Garrett, 2006, p. 206). Castells contends that the more movements can make use of these technologies, the easier it is to convey their messages, raising the consciousness of the community and finally forming a contested terrain within the public sphere (2012, p. 237). Digital technologies influence social movements' functions, both internal and external, affecting their dynamics, cohesion and collective identity (Flesher Fominaya & Gillan, 2017).

Finally, digital technologies lower the level of formal engagement, resources and affordances for social movement organisers (Shirky, 2009, 2011). Indeed, despite the persistence of digital inequalities (discussed in Chapter 2), many researchers have argued that social media is a particularly important tool for mobilising social movements among 'resource poor' actors (Eltantawy & Wiest, 2011). Moreover, some social movement scholars have gone further, identifying the different repertoires employed by well-resourced and resource-poor individuals, finding that for the former social media is merely a tool that facilitates familiar strategies and organisational activities, while for the latter social media enables entirely new opportunities to engage in activism (Bennett & Segerberg, 2012).

Visual Communication and 'Bearing Witness'

Among the new repertoires of collective action are the multiple functions of images, or 'visual communication' (discussed in Chapters 2 and 5), in activating public engagement and participation. It has long been understood that the use of images offers creative forms of collective action that can be integral in achieving political change (Micheletti & Stolle, 2007). In the context of informational capitalism, the most successful global justice movements have been known to employ tactics that produce 'highly visible, theatrical images for mass mediated consumption' (Juris, 2004, p. 58). When evoked in activism, imagery is often a tool that offers autonomous, collective, open-ended, theatrical participation focused on political or social issues (Duncombe, 2007). When compared to written forms of communication, these options allow for messages of injustice to reach audiences well beyond commonly heterogeneous groups of activists (Juris, 2004) to include groups with little attachment to justice issues (Micheletti & Stolle, 2007).

The features of digital society, then, increase the capacity of everyday citizens to witness, record, share and respond to injustices. Indeed, as discussed in Chapters 4 and 5, as individuals are now constantly connected through internet and camera-enabled devices that are always at hand, so too is there a dominant technosocial practice of visually documenting everything from the most banal of day-to-day experiences through to the most brutal. While imagery intended to humanise and elicit empathy for victims of social injustices (and thereby call audiences to action) has long been deliberately deployed in activist movements, in digital society it is increasingly citizen 'eye-witness' images that play a role in activating others to support a cause.

The parallels and differences between the responses to the assault of Rodney King in Los Angeles on 3 March 1991, and the death of Michael Brown nearly 25 years later, further illustrate the power of visual communication in enhancing the efforts of activists. Rodney King's initial contact with police on the day he died was suspected criminal behaviour as he led police on a high-speed car chase along a major freeway (Jacobs, 1996). When eventually stopped by police, King was tasered, then clubbed by three officers 56 times and kicked six times in the head and body in an assault that reportedly lasted 15 minutes (Davis, 1994). In addition to this police brutality, at least 17 other police officers were known to have witnessed the incident but did not intervene (Jacobs, 1996). The assault of Rodney King was caught on camera by a bystander, George Holliday. On 29 April 1992, a year after the initial assault, a majority white jury found the four officers not guilty. The acquittal was followed by three days of riots, looting, arson and extreme violence across the city of Los Angeles, resulting in 55 deaths and over 2,000 injuries (Sastry & Bates, 2017).

It is important to clarify here that the beating of Rodney King, and the subsequent 'LA riots' in 1992, took place in a mediated environment (Van Loon, 1997). Without a member of the public recording the video of King being beaten by members of the LAPD, the incident would have been overlooked, and subsequent events (police being charged, found not guilty and the public violence that resulted) may not have taken place (Van Loon, 1997). In 1992, the video in the hands of George Holliday would never have been able to reach the public directly. It was only after the police displayed no interest in the recording that Holliday contacted a television station, and the recording was subsequently broadcast into homes across the nation and worldwide. This video of police brutality was one of the first of its kind, and it has been described as a significant turning point in the national conversation about police and racial inequality in America. Again, in the pre-digital era, the limitations of video-recording and the constraints of media broadcasting technologies constrained responses to injustices. In contrast, stories and video of Michael Brown's death were shared directly with the public because of the lower thresholds of participation, access and distribution that digital technologies allow.

Although both instances of police brutality resulted in public protest and violence, the use of digital technology displays distinct differences in the evolution of movement mobilisation. King's victimisation highlighted LAPD apathy towards police violence against African Americans but also would become 'the most well-known case of police use of force in history' (Martin, 2005) with the assistance of the broadcast media, and this created a groundswell of public response (Davis & Frommer, 1993). The riots that followed the acquittal of the police officers involved constant media reporting, but were also portrayed as dispersed, disorganised and decentralised violence, rather than a civil rights moment or movement. While non-violent protesters could be found, their voices were overwhelmed by media representations of riots, looting, violence and death (Fiske, 1994). In comparison, the mediated response to Brown's death was more egalitarian, with the footage distributed privately through social media as well as publicly on traditional media platforms. The opportunity to converse in public and private through digital media gave organisers of the protest greater flexibility in responding to police tactics and presenting a coherent narrative to journalists (Barnard, 2017).

The unrest in Ferguson following the death of Michael Brown and acquittal of his killer focused on police brutality; in contrast, the response to King and the LA violence also came to represent the grievances of the Black and Latino community towards a plethora of broader social and economic issues in the community (Stevenson, 2013; Twomey, 2004). This lack of cohesion resulted in a mediated event defined by violence and journalistic interpretation (Twomey, 2004), rather than the voices of those involved in protests, resistances and rebellion. In contrast, despite media reports and criticism towards the violence in Ferguson, the aims and purpose of protesters were widely acknowledged and understood by the general public. While digital technology may not account for all of the reasons, social media, smartphones and other internet-based technologies aided in providing organisers, protesters and the public with opportunities to account for the happenings in the town. For organisers and protesters, social media and live-streaming became a viable platform for mobilising activists in response to police tactics (Bonilla & Rosa, 2015). As Anthropologists Yarimar Bonilla and Jonathan Rosa (2015) also noted, the use of #Ferguson on Twitter and the live-streaming (and post-event 'vines') also created a focus through the shared temporality experienced by those following these trends. As Barnard argues, the network's 'use of common platforms and hashtags to document, contextualise, and amplify cases of police violence against people of colour helped link together individual cases, revealing an undeniable pattern explained only by structural racism' (2017, p. 5). Moreover, journalists were key to the movement, both in the distribution of imagery via hashtags and in allowing the voices of participants to be heard (Barnard, 2017). This allowed those monitoring the events to follow them as they unfolded, rally supporters to join various hashtag campaigns and bear witness to the tear-gassing and arrests of participants (Bonilla & Rosa, 2015, p. 7). Unlike the LA riots of 1992, which were marred by perceptions of 'directionless violence', the response in Ferguson was able to leverage the opportunities afforded by digital technology to create a united messaging. Moreover, these uses of technologies created a 'collective effervescence' or 'eventfulness' that created the momentum for the sustained effect of #BlackLivesMatter (Bonilla & Rosa, 2015).

Aside from petitions and #hashtag activism, the Million Hoodies movement (www.millionhoodies.net) further highlights how visual symbols can become central for activists. The movement, like #BlackLivesMatter, was established in response to Martin's death and the mainstream media's inadequate reporting about the events surrounding it. Emerging from a Change.org petition, Million Hoodies called for traditional protests in response to Martin's death by organising participants through YouTube, Facebook and Twitter. What would result was not just a protest, but also powerful images shared on social media displaying images of supporters wearing hoodies in solidarity with the justice movement but not necessarily members of the physical protest. This imagery was expanded when high-profile athletes, notably LeBron James and other NBA stars, became involved with the movements, sharing images in solidarity and raising awareness amongst NBA fans. The distribution of 'selfies' as solidarity with a Million Hoodies demonstrates how the ubiquity of technologies allows images to play a central role in contemporary activism. Unlike previous camera (particularly video) technologies that were restrictive due to portability and cost, smartphones and internet access mean 'anyone can take and share a selfie on an expanding number of social network platforms' (Iqani & Schroeder, 2016, p. 407). Just as Million Hoodies was extended by the 'selfie' phenomena, images shared on Facebook and Twitter of protests have been embraced by the powerless to make their victimisation, vulnerability and repression visible (Senft & Baym, 2015). Moreover, sharing images represents a shared experience by converging networks of activists and users. The resulting effect is the development of a common identity and consciousness that may lead to sympathetic media coverage (Araiza, Sturm, Istek, & Bock, 2016). From the revolution during the Arab Spring (Aday et al., 2012) through to Ferguson and beyond (Bonilla & Rosa, 2015; Freelon et al. 2016), the use of images has been key in providing a voice and evidence that was not available in previous eras reliant on traditional governmental and media power.

The powerful imagery that social media platforms offer to activism can be further understood through the concept of the 'ethical spectacle'. For media scholar Stephen Duncombe (2007), the ethical spectacle is viewed in the context of performance and embodiment of roles. Such events are defined by tactile, creative and bodily engaged performances that raise awareness or open discussion towards an issue. While this suggests an incompatibility with social media, its relation to this discussion lies in the participatory nature of the behaviour. Social media is particularly relevant here, as it allows for active participation in the creation and symbolic performance of spectacles that can involve different modes of performance, are adaptable to different requirements and situations, and are presentable to a ready audience (Duncombe, 2007, pp. 124–152). In effect, social media audiences are drawn to the ethical spectacle and called not only to bear witness to the injustice but to take action (discussed in Chapter 5).

Amplification, Virality and 'Timeless Time'

The transformation from hashtag activism to social movement undertaken by the likes of #BlackLivesMatter and Million Hoodies demonstrates how digital technologies amplify both the message and the movement. When discussing amplification within digital society, the tendency is to discuss the role of technology in enabling social movements to strategically have their 'voice' heard through larger networks of followers (Grabowicz, Ramasco, Moro, Pujol, & Eguiluz, 2012). While this remains true, digital media also allow for strategic innovation by activist organisations, such as the development of new media interventions to increase their leverage within digital society (Karpf, 2016).

An example is the manner in which Million Hoodies adapted technological innovations to develop an app for reporting police misconduct (Million Hoodies Movement for Justice, 2017), further demonstrating how a movement's power, success and influence may be extended through the social use of technology (Karpf, 2016). In adapting in this way, social movements evolve from reacting to individual incidents to drawing together patterns of injustices that better demonstrate the need for substantive social change. As such, activist voices in digital society can be amplified beyond social networks in a way that challenges existing power structures (Freelon et al. 2016). Juris has likewise highlighted these 'politics of scale' that networked activism allows: meaning that diverse local calls for justice are enabled by directly linking with global activists around common objectives (2004, p. 347). While this at first may seem like diversification, such networking creates a unity that allows for open collaboration on decision-making, sharing of information and distribution of the message.

Yet, in digital society, amplification of a social movement's messages is not only a function of the strategies and voice of activists themselves. Rather, amplification results from the interaction of human agency with non-human actants across hybrid technosocial networks (see Chapters 5 and 7). Indeed, in earlier chapters, we have discussed the nature of 'algorithmic sociality', referring to the profit-driven and automated logics of social media content curation, which seek to elicit individuals' engagement within a network. As a result of this 'invisible hand' (Zuboff, 2015), some content is more likely than others to be actively disseminated throughout social media networks by algorithms that are designed to maximise users' time spent with eyes on the screen (thereby increasing advertising revenue of the platform). In this way, social media content that elicits an active initial response, such as anger expressed through 'likes' and 'shares' in response to a post about the unjust killing of another African-American person, is likely to be widely and rapidly disseminated throughout a network. Arguably, there are both positive and negative implications of such algorithmic sociality: on the one hand, when social media content 'goes viral' it is more likely to then attract the attention of mainstream news media, further escalating the amplifying effect. Yet, on the other hand, there are limits to the potential for social media discourse to disrupt mainstream narratives if amplification and virality are, at least in part, aligned with non-social justice logics of profit-margins and advertising revenue.

While the mass media reporting of an individual incident of police brutality may come to a close, the record is preserved. And multiple digital archives of images and first-hand accounts on social media and other content-sharing platforms ensure its longevity. As discussed in Chapter 5, such permanence is characteristic of digital society and, in turn, facilitates an ongoing witnessing, memorialisation and citizen participation through revisiting the content and through its continued redistribution. To extend Castells' (1996) concepts of 'timeless time' and a 'forever universe', the digitised spectacle allows an unending witnessing, and vicarious experiencing, of traumatic events repeatedly over both distance and time (also discussed in Chapter 4). Yet, in the case of social justice movements, this permanence serves a further function: there is power in being able to link multiple incidents of injustice and in recalling visually, as well as discursively, the painful harms that occurred. By retrospectively being able to connect, link and recirculate images, eye-witness accounts, protest information and campaign messages, disparate elements of activity over time and place are able to be unified. In the case of #BlackLivesMatter, digital technologies enable the images of Trayvon Martin, Michael Brown, Eric Garner, Freddie Gary, Oscar Grant and many others to be drawn together and recirculated, in turn making the systemic nature of the harms, and the racial inequalities they embody, undeniable.

Challenges and Implications

Digital technologies have emerged as central to the uptake and spread of many contemporary social movements. Key features of digital society, such as visual communication, amplification, permanence and timeless time, have arguably facilitated local, and even global, networks of activists, who may be leaderless but who nonetheless share, in common, overarching goals. Though an optimistic perspective on the potential of online participation to act as a 'virtual town square' (Kavanaugh, Perez-Quinones, Tedesco & Sanders, 2010) and extend democratic engagement among otherwise marginalised groups is highly comforting, it is not without criticism. As discussed in Chapter 2, internet scholar Evgeny Morozov (2009, 2011) has famously urged caution in overstating the potential of the internet, social media and online activism as a substantive force for freedom. Indeed, for Morozov, just as these networks *facilitate* democracy so too do they *endanger* it, through authoritarianism in the form of consumerism and corporatisation which have only expanded in the digital age (as discussed in Chapter 3). Ultimately, Morozov's warning reminds us that *we cannot tweet our way to freedom* (Morozov, 2011).

We do not suggest that #BlackLivesMatter, or the many other examples of activism in digital society, should too readily and disparagingly be reduced in either their substance or impact to 140 or 280 character lengths of text. Yet it is also the case that, as a social movement, #BlackLivesMatter has also been the subject of fierce anti-black resistance, political polarisation, misinformation and hate speech (discussed in Chapter 6). Examples of this resistance can be seen in the counter campaigns that have arisen in response to #BlackLivesMatter, and co-opting the slogan, including: #AllLivesMatter, #BlueLivesMatter, and #WhiteLivesMatter (Carney, 2016; Gallagher, Reagan, Danforth, & Dodds, 2016; Langford & Speight, 2015). American sociologist and activist Nikita Carney (2016) describes the ways in which #AllLivesMatter, while appearing 'neutral', is in fact a reflection of a contemporary form of colourblind, neo-liberal racism. Carney (2016) writes:

> color-blind racism appears egalitarian on the surface with its assertion that all people are the same. However, adherence to this postracial ideology while both structural and interpersonal racism persist effaces the struggles of people of color by claiming that racism is a thing of the past. This dangerous liberal ideology provides a false sense of comfort to those who do not face racial oppression in their everyday lives (p. 186).

Carney's argument highlights how racist ideology can function and be reproduced in subtle and systemic ways, as well as in ways that might be more overtly recognisable as 'hate speech'. Yet such rhetoric carries powerful socio-cultural and socio-political significance in the context of struggles for racial equality. American philosopher and gender theorist Judith Butler, whose work on the politics of speech is globally renowned, also spoke about the importance of #BlackLivesMatter in an interview published in the *New York Times* (Yancy & Butler, 2015). In the interview, titled 'What's Wrong with "All Lives Matter"' Butler (2015) says:

> When we are talking about racism, and anti-black racism in the United States, we have to remember that under slavery black lives were considered only a fraction of a human life, so the prevailing way of valuing lives assumed that some lives mattered more, were more human, more worthy, more deserving of life and freedom ... When some people rejoin with "All Lives

Matter" they misunderstand the problem, but not because their message is untrue. It is true that all lives matter, but it is equally true that not all lives are understood to matter which is precisely why it is most important to name the lives that have not mattered, and are struggling to matter in the way they deserve (n.p.).

As so poignantly expressed by Butler and others (Langford & Speight, 2015), #AllLivesMatter is not in any way a 'neutral' statement: it is a statement of erasure, a 'colourblind' statement, that does more than assert the value of all life. #AllLivesMatter in response to #BlackLivesMatter fails to recognise the ongoing systemic racial injustices against African Americans that continue the legacy of slavery in which black lives mattered less than white lives. The point is further made by Garza (2014, p. 3) that there is nothing lost in the broader US community getting behind #BlackLivesMatter; that freedom from injustice benefits everyone:

> #BlackLivesMatter doesn't mean your life isn't important — it means that Black lives, which are seen as without value within White supremacy, are important to your liberation. Given the disproportionate impact state violence has on Black lives, we understand that when Black people in this country get free, the benefits will be wide reaching and transformative for society as a whole . . . When Black people get free, everybody gets free.

Yet, just as we have suggested that characteristics of digital society such as perpetual contact, permanence, visual conversations and algorithmic sociality can beneficially amplify the efforts of social justice activists, so too are they used to spread misinformation and hate. The potential of these counter-movements to further polarise race-relations and exacerbate violent tensions in the United States is very real. #BlueLivesMatter, for example, seeks to recognise the police officers whose lives have been lost in the line of duty. Throughout 2016 and 2017, more than 30 bills have been introduced in the United States, seeking to classify violent attacks on police as 'hate crimes' (Craven, 2017). Then presidential candidate Donald Trump moreover also expressed countering views to the #BlackLivesMatter movement, saying: 'The first time I heard it I said, "You have to be kidding" . . . I think it's a very, very, very divisive term. There's no question about it' (in Siddiqui, 2016). Indeed, as discussed in Chapters 1 and 6, under President Trump's administration, hate crimes against racial and religious minorities have demonstrably increased. While #AllLivesMatter may be colourblind racism, the hashtag #WhiteLivesMatter makes explicit a racial supremacist framing of resistance. In their analysis of Twitter context using the counter-movement hashtag, Catherine Langford and Montené Speight (2015) describe the tweets as characterising African Americans as 'thugs', 'racists' and 'terrorists', while white citizens are seen as 'under attack', 'oppressed' and needing to defend and protect 'their' people and heritage.

In addition to the palpable resistance directed towards the #BlackLivesMatter movement, a further challenge to social movements in digital society is their characteristically different organisational structure from movements in the pre-digital age. As discussed in Chapter 7, several scholars have described social movements in digital society as 'multiplicitous', 'horizontal', 'leaderless' and 'rhizomatic'. Drawing on French philosopher Gilles Deleuze and his collaborator Felix Guattari's (1980) metaphor of the rhizome, such scholars seek to emphasise the non-hierarchical, non-symmetrical and heterogeneous structures of activism in digital society, in which there are 'multiple entranceways and exits' (Deleuze & Guattari, 1980). It could certainly be argued that there are fundamental limitations to such social movements: in particular, that they may lack the cohesion, sustainability and, therefore, longer-term impact associated with more readily identifiable organisations and movement leaders.

Yet, arguably, to describe social movements as 'rhizomatic' is also to acknowledge the complexity of social justice-seeking and social change in digital society. As Deleuze and Guattari (1980/2004) describe:

> Unlike a structure, which is defined by a set of points and biunivocal relationships between positions, the rhizome is made only of lines: lines of segmentarity and stratification as its dimensions, and the line of flight or deterritorialization as the maximum dimension after which the multiplicity undergoes metamorphosis, changes in nature . . . The rhizome operates by variation, expansion, conquest, capture, offshoots (p. 23).

For Castells, too, 'networked' social movements can be explored through the metaphor of the rhizome, 'in the sense that they are always there in the Internet and then emerge in different forms in institutions, urban space, go underground, and so forth . . . the notion of the rhizome is crucial' (Castells & Kumar, 2014). As sociologists Andrew Robinson and Simon Tormey (2005) articulate, there are further advantages to rhizomatic social movements in digital society.

> The proliferation of rhizomes is also an effective way of multiplying points of challenge so as to reduce the effectiveness of measures of repression. As any gardener who has tried to eliminate [weeds] knows, a rhizome system is very difficult to reach because, when a rhizome is destroyed, others will form and re-link, re-forming the networks which have been damaged. An arborescent organization, in contrast, can be cut down far more easily (p. 221).

In the context of both overt and subtle racist challenges to the efforts of #BlackLivesMatter activists to fight systemic inequalities, it is perhaps encouraging to position such contemporary social movements in this way: characteristically resistant to measures of repression.

Conclusion

Operationally, networked social movements differ from the traditions of protest and rebellion in pre-digital societies. Exploring social movements such as #BlackLivesMatter provides particular insights into how technology has shifted the repertoires of collective action in a digital society. Although initially a post on Facebook and a hashtag on Twitter, #BlackLivesMatter provides an example of how activists adopting social media technologies, in particular, have moved beyond practices of cyber-protest that characterise earlier social movement research. The repertoires and successes of contemporary movements allow an understanding of digital technologies as central to such movements, not simply extensions of them. Indeed, key characteristics of digital society, such as perpetual contact, permanence, visual conversations and algorithmic sociality, can have the benefit of amplifying the efforts of social justice activists. We are not so naïve as to imagine that crime and social justice movements in digital society do not face challenges, particularly in light of persistent structures of systemic inequality. Rather, the multiplicity of these 'rhizomatic' movements provides a cause for optimism that multiple lines of activity are able to spread in both socio-cultural and socio-political influence and action. Yet what are the implications of the discussion here for progressing a digital criminology?

As we suggested in the opening of this chapter, in digital society, which is characterised by fundamental challenges to the regulatory role of nation states, criminologists ought rightly to be concerned with harms and with responses to harms beyond those legislated by the state. Yet, even with a more narrow reading of the core concerns of criminology, the ways in which activist repertoires engage with triggering incidents of criminal violence — whether by the state as discussed here, or by citizens as discussed in Chapter 7 — should rightly be the focus of a digital criminology. Seeking to understand how such technosocial justice movements might enable substantive social, cultural and political change can further enhance analyses of crime and justice in digital society.

Note

1   Meagan Hockaday of Oxnard, California, and Janisha Fonville of Charlotte, North Carolina.

Recommended Further Reading

Bonilla, Y., & Rosa, J. (2015). #Ferguson: Digital protest, hashtag ethnography, and the racial politics of social media in the United States. *American Ethnologist, 42*(1), 4–17.

Brown, M., Ray, R., Summers, E., & Fraistat, N. (2017). #SayHerName: A case study of intersectional social media activism. *Ethnic and Racial Studies*, 1–15.

Garza, A. (2014). A herstory of the #BlackLivesMatter movement by Alicia Garza. *The Feminist Wire*, 7.

Lebron, C. (2017). *The making of Black Lives Matter: A brief history of an idea.* New York, NY: Oxford University Press.

References

Aday, S., Farrell, H., Lynch, M., Sides, J., & Freelon, D. (2012). *New Media and Conflict after the Arab Spring.* Washington, DC: United States Institute of Peace.

Ali, S. (2017, April 26). Tamir rice shooting: Newly released interview reveals cop's shifting story, NBC news. Available at: www.nbcnews.com/news/us-news/newly-released-interview-footage-reveal-shifting-stories-officers-who-shot-n751401 (last accessed 29 November 2017).

Aloi, D. (2015). Cornell Chronicle. November 19, 2017. Available at: www.news.cornell.edu/stories/2015/10/black-lives-matter-teach-aims-inspire-inform (last accessed 29 November 2017).

Anderson, M., & Hitlin, P. (2016). 3. The hashtag #BlackLivesMatter emerges: Social activism on Twitter. Pew Research Center: Internet, Science & Tech. Available at: www.pewinternet.org/2016/08/15/the-hashtag-blacklivesmatter-emerges-social-activism-on-twitter/#fn-16486-8

Araiza, J. A., Sturm, H. A., Istek, P., & Bock, M. A. (2016). Hands up, don't shoot, whose side are you on? Journalists tweeting the Ferguson protests. *Cultural Studies – Critical Methodologies, 16*(3), 305–312.

Associated Press. (2014, May 22). Fruitvale Station trial ends as Bart settles with Oscar Grant's friends. *The Guardian.* Available at: www.theguardian.com/world/2014/may/21/fruitvale-station-oscar-grant-trial-settlement (last accessed 29 November 2017).

Atton, C. (2003). Reshaping social movement media for a new millennium. *Social Movement Studies, 2*(1), 3–15.

Baker, A., Goodman, D., & Mueller, B. (2015, June 13). Beyond the chokehold: The path to Eric Garner's death. *New York Times.* Available at: www.nytimes.com/2015/06/14/nyregion/eric-garner-police-chokehold-staten-island.html (last accessed 29 November 2017).

Barnard, S. R. (2017). Tweeting #Ferguson: Mediatized fields and the new activist journalist. *New Media & Society.* Advance online publication. doi: 10.1177/1461444817712723.

Baylor, A. (2016). Chapter 10: #SayHerName captured: Using video to challenge law enforcement violence against women. In M. Wojcik (Ed.), *The state of criminal justice.* Washington, DC: American Bar Association.

BBC. (2016, May 23). Freddie Gray's death in police custody—what we know. BBC News. *US and Canada*. Available at: www.bbc.com/news/world-us-canada-32400497 (last accessed 29 November 2017).

Bennett, L. W. (2003). Communicating global activism: Strengths and vulnerabilities of networked politics. *Information, Communication & Society 6*(2), 143e168.

Bennett, W. L., & Segerberg, A. (2012). *The logic of connective action: Digital media and the personalization of contentious politics*. Cambridge, UK: Cambridge University Press.

Bobo, L. (2015). Foreword: The racial double homicide of Trayvon Martin. In D. Johnson, P. Warren, & A. Farrell, *Deadly injustice: Trayvon Martin, race, and the criminal justice system* (pp. xi–xv). New York, NY: New York University Press.

Bonilla, Y., & Rosa, J. (2015). #Ferguson: Digital protest, hashtag ethnography, and the racial politics of social media in the United States. *American Ethnologist, 42*(1), 4–17.

Bosman, J. & Goldstein, J. (2014, August 23). Timeline for a Body: 4 Hours in the Middle of a Ferguson Street, *New York Times*. Available at: www.nytimes.com/2014/08/24/us/michael-brown-a-bodys-timeline-4-hours-on-a-ferguson-street.html (last accessed 29 November 2017).

Botelho, G. (2012, May 23). What happened the night Trayvon Martin died. *CNN*. Available at: www.edition.cnn.com/2012/05/18/justice/florida-teen-shooting-details

Boyd, D. (2008). Digital handshakes in networked publics: Why politicians must interact, not broadcast. In B. Rigby (Ed.), *Mobilizing generation 2.0: A practical guide to using Web 2.0 technologies to recruit, organize and engage youth* (pp. 91–94). San Francisco: Jossey-Bass.

Brown, M., Ray, R., Summers, E., & Fraistat, N. (2017). #SayHerName: A case study of intersectional social media activism. *Ethnic and Racial Studies, 40*(1), 1831–1846.

Bruns, A., Highfield, T., & Lind, R. A. (2012). Blogs, Twitter, and breaking news: The produsage of citizen journalism. *Produsing theory in a digital world: The Intersection of Audiences and Production in Contemporary Theory, 80*(2012), 15–32.

Buchanan, L., Fessenden, F., Lai, K. K. R., Park, H., Parlapiano, A., Tse, A., … Yourish, K. (2017, November 19). What happened in Ferguson? Available at: www.nytimes.com/interactive/2014/08/13/us/ferguson-missouri-town-under-siege-after-police-shooting.html (last accessed 29 November 2017).

Campbell, P. (2018). Occupy, black lives matter and suspended mediation: Young people's battles for recognition in/between digital and non-digital spaces. *Young, 26*(2), 145–160.

Carney, N. (2016). All lives matter, but so does race: Black lives matter and the evolving role of social media. *Humanity & Society, 40*(2), 180–199.

Castells, M. (1996). *The Information Age: Economy, Society and Culture. Volume I – the Rise of the Network Society*. Oxford: Blackwell.

Castells, M. (1997). *The Power of Identity* (2nd ed., 2004). Oxford: Blackwell.

Castells, M. (2001). *The Internet galaxy: Reflections on the Internet, business and society*. Oxford: Oxford University Press.

Castells, M. (2012). *Networks of outrage and hope: Social movements in the Internet age*. Cambridge: Polity Press.

Castells, M., & Kumar, M. (2014). A conversation with Manuel Castells. *Berkeley Planning Journal, 27*(1), 93–99.

Chang, H. C. (2010). A new perspective on Twitter hashtag use: Diffusion of innovation theory. *Proceedings of the Association for Information Science and Technology, 47*(1), 1–4.

Clark, L. (2016). Participants on the Margins: #BlackLivesMatter and the Role That Shared Artifacts of Engagement Played Among Minoritized Political Newcomers on Snapchat, Facebook, and Twitter, *International Journal of Communication, 10*(2016), 235–253.

Cobb, J. (2016). The matter of black lives. Available at: www.newyorker.com/magazine/2016/03/14/where-is-black-lives-matter-headed (last accessed 29 November 2017).

Cox, J. M. (2017). The source of a movement: Making the case for social media as an informational source using black lives matter. *Ethnic and Racial Studies, 40*(11), 1847–1854.

Craven, J. (2017, March 1). 32 Blue lives matter bills have been introduced across 14 States this year, *Huffington Post*. Available at: www.huffingtonpost.com.au/entry/blue-black-lives-matter-police-bills-states_us_58b61488e4b0780bac2e31b8 (last accessed 29 November 2017).

Crenshaw, K. (1989). Demarginalizing the intersection of race and sex: A black feminist critique of antidiscrimination doctrine, feminist theory and antiracist politics. *University of Chicago Legal Forum*, (1989), 139–168.

Crenshaw, K. (1991). Mapping the margins: Intersectionality, identity politics, and violence against women of color. *Stanford Law Review*, *43*(6), 1241–1299.

Crenshaw, K., & Ritchie, A. (2015). *Say her name: Resisting police brutality against black women*. Prepared for African American Policy Forum, New York, NY: Centre for Intersectionality and Social Policy Studies, Columbia University.

Davis, P. (1994). Rodney King and the decriminalization of police brutality in America: Direct and judicial access to the grand Jury as remedies for victims of police brutality when the prosecutor declines to prosecute. *Maryland Law Review*, *53*, 271.

Davis, M., & Frommer, M. (1993). An interview with Mike Davis. *Chicago Review*, *38*(4), 21–43.

Deleuze, G., & Guattari, F. (1980). *A thousand plateaus: Capitalism and schizophrenia*. Paris: Minuit.

Deleuze, G. & Guattari, F. (2004, ed.) *A Thousand Plateaus: Capitalism and Schizophrenia*. Translation and foreword by Brian Massumi. London: Continuum.

Diani, M. (1992). The concept of social movement. *The Sociological Review*, *40*(1), 1–25.

Duncombe, S. (2007). *Dream: Re-Imagining Progressive Politics in an Age of Fantasy*. New York, NY: The New Press.

Eltantawy, N., & Wiest, J. B. (2011). The Arab spring| social media in the Egyptian revolution: Reconsidering resource mobilization theory. *International Journal of Communication*, *5*, 18.

Embrick, D. G. (2015). Two nations, revisited: The lynching of black and brown bodies, police brutality, and racial control in 'post-racial' Amerikkka. *Critical Sociology*, *41*(6), 835–843.

Ennis, J. G. (1987). Fields of action: Structure in movements' tactical repertoires. *Sociological Forum*, *2*(3), 520–533.

Fiske, J. (1994). Radical shopping in Los Angeles: Race, media and the sphere of consumption. *Media, Culture & Society*, *16*(3), 469–486.

Flesher Fominaya, C., & Gillan, K. (2017). Navigating the technology-media-movements complex. *Social Movement Studies*, *16*(4), 383–402.

Fraser, N. (1990). Rethinking the public sphere: A contribution to the critique of actually existing democracy. *Social Text*, (25/26), 56–80.

Freelon, D., McIlwain, C. D., & Clark, M. D. (2016). *Beyond the hashtags: #Ferguson, #Blacklivesmatter, and the online struggle for offline justice*. Washington, DC: Centre for Media & Social Impact, American University. Available at: www.cmsimpact.org/resource/beyond-hashtags-ferguson-blacklivesmatter-online-struggle-offline-justice/ (last accessed 29 November 2017).

Freelon, D., McIlwain, C. D., & Clark, M. (2018). Quantifying the power and consequences of social media protest. *New Media & Society*, *20*(3), 990–1011.

Gallagher, R. J., Reagan, A. J., Danforth, C. M., & Dodds, P. S. (2016). Divergent discourse between protests and counter-protests:# BlackLivesMatter and# AllLivesMatter. Available at: www.arxiv.org/abs/1606.06820 (last accessed 29 November 2017).

Garza, A. (2014). A herstory of the #BlackLivesMatter movement by Alicia Garza. *The Feminist Wire*, 7.

Ghonim, W. (2015). Available at: www.ted.com/talks/wael_ghonim_let_s_design_social_media_that_drives_real_change/transcript

Grabowicz, P. A., Ramasco, J. J., Moro, E., Pujol, J. M., & Eguiluz, V. M. (2012). Social features of online networks: The strength of intermediary ties in online social media. *PLoS ONE*, *7*(1), 1–9.

Higgins, I., & Brennan, B. (2017, November 01). *How black lives matter is inspiring aboriginal activists*. Retrieved November 19, 2017, from www.abc.net.au/news/2017-11-01/how-black-lives-matter-is-inspiring-aboriginal-australians/9107314 (last accessed 29 November 2017).

Hockin, S., & Brunson, R. (2016). The revolution might not be televised (but it will be lived streamed): Future directions for research on police–minority relations. *Race and Justice*. Advance online publication. doi: 10.1177/2153368716676320.

Howard, P. N., & Hussain, M. M. (2011). The role of digital media. *Journal of Democracy*, *22*(3), 35–48.

Huggins, B. (2017, November 06). *Speech: Black lives matter in Australia, too*. Retrieved November 18, 2017, from www.themandarin.com.au/85735-speech-black-lives-matter-in-australia-too/ (last accessed 29 November 2017).

Ince, J., Rojas, F., & Davis, C. (2017). The social media response to black lives matter: How Twitter users interact with black lives matter through hashtag use. *Ethnic and Racial Studies*, *40*(11), 1814–1830.

Iqani, M., & Schroeder, J. (2016). #selfie: Digital self-portraits as commodity form and consumption practice. *Consumption Markets & Culture*, *19*(5), 405–415.

Jackson, S. J., & Foucault Welles, B. (2016). #Ferguson is everywhere: Initiators in emerging counterpublic networks. *Information, Communication & Society*, *19*(3), 397–418.

Jacobs, R. (1996). Civil society and crisis: Culture, discourse, and the Rodney King beating. *American Journal of Sociology*, *101*(5), 1238–1272.

Juris, J. (2004). Networked social movements: Global movements for global justice. In M. Castells (Ed.), *The network society: A cross-cultural perspective* (pp. 341–362). Cheltenham, UK: Edward Elgar.

Juris, J. (2005). The new digital media and activist networking within anti-corporate globalization movements. *Annals of the American Academy of Political and Social Science*, *597*, 189–208.

Juris, J. (2008). *Networking futures: The movements against corporate globalization*. Durham, NC: Duke University Press.

Juris, J. (2012). Reflections on #Occupy everywhere: Social media, public space, and emerging logics of aggregation. *American Ethnologist*, *39*(2), 259–279.

Jurkowitz, M., & Vogt, N. (2013). On Twitter: Anger greets the Zimmerman verdict. Pew Research Center. Available at: www.pewresearch.org/fact-tank/2013/07/17/on-twitter-anger-greets-the-zimmerman-verdict/ (last accessed 29 November 2017).

Karpf, D. (2016). *Analytic activism: Digital listening and the new political strategy*. New York, NY: Oxford University Press.

Kavanaugh, A., Perez-Quinones, M. A., Tedesco, J. and Sanders, W. (2010). Toward a virtual town square in the era of Web 2.0. In J. Hunsinger, L. Klastrup, & M. Allen (Eds.) *International handbook of Internet research* (pp. 279–294). Surrey: Springer.

Kelly Garrett, R. (2006). Protest in an information society: A review of literature on social movements and new ICTs. *Information, Communication & Society*, *9*(02), 202–224.

Khaleeli, H. (2016, May 31). #SayHerName: Why Kimberle Crenshaw is fighting for forgotten women. *The Guardian*.

Khondker, H. H. (2011). Role of the new media in the Arab Spring. *Globalizations*, *8*(5), 675–679.

Klein, R. (2014, December 1). High school students around the country are walking out of class for Ferguson. *The Huffington post*. Available at: www.huffingtonpost.com/2014/12/01/high-school-students-protest-ferguson_n_6249802.html (last accessed 29 November 2017).

Langford, C. L., & Speight, M. (2015). #BlackLivesMatter: Epistemic positioning, challenges, and possibilities. *Journal of Contemporary Rhetoric*, *5*(3/4), 78–89.

Lim, M. (2012). Clicks, cabs, and coffee houses: Social media and oppositional movements in Egypt, 2004–2011. *Journal of Communication*, *62*(2), 231–248.

Loader, B. D., & Mercea, D. (2011). Networking democracy? Social media innovations and participatory politics. *Information, Communication & Society*, *14*(6), 757–769.

Lowery, W. (2017). *They Can't Kill Us All: The Story of Black Lives Matter*. New York, NY: Penguin Books.

Martin, B. (2005). The beating of Rodney King: The dynamics of backfire. *Critical Criminology*, *13*(3), 307–326.

McMurtry-Chubb, T. A. (2015). #SayHerName #BlackWomensLivesMatter: State violence in policing the black female body. *Mercer Law Review*, *67*, 651.

Melucci, A. (1989). *Nomads of the present: Social movements and individual needs in contemporary society*. Philadelphia: Temple University Press.

Messina, C. (2007). (@chrismessina) August 23, 2007.

Micheletti, M., & Stolle, D. (2007). Mobilizing Consumers to Take Responsibility for Global Social Justice. *The Annals of the American Academy of Political and Social Science*, *611*(1), 157–175.

Million Hoodies Movement for Justice. (2017). About us. Available at: www.millionhoodies.net/about/ (last accessed 29 November 2017).

Mirzoeff, N. D. (2015, August 10). *#BlackLivesMatter is breathing new life into the die-in*. Available at: www.newrepublic.com/article/122513/blacklivesmatter-breathing-new-life-die (last accessed 19 November 2017).

Morozov, E. (2009). Iran: Downside to the "Twitter Revolution." *Dissent, 56*(4), 10–14.

Morozov, E. (2011). *The net delusion: The dark side of Internet freedom.* New York, NY: PublicAffairs.

Papacharissi, Z. (2015). *Affective publics: Sentiment, technology, and politics.* New York, NY: Oxford University Press.

Peelo, M. (2006). Framing homicide narratives in newspapers: Mediated witness and the construction of virtual victimhood. *Crime, Media, Culture, 2*(2), 159–175.

Pew Research Center. (2016). The hashtag #BlackLivesMatter emerges: Social activism on Twitter. *Social media conversations about race.* Pew Internet Center. Available at: www.pewinternet.org/2016/08/15/social-media-conversations-about-race/ (last accessed 29 November 2017).

Postmes, T., & Brunsting, S. (2002). Collective action in the age of the Internet: Mass communication and online mobilization. *Social Science Computer Review, 20*(3), 290–301.

Ramaswamy, C. (2017, February 13). Trayvon Martin's parents, five years on: 'Racism is alive and well in America'. *The Guardian.* Available at: www.theguardian.com/us-news/2017/feb/13/trayvon-martin-parents-racism-alive-and-well-in-america (last accessed 29 November 2017).

Ray, R., Brown, M., & Laybourn, W. (2017). The evolution of #BlackLivesMatter on Twitter: Social movements, big data, and race. *Ethnic and Racial Studies, 40*(11), 1795–1796.

Richardson, L. S. (2014). Police racial violence: Lessons from social psychology. *Fordham Law Review, 83*(6), 2961.

Rickford, R. (2016). Black lives matter: Toward a modern practice of mass struggle. *New Labor Forum, 25*(1), 34–42.

Ries, B. (2014). This person live-tweeted Michael Brown's killing. Available at: www.mashable.com/2014/08/15/live-tweet-michael-brown-killing-ferguson/#B2qgDb599uq0 (last accessed 29 November 2017).

Robinson A., & Tormey S. (2005). 'Horizontals', 'Verticals' and the Conflicting Logics of Transformative Politics. In P. Hayden, & C. el-Ojeili (Eds.) *Confronting Globalization.* International Political Economy Series (pp. 208–226). London: Palgrave Macmillan.

Rolfe, B. (2005). Building an electronic repertoire of contention. *Social Movement Studies, 4*(1), 65–74.

Sastry, A., & Bates, K. (2017, April 26). When LA erupted in anger: A look back at the Rodney King riots. *NPR.* Available at: www.npr.org/2017/04/26/524744989/when-la-erupted-in-anger-a-look-back-at-the-rodney-king-riots (last accessed 29 November 2017).

Scott, K. (2015). The pragmatics of hashtags: Inference and conversational style on Twitter. *Journal of Pragmatics, 81*, 8–20.

Senft, T. M., & Baym, N. K. (2015). Selfies introduction – What does the selfie say? Investigating a global phenomenon. *International Journal of Communication, 9*, 1588–1606.

Shirky, C. (2009). *Here comes everybody: How change happens when people come together.* London: Penguin.

Shirky, C. (2011). The political power of social media: Technology, the public sphere, and political change. *Foreign Affairs, 90*(1), 28–41.

Siddiqui, S. (2016, July 13). Donald Trump strikes muddled note on 'divisive' Black Lives Matter. *The Guardian* [online]. Available at: www.theguardian.com/us-news/2016/jul/13/donald-trump-strikes-muddled-note-on-divisive-black-lives-matter (last accessed 29 November 2017).

Stevenson, B. (2013). *The contested murder of Latasha Harlins: Justice, gender, and the origins of the LA riots.* New York, NY: Oxford University Press.

Tilly, C. (1977). *Repertoires of contention in America and Britian, 1750–1830.* Center for Research on Social Organisation (CRSO) (Working Paper No. 1151). Michigan, MI: University of Michigan.

Tilly, C. (1986). European violence and collective action since 1700. *Social Research, 53*(1), 159–184.

Tilly, C. (1993). Contentious repertoires in Great Britain, 1758–1834. *Social Science History, 17*(2), 253–280.

Tilly, C., & Wood, L. J. (2015). *Social movements 1768–2012.* New York, NY: Routledge.

Tometi, O., & Lenoir, G. (2015). *Black lives matter is not a civil rights movement.* Available at: www.time.com/4144655/international-human-rightsday-black-lives-matter/ (last accessed 2 October 2017).

Tonkin, E., Pfeiffer, H. D., & Tourte, G. (2012). Twitter, information sharing and the London riots? *Bulletin of the Association for Information Science and Technology, 38*(2), 49–57.

Towns, A. R. (2016). Geographies of Pain: #SayHerName and the fear of black women's mobility. *Women's Studies in Communication, 39*(2), 122–126.

Twomey, J. L. (2004). Searching for a legacy: The Los Angeles Times, collective memory and the 10th anniversary of the 1992 LA "Riots". *Race, Gender & Class, 11*(1), 75–93.

Van Laer, J., & Van Aelst, P. (2009). Cyber protest and civil society: The Internet and action repertoires of social movements. In Y. Jewkes, & M. Yar (Eds.), *Handbook of Internet crime* (pp. 230–254). Portland, OR: Willan Publishing.

Van Laer, J., & Van Aelst, P. (2010). Internet and social movement action repertoires. *Information, Communication & Society, 13*(8), 1146–1171.

Van Loon, J. (1997). Chronotopes: Of/in the televisualization of the 1992 Los Angeles riots. *Theory, Culture & Society, 14*(2), 89–104.

Vegh, S. (2003). Classifying forms of online activism: The case of cyberprotests against the World Bank. In M. McCaughey, & M. D. Ayers (Eds.), *Cyberactivism: Online activism in theory and practice* (pp. 71–95). New York, NY: Routledge.

Warner, M. (2002). *Publics and Counterpublics*. New York, NY: Zone Books.

Williams, S. (2016). #SayHerName: Using digital activism to document violence against black women. *Feminist Media Studies, 16*(5), 922–925.

Workneh, L. (2015). #SayHerName: Why we should declare that Black women and girls matter too, *The Huffington Post*. Available at: www.huffingtonpost.com.au/entry/black-women-matter_n_7363064 (last accessed 29 November 2017).

Yancy, G., & Butler, J. (2015, January 12). What's wrong with 'All Lives Matter'? *New York Times*.

Yar, M. (2012). Crime, media and the will-to-representation: Reconsidering relationships in the new media age. *Crime, Media, Culture, 8*(3), 245–260.

Zappavigna, M. (2012). *Discourse of Twitter and social media-how we use language to create affiliation on the web*. London: Continuum International Publishing Group.

Zappavigna, M. (2015). Searchable talk: the linguistic functions of hashtags. *Social Semiotics, 25*(3), 274–291.

Zuboff, S. (2015). Big other: surveillance capitalism and the prospects of an information civilization. *Journal of Information Technology, 30*(1), 75–89.

9

CONCLUSION

Crime and Justice in Digital Society

Introduction

Digital Criminology invites an exploration of the ways in which technosocial cultures and practices come to bear not only on crime, deviance and (in)justice, but on social harms, social justice, inequality and meaning-making in digital society. This book has offered a framework for extending criminological engagement beyond the conventional foci of 'cyber' crime towards a critical and cultural orientation to examining crime and justice in digital society. Investigating the role(s) of an array of technological tools and technosocial practices in not only the commission of crimes but also the emergence of new harms, the extension of cultures of hate and structural inequalities, as well as issues of justice, citizen participation and crime policy activism are all within the scope of a digital criminology. Yet, to engage in the conceptual and empirical work required for this endeavour, criminology must engage more thoroughly with interdisciplinary perspectives from across science and technology, politics, cultural studies, and media and communications, in seeking to understand and respond to crime, deviance, justice and injustice in digital society. In this, our concluding chapter, we draw together some of the key concepts, tools and issues that we have examined throughout this book, as well as identifying some future directions for the continued development of a digital criminology.

What is Digital Criminology?

Our original concept for this book was driven by our concern that studies of the integration of the digital in practices, cultures and structures of crime and justice have been under-developed within criminology generally, and cybercriminologies in particular. Despite remarkable social shifts since the advent of the 'social web', within criminology there has been little conceptual or empirical analysis that has sought to integrate what we know about crime and justice from our critical and cultural subfields with knowledge gained from a plethora of theoretical tools in science, technology, sociology, politics, media and cultural studies. The persistence of the conventional scope of computer criminologies and cybercriminologies has led to the comparative neglect of areas such as: the role of technologies in a wide range of offending and victimisation; the increasingly embedded nature of digital technologies in crime and justice; the online victimisation of marginalised communities (such as on the basis of race, gender and sexuality); and persistent social and digital inequalities as they relate to crime and justice. In addition, there are rapidly emerging topics to explore, including online justice movements, digital vigilantism, and 'open-source' policing (i.e. social network surveillance). We suggest that these are appropriate issues for empirical analysis and theorisation in criminology, and that there is much to be gained by moving beyond a relatively narrowly defined, cyber-oriented criminology towards an exploration of the broad implications of digital technologies embedded in emerging technosocial practices that are shaping crime, deviance, criminalisation, justice and community responses to crime in various ways.

The first step towards this is to understand that a digital criminology, as we propose it, is not limited to the commission of crimes. There has been a tendency to study digital technology in a criminological context largely in terms of the motivated offender, which has caused new digital technologies to be viewed primarily as potential threats to the general public and opportunities for offending. While we would argue that most, if not all, crime is now fundamentally technological at some level, technology is not being used disproportionately in the commission of crime. Rather, technology has become embedded throughout society, including: in cultures and subcultures of deviance; in the sense-making of crime by a globally networked public; throughout formal and informal justice responses; and in practices of crime and justice policy advocacy and activism. These uses simply reflect the reality that technology is ubiquitous in the cultures and norms of a digital society. Given this ubiquity, it is important to avoid either social or technological determinism. In Chapter 1, we highlighted sociologist Manuel Castells' concept of the 'network society' to remind us that 'technology does not determine society . . . nor does society script the course of technological change'. Similarly, it can be said that technology does not determine patterns of crime and deviance, nor do crime and deviance shape how technology will be used. A thorough-going account of digital technology and crime will also consider how it is used to understand crime, shape crime policy and enable new kinds of crime responses.

A further vital step towards the digital criminological approach is to overcome the digital dualism that views the world in terms of separate online and offline spheres of activity. In a digitally mediated society, crime is no longer conceptually distinct from digital technology. The social practices through which crime is represented and understood require digital tools. Even a person who has no smart-phone, no computer, no social media identity and avoids (digital) television will still be reading print newspapers or talking to people who have drawn information through digital networks. Most aspects of an individual's identity that are recorded in some way will be stored on digital databases. The process of constructing the social meaning of crime is a digital process, even if the final stage of mediation is analogue, verbal or brutally corporeal. The 'digital' in digital society and digital criminology is not just an interface provided by a phone or a computer, it is deeply enmeshed and indeed constitutive of our everyday lives. Criminology that does not engage with digital society looks increasingly incomplete.

Throughout this book, we have sought to position digital criminology as an interdisciplinary set of tools and analyses that can be brought to all fields within the discipline, not as a sub-discipline. Technosocial practices, cultures and structures are implicated in most forms of crime and justice in contemporary society. This can be seen most obviously in social media usage. Not only do most offenders and victims have social media identities, these platforms are now ubiquitous in informing the public, policy-makers and politicians about the nature of crime and how justice may be pursued. And the ways in which digital technologies are enmeshed with the social, structural and cultural practices of law, crime and justice are many and varied — extending well beyond the politics of social media. Digital social systems will also inform how crime and justice processes continue to scale, both in terms of *intensity*, as technology continues to be integrated into every aspect of our everyday lives, and *spatially,* as global networks continue to extend and challenge our experiences of place.

Towards a *Digital Criminology*

Ultimately, what we've presented throughout this book is an *invitation* — the beginning of a shared scholarly conversation — that seeks to further develop a critical and cultural criminological approach to crime and justice in digital society. As such, we make no claim to have presented a comprehensive account of everything that a digital criminology might encompass. It is our intention that the case study issues and the assortment of interdisciplinary tools that we have explored here represent a launching-pad and a motivation for further development in the field. In Chapter 1, we outlined seven initial avenues for exploration by a digital criminology: spectatorship, investigation and evidence, justice and 'digilantism', surveillance, embodied harms, engagement, and inequalities. Each of these avenues has come to the fore in varying ways and to different degrees throughout the case studies examined in this book. Their exploration in our case study chapters has been further framed by our initial conceptual chapters, which establish the foundation for our pursuit of a digital criminology.

From the outset of this book, we have grappled with how criminology might engage conceptually and empirically with crime and justice in ways that extend beyond the common dualism that positions 'cyber' space as distinct from 'real' or terrestrial, corporeal space. To theorise alongside, yet against, such binary categories is a challenge for digital criminology. As we discuss in Chapter 1, we use 'digital society' (rather than digital age or era) purposefully, to draw the criminological imagination towards an exploration of the social inequalities, socio-cultural practices and socio-political factors that underpin crime and justice and that demonstrably persist as our lives become increasingly integrated with the digital. Technosociality, meanwhile, further positions technologies neither as mere tools of human action and interaction, nor as determinant of human action and interaction, but rather, captures the mutually constitutive nature of technology and society (Brown, 2006; Powell & Henry, 2017; Wajcman, 1991). For us, the concepts of digital society and technosociality are vital cornerstones of a digital criminological approach. We extend these concepts in Chapter 2, discussing some of the many theoretical affinities for digital criminology that incorporate concepts and approaches from across studies in science, technology, sociology, politics, media and cultural studies. Inspired in part by the work of criminologist Sheila Brown (2006), we have sought to examine crime and justice through a conceptual lens that understands all experience as digitally mediated: the difference being better viewed as one of extent rather than one of kind. With this as our foundational basis, throughout the remaining chapters in this book, we have variously been informed by and explicitly drawn on: Manuel Castells' concept of the network society, Judy Wajcman's critiques of technology as socially 'neutral', Nancy Fraser's work on meanings of justice and the operation of counterpublics, Bruno Latour's Actor–Network Theory (ANT), and Gilles Deleuze and Félix Guattari's metaphor of the rhizome, among others. Indeed, the nature of human and non-human interaction in networks, and the implications of these for amplifying, even constituting, criminal practices and cultures, is a key thread that continues through this book. In Chapter 2, we discuss 'algorithmic sociality' as a shorthand to refer to the automated and interactive processes of joint human–machine content curation that are determining how we experience and enact social relations (Smith, 2017). In short, every time we click 'like', we are simultaneously responding to, and reinforcing, a social algorithm that will determine not only which content we continue to be presented with, but also the content presented to others who are 'like us'. This mutual shaping of our content tastes and preferences is likely to have productive and reproductive effects on our production and consumption of crime and criminality: a theme we continue to examine in our later case study chapters.

Throughout this book, we have also sought to highlight the profit-driven imperatives that inform the regulation of digital society by its 'corporate sovereigns'. The global nature of digital society and its implications for crime and justice are discussed in detail in Chapter 3. Indeed, the power of the transnational corporations poses a range of challenges for the oversight of their economic activities within nation states. Not only can powerful corporations elude regulation, but also the pursuit of their interests can engender forms of transnational regulation that are imposed on states. The emergence of the corporate behemoths of Silicon Valley on the back of the disruptive and immensely profitable digital economy has only served to accelerate and intensify these dynamics (Taplin, 2017). This is, in part, due to the hyperfluidity of digital data, finance and capital, which gives it an advantage over the human labour force, which is less mobile, though also required to be increasingly flexible (Roberts, 2015). This can give rise to multiple parallel modes of regulation — each with their own normative entailments — that citizens traverse as they interact across digital networks.

In Chapter 3, we also further elaborate on the influence of global networks on shifts in temporality and spatiality: key themes that continue to feature throughout the case study chapters of this book. Perhaps, in particular, temporal and spatial shifts are a key context for Chapter 4, in which we explore the capacity for everyday citizens to follow, engage with and even participate in investigations of 'crime in real time'. These technosocial practices are, we suggest, influencing individuals' perceptions and meaning-making in response to crime, as well as formal and informal justice responses. For example, the capacity for citizens to generate information sources of their own and to follow crime in real time represents a significant shift in the traditional relationship between media producers and audiences that has previously been characterised by a hierarchy of official knowledge sources on crime. Furthermore, these 'participatory' engagements are often immediate and reflexive, developing and changing as new information is made available; having the capacity to influence official police investigations as well as media reporting on crime events as they unfold. In Chapter 4, we explore some key case studies that exemplify the concept of citizen engagement and participation with crime events in real time, including: the 2015 Paris (France) attacks, the 2013 Boston (USA) marathon bombing, the 2011 London (England) riots and the 2012 murder of Jill Meagher in Melbourne (Australia). Following crime in real time can lead to unintended and potentially harmful effects: leading to the misidentification of suspects as a result of 'crowdsourced' investigations, as well as vigilantism and interfering in the due process rights of accused persons. Yet a further unintended impact of citizen engagement and participation in crime events in digital society is the potential for an amplification of populist punitiveness; a concept well familiar to criminologists' concerned about both media and public opinion being co-opted to support punitive 'law and order' policy agendas.

Populist crime and justice politics are increasingly amplified through the combination of greater citizen participation via social media and other platforms, as well as the interaction of mainstream news media with 'what's trending'. As we discuss in Chapter 4, there is potential for digital society to amplify the politics of punitive populism as citizens' engage with crime and justice in new participatory ways. Yet, as argued by criminologists such as Russell Hogg and Julia Quilter, it may be possible to rescue populism from its critics and for crime and justice politics to adapt the repertoires of populism in ways that service progressive policy change. Criminologists arguably need to engage with crime and justice policy debates in more accessible, public and 'populist' ways. Indeed, it appears there may be a role for a new kind of 'public' criminology in the context of digital society — a point we elaborate on further below.

Some traditional criminological concepts arguably take on new and/or amplified meanings in the context of digital society. Cultural and (in particular) visual criminologies have engaged with the affectual and political implications of mediated witnessing (Peelo, 2006; Wood, 2017), as well as the mass media spectacle that is characteristic of 'mega cases' (Soothill, Peelo, Pearson, & Francis, 2004) and 'signal crimes' (Innes, 2004). While criminologists have analysed the significance and lasting meanings of crime images, such as the World Trade Center terror attacks of 11 September 2001 and the 2003 Abu Ghraib torture images, among others (see Brown, 2014; Carrabine, 2012; Hayward, 2009; Young, 2007, 2014), in Chapters 4 and 5, we further explore the ways in which public production and consumption of crime images and engagement with meaning-making seem to be shifting in digital society. From the 2011 London riots, to the 2012 Steubenville Ohio sexual assault images, to the 2013 Boston Marathon bombing, to the 2013 #BlackLivesMatter movement, to the 2014 rape meme #JadaPose, to the 2015 photo taken by convicted college rapist Brock Turner, to the 2016 rapes that were broadcast by live-streaming video, to the 2017 murders that were video-streamed on Facebook Live — our relationship with the visual is shifting in powerful ways that will shape our experience of, perceptions of, and cultural reproduction of, crime and justice. In the context of digital society, in which images are made available by everyday participants and witnesses to extraordinary events, the *spectacle* of crime has taken on new forms. While the mass media spectacle may come to a close, in digital society the record is preserved through multiple digital archives of images and first-hand accounts on social media and other content-sharing platforms, enabling an ongoing witnessing, memorialisation and citizen participation through revisiting and redistributing the content. In this way, there is a seemingly unending vicarious re-experiencing of traumatic public events over both distance and time. This immersion, amplification and extension, or 'forever time', of trauma in the aftermath of a crime event can also be understood as an unintended effect of algorithmic sociality and the digital permanence that is characteristic of digital society.

The interaction of human and non-human agency are perhaps most observable in the spread of 'memetic deviance', discussed in Chapter 5, in which the participatory logics of mimicry, along with the automated distribution of popular or visually engaging content, can lead to the rapid replication of deviant, sometimes criminal, practices throughout a social network. As we suggest, in effect, the algorithms that push content into the view of selected human users therefore contribute to the production and reproduction of social and power relations throughout networks. Though we have drawn on case examples of criminal selfies, in particular sexual assault images, as well as 'fight videos' in our earlier discussions, there are many other possible examples of algorithmic sociality as it relates to crime and deviance that might be the subject of continued research within a digital criminology. Where once criminologists examined the choices of rational offenders, and their differential associations with deviant peer networks, increasingly deviant networks are comprised of both human and algorithmic 'peers'.

In Chapter 6, we consider the effects of immersion, amplification and automation in the concept of networked hate. The chapter discusses racial, religious, gender and class manifestations of networked hate — exploring the interaction of technosocial norms and practices with social structures of inequality and disadvantage. It is clear that the role of technology, namely the systems, algorithms and databases of social media and other communications companies, play a vital role in enabling the norms and practices of networked hate. Yet, as we discuss, the nature of this relationship is complex: technology cannot be understood as *causing* the norms and practices of hate, but neither is technology insignificant in examining recent manifestations of such hate. A digital criminological approach to hate requires a nuanced analysis that moves beyond the dichotomy of 'online' hate and 'offline' hate. Even when hate manifests as mass movements that are highly visible on the streets of cities, such events are, in many respects, digitally produced and mediated phenomena.

We suggest that a digital criminological account of networked hate requires examination of the phenomenon as resulting from ongoing cycles of social and technological co-production. Indeed, in the context of digital society, it is fundamental to recognise that technologies themselves are not neutral tools in the hands of societal biases and inequalities. Rather, biases and inequalities are (inadvertently) built into the codes and algorithms that, in turn, learn and are refined from their continued engagement with human agency. Yet, importantly, just as a combination of human and non-human actors are involved in this co-production of networked hate, so too can algorithms be harnessed in responding to such hate. For example, the process of identifying and removing content can be automated, or the actual user experience of software can be reshaped, changing the interaction between technology and society in a way that has flow-on effects for the norms and practices that continue to be produced and reproduced. While we are ultimately optimistic for a combination of social and technical strategies to challenge the norms and practices of networked hate, it is not possible that, as a society, we can simply code our way out of the complex histories and ongoing practices of institutionalised bigotry and inequality.

A cautious optimism is the approach we continue to take as we delve into informal justice, 'digilantism' and justice activism in Chapters 7 and 8. Though vigilantism is a contested concept within criminology, and indeed such citizen-led 'justice' can lead to very unjust outcomes, in Chapter 7, we examine both the risks and potential benefits of informal justice practices in the context of digital society. We discuss a range of case study examples where victim-survivors and their advocates have sought some form of public validation of the wrongs they've experienced through civil society spaces, including online platforms. This is as opposed to seeking formal justice through the police, court and prison systems (though the two are, of course, not mutually exclusive). Indeed, we consider an emerging set of practices, occurring largely via participatory and social media, that constitute a digital vigilantism (or 'digilantism'), including those engaged in by victim-survivors of interpersonal violence (such as domestic and sexual violence and sexual harassment) as well as democratic digilantism and hacktivism. There are clear tensions, we suggest, in such practices, which might include simply sharing one's own experience of victimisation, naming and shaming alleged perpetrators and/or engaging in online harassment of those suspected of committing harms. On the one hand, for victim-survivors of domestic and sexual violence, who are frequently failed by the formal criminal justice system, seeking some form of recognition by a community of peers may meet some of their justice needs. Likewise, when citizens take to social media to bear witness to wrongs committed by state officials and demand action to protect the rights of citizens, naming and shaming of those who have perpetrated such harms may be well justified — and even serve the interests of the broader community. On the other hand, a range of embodied harms may be experienced by those misidentified, suspected or convicted perpetrators, whose punishment in digital society may not necessarily be proportionate to the crime. Again, we analyse emerging forms of informal justice and digilantism through the lens of technosociality and the interaction of human and non-human actors in deciding which justice-seeking content 'goes viral' throughout the network. Key concepts developed earlier in the book, such as algorithmic sociality, are again drawn upon to understand how it is that some informal and digilante practices might produce a kind of 'viral justice'.

In Chapter 8, our final case study discussion, we end on a more hopeful analysis of the vital role of social justice activism in digital society. Through an in-depth discussion of the #BlackLivesMatter movement, we draw together many of the themes developed throughout the book in order to advocate that 'hashtag activism' can produce effects that are much more than the sum of thousands, even millions, of people tweeting into the ether. Rather, we suggest that key characteristics of digital society, such as perpetual contact, permanence, visual conversations and algorithmic sociality, can have the benefit of amplifying the efforts of social justice activists. Drawing not only on Castells' but also the work of Deleuze and Guattari, we engage with the concepts of rhizomatic justice movements as a metaphor representing the characteristic multiplicity of social justice activism in digital society. Though we are not so naïve as to imagine that movements do not face real challenges in overcoming persistent structures of systemic inequality, we suggest a more optimistic reading of capacity for technosocial justice movements to enable substantive social, cultural and political change.

Further Avenues for *Digital Criminology*

There are naturally many more issues, concepts and analyses of crime and justice in digital society still to be explored, and in this final section, we suggest some further areas that we believe will also feature in digital criminological research as it develops into the future.

The technological race for immediacy and to automate is present in every aspect of our everyday lives, and justice responses are no exception. Take, for example, developments in 'chatbots', computer programs that are designed to simulate conversation with human users. The concept itself is not new: any internet user who has engaged in online shopping has probably experienced the pop-up box from an automated 'salesperson' who is only too eager for you to type in questions for it to answer. Yet the extension of chatbots into legal education and advice practices is a rapidly developing field of innovation — a technosocial solution to the ongoing problem of a justice system failing to meet user demand. For example, in the UK in August of 2015, then 18-year-old IT student Joshua Browder developed a chatbot called *DoNotPay* (donotpay.co.uk) to assist people in contesting their parking tickets (Sehmer, 2015). The concept soon developed into the 'world's first robot lawyer', providing answers to common legal questions and assisting to complete forms in civil matters from traffic violations, to landlord disputes, and soon marriages, bankruptcies and divorces (Mannes, 2017). Meanwhile, in Australia in November 2017, technology developers at Good Hood launched a text-message-based chatbot to assist victims of domestic and sexual violence. *Hello Cass* enables victims to ask difficult questions via SMS on their smartphones without the need to go to a website or download a specific software application and is being piloted in collaboration with leading local support services (Brown, 2017). Perhaps, eventually, our mobile phones and other internet-enabled devices (such as Amazon Echo, Google Home and Apple HomePod) will monitor our communications and automatically contact support helplines, even call emergency services, if they detect a problem behaviour or crisis. In a service system that is under-funded to deliver a human response to victims in crisis, the idea of automating advice and support 'with a few simple clicks' is certainly appealing (Coade, 2017, n.p.). Yet, as technology scholars in other fields have asked about the automation of allied human services and caring professions (Wajcman, 1991, 2014), is it correct to assume — as such automation inevitably does — that people in need would rather *not* engage with the empathy and contact of another human person?

A further area for digital criminological research lies in the rapidly developing field of augmented reality (AR), which refers to technologies that overlay computer-generated content on a user's view of the real world (such as via their smartphone, a tablet, goggles or digital glasses), providing a kind of composite view. AR games such as Google's Ingress and Pokemon Go have begun to attract the attention of criminologists, legal scholars and police investigators alike (Cowper & Buerger, 2003; Powell, 2012). According to media reports in both the United States and the UK, Pokemon Go has been linked to hundreds of reported crimes, with players being lured into isolated areas and subsequently robbed and/or assaulted while they tried to catch virtual Pokemons (Mullen, 2016; Yuhas, 2016). More positively, police in several jurisdictions have reported using AR to supplement their investigations of crime scenes (Datcu, Lukosch, & Lukosch, 2016; Streefkerk, Houben, van Amerongen, ter Haar, & Dijk, 2013). Meanwhile, in the United States, police agencies have long identified the utility of an AR adaptation of 'Identification Friend or Foe' (IFF) technologies currently used by the military for everyday police patrols (Cowper & Buerger, 2003; Reed, 2008). Their motivation for use of IFF is the idea that, if local police were assisted with a digital overlay of information about the identities of potential suspects (such as via digital goggles, glasses or even vehicle windscreens), it would assist in preventing the misuse of lethal force.

Yet, some scholars have expressed concern that, if such technologies were to become widespread, they would have the further effect of extending privacy violations, surveillance and dataveillance of citizens by the state (Roesner, Denning, Newell, Kohno, & Calo, 2014). Indeed, questions have already been raised about the 'profiling' that may occur based on facial recognition and other automated surveillance technologies, including police-worn body cameras (Atkins, 2016; Gates, 2011). It would also seem important to question whether such identification and surveillance technologies may, in practice, contribute to racial profiling in criminal justice responses, discussed further below.

As we have discussed in this book, big data is big business. The potential implications of big data analytics, including social network data, for crime and justice are extensive and are yet to receive an in-depth treatment by criminologists. Yet, clearly big data, and in particular the emergence of 'predictive policing' (Haberman & Ratcliffe, 2012; Pearsall, 2010; Perry, 2013), including the increasingly automated calculations of offender risk profiles (on which bail and parole decisions may be made), and 'crime sensing' via social media (Williams, Burnap, & Sloan, 2017), are important issues for digital criminology (Chan & Bennett Moses, 2016; Smith, Bennett Moses, & Chan, 2017). The promise that big data might make the administration of criminal justice smarter is certainly tempting. But Australian criminologist Professor Janet Chan and her colleagues (Smith, Bennett Moses & Chan, 2017) have identified that there are 'feedback loop' problems inherent in algorithmic and 'predictive' criminal justice responses, such as the allocation of police patrols, for instance:

> If there are initial biases in the crimes noticed by police (for example racial bias affecting initial patrolling patterns), then this will be fed back into the algorithm and 'confirm' police biases (p. 33).

Chan's critique highlights the challenges inherent in predictive justice: the arguably flawed assumption that technology is neutral. Yet, as Wajcman (1991) has frequently pointed out in relation to gender, the same biases that exist within our societies are built into the systems that are developed, refined, implemented, used and learn through human–technology interaction in our societies. In the case of predictive policing and risk calculations, data are generated based on forensic samples that are already over-represented by those in our communities who are subject to greater police and criminal justice scrutiny. They are therefore likely to generate a feedback loop of racial, class and education biases that become self-fulfilling prophecies, arguably amplifying social inequalities that are already endemic in crime and justice.

While digital technologies benefit from global mobility, the technologies that result play a vital role in regulating the mobility of people, services and goods. Border security is a form of contemporary governance that can be understood as a fundamentally logistical practice, managing supply chains — licit or illicit — in order to enable and control mobility (Chambers, 2017). Critical criminologists, such as Pickering and Weber's (2006) ongoing concern with the harms that occur in border crossings, have highlighted the vital role that technology plays in this regulation of human movement. Chief amongst these is the use of biometric technologies to authenticate and verify as part of a system of global surveillance (Wilson, 2006, 2007). The specific concern of biometrics with the body as means of verification when crossing borders is a powerful example of how technology is deeply enmeshed in everyday life, determining not only whether individuals have criminal histories but also whether they are likely to be productive and beneficial for the society they are seeking to enter (Epstein, 2007, 2008). A common finding among all these works on technology and borders is that spatial control is enacted through borders but does not start and end at the border; the border becomes a technology that regulates wherever suspect foreign identities are encountered (Cameron, 2013).

In a digital society, however, the *global* is not simply 'out there' beyond the territorial borders. Networked digital technology offers a constant connection across the globe — and an accompanying trail of metadata. Biometric border technologies now allow borders to be 'portable'; they can be far beyond and far within the geographical territorial boundary that traditionally demarcated the border (Amoore, 2006, p. 338). Borders, in this sense 'are not where they are supposed to be' (Vaughn-Williams, 2012, p. 14). This can be seen in the United States Visitor and Immigration Status Indicator Technology (US-VISIT) program (Muller, 2010). According to the initial media release

> the end vision for the Smart Border Alliance solution is built around the concept of a virtual border. The virtual border is designed to operate far beyond US boundaries ... the virtual border makes US border inspectors the last line of defense, not the first.
>
> (Accenture, 2004)

This bold conceptual vision has been implemented using expansive and detailed data-mining that begins prior to the potential visitor's departure from home (Lahav, 2008). This means the border has been effectively spatially and temporally shifted, as automated algorithms assess risk suggested by visitors' metadata and determine whether they can enter when they purchase a ticket or apply for a visa (Bennett, 2005). Border technology, however, does not stop there; it is able to track the movement and activities of travellers within the United States for the duration of their trip, assessing financial and other digital metadata (Amoore & de Goede, 2005). Technologies such as these offer 'new ways of visualizing and governing deviant populations' that will grow ever more detailed as more data are collected and ever more expansive in their reach as collection technologies improve (Valverde & Mopas, 2004, p. 240). Considering these technologies will increasingly govern everyday life and institute new modes of citizenship, the interaction of digital technologies and new security repertoires at borders ought to be a concern of digital criminology.

Finally, as we alluded to in our discussion earlier, there is arguably a need for a new kind of 'public' criminology. For more than ten years, the utility of 'public criminology' has been advocated by criminologists (and by sociologists such as Michael Burawoy, 2005) who define their role as reaching beyond academia and into policy advocacy and justice activism (Currie, 2007; Feilzer, 2009; Groombridge, 2007; Loader & Sparks, 2013; Mopas & Moore, 2012; Tonry, 2010; Turner, 2013; see also 'newsmaking criminology', Barak, 1988). In short, public criminology 'takes as part of its defining mission a more vigorous, systematic and effective intervention in the world of social policy and social action' (Currie, 2007, p. 176), and to embrace this mission, we will need to do more than convince policy- and lawmakers — we will have to convince the hearts and minds of the public. American Professor of Criminology Elliott Currie, whose 2007 essay *Against Marginality: Towards a Public Criminology* was among the first in the field, further identified part of the problem facing criminologists:

> How do we define the main job of the criminologist? Too often, we privilege what we think of as 'original' research — especially that which can get us published in peer-reviewed research journals — at the expense of two other things that I think are essential parts of any intellectual enterprise: making *sense* of the mass of research we generate, through analytical and synthetic work, and *disseminating* that work to a broader and potentially more efficacious audience than ourselves. In other words, we spend a great deal of time generating 'findings', but we spend altogether too little time talking among ourselves and to wider and more diverse publics about what we think those findings *mean*.
>
> (2007, p. 180, emphasis in original)

The call for a public criminology, then, is not only a call for criminologists to step down from the ivory 'pure research' tower and get involved in the development and advocacy of pragmatic policy solutions for a greater public good (Haines & Sutton, 2000). It is also a specific call to communicate effectively with the public and the media (Tonry, 2010).

Yet what does public criminology look like in digital society? The literature at the time of writing is surprisingly scant. Among the more recent and in-depth treatments of public criminology, a 2011 book by Ian Loader and Richard Sparks makes no mention of 'social media' and includes just one passing reference to the 'internet'. In a rare example, in the journal *Radical Criminology*, Professor Christopher Schneider described public reactions and perceptions of crime and justice expressed during the 2011 Vancouver Stanley Cup riots. Schneider (2015, p. 40) observed that 'public debates …

can now emerge even during the commission of a criminal event' — a characteristic that we describe as following and responding to 'crime in real time', in Chapter 4. During such crime events, many contested public sentiments, including punitiveness, may play out in networked publics. For Schneider (2015), this represents a unique opportunity for public criminologists:

> By understanding where public perceptions come from, and by directly contributing our scientific explanations to online public debates, criminologists can now provide insights to publics in direct ways not possible in the recent past. These "interventions" in public life may then contribute to harm reduction among the very publics that we serve. Future work in public criminology might develop strategies for entering public debates online, and perhaps test the effectiveness of such approaches (p. 42).

Anecdotally at least, it is apparent that some criminologists are indeed entering into public discussions on platforms such as Twitter and Facebook, both to communicate their research findings and to engage in commentary and public policy debates. Yet empirical analyses regarding the scale and nature of such engagements, as well as evidence of their impact on policy or media framings of crime and justice, remain areas for future research. Such research has, however, been undertaken in sociology by Christopher Schneider and Deana Simonetto (2017), who found that most Twitter engagements by 'public sociologists' were far more focused on content generation based on their own research findings than on genuine engagement with a broader public. The challenge, then, appears to have been set for a genuine engagement in crime and justice debates by a digital *public* criminology.

Conclusion

Early on in this book, we asked a long-standing question for criminologists: Are we defenders of order or guardians of human rights?[1] It has been our intention to suggest a framework for the study of crime and justice in digital society that is oriented towards the latter. We have sought to draw explicitly on existing critical and cultural criminologies, as well as on interdisciplinary concepts from science, technology, sociology, politics, media and cultural studies. As such, our focus for a digital criminology is beyond the narrowly defined set of criminal harms and justice processes within a territorially bounded state. Critical engagement with crime and justice in a digital society allows for further exploration of the personal, social and political implications of the immersion of technology in our daily experiences and interactions with others, including in the crime perpetration and victimisation, as well as formal and informal (or 'citizen led') justice responses, among many other issues and focus areas.

In digital society, the need for criminology to challenge its insularity and once again engage dialogically with other disciplines, as identified at the outset of this book, is not just imperative for continued *development* of our field but also for its continued *relevance* (Garland, 2011). When we understand the digital as an embedded part of the larger social entity and acknowledge the incorporation of digital technologies, media and networks in our everyday lives, this imperative becomes increasingly clear. In *Digital Criminology*, we have invited the wider criminological community to develop a way forward. We hope that our colleagues in criminology, both those established in their careers and a new generation of scholars, will take up the challenge of further expanding the foci, tools and analyses of crime, justice and injustice in digital society.

As we move into an increasingly digital society, it is worth reminding ourselves that we are only in the very early stages of a normative order structured by these technologies. The communications platforms that we use to connect to friends, family, colleagues and community are barely a decade old, and there is a long and varied future to come. Digital technology is often thought of as either an intrusion on our lives or a tool to be used in aid of either fair or foul play. The socio-technical approach we have adopted in *Digital Criminology* has sort to reconcile the prospect of these new technologies in our lives but, in so doing, does not simply treat it as neutral. Understanding that society and technology will continue to co-produce one another gives cause for greater investment in this digital society. What should the digital future look like? How should it structure our cities? Should technology be a source of greater social division and inequality, or a means towards overcoming it? The concepts and case studies in this book have not always provided much cause for optimism on these fronts, and current configurations of digital social systems hold many challenges. The case for optimism requires not only greater investment in software and hardware but the energy and engagement that can foster an active sense of citizenship embedded within the digitally mediated social relations. Such a sense of digital citizenship, we suggest, is a vital foundation for a digital criminology.

Note

1 A question originally posed by Schwendinger & Schwendinger (1970) in the form of their article *Defenders of Order or Guardians of Human Rights?*

References

Accenture. (2004). US Department of Homeland Security Awards Accenture-Led smart border alliance the contract to develop and implement US-visit program. Available at: https://newsroom.accenture.com/news/us-department-homeland-security-awards-accenture-led-smart-border-alliance-contract-to-develop-and-implement-us-visit-program.htm (last accessed 9 March 2018).

Amoore, L. (2006). Biometric borders: Governing mobilities in the war on terror. *Political Geography, 25*(3), 336–351.

Amoore, L., & de Goede, M. (2005). Governance, risk and dataveillance in the war on terror. *Crime, Law & Social Change, 43*(2–3), 149–173.

Atkins, E. (2016, July 1). #Blacklivesrecorded: Will the Darling Savior of police brutality be the downfall of modern privacy? Available at: www.ssrn.com/abstract=2803588 (last accessed 29 November 2017).

Barak, G. (1988). Newsmaking criminology: Reflections on the media, intellectuals and crime. *Justice Quarterly, 5*(4), 565–585.

Bennett, C. J. (2005). What happens when you book an airline ticket? The collection and processing of passenger data post-9/11. In M. B. Salter, & E. Zureik (Eds.), *Global surveillance and policing: Borders, security, identity* (pp. 113–138). Devon: Willan Publishing.

Brown, M. (2014). Visual criminology and carceral studies: Counter-images in the carceral age. *Theoretical Criminology, 18*(2), 176–197.

Brown, S. (2006). The criminology of hybrids: Rethinking crime and law in technosocial networks. *Theoretical Criminology, 10*(2), 223–244.

Brown, S. (2017). Hello Cass chatbot developed to help people experiencing domestic violence. Available at: www.abc.net.au/news/2017-11-06/hello-cass-chatbot-helps-people-experiencing-violence/9114986 (last accessed 29 November 2017).

Burawoy, M. (2005). For public sociology. *American Sociological Review, 70*(1), 4–28.

Cameron, R. (2013). *Subjects of security: Domestic effects of foreign policy in the war on terror.* Basingstoke: Palgrave.

Carrabine, E. (2012). Just images: Aesthetics, ethics and visual criminology. *The British Journal of Criminology*, *52*(3), 463–489.

Chambers, P. (2017). *Border security: Shores of politics, horizons of justice*. Abingdon, Oxon: Routledge.

Chan, J., & Bennett Moses, L. (2016). Is big data challenging criminology? *Theoretical Criminology*, *20*(1), 21–39.

Coade, M. (2017). The AI platform creating a safe space for DV victims to get help. Available at: www.law-yersweekly.com.au/newlaw/21657-the-ai-platform-creating-a-safe-space-for-dv-victims-to-get-help (last accessed 29 November 2017).

Cowper, T., & Buerger, M. (2003). *Improving our view of the world: Police and augmented reality technology*. Washington, DC: US Federal Bureau of Investigation.

Currie, E. (2007). Against marginality: Arguments for a public criminology. *Theoretical Criminology*, *11*(2), 175–190.

Datcu, D., Lukosch, S. G., & Lukosch, H. K. (2016, November). Handheld augmented reality for distributed collaborative crime scene investigation. In *Proceedings of the 19th International Conference on Supporting Group Work* (pp. 267–276), Sanibel Island, Florida, November 13–16. ACM.

Epstein, C. (2007). Guilty bodies, productive bodies, destructive bodies: Crossing the biometric borders. *International Political Sociology*, *1*(2), 149–164.

Epstein, C. (2008). Embodying risk: Using biometrics to protect the borders. In L. Amoore, & M. de Goede (Eds.), *Risk and the war on terror* (pp. 178–193). Abingdon, Oxon: Routledge.

Feilzer, M. (2009). The importance of telling a good story: An experiment in public criminology. *The Howard Journal of Crime and Justice*, *48*(5), 472–484.

Garland, D. (2011). Criminology's place in the academic field. In M. Bosworth, & C. Hoyle (Eds.), *What is criminology?* (pp. 298–317). Oxford: Oxford University Press.

Gates, K. A. (2011). *Our biometric future: Facial recognition technology and the culture of surveillance*. New York, NY: NYU Press.

Groombridge, N. (2007). Criminologists say . . .: An analysis of UK national press coverage of criminology and criminologists and a contribution to the debate on 'Public Criminology'. *The Howard Journal of Crime and Justice*, *46*(5), 459–475.

Haberman, C. P., & Ratcliffe, J. H. (2012). The predictive policing challenges of near repeat armed street robberies. *Policing: A Journal of Policy and Practice*, *6*(2), 151–166.

Haines, F., & Sutton, A. (2000). Criminology as religion? Profane thoughts about sacred values. *British Journal of Criminology*, *40*(1), 146–162.

Hayward, K. (2009). Visual criminology: Cultural criminology-style: Keith Hayward makes the case for 'visual criminology'. *Criminal Justice Matters*, *78*(1), 12–14.

Innes, M. (2004). Signal crimes and signal disorders: Notes on deviance as communicative action. *The British Journal of Sociology*, *55*(3), 335–355.

Lahav, G. (2008). Mobility and border security: The U.S. aviation system, the state, and the rise of public-private partnerships. In M. B. Salter (ed.), *Politics at the airport* (pp. 77–104). Minneapolis, MN: University of Minnesota Press.

Loader, I., & Sparks, R. (2013). *Public criminology?* London: Routledge.

Mannes, K. (2017). DoNotPay launches 1,000 new bots to help you with your legal problems. Available at: www.techcrunch.com/2017/07/12/donotpay-launches-1000-new-bots-to-help-you-with-your-legal-problems/ (last accessed 29 November 2017).

Mopas, M., & Moore, D. (2012). Talking heads and bleeding hearts: Newsmaking, emotion and public criminology in the wake of a sexual assault. *Critical Criminology*, *20*(2), 183–196.

Mullen, T. (2016, August 26). Hundreds of Pokemon Go incidents logged by police. *BBC News UK*. Available at: www.bbc.com/news/uk-england-37183161 (last accessed 29 November 2017).

Muller, B. (2010). *Security, risk and the biometric state: Governing borders and bodies*. Abingdon, Oxon: Routledge.

Pearsall, B. (2010). Predictive policing: The future of law enforcement. *National Institute of Justice Journal*, *266*(1), 16–19.

Peelo, M. (2006). Framing homicide narratives in newspapers: Mediated witness and the construction of virtual victimhood. *Crime, Media, Culture*, *2*(2), 159–175.

Perry, W. L. (2013). *Predictive policing: The role of crime forecasting in law enforcement operations*. Santa Monica, CA: Rand Corporation.

Pickering, S., & Weber, L. (2006). Borders, mobility and technologies of control. In S. Pickering, & L. Weber (Eds.), *Borders, mobility and technologies of control* (pp. 1–21). Dordrecht: Springer.

Powell, A. (2012, November 29). Turf war: Pick your side and get outside with Google's Ingress. *The Conversation*. Available at: www.theconversation.com/turf-war-pick-your-side-and-get-outside-with-googles-ingress-11006 (last accessed 29 November 2017).

Powell, A., & Henry, N. (2017). *Sexual violence in a digital age*. Basingstoke, UK: Palgrave Macmillan.

Reed, B. (2008). Future technology in law enforcement. *FBI Law Enforcement Bulletin, 77*(5), 15.

Roberts, J. M. (2015). *Digital publics: Cultural political economy, financialisation and creative organisational politics*. New York, NY: Routledge.

Roesner, F., Denning, T., Newell, B. C., Kohno, T., & Calo, R. (2014). Augmented reality: Hard problems of law and policy. In Proceedings of the 2014 ACM International Joint Conference on Pervasive and Ubiquitous Computing: Adjunct Publication (pp. 1283–1288). Seattle, Washington, September 13–17, ACM.

Schneider, C. J. (2015). Public criminology and the 2011 Vancouver riot: Public perceptions of crime and justice in the 21st century. *Radical Criminology, 5*, 21–45.

Schneider, C. J., & Simonetto, D. (2017). Public sociology on Twitter: A space for public pedagogy? *The American Sociologist, 48*(2), 233–245.

Schwendinger, H., & Schwendinger, J. (1970). Defenders of order or guardians of human rights? *Issues Criminology, 5*(2), 123–157.

Sehmer, A. (2015, December 29). Teenager's parking appeals website saves motorists £2m after overturning thousands of fines. *The Independent*. Available at: www.independent.co.uk/news/uk/home-news/teenagers-parking-appeals-website-saves-motorists-2m-after-overturning-thousands-of-fines-a6789711.html (last accessed 29 November 2017).

Smith, D. R. (2017). The tragedy of self in digitised popular culture: The existential consequences of digital fame on YouTube. *Qualitative Research, 17*(6), 699–714.

Smith, G. J., Bennett Moses, L., & Chan, J. (2017). The challenges of doing criminology in the big data era: Towards a digital and data-driven approach. *The British Journal of Criminology, 57*(2), 259–274.

Soothill, K., Peelo, M., Pearson, J., & Francis, B. (2004). The reporting trajectories of top homicide cases in the media: A case study of the times. *The Howard Journal of Crime and Justice, 43*(1), 1–14.

Streefkerk, J. W., Houben, M., van Amerongen, P., ter Haar, F., & Dijk, J. (2013). The ART of CSI: An augmented reality tool (ART) to annotate crime scenes in forensic investigation. In *International conference on virtual, augmented and mixed reality* (pp. 330–339). Berlin, Heidelberg: Springer.

Taplin, J. (2017). *Move fast and break things: How Google, Facebook and Amazon cornered culture and undermined democracy*. London: Macmillan.

Tonry, M. (2010). "Public criminology" and evidence-based policy. *Criminology & Public Policy, 9*(4), 783–797.

Turner, E. (2013). Beyond 'facts' and 'values' rethinking some recent debates about the public role of criminology. *The British Journal of Criminology, 53*(1), 149–166.

Valverde, M., & Mopas, M. (2004) Insecurity and the dream of targeted governance. In W. Larner, & W. Waters (Eds.), *Global governmentality: Governing international spaces* (pp. 233–250) London: Routledge.

Vaughn-Williams, N. (2012). *Border politics: The limits of sovereign power*. Edinburgh: Edinburgh University Press.

Wajcman, J. (1991). *Feminism confronts technology*. University Park, PA: Pennsylvania State University Press.

Wajcman, J. (2014). *Pressed for time: The acceleration of life in digital capitalism*. Chicago, IL: University of Chicago Press.

Williams, M. L., Burnap, P., & Sloan, L. (2017). Crime sensing with big data: The affordances and limitations of using open-source communications to estimate crime patterns. *The British Journal of Criminology, 57*(2), 320–340.

Wilson, D. (2006). Biometrics, Borders and the Ideal Suspect. In S. Pickering, & L. Weber (Eds.), *Borders, mobility and technologies of control* (pp. 87–109). Dordrecht: Springer.

Wilson, D. (2007). Australian Biometrics and Global Surveillance. *International Criminal Justice Review*, *17*(3), 207–219.

Wood, M. A. (2017). Antisocial media and algorithmic deviancy amplification: Analysing the id of Facebook's technological unconscious. *Theoretical Criminology*, *21*(2), 168–185.

Young, A. (2007). Images in the aftermath of trauma: Responding to September 11th. *Crime, Media, Culture*, *3*(1), 30–48.

Young, A. (2014). From object to encounter: Aesthetic politics and visual criminology. *Theoretical Criminology*, *18*(2), 159–175.

Yuhas, A. (2016, July 11). Pokémon Go: Armed robbers use mobile game to lure players into trap. *The Guardian*. Available at: www.theguardian.com/technology/2016/jul/10/pokemon-go-armed-robbers-dead-body (last accessed 29 November 2017).

INDEX